GW00471800

# THE STOCK EXCHANGES OF IRELAND

# STUDIES IN FINANCIAL AND ECONOMIC HISTORY

ISSN 0950-2211

General Editors: Philip Cottrell and W. A. Thomas

Volume 1

Grateful acknowledgement is made to
The Irish Stock Exchange
for a subvention in aid of publication

# THE
# STOCK EXCHANGES
# OF
# IRELAND

## W. A. THOMAS

FRANCIS CAIRNS

Published by Francis Cairns (Publications) Ltd

c/o The University, P.O. Box 147, Liverpool L69 3BX, Great Britain

and

27 South Main Street,Wolfeboro, New Hampshire 03894, U.S.A.


First published 1986

Copyright © W.A. Thomas, 1986



All rights reserved. No part of this publication may be reproduced, stored in a retrieval system, or transmitted, in any form or
by any means, electronic, mechanical, photocopying, recording,
or otherwise, without the prior permission of the Publisher.

*British Library Cataloguing in Publication Data*

Thomas, W.A.
    The Stock exchanges of Ireland
    1. Stock-exchange—Ireland—History
    I. Title
    332.64′ 2415        HG5450.3.A3

    ISBN 0-905205-34-0


*Library of Congress Cataloging-in-Publication Data*

Thomas, William Arthur.
    The stock exchanges of Ireland.

    Includes index.
    1. Stock-exchange—Ireland—History.  I. Title.
    HG5450.3.A3T48  1986        332.64′ 2415        86-18395
    ISBN 0-905205-34-0

Printed in Great Britain by
Redwood Burn Ltd, Trowbridge, Wiltshire

*to two splendid teachers and scholars*

*E. VICTOR MORGAN and L. S. PRESSNELL*

# CONTENTS

List of illustrations and plates viii
Foreword ix
Acknowledgements xi

1. The Background 1
2. Annuities, Tontines and Lotteries 16
3. Supply, Demand and the Market 39
4. Organisation 55
5. Domestic Matters 74
6. Irish Railway Shares 99
7. Government and other Fixed Interest Stocks 116
8. Irish Joint Stock Companies 135
9. Irish Government Securities 164
10. The Industrial Share Market 182
11. Amalgamation and Unification 203
12. The Belfast Stock Exchange 219

Appendixes 255
   1. Public Loans raised in Ireland 1760 to 1793, 255
   2. Irish Tontine Annuities (1773, 1775, 1777):
      Distribution of Subscriptions, 256
   3. Public Loans raised in Ireland 1793 to 1814, 257
   4. Loans raised in Great Britain for Ireland 1798 to
      1816, 259
   5. Transfers of Stock between Ireland and England 1818
      to 1863, 260
   6. Large Limited Company Registrations in Ireland 1887
      to 1897, Dublin and Cork, 262
   7. Turnover on The Stock Exchange – Irish, 264
   8. Turnover on The Stock Exchange – Northern Ireland,
      264
Index 267

# ILLUSTRATIONS

1. A proposal for the 1797 Lottery      27
2. Charles Tisdall's Memorial to the Lord Lieutenant for a broker's licence, 1815      76
3. The "Certificate of Merchants" supporting Charles Tisdall's application      77
4. A Broker's Licence, 1913      84
5. A Broker's Licence, 1925      85
6. An Apprenticed Clerk's Indenture, 1876      87
7. Cork Stock Exchange Daily Price List, 1888      152
8. Prospectus of The "Grappler" Pneumatic Tyre & Cycle Co. Ltd., 1893      155
9. Belfast Stock Exchange Daily List, 1898      243

## PLATES
(between pages 212 and 213)

1. The Commercial Buildings, Dame Street (print by James Malton, Dublin)
2. Members of the Dublin Stock Exchange, 1896 (photo: Bestick Williams)
3. The Belfast Call Over after the War (photo: Belfast Newsletter Ltd.)
4. The Call Over, 1952 (photo: Irish Press Ltd.)
5. Presiding at the Call Over
6. Launching the Smaller Companies Market, 1986 (photo: Lensmen Ltd.)
7. The Introduction of the New Technology (photo: Lensmen Ltd.)
8. The Committee at Work, 1986 (photo: K. O' Farrell, Skibbereen)

# FOREWORD

## by

## ANGUS McDONNELL, PRESIDENT OF THE IRISH STOCK EXCHANGE

In writing the foreword to this book, I felt that the history of the Irish Stock Exchange has been intertwined with both the political and economic life of Ireland from the time of Wolfe Tone to the present day.

The market in Ireland has always been a forerunner in the economic development of this country and has financed most of the major capital programmes in the last century. This role has been continued to the present day with the financing through the market of almost all the major Irish institutions.

It is interesting to reflect that way back in 1799 the Irish Parliament was passing an Act, probably the first in the world, for the better regulation of Stockbrokers, and that almost 200 years later the same subject of Investor Protection and Regulation is still occupying the minds of Stock Exchange Regulators throughout the world.

The timing of this book, in Stock Exchange terms, coincides with probably one of the most interesting periods this century as far as market development is concerned. The future for us in Ireland will consist of the better aspects of the old and new combined so as to continue to strengthen our position as the regulated market of this country.

The realisation of the Government that wider share ownership and worker participation is an essential part of the fabric of the modern industrial society shows that the Government also sees the beginning of a new era in Stock Exchange development.

I would like to commend Arthur Thomas for writing this book at this time of great change. I know it will make interesting and entertaining general reading and also will be most useful to the students of economic, social and political history in this country.

June 1986

# ACKNOWLEDGEMENTS

I am indebted to the S.S.R.C., the University of Liverpool, and The Stock Exchange for financial assistance which enabled me to undertake the research for this book. My other debts are of a more personal nature.

For several years I harboured the idea of writing a history of the Irish markets. The opportunity to do so arose in 1975 when the General Manager of the Irish Unit, John Leeson, invited me to help with the preparation of a brief history of the Dublin Stock Exchange. It was soon obvious that the wealth of material available merited a much fuller account. From then on I received generous assistance from many quarters.

The Committee of the Irish Unit kindly allowed me full access to all their records and for this I am most grateful. Several members of the Committee displayed a keen interest in the progress of my work. In particular, Donald C. Goodbody opened many "doors" for me and his encouragement was much appreciated. I also have good cause to remember the interest and support of the late Brendan Briscoe, a former President and for many years the Government Broker. Several members helped greatly by readily supplying details of their firms' history; J.A. Garvey, T.V. Murphy, D.C. Morrogh, Kenneth Beaton, J.K. Martin and D.C. Goodbody. Indeed, John L. Gageby valiantly read the entire manuscript and his labours and suggestions are greatly appreciated.

A.E. 'Ted' Hutson, Assistant General Manager, (who served the Stock Exchange for over half a century) rendered many services with characteristic good humour and some splendid anecdotes. Similarly, the present General Manager, Patrick Gowran, obliged with countless favours, large and small, and gave the whole venture his enthusiastic support. His genial hospitality on my visits to Dublin will long be remembered.

Other institutions in Dublin also left me in their debt. The Court of Directors of the Bank of Ireland kindly allowed me to consult their early records and the Secretary to the Court, John Rudd, gave me every facility on my visits to the Bank. The staff at the State Paper Office, Companies Office, and the National Library all answered my queries with great efficiency and friendliness.

I am also indebted to the Committee of the Northern Ireland Unit of The Stock Exchange for giving me access to all their records, and to the staff there for every assistance on two visits to the city some years ago. The present General Manager, Robin J. Moore, kindly answered several enquiries by post. Michael Sweetnam, of the Bank of Ireland, Donegall Place, gave much help as to the operation of the Belfast Register. To all I am most grateful. Nearer home, Peter Davis, of The Stock Exchange, London, helped to guide the financial pilgrimage of the book to a happy close. John Leeson, also of The Stock Exchange, London, gave valuable assistance as indeed he has done throughout.

My other debts are in Liverpool. Professor Patrick Minford gave enthusiastic support and had the foresight to have at hand in the Department the appropriate computer technology just at the right moment. It might be a mere terminal to some but to me it has been a wondrous facility for converting several hundred pages of manuscript into 922,804 bytes. However, without the patient guidance of Anupam Rastogi I would never have mastered some of its mysterious ways. Jane Lucas, hard pressed with Departmental duties, found time to help put the work on to the plastic page. I am most grateful. The graphs show the expert hand of Simon Blackman. Faults, omissions and infelicities of expression that remain are all my own.

At this point the purists of presentation will be looking for a lengthy introduction. There is none. The book has one great purpose — to complete the history of the Stock Exchanges of these islands. It is the last in a trilogy. "Digon i'r diwrnod....".

Liverpool, 1986                                          W. A. Thomas.

CHAPTER 1

★

# THE BACKGROUND

By the close of the eighteenth century Dublin had become one of the most impressive capitals of Europe and the second largest city in the British Isles. Its population had increased from around 115,000 in 1750 to 180,000 in 1800. Its domestic importance was boosted by greater parliamentary independence, the port expanded with the growth of trade and it was the undoubted financial centre of the country. Greater prosperity produced an imposing display of public buildings, among them the Law Courts and the Customs House, and the Irish nobility, with London residences beyond their means, contributed a matching array of spacious and elegant private terraces.

Dublin's growth reflected the relative prosperity of Ireland during the closing decades of the eighteenth century. With rising prices and greater freedom of trade from 1780 onwards, agricultural output and exports rose, and commercial and industrial activity increased, both in old and new manufacturing industries. The linen trade recovered from depression, wool and silk continued to prosper, while brewing and distilling went on expanding.

Contributing to this increased prosperity was the inclination of the landowning aristocracy (the Anglo-Irish protestant families were thought to hold about three-quarters of the land) to spend a lärger proportion of their rental income at home rather than abroad; it was estimated that in 1750 about £$\frac{3}{4}$ mn was leaving Ireland. To cater for this demand Dublin could boast a wide range of luxury goods producers, among them silversmiths and goldsmiths, jewellers and silk manufacturers. Such startling growth in city and country continued against a background of war and turbulence; in Europe the prolonged Napoleonic War and at home the Rebellion of 1798

1

followed later by the Act of Union.

Until the constitutional changes of 1782 and the commencement of Grattan's Parliament, the Irish legislature enjoyed few powers with virtually all legislation being closely controlled by the Privy Council in London. The administration, consisting of the Lord Lieutenant and senior officials, spent most of their time and their high salaries there. The running of the country was directed from Whitehall, while the economy was subordinated to that of England by various enactments.

The American War of Independence helped to change the situation. The government in London realised that it would be necessary to appease public opinion in Ireland, while the Protestants, with some Catholic support, took the opportunity to form an armed body, the Irish Volunteers. The arms were to defend the shores of Ireland against foreign invasion, but the movement really served to demand constitutional changes, eloquently argued by Henry Grattan, for Ireland. As a result several important changes followed, including much greater commercial freedom for Irish manu-facturers and agricultural produce. Significantly, the London government conceded legislative independence in 1782. In May of that year it repealed an Act of the Irish Parliament, 10 Henry VII, c.4 (1494), and in so doing established the sole right of the Irish Parliament to legislate for Ireland, while the final jurisdiction of the Irish House of Lords was also granted. As a result of this change the Chief Governor and Council in Ireland lost the power to originate and alter parliamentary bills. Henceforth bills were transmitted to the King who had the power to approve or reject but not alter them.[1] A year later the Castle authorities agreed to allow annual instead of biennial sessions of the Irish Parliament.

But legislative independence was not accompanied by an Irish Executive responsible to the Irish House of Commons. The executive, consisting of the Lord Lieutenant and a small group of officials — the so called 'Irish Cabinet' — continued to carry out policy which was directed largely from London. They were administrators not ministers. But the constitutional changes of 1782 did not leave the position and the character of the executive entirely unaffected. The concession of annual parliaments made Castle management of the House of Commons more important, and in order to carry through its measures, or resist bills it found objectionable, bribery and patronage continued to be extensively used. The patronage exercised by the government was reflected in the increased civil list pensions and other sinecured posts held by members of the Commons. The executive was enlarged and strengthened but at least some benefit came from this in that "several lucrative offices once held by English absentees were now restored to Ireland".[2] The most notable was the appointment in 1784 of John Foster as Chancellor of the Irish Exchequer, an office held for over twenty years as a sinecure by 'single speech' Hamilton. William Gerard Hamilton was appointed Chancellor 'for life' in 1763. He treated his office as a mere sinecure, leaving the management of the national finances to one of his colleagues, the Attorney General, "a busy lawyer who had no special knowledge of the subject". For this neglect of his duties he received a princely salary of IR£1,800 a year.[3]

Legislative independence did not bring financial control either. The House of Commons had little more control of finance than it did before 1782, and this situation remained unchanged until 1793.[4] Though modelled on the early English Exchequer the Irish Office did not develop along the same lines. Before 1793 it retained a very complex organisation where many offices continued to be filled even when the accompanying duties had long since disappeared, that is, they became profitable sinecured posts for favoured members of the legislature who supported the Castle. Since the payment of money from the Exchequer was made on the authority of a King's Letter countersigned by the British Treasury, the House of Commons was left with little or no control over expenditure. Any suggestions for imposing parliamentary control were viewed as attacks on the royal prerogative. In the meanwhile civil expenditure was continuously expanded without any need to obtain the approval of the House of Commons. At least from 1783 onwards funds to meet expenditure were voted on an annual basis which permitted the House of Commons some influence on the timing and detailed composition of money bills. Also, when John Foster became Chancellor in 1784, although general guidance no doubt came from Whitehall, he was not prepared to act as a mere agent but demanded some share in making as well as executing policy. Even when the office was held from 1785 to 1799 by his friend Sir John Parnell, member for the Queen's County, Foster's influence on financial affairs remained considerable; the allegation that Sir John was 'notoriously indolent' is not entirely fair judging by his labours to raise loans after 1793 and his competent parliamentary performance in financial debates.[5]

The revenue to meet expenditure was collected under the supervision of the Revenue Commissioners who also treated their offices as well paid sinecures. It was a very costly operation absorbing a fifth of the total proceeds, while the officers of the several branches of the Revenue were invariably inefficient and frequently dishonest. The money collected was paid into the Treasury where it was held by an officer called the Teller of the Exchequer. By custom — a highly dangerous one — he could use such balances for his private gain, the only restraint being that if the balances in hand exceeded £30,000 the interest on any excess was to be devoted to public use. Even after the requirement, introduced in 1783, that all receipts were to be promptly lodged with the newly established Bank of Ireland, the Teller apparently continued to hold large balances for some time but at least on some occasions they were used for an arguably "public purpose". It was not until 1813 that the Treasury insisted on full compliance with the order of 1783.[6]

Despite frequent criticism, and suggestions for reform pressed fervently and diligently by John Forbes, change did not come until 1793. The proposals which were made then revolved around setting up a general revenue fund — a Consolidated Fund on the British model — into which all revenue would be paid, and there was to be a limited Civil List with the provision that any additional expenditure had to be duly authorised by the House of Commons and not by the King. The war with France and the voting of large supplies to increase the size of the army, prompted the Chancellor of the Exchequer to introduce a bill "that would regulate the issue from the Treasury of all public money — would add and confirm the authority of Parliament over their grants — and would lessen the expenditure of the nation and the influence of the crown".[7] His aim was to ensure that control of the Treasury would rest with the Irish House of Commons and nowhere else.

The legislation, the Consolidation Fund Act (33 Geo. 3, c. 34), provided for a general fund for all unappropriated duties and from this a fixed sum was allowed to the Civil List and pensions, and the latter was to be gradually reduced. The expenditure of all public funds was placed under the direction of the House of Commons, while the long established system of King's Letters and Warrants was abolished. Thus, in 1794-95 an appropriation of funds was made by the House of Commons with specific sums voted for each service. Later legislation provided for the appointment of Treasury Commissioners to replace the wasteful and sinecured officialdom, and it also prohibited holders of profit under the Crown, or recipients of pensions, from continuing in parliament (re-election, however, was not prohibited). Regulations were also framed for the strict control of the receipt and issue of public money, with all official accounts being kept at the Bank of Ireland. These reforms involved a considerable degree of financial independence but the influence of the Castle was not entirely removed, while their effectiveness in controlling expenditure was compromised by the rapid growth of military activity with the start of the Napoleonic Wars.

There were three main areas of expenditure at this time — civil, military and interest on the public debt. Civil expenditure accounted for about 30% of total expenditure in the period 1770-82, the bulk of it going on "salaries and expenses of State Officers, law and other Civil offices and Incidental expenses", and on "Pensions", in roughly equal amounts. The other important item within civil expenditure were the much criticised parliamentary grants (during 1770-82 they represented about 6% of all expenditure). Prior to Grattan's Parliament they were little more than gifts to private individuals masquerading as grants for public works and the promotion of various manufactures. The use of such generous payments had been prompted in the 1750s by the desire not to show a large surplus in the annual accounts.[8] In the decade before 1793 the proportion of total expenditure absorbed by civilian uses rose to some 43%. Generally, however, this period was regarded as one in which spending was held in check by restrictions on absentee offices, the pension list was constantly scrutinized by parliament and the administration of public funds was improved.

With the coming of war civil expenditure, while it continued to grow, only represented about a fifth of all expenditure. Military spending in the war years rose quickly from around £600,000 in 1793 to a peak of £4.6mn in 1800. For the period 1794-1801 it represented about 66% of total expenditure, a considerable increase on the 46% of the previous decade. In an earlier period, 1770-1783, military expenditure represented some 65% of total expenditure, reflecting the frequent complaint that the military establishment was larger in proportion to the size of the country than was the case in England, a criticism heightened by absentee officers and the frequent use of paid Irish troops abroad.

The final item, interest on the debt, amounted to a modest 6½% of expenditure during 1770-82 (annual average), rising to 13% in the closing years of the century, from 1794-1801. While debt interest was normally about a fifth of civil expenditure in the period before 1793, the great increase in government borrowing needed to finance wartime spending meant that, at the time of the Union, interest payments were running at almost the same level as the entire budget for civil purposes.

The revenue to meet all this expenditure came from several sources. The main source was "Customs and Excise, including Quit Rents, and other Revenue of Crown Lands, and Taxes under the Management of Excise". During 1770-82 this produced some 93% of all net income, the remainder coming from such varied sources as stamps, licences, and taxes on the salaries and pensions of absentees and others. The net income for this period remained relatively stable but since expenditure was increasing there was an annual deficit of about £125,000 which was financed by borrowing. With the somewhat greater stringency of the Grattan Parliament revenue kept pace with expenditure so that the annual average deficiency for 1783-93 stood at a mere £51,000. Revenue was made more buoyant in the mid-1780s by imposing new duties and licences, while the yield from a more prosperous economy produced an income of over £1.0mn in 1793. With the relatively balanced budgets for this period there was thus less net borrowing (that is, new debt less that paid off). However, the growth of military spending after 1793 and particularly that associated with the Rebellion of 1798, meant that traditional sources of revenue which were dependent on peacetime trade simply could not keep pace with expenditure levels. The average annual deficit for the year 1793-1801 was £500,000, and attempts to stem the deficit by imposing additional duties in 1797, including very unpopular duties on items of common consumption, made little impression on the need to borrow heavily. From a figure of £400,000 in 1794 the deficit reached £3.6mn in 1800, and this was covered by borrowing, that is, by increasing the national debt.

The permanent debt of Ireland started in 1716 with a loan of IR£50,000 (£46,153 British) at 8%, payable half yearly, and it was raised in response to a fear that a rebellion might take place. Before this the Irish parliament had been careful to avoid any deficits, and thus borrowing, and went to some lengths to find fiscal alternatives. By a series of irregular borrowings after 1716, and with interest rates falling gradually from 8% to 4%, the debt increased to IR£378,000 by 1749. In the next few years large budget surpluses enabled a great deal of this debt to be paid off, and by 1753 the entire debt had been discharged — an enviable national achievement.[9] But this was not to last for long.

When government borrowing resumed in 1760 the pace was indeed lively. By Lady Day (March 25th) 1763 the total debt created, all in 5% debentures, amounted to IR£550,000, and by 1769 further loans on debentures brought the total debt to IR£640,000. Constant additions to the military establishment required annual loans during the 1770s and for the most part these took the form of debentures paying 4% interest. On three occasions, 1773, 1775, and 1777, they were augmented by three loans on tontine life annuities, involving sums of IR£265,000, IR£175,000 and IR£300,000 respectively. Unlike earlier English tontine loans these were popular not only in Ireland but on the continent as well. In 1780 and 1781 the "deficiencies in Aid" were partly financed by two lottery loans, the only instances in Ireland where lottery prizes were funded, that is, the prizes took the form of government securities, 4% debentures. The amount of stock created for this purpose in the two years was IR£210,000 and IR£105,000 with IR£300,000 being raised through the sales of IR£5 tickets. Thus, as a result of these operations the total debt had risen to IR£1,267,000 by March 26 1782.

For a brief spell, from 1782 to 1793, the total debt outstanding in the form of debenture stock actually fell. This was due in part to the conversion in 1783 of IR£600,000 4% debentures into Bank of Ireland stock. When the Bank of Ireland was formed in 1782 the public were invited to subscribe for the new Bank stock either in cash or by depositing government securities (debentures) which were accepted at their par value, £100. Since the market price of debentures was around £80 the entire subscription was completed by people buying government debentures and tendering them for Bank stock. In effect the entire capital subscribed by the public was lent by the Bank to the government in return for an annual payment of £24,000.

The other reason for the fall in the volume of debt was the virtual balancing of government income and expenditure. Such borrowing as was undertaken, apart from one modest issue of IR£150,000 in 4% debentures with a short annuity attached, was concerned with the repayment of Treasury bills falling due, while the largest operation by far was the successful conversion of IR£1,118,240 4% debentures to a 3½% basis in

1787. This ambitious project was prompted by the rise of the funds, debentures having risen to par, in response to the conservative financial policies of the government. The reduction in the interest burden for the government of about IR£5,000 a year was "affected by calling in the debentures and issuing others to a similar amount to certain Contractors, who were in consideration granted the Lotteries of 1787, 1788 and 1789".[10] Thus, at March 25 1792, the funded debt of Ireland stood at IR£1,118,240, in 3½% debentures, together with IR£600,000 of debt due to the Bank of Ireland. This represented the total permanent debt of the country and provision had to be made for the regular payment of interest at a fixed date every year.

War expenditure soon produced large "deficiencies in Aids" and eventually forced the government to make separate loans in London. War borrowing began with a loan of IR£350,000 in 5% debentures, followed a year later in 1794, by a larger loan of IR£487,983, in 5% debentures, the interest being payable at the Exchequer in Ireland and there was a short annuity attached as an additional attraction to persuade investors to lend their money to the government. To make Irish offers more attractive to English investors a large tranche of IR£541,666 was made payable at the Bank of England, this particular loan being taken by Robert Shaw, who "must have sent at least half of it in specie", that is, gold coin or bullion, back to Ireland. Two other loans followed in 1795, one of IR£400,000 in Ireland of 5% debentures but the balance of the deficit was met by a separate loan made in London amounting to IR£1,191,600 in stock transferable at the Bank of England, both loans having a short annuity attached to them. Increasing dependence on London arose because the demands of the Dublin Treasury exceeded the local supply of funds; as John Puget, London agent to the Bank of Ireland, expressed it to the 1797 Lords' Committee of Secrecy on the Bank of England, "I do not believe a loan of £1,200,000 could have been made in Ireland in 1795, in addition to the other loan made there.....".[11]

An attempt to repeat the 1795 pattern of borrowing ran into severe difficulties a year later, on both domestic and more distant fronts. The home loan of IR£860,000, taken by the contractor Robert Shaw, realised only IR£640,000, since the last two deposits were not paid "by those who had undertaken the loan, in consequence of the difficulty of raising money". Nobody wanted to buy government securities when news came of a French fleet in Bantry Bay and with an invasion imminent. The London loan of 5% stock transferable at the Bank of England, with an attractive short annuity of £4.15s% for 13½ years, produced only IR£325,000 out of the intended IR£500,000. The loan, taken by Robert Curtis, came to an abrupt close "when the Governor and Deputy Governor of the Bank of England objected to the transmission of any more specie to this country (Ireland) — they complained that the loans to Ireland diminished the quantity of gold in the London market, and declared that they must take care of their own interest in that respect in preference to the interest of Ireland".[12] It was probably this experience which produced the change from direct borrowing by the Irish Treasury in London to that of "agency" borrowing through the British Treasury.

By March 25 1797, the debt, excluding that owed to the Bank of Ireland, amounted to IR£5,255,026. Further large home loans followed, prompted by the Treasury's needs, and the feeling expressed by Sir John Parnell that he had "reason to believe that the certainty of some money being borrowed in Ireland would facilitate the negotiation here" (London).[13] It was thought that London investors would be more willing to put up money if they saw Irish ones sharing the risks with them. The home loans were issued to contractors at heavy discounts, or more elegantly put "when the difficulty of raising loans increased, capitals were assigned to the creditors much higher than the sum advanced".[14] The 1797 loan was issued at 63, the one for 1798 at 61, both in 5% debentures. The Chancellor, Sir John, confessed that the "terms, bad as they were for Government, were made necessary....by the situation of the two countries: the other terms which had been offered, the monied men had not thought proper to accept".[15] The doubts of the "monied men" were greatly increased by the Rebellion of 1798 when the United Irishmen led by Wolfe Tone sought to make Ireland into a republic on French lines, independent from Britain. Such ambitions made William Pitt intent on securing the legislative union of Ireland and Britain so as to remove any threats from across the Irish Sea.

On a falling market the choice was open to the government to issue stock of the same denomination as the money lent, that is, issue a stock at $7\frac{3}{4}\%$ interest for £100 rather than 5% stock at a price of 63 or so. However, the contractors preferred loans in a low price stock since the public were reported to have a "taste" for them, hoping for future falls in interest rates, while issuing more of the same denomination ensured a better sale because a large quantity of such stock was already on the market.[16] Public enthusiasm, however, was in contrast to some opposition in the Irish House of Commons. The issue of stock at such a large discount produced sufficient benefit for the lender by way of a yield of £17 18s. 9d. on 5% debentures at 63, but "besides this", complained a critic, "the public creditor will also receive a premium of 37l.... [and] the loss which the public would sustain by this transaction was enormous".[17] But the government also had an interest in issuing stock at a large discount. Interest rates would have to fall a great deal to absorb the margin between the issue price and par (£100), thus allowing the government to buy in stock below par value. It would do this in order to reduce the amount of debt outstanding in the hands of the public and thus lessen somewhat the annual interest payments it had to make. Issuing stock with a high coupon rate, at par, would mean that if interest rates fell the stock would then stand at a premium above the par value and at such prices the government would certainly be disinclined to buy from the market.

To help the government financially in this difficult period its issues on the market were supplemented in 1797 by a loan of IR£500,000 from the Bank of Ireland, at 5%, which represented a further increase in the capital of the Bank. Two large loans were also made to the market in 1799 and 1800, at 74 and 85 respectively, both in 5% debentures to which was attached a premium in Exchequer Bills. Thus by January 1 1801, the total debt of Ireland, funded in Ireland, amounted to IR£12,417,806, together with a debt of IR£1,100,000 due to the Bank of Ireland.

However, this was not the total borrowing of the Irish Government. Having exhausted its credit with the Bank of Ireland and particularly on the local market, the government increasingly turned to the large London market. Between 1797 and 1801 several big loans were raised by the issue of debt funded in Great Britain. These were loans raised in Great Britain for the separate service of Ireland, the annual interest of the debt so created being met by the Irish Exchequer who periodically remitted sums for this purpose to the British Treasury. In the period from March 25 1797 to January 5 1801, the debt of Ireland funded in Great Britain was issued to the nominal total of £15,315,000, the actual sum raised being £8,500,000, in British currency. The sums for Ireland were raised as part of British loans, the amounts being remitted from the British Exchequer (see below). The inclusion of an element of Irish borrowing in the British loans obviously simplified the borrowing programme, and no doubt procured the capital for Ireland at a more favourable rate of interest than if the loans were made separately (if they could have been made at all in that way) in competition with British loans. In terms of interest payments the needs of war time expenditure increased the sum paid on the total public debt from £132,000 in 1793 (10% of total government expenditure) to £915,000 in 1801 (20% of total government expenditure). Whereas about a third of the former sum was paid in London and elsewhere, by 1801 that proportion had risen to nearly a half.[18]

The other important element in government borrowing was the unfunded debt, that is, short term and temporary debt, which in the case of Ireland consisted largely of Treasury bills. These were first issued in 1779 by authority of the act, 19 and 20 George III, c. 2, the amount raised being IR£100,000 at 3d. per day interest, or £4 11s. 3d. per annum. None were issued for under £100, while their maturity ranged from one to five years. Within a few years of their introduction the government was relying heavily on them either to finance the deficit temporarily or to pay off debentures, so that by 1785 bills amounted to about half of the total funded debt, the amount outstanding being IR£795,755.[19] In the period to 1792 the total outstanding stabilized around IR£630,000, maturing bills being replaced by new bills issued at 2½d. per day interest as against 3d.[20] War requirements produced heavy reliance on bill finance and by 1801 the unfunded debt stood at IR£1,435,783, most of the bills issued at 5% and 6% interest. They were always a popular form of investment since they could be easily traded — "being distributed among those who are willing to advance their value they form a kind of circulating medium", and they could be tendered in payment to the government either in settlement of a debt or for new loans offered to the market.[21] Even London financial interests regarded them as an attractive security. To obtain funds quickly large blocks were also issued to the Bank of Ireland and by April 1797 government indebtedness to the Bank for Treasury bills was IR£704,000, prompting the latter to refuse further accommodation to the government on this basis.[22] It was one reason for resorting to the London market at that time.

An interesting aspect of the loans raised outside Ireland was the way in which they were remitted to Dublin. Several methods were available and all were employed at various times. Gold could be transported, an expensive and risky procedure. Sending bank notes was slightly less difficult. The safest way was to use bills of exchange since this merely involved claims on money.

Part of the separate loans raised for Ireland in London between 1794 and 1797, and the loans raised for the service of Ireland as part of British loans after that, were left in London to pay interest due on annuities and previous loans, which meant that no remittances across the exchanges were needed on account of interest payments due in London. The residue of the loans were then remitted to Ireland. Up until the suspension of specie payments in 1797 the London agent of the Irish Treasury, John Puget, remitted large sums in gold. Of the two loans made in 1794 and 1795, for a total of £1.6mn, "upwards to £1,200,000 was remitted in Specie".[23] The last separate loan for Ireland in 1796-97, which was cut short at £300,000, led to "about 80,000l." in specie being sent to Dublin; this was part of the alarming run on the Bank of England which resulted in the suspension of the convertibility of Bank of England notes into gold in February 1779 and which was applied to the Bank of Ireland in the following month.[24] According to John Puget's evidence to the 1804 Committee on the Irish Currency the expense of transmitting money from England to Ireland was "Seven shillings and sixpence per cent carriage and insurance to Holyhead; 2s. per cent freight to Dublin, without any expense of insurance, or any other charge; but if insured, from 5s. to 7s. per cent", while his firm Puget & Bainbridge, charged the government and the Bank of Ireland ¼% commission.[25] The practice was to sent the gold "in proper carriages and attended by a sufficient guard to Holyhead, with one or two confidential persons to see it shipped on board the Packet. A cutter is to attend the Packet for protection and the money is not to be put on board until the cutter arrives and is ready to sail. [The] Confidential person to come over in the cutter and the guard to stay at the 'Head until the money is shipped".[26]

Less frequently used was the transmission of Bank of England notes to the Treasury of Ireland. In 1797 the Bank of Ireland, as agents to the Treasury, received about £400,000 in Bank of England notes as part of the £1.2mn remitted at the time, the notes being exchanged at 6%, that is, £106 Irish for £100 British. The notes were then sold to such persons in Dublin as applied for them. The rate, 6%, "was more favourable to Government..... than that upon the Exchange of Dublin", the exchange of Dublin on London at the time going as low as 4½%.[27]

A simple and safe channel for transmitting funds to Dublin was to buy in London bills of exchange payable in Dublin and transmit them to the Bank of Ireland for the account of the Treasury so that when presented for payment the Treasury would receive cash. However, after the introduction of borrowing in London through the agency of the British Treasury, another method became more general and involved the Lords of the Treasury drawing on their London agents, Puget & Bainbridge. These were appropriately called "Their Lordships Drafts".[28] When a loan was made in London, part of which was for Ireland, it was arranged between the two Treasuries at what periods the portion due to Ireland should be paid in London. At such times, therefore, the Irish Treasury could avail themselves of the funds by drawing bills on their London agent who received the money on their behalf. The bills drawn on London were then offered for sale in Dublin to anyone who wanted to obtain funds in London. Thus, the Irish Treasury got funds in Dublin in exchange for a claim on funds in London.

The procedure followed is of interest because it reveals that several names, later to feature in the origins of the Stock Exchange, were involved in financial affairs for some years before this. Briefly, the practice was as follows. The Lords of the Treasury gave notice that they intended to issue bills either by telling the "great number of people [who] came to inquire", or "notice was at times given on the Royal Exchange". The amounts drawn by the Treasury depended on the funds available in England and the short term fiscal needs of the Exchequer. However, "in all cases where the Treasury have been at ease in their circumstances, the amount in their power to draw has been given in such proportions as it was thought would be most likely to regulate and steady the Exchange, say 30 to £40,000 a week. In cases of necessity £140,000 or more have been drawn in a week."[29] Generally the period of the drawing was from a month to six weeks or more, the practice being to extend the period of drawing, consistent with the financial position, so as to "regulate and steady the Exchanges".[30]

Following the notification of the drawing application was made by individuals who wanted such bills. Frequently about 50 persons would appear "in the waiting room at one time" and bills were given to those "who first pressed nearest to get in their names...[and] each came with a slip in his hand". Those not able "to press near enough and were disappointed" usually received preference at the next drawing, and for some time in 1803

James Crofton, Chief Clerk of the Irish Treasury, "entered in a book the names of all Persons who applied for Bills, with a view that every person might be accommodated in his turn". Among those who sought such drafts in 1803, were such prominent Dublin names as Pim, Hone, La Touche, Beresford, Jeremiah D'Olier and Thomas Williams (of the Bank of Ireland), Sir. W. G. Newcomen, Leland Crosthwait, the Archbishop of Dublin, and the following prominent Dublin stockbrokers, Samuel Bruce, William Deey, Richard Williams and James Gibbons.[31]

The days of drawing were Tuesdays, Thursdays and Saturdays, the proceeding days being the regular "Exchanges" days at the Royal Exchange, and the prices which were made there "in some measure influenced the price to be fixed by the Lords of the Treasury" for the bills on offer. The rate they drew at was based on information brought to their Lordships by a leading Dublin broker; "There is a broker in the employ of the Lords of the Treasury (Mr. Robert Deey) whose business it is to attend the public Exchange, and on the morning following to report the courses of that day; this report is laid before the Lords of the Treasury, and they fix the price being never higher, generally the lowest of the prices reported".[32] In some instances bills were drawn at lower rates than market levels but this arose from the "absolute necessity of providing funds...which could at that time be provided in no other manner than holding out a temptation to the Merchants, Bankers and Dealers, to come in for a larger sum". Usually the discount on market levels was between $\frac{1}{4}$ and 1%, seldom as much as 1%.[33] Initially the drafts were drawn for three days sight, but from about 1802 they were generally made payable at 21 days sight. This simple change meant that it was possible for the Dublin Treasury to receive funds about a month before payment was made in London and it was interest free. It also enabled them to draw over a longer period which induced less fluctuation on the Exchanges.[34] Up until 1802 the Treasury drew for any sum demanded but found that "speculators in Exchange had great advantage, by taking the power out of the Lords of the Treasury in a short period, and thereby having the markets under their control". To remove "this evil it was thought advisable to limit the amount of Bills delivered to £1,000 for each person".[35]

# NOTES

1. Poynings' Law, an act passed by the Irish Parliament in 1494, and later amended, required that all Irish bills had to be submitted by the Chief Governor and Council in Ireland to the King and Council in England, for approval, alteration or to be suppressed altogether. Only bills approved by the King were then presented to the Irish parliament, which might reject or accept them as they stood; J.C. Beckett, *The Making of Modern Ireland 1603-1923*, (1966), p. 51.

2. ibid., p. 235.

3. To confer the office on John Foster in 1784, the government had to buy it back from Hamilton with the promise of a pension of IR£2,500 a year; see W.E.H. Lecky, *A History of Ireland in the Eighteenth Century*, Vol. 2, (1892), p. 409: D.N.B., Vol. 8, pp. 1116-17.

4. For a detailed discussion see T.J. Kiernan, *History of the Financial Administration of Ireland to 1817*, (1930), chapter 10.

5. A.P.W. Malcomson, *John Foster : The Politics of the Anglo-Irish Ascendancy*, (1978), pp. 46-58. Sir John Parnell was dismissed from the Chancellorship in 1799 because he opposed the Union proposals.

6. It was brought to light in 1813 that the Deputy Teller had the use of about £200,000 of public money; Kiernan, op.cit., p. 326.

7. *The Parliamentary Register, or Histories of the Proceedings and Debates of the House of Commons of Ireland*, 1793, Vol. 13, p. 431.

8. For a detailed description see G. O'Brien, *Economic History of Ireland in the Eighteenth Century*, (1918), pp. 322-25. Particulars of the payments made are given in Accounts Relating to the Public Income and Expenditure of Great Britain and Ireland, B.P.P., 1868-69, Commons, Vol. 35, Accounts and Papers (2), covering the years 1769-1801. The largest grants in the early years were bounties on linen and hemp manufactures, with bounties on the home sale of Irish manufactures increasing in size in the 1780s. Grants to inland navigation became important from 1790 onwards.

9. An event which produced a constitutional wrangle involving the niceties of the relationship between the Irish parliament and the King; see Kiernan. op. cit., pp. 157-58.

10. "The Debt of Ireland – Funded in Ireland (Irish Currency)", Report of the Proceedings of the Commissioners of the National Debt from 1786 to March 1890, B.P.P., 1890-91, Vol. XLVIII, p. 144.

11. Report of the Lords' Committee of Secrecy, 1797, Minutes, B.P.P., 1810, (17), Vol. 3, p. 56.

12. *Parliamentary Register*, op.cit., 1797, Vol. 17, p. 470.

13. Letter to John Foster, 1796-97, State Paper Office, O.P./22/22/14.

14. Robert Hamilton, *An Enquiry Concerning The Rise and Progress, the Redemption and Present State, and the Management of the National Debt of Great Britain and Ireland*, (1818), p. 244.

15. *Parliamentary Register*, op. cit., 1797, Vol. 17, p. 469.

16. Henry Parnell, *Financial Reform*, (1830), p. 242.

17. *Parliamentary Register*, op. cit., Vol. 17, p. 473. Sir John M'Cartney proposed the issue of short term bills rather than perpetual annuities at a large discount. In reply to the criticism the Chancellor pointed out that by the late act the government were "enabled to purchase in their own securities on the best terms"; ibid., p. 475. An issue at par with a high coupon rate would lead to a premium if interest rates fell, and the government would not be keen to buy stock at such prices.

18.   In 1801 interest and management of Irish debt funded in England amounted to £307,000 out of total interest payments on the public debts of £915,000; English investors also held stocks and debentures funded in Ireland. For details see "Accounts Relating to the Public Income and Expenditure of Great Britain and Ireland," B.P.P., 1868-69, Vol. 35, Accounts and Papers (2).

19.   An attempt in 1784 to exchange Treasury bills, which bore interest at £4 11s. 3d. p.a., for 4% debentures, with a payment in money by way of a premium, failed lamentably; see "Accounts Relating to the Public Income and Expenditure...", op. cit., p. 543.

20.   For details of schemes involving Treasury bills, see F.G. Hall, *The Bank of Ireland 1783-1946*, (1949), pp. 59-61.

21.   Hamilton, op. cit., p. 169.

22.   Hall, op. cit., p. 67. The correspondence on the subject between the Bank of Ireland and the Treasury is given in *Journals of the Irish House of Commons*, Vol. XVII, pp. ccxxxvi-ccxxxix.

23.   Evidence of John Puget to the Lords' Committee on Secrecy, 1797, op. cit., pp. 30-31.

24.   F.W. Fetter, *The Irish Pound 1797-1826*, (1955), pp. 12-13.

25.   Report, Minutes of Evidence, and Appendix of the Committee on the Circulating Paper, the Specie and the Current Coin of Ireland, and also on the Exchange between that part of the United Kingdom and Great Britain, 1804, B.P.P., 1826, (407), Vol. 461, p. 20.

26.   Bank of Ireland, Minutes of the Court of Directors, April 7, 1795.

27.   Evidence of Jeremiah D'Olier, formerly Governor of the Bank of Ireland (1799-1801), 1804 Committee on Irish Currency, op.cit., p. 96.

28.   This method was departed from in 1800 when some Irish merchants in England induced the government to accept part of the loan due to Ireland in Bank of Ireland notes exchangeable at the Bank of England at 9½%, when the market exchange rate was 13¾% - 14%. While this concession lasted it produced a lowering of the exchange rate and considerable uncertainty in the market. The Chancellor, Mr. Pitt, agreed to the concession because several merchants in the Irish trade in London represented "to him the difficulties which were growing in the commercial intercourse between Great Britain and Ireland in consequence of the high Exchange". The effect of the measure was to reduce the rate to 9½% so that "all the remittances out of Ireland whether for payment of imports, or of rents of absentees, or for remittances to the Bank of England passed over at this Exchange and continued to do so, so long as the Exchange of Bank of Ireland notes continued at the Bank of England". The rate of Dublin on London was at a 9% level from October to December 1800; thereafter it rose to a peak of 15% in July 1801. In the 1801 administration of Addington the practice was dropped, the government being anxious to obtain the profits of exchange on the appreciating British pound. See the evidence of Walter Borrowes, London Merchant, 1804 Committee on Irish Currency, op. cit., p. 29.

29.   Evidence of James Crofton, Chief Clerk of the Irish Treasury, to the 1804 Committee on Irish Currency, op. cit., p. 67. Appendix Q of the Report gives the amounts drawn by the Treasury between January 1803 and March 1804; the sums were mostly in the £10,000 to £30,000 range, by far the largest being £113,300 for March 15 1801.

30.   In 1803 when the Treasury were drawing the fluctuation in the Exchange was about 1%; when they were not drawing it was about 4%; ibid., p. 70.

31.   ibid., Appendix No. 4. When the Treasury was able to meet all demands it was no longer necessary to keep such a waiting list.

32.   ibid., p. 66.

33.   The Treasury discouraged persons from selling drafts on the Exchange, or retailing them in small sums at a profit, by refusing to supply further bills; ibid., p. 68.

34.   Evidence of John Puget to the 1804 Committee on Irish Currency, op. cit., p. 126. John Puget observed that "the Treasury got no allowance in the Exchange from the takers of their Bills for the difference of drawing at three days sight instead of twenty one days sight"; that is, there was no advantage for the Treasury in offering money in London within three days — the buyers of bills were not prepared to pay more for them.

35.   Evidence of James Crofton, op. cit., p. 67. In 1804 bills of £500 were issued.

CHAPTER TWO

# ANNUITIES,
# TONTINES AND LOTTERIES

Modern governments resort to many kinds of lures and devices in order to persuade savers to part with their funds. Their eighteenth century counterparts were equally inventive in this direction. When the rate of interest by itself was not sufficient to entice public demand for the securities offered, various bonuses were attached to the loans as an additional inducement. If it was thought that investors needed a speculative lure the Treasury was not reluctant to appeal to the gambling instinct of the public. Lotteries served this end quite successfully. As at all times the compulsion to gamble is infinitely more prevalent than the ability to invest. A variation on the same approach, but more complex in their workings and more select in their appeal, were the tontine loans which the Irish Treasury resorted to. These offered the rewarding prospect of large returns should the other subscribers or their nominees have the misfortune to die early. Their appeal was very much the same as that of the lottery, a large gain for a modest outlay, except one had to wait a little longer for it. During the last quarter of the eighteenth century the Irish Government exploited all the above financial inducements in its borrowing activity, and in so doing drew upon the services of several gentlemen involved with financial matters and who later emerged as leading Dublin stockbrokers.

The form of security used for loans made in Ireland before 1731 appears to have been merely a receipt issued by the Treasury for the amount of money lent. In practice it was a very convenient instrument since the authorising legislation allowed the holder to transfer it to another person simply by endorsement. Both the principal and interest were charged on 'Aids' granted by the Irish Parliament.

In 1731 the type of security issued was altered by act of parliament (5 Geo. II, c. 2, s. 7). All existing Treasury receipts were called in and instead more formal "Treasury orders or receipts termed Debentures", numbered "arithmetically", were issued. It was also provided, with a view to reducing the amount of debt outstanding, that if a revenue surplus of £5,000 developed, then debentures drawn by lot could be paid off. The interest on debentures was supposed to cease with the current half yearly day of payment, but "whether from ignorance or negligence it not infrequently happened that some considerable time elapsed between the cessation of the interest and the presentation of the debentures for the payment of principal".[1] Of the total amount of IR£4,013,190 raised by loans between 1760 and 1793, threequarters constituted funded debt in the form of loan debentures.

Loan debentures transferable by endorsement, effectively a bearer security, proved a particularly popular instrument and when in 1797 facilities were made available to convert them into government stock transferable by inscription, the response was somewhat lethargic.

Irish investors preferred debentures for several reasons. Transfer by endorsement was a useful attribute which required the minimum of work and dispensed with the services of a third party, such as power of attorney. The debentures were also widely used as security for bank loans. Borrowers from the Bank of Ireland were required to lodge as "collateral security Government Debentures which if the loan was not repaid could be disposed of at market prices".[2] A further point in their favour was that the Bank of Ireland would not accept inscribed stock as collateral security when the transfer books were shut since for that period a transfer could not take place. Debentures had no such drawbacks. Finally, the interest was paid half yearly, on a calendar basis, and paid at the Treasury (from 1806 it was paid at the Bank of Ireland). Since many Irish investors appear to have been eager to cling to these advantages, debentures did not finally disappear until the old Funded Debt in Ireland at different rates of interest was either paid off or converted under the several conversion schemes of 1822, 1824 and 1844.[3]

The preamble to the act 37 George III, c. 54 claimed that "it may be advantageous and satisfactory to persons holding debentures... if the principal sums therein were turned into stock, to be called government-stock, such stock to be entered in books, to be kept in the Bank of Ireland... and if the dividends or interest payable thereon, were paid at the said bank half-yearly". In the Irish House of Commons the Chancellor of the Exchequer, Sir John Parnell, noted two benefits for the holders of debentures who opted for the new arrangements; "The advantage to the holders would be, that they would not be liable to lose their securities which depended on the preservation of the parchments. Another advantage would be, that the holder of the stock might dispose of any portion of it as he pleased, which he could not do if he held debentures".[4] The change was

"satisfactory" from the standpoint of the government since the growth of
the debt obviously imposed administrative strains on the Treasury. But
probably more significant was that arrangements had been made to
establish a Sinking Fund (see Chapter 3) and its operation would be greatly
assisted if "the entries of... principal sum or stock in the books...and of every
assignment or transfer...shall be evidence of the right and title thereto...".[5]
Debentures written on parchment were hardly suitable for the kind of
transactions the Treasury had in store.

Following the passing of the act, debenture holders were invited to bring
their debentures to the Bank of Ireland and have them "entered in books",
and the debentures were then cancelled. The debentures deposited at the
Bank and converted into stock were "stamped with the words BANK OF
IRELAND in red oil colour", and according to the act they were to be
transmitted within seven days of receipt to the Treasury for cancellation.[6]

Under the new system a change of ownership entailed the signing of the
transfer books by the person assigning or transferring, or their attorney
"lawfully authorized in writing", the entry to be undersigned by the person
to whom the stock was transferred or by his attorney. While cumbersome
compared with bearer stocks, inscription was not entirely novel to Irish
investors since they were accustomed to the ownership of British government stocks transferable in person or by granting power of attorney.[7] To
remove the obstacle that interest was paid at different dates by the Treasury
on debentures and by the Bank on the newly created inscribed stock, the
Treasury arranged that interest due on debentures brought to the Bank
could be paid by the Bank who was later reimbursed by the Treasury.[8]
Interest on debentures not offered for conversion continued to be paid at the
Treasury.

To cope with the increased volume of work involved the Bank of Ireland
decided to move the transfer business from the Secretary's Office to a
separate office and an adjacent property was acquired for that purpose. The
Transfer Office was open from eleven until two o'clock, and following the
"great increase in business" a Transfer Officer was appointed to "see the
Transfers of government and Bank stock made, keep correct duplicate
books in the safe provided by the government and the Treasury, post and
compare the additional transfers weekly and transact every business relative
thereto as directed by Act of Parliament".[9]

The debentures issued between 1761 and 1801, and funded in Ireland,
ranged from the "Old 3½%", through the "old Four per cents", to the
"Irish Fives". The latter stock belonged to the Napoleonic War period, the
first major loan appearing in 1793 and by 1800 IR£11,115,206 of stock had
been created involving loans of IR£10,083,175 in twelve separate issues.
Four loans to the sum of IR£550,000 were made in 5% debentures during
1761-63, but the rate was reduced to 4% in two conversions a few years later.
Old Irish Fours formed the bulk of the funded debt between 1765 and 1789,

the biggest volume outstanding being in 1783 with a total of IR£1,527,600; in 1784 IR£600,000 was converted into Bank of Ireland stock as part of the subscription to the capital of the Bank. Some of the stock was paid off but most of it was converted to 3½% stock in the great conversion operation of 1787-88. Further loans were made later at 4% but they were mostly small and for local purposes. The Old 3½% debentures dated from the 1787-88 conversion; a small issue at 3½% was made in 1769 but paid off a year later (see Appendix 1 for the various issues).[10]

With the increase in the amount of government borrowing after 1793 part of the issues were made payable at the Bank of England, in addition to the normal facility of being payable at the Exchequer in Ireland. This provision was introduced in order to increase the attractiveness of Irish Funds to English investors and to non-resident Irish holders. Money was remitted to London to pay interest to those subscribers who indicated that they wanted to be paid there, "such interest and annuities to be paid according to the rate that money is current for in Ireland".[11] In 1795 a large loan of over IR£2mn was made transferable at the Bank of England for English subscribers ("subscription to stock to be entered in books to be kept by the Governor and Company of the Bank of England"), and the truncated loan of 1796 was also put into the inscribed form transferable in London. However, when borrowing needs exceeded domestic lending ability, and while separate Irish loans in London would only be possible on very prohibitive terms, the loans of 1798 to 1801 (raising £8.5 million with a nominal capital of £15.3mn, mostly at 3%) took the form of inscribed stock transferable and payable at the Bank of England, and funded in Great Britain. The stocks involved were 3% Consols, Reduced Three percents, and 4% Consols.

With the exception of the three Irish Tontines of 1773, 1775 and 1777, annuities created in Ireland "as a collateral inducement to the Public Creditor to subscribe to loans ... [were] ... neither numerous nor important".[12] Only seven of the loans made between 1786-97 had short annuities and apart from the 1786 loan on 4% debentures (with a short annuity of £1.10s% for 12 years), the others were inducements associated with wartime issues. The four annuities linked to loans made between 1794-95 ranged around the 1½% level for periods of about 15 years. The 5% loan of 1796 had a short annuity of £4 15s. per cent for 13½ years, while the loan of IR£500,000 a year later from the Bank of Ireland had a short annuity of £3 12s. 6d. per cent for 19 years, both indicating the difficulty of raising funds at the time.

The only departure from the use of perpetual annuities for long term borrowing, that is, the debentures described earlier, was the use of terminable life annuities associated with the three tontine schemes of the mid 1770s. From the standpoint of the Treasury, life annuities (payment ceased with the death of the subscriber or his nominee in the case of a tontine) had certain attractions since reducing the amount of debt outstanding was more easily secured than by the use of perpetual annuities; as the Reverend Dr. Richard Price put the case against perpetual debt — "It is obvious that accumulating debt so rapidly, and mortgaging posterity for eternity in order to pay the interest of it must in the end prove destructive".[13] Life annuities, however, involved a slightly higher annual charge since the value of the annuity was continually falling ,and as Adam Smith pointed out "An annuity for a long term of years will not find nearly the same number of purchasers" as a perpetual one. Lenders on the other hand generally preferred perpetual annuities redeemable by parliament. It was a more convenient transferable stock and enjoyed a freer market than life annuities since in their case the value of the unexpired part could not be calculated with any confidence. Perpetual stock also had an advantage for the government since it could be redeemed at the government's option and thus offered an opportunity for conversion to a lower rate of interest, which was not possible with life annuities.

The attraction of tontine life annuities for the borrower was that while the "liberation of the public revenue" did not occur until, as the act quaintly put it, the "death of all the annuitants comprehended in one lot", for the same outlay more money could be raised than by the issue of annuities for separate lives. An annuity with the right of survivorship attached (a tontine annuity) was worth more than an equal annuity for a separate life and generally sold for something more than it was worth. In European countries where life annuities were more widely used, tontines were preferred on this account: "The expedient which will raise the most money is almost always preferred to that which is likely to bring about in the speediest manner the liberation of the public revenue".

Tontines were the invention of the Neapolitan, Lorenzo Tonti, who successfully proposed his scheme to Cardinal Mazarin in 1653, and the first French tontine appeared in 1689. The general principle is that a fixed annual amount by way of interest should be divided among the lenders in proportion to their subscription and they receive such payment for the duration of any life they nominate, their own or someone else. On the death of a nominee his or her share is divided among the surviving subscribers.

The first English tontine was made in 1693 and was linked to the beginnings of the National Debt, raising about a tenth of the proposed sum. The next, in 1766, was an almost total failure, while the attempt of 1789 was only rescued by the extensive use of government nominees.[14] By contrast the three Irish tontines, of 1773, 1775 and 1777, were remarkable in that they were carried out successfully.

The first Irish tontine of 1773, established by 13 & 14 Geo. III, c. 5 (Irish) was for IR£265,000 in sums of £100 each with annuities of 6%. It offered the benefit of survivorship in three classes; persons of the age of 40 years and upwards, from 20 to 39 years, and under 20 years.[15] However, no subscriber was to receive by benefit of survivorship an annuity in excess of the principal sum originally advanced. Even so it was an appealing prospect. Subscribers could nominate one life for every £100 subscribed, or one life to the total amount subscribed in multiples of £100. When the subscribers had completed the payments (£20 down, and two instalments of £40) they received from the Treasury "one or more debentures, in which shall be mentioned and expressed the names and surnames, additions, places of abode, ages and other descriptions of the nominee or nominees". Such debentures could be assignable by "any writing under hand and seal, such transfers to be notified to the Treasury" who kept the appropriate record books.

Subscribers were required to notify the death of their nominees within a month and to return "the Debentures if in their hands within three months under penalty of £20", while failure to claim the annuity for three years led to forfeiture, although in practice some leniency was shown to proprietors who neglected to do so.[16] To keep the accounting manageable no additional distribution was made among the survivors in any class until a sufficient sum had accrued by the "fall of lives" to pay an extra ½% interest. Initially subscriptions were received at the Dublin Treasury but it was found that many investors in England were eager to subscribe but they were discouraged by the trouble and expense of obtaining their annuity due to the currency exchange. To meet the needs of English investors a further act (13 & 14 Geo. 3, c. 7) empowered the Lord Lieutenant to appoint an agent to pay the annuities in London and to receive subscriptions there. English subscribers paid in sterling the sum of £92 6s. 1d. and received an annuity of £5 10s. 9d.; the Irish government absorbed the cost or took the benefit of fluctuations in the exchange rate.

The second tontine of 1775 was for IR£175,000 at 6%, on somewhat similar terms to its predecessor. However, to add to its attractiveness there was no restriction on the benefit of survivorship; "the entire interest of the sum advanced shall be paid to the subscriber, his or her assignee or assignees, whose nominee shall be the survivor of the nominees of each class, during the life of such surviving nominee".[17] Such a prospect was indeed a considerable enticement. The third tontine of 1777 was for IR£300,000 at 7½% and similar to the 1775 issue. At first it was intended to pay an annuity of 6% but only IR£47,000 was raised on these terms in three weeks and to revive interest the annuity was raised to 7½%, a move which produced a full subscription in a few days.[18]

Subscribers to the annuities, if they were resident in Ireland, could obtain their half yearly payment by the personal appearance of the nominee at the Treasury along with the debenture. This occasioned little difficulty where subscribers had nominated their own life. However, if they nominated someone else payment could be made on producing "a certificate of the life of...(the)....respective nominee, signed by the minister, or in his absence by the curate of the parish, where such nominee shall be then living upon the day when the said half yearly half payment shall become due".[19] For all subscribers "resident beyond the seas", and there were quite a lot, payment was made on the appearance of the subscriber and nominee, or the agent of the former acting under power of attorney, and he had to produce the necessary certificate of the existence of the nominee at the office duly set up in London. At the time of completing their payments subscribers were asked to indicate if they wanted the annuity paid in London.

The first agent authorized by the Lord Lieutenant to act in London was the firm of Brown, Collinson & Co., but when it failed in 1781 the banking house of Boldero, Kendall, Adey & Co. took over the work.[20] After the Union the agency was transferred to Rogerson Cotter Esq., who continued to use the offices of Boldero until 1811 when the firm ceased to be bankers to the Tontine Office. The office then move from Cornhill to premises in Bridge Street, Blackfriars, remaining there until 1832, when payment of the annuities devolved to the National Debt Commissioners.

Money for the half yearly payment of the annuities was paid into an account (under the title 'Irish Tontine Annuities payable in London') at Boldero's by the Treasury's London agent, Puget & Bainbridge. Between 1802-10 the Treasury sent over £20,000 (British money) every six months; in 1796 it had been £18,000. It was then the practice to take "in the morning of each day a sum of money from Messers Boldero & Co" to pay the annuitants who applied for their dividend, and return the balance remaining to the account in the evening, the sum used up being charged to the Tontine Account.[21] The sum sent from Ireland was generally more than adequate to meet the requests for payment which left a large balance in Boldero's hands, an estimated accumulated balance between 1802 and 1810 of around £12,000. Earlier, however, Boldero's had paid out more than they had received, the Treasury having remitted less than the full half yearly payment. The precise amounts of the dividends to be paid were decided by the long serving Mr. F. Standish, "Clerk, Life Annuities"; "Mr. Standish had ever made the half yearly statements himself". They were based on knowledge of deaths and lapses of claims to an annuity both in Ireland and elsewhere, the increased dividends which then arose being notified to the London office about a week after the half year, "according as the post happens to come from Ireland".[22]

Since increases in the amount of the dividend depended on the death of nominees, or of forfeitures where no dividend was claimed for three years, the reporting of these occurrences was a matter of some importance, particularly to the surviving subscribers. However, they were attended with considerable problems. On the death of a nominee a subscriber had no further interest in the tontine but there were considerable delays before the appropriate notice (the burial certificate) was received by the Tontine Office.[23] A list of persons who had not received a dividend for some years was also kept, but these names were not put on the list of deaths or forfeitures. Contrary to the provisions of the acts it was the custom "not to bring to account the forfeited shares for a considerable time after the lapse of three years.....to afford time to the proprietors to produce proof if in their power, for the preservation of such shares." During the war years the appropriate half yearly certificates frequently did not appear due to the difficulty with foreign correspondence and it was thought proper to allow them extra time; one subscriber sent his certificate from Madras but the ship sank and his claim was heard by H. T. Clements and John Foster, who granted it. To overcome the difficulties arising from delays in getting certificates to London, an act was passed in 1809 which granted relief for lapsed claims where the "war and the difficulty of correspondency was the cause and the only cause of the failure to claim dividends".[24]

The other great problem was the collective certificates of nominees submitted on behalf of overseas subscribers by their London agents. The outstanding one was the "grand certificate" presented by Thellusson & Co. in 1811 for 91 lives. This vouched for nominees in Geneva and was duly signed by a local clergyman. It was acknowledged at the time that many of the nominees had no interest in the annuities — several young ladies were nominated since the "Genevese never die" — and by 1810 many were married although described as single on the certificate, while several had moved to other countries. This collective certificate had been "amicably" agreed between Thellusson & Co. and the Lord Commissioners of the Irish Treasury at the time of creating the tontines, and the agency houses undertook the preparation of such testimony.

While the agents had no interest in practising deceit it is doubtful, given the nature of the arrangement, if considerable accuracy could have been persistently maintained. One of Boldero's clerks, William Carr, took faith in that "there is a confidence to be put in the house that brings it". However, the Committee on the Irish Tontine Annuities of 1812 was less trusting in its Report, claiming "that there is sufficient reason to doubt the accuracy of a certificate from Geneva in which have been constantly inserted the names of nearly eighty female nominees, without any change or addition of name from the years of infancy; and for years past without any mention of any place of residence". To remedy the obvious deficiencies of the collective certificates the 1812 Tontine Committee recommended using a more accurate certificate and urged greater caution in their acceptance.[25] By this means, along with other reforms designed to cure the "want of method, laxity of regulation, and negligence" which had "prevailed to a most culpable degree", the Committee hoped that dividends would not be paid out to individuals no longer entitled to them, and that thereby the "great surprise and disappointment", because dividends had not increased in line with expectations, would be greatly reduced.

The death of the long serving Mr. Standish in 1811 produced further changes which were designed to improve the administration of the tontines.

The event led the Lords of the Irish Treasury to realise that considerable delays had occurred in the transmission of the books of half yearly payments to Dublin from London, and that they, "appear in such a form that no efficient check can be made on the Payments to each individual". Accordingly, they directed Rogerson Cotter to adopt an improved system of accounting similar to that used in Dublin which involved "paying each Annuitant by a Draft from the Tontine Office". This would preserve the accuracy of the cash account; it certainly had been misused by William Carr who appropriated some £2,000 for his own use. The new drafts were on Messers Puget & Bainbridge and provided a means of checking the accounts of the Tontine Office since both would have to agree. However, Boldero's were not prepared to accept from Puget & Bainbridge a sum less than the full amount of the half yearly annuity and the Treasury responded in July 1811 by taking the account from them and returning their security. The new arrangement would have meant ending the "large, unnecessary Balance in the House of Boldero & Co.", and it was probably the loss of these funds that prompted them to refuse to accept any sum less than the full half yearly annuity payment.[26]

Despite their speculative appeal and their success in Ireland, tontines were complicated and cumbersome to operate. No doubt these drawbacks prompted the government to turn to the lottery as a source of funds. It possessed even greater appeal for all investors, large and small. In England, early lotteries had been used mainly as a means of helping to raise loans, lottery tickets being given to subscribers, while the prizes were usually an additional allotment of the capital stock issued.[27] The first lottery to produce a source of profit appeared in 1755 where the amount of stock allowed as prizes was less than the total sum paid; it was greatly oversubscribed, so much so that "the crowd of persons at the Bank [of England] to subscribe was so great that the counters were broken by their eagerness to get at the books".[28] However, later lotteries on the same lines failed and a further attempt at a lottery for revenue was not made until 1768 when Lord North offered cash prizes rather than stock. The prospect of such large cash prizes proved an irresistible lure. Thereafter, lotteries became a regular source of revenue, except during the American War of Independence when they were linked with loans. The lottery remained a popular annual event until 1824 when buoyant government revenue (and a long standing campaign against it) saw its demise. One feature of lotteries was that the money paid for tickets was received in one year and the prizes paid out the next. The government thus not only benefited from the net profit made but also had the use of a large sum of money interest free, which was generally used to pay off short term debt.[29]

State lotteries were first used in Ireland in 1780 and for the next twenty years, with the exception of 1784, there was a separate lottery modelled on that used in London. It was a device which the Irish Chancellor of the

Exchequer considered as a "measure highly beneficial to the country; first, it was a tax voluntarily paid, and of which two thirds was paid from other nations; and next, it prevented every year the borrowing of £200,000 because the purchase of each succeeding year's lottery paid the prizes of the year preceding".[30]

The first two lotteries in 1780 and 1781, took the form of lottery loans. The 1780 lottery was for an issue of 40,000 tickets of £5 each, raising IR£200,000, with a "further 2000 as a *douceur*"; that is, contributors received an extra ticket for every twenty tickets bought. Prizes amounting to IR£210,000 in 4% lottery debentures were divided among the fortunate ticket holders. There were two first prizes of IR£10,000, two prizes of IR£5,000, five of IR£2,000, etc., ending with 13,000 of IR£10.[31] In the next year there was a similar lottery loan for IR£100,000 (20,000 tickets at £5) the prizes being funded to the sum of IR£105,000 in 4% lottery debentures. The prizes in all the other lotteries were paid in cash.

The lotteries held between 1782 and 1789 were "allowed in aid of a loan", that is, to help in the successful floatation of an issue. In the case of the 1782 lotteries (there were two in that year) it was to aid the sale of IR£130,000 in 4% debentures, with 40 tickets distributed, at IR£5 each to the lender of IR£130, making a lottery of IR£200,000. The lottery was drawn on June 24 1782 but the prize holders did not receive their cash from the Treasury until January 1 1783. Similar intentions and conditions attached to the lotteries of the next six years, the lottery being an additional attraction for the loan subscribers. The lotteries of 1783, 1785, and 1786 were for around IR£160,000 in prizes, while the three lotteries of 1787-89 were for IR£200,000, all three being associated with the conversion in 1787-88 of IR£1,118,240 of 4% debentures to $3\frac{1}{2}$% ("to fine down the interest of the debt"). As a reward for taking up the entire issue of $3\frac{1}{2}$% debentures "certain contractors" were granted three lotteries; the Chancellor of the Exchequer noted that "better terms were obtained than if a contract had been entered into for a single year"[32] The 4% debentures, standing around par, were called in and debentures at $3\frac{1}{2}$% issued to the contractors who sold them at 90. The loss of £10 on each exchange of £100 nominal was covered by the profit from the sale of the lottery tickets which went for "fifty percent above their real value". The 1787 lottery produced a profit of about IR£30,000, while the two lotteries of 1788-89 brought a further £50,000. The Chancellor was content with the result and was glad to "see gentlemen who, with so much spirit, had undertaken to negotiate a prodigious sum of money for the state gain something for their trouble".[33]

The main purpose of most of the early lotteries was to act as the classical *douceur* (bribe), the main financial gain to the Exchequer taking the form of an interest free loan for the period between receiving the money from the sale of lottery tickets and the payment of the prizes. However, the lotteries held from 1790 onwards were not "allowed in aid of loans" but rather were designed for the direct support of the government. The lotteries of 1790-96 offered 40,000 tickets with IR£200,000 in prizes, and those from 1797-1800 had 60,000 tickets with IR£300,000 in prize money, and there were usually two lotteries a year. The total receipts from a lottery generally exceeded the prize money by about IR£75,000, which, less expenses, left the Treasury with a gain of around IR£70,000.[34] The profit came from the sale of lottery tickets to the contractors at a premium over the usual nominal value of £5.[35]

The first lotteries, from 1780 to 1786, were conducted on an open basis, the tickets being bought along with the subscription to the loans, or separately, but in both cases from the Treasury. It was not, however, a procedure which commended itself to the Chancellor of the Exchequer who felt that "while the lottery remained in the hands of the government, to deal out tickets to individuals, no good effect was ever produced from it".[36] The change to the practice of a "close bargain" was made in 1787, with the granting of the lottery to the contractors who undertook the conversion scheme.

Under the new procedure the Chancellor gave "notice to every Banker in Ireland and notice was also given to several Bankers in England, and the lottery was disposed of by way of auction, the highest bidder had it".[37] The proposals of the rival bidders were received on an appointed day and opened by the Chief Secretary in his apartments in the Castle, "in the Presence of the Proposers or their Agents, and the Lottery or Lotteries given to the Person who shall make the highest offer per Ticket for the Lottery, or two Lotteries, provided it shall not be less than the Sum mentioned in a Paper previously sealed up, to be opened in the Presence of the Proposers or their Agents, (if opened) at the Time the Proposals shall be read".[38] The amount of the deposit, and number of further instalments varied somewhat, the former ranging from 15% to 25%, and the latter from five to seven payments. Following the April auction, the draw was held in October and the prizes paid out the following June. If there were two lotteries within the year the draw was held in July and November, and the prizes paid in March and June of the following year.

Using contractors placated some of the critics, and irritated others. If they were to "have the plagues of a lottery let us take care to have the profits of it also". The "close bargain" ensured that benefit. On the other hand, the procedure tended to raise "the lottery fever so much higher than it had been by ... open subscription" and made it more expensive to obtain a ticket. But the Chancellor of the Exchequer "would not make any apology to the gentlemen who had been disappointed of shares in it, because he was convinced they were better satisfied to see the good effect produced to the national credit, than they would have been by any little emolument that could possibly accrue from a share".[39]

The contractors for the lotteries came from a variety of backgrounds. Since none "but great speculatists....would venture to engage in such a

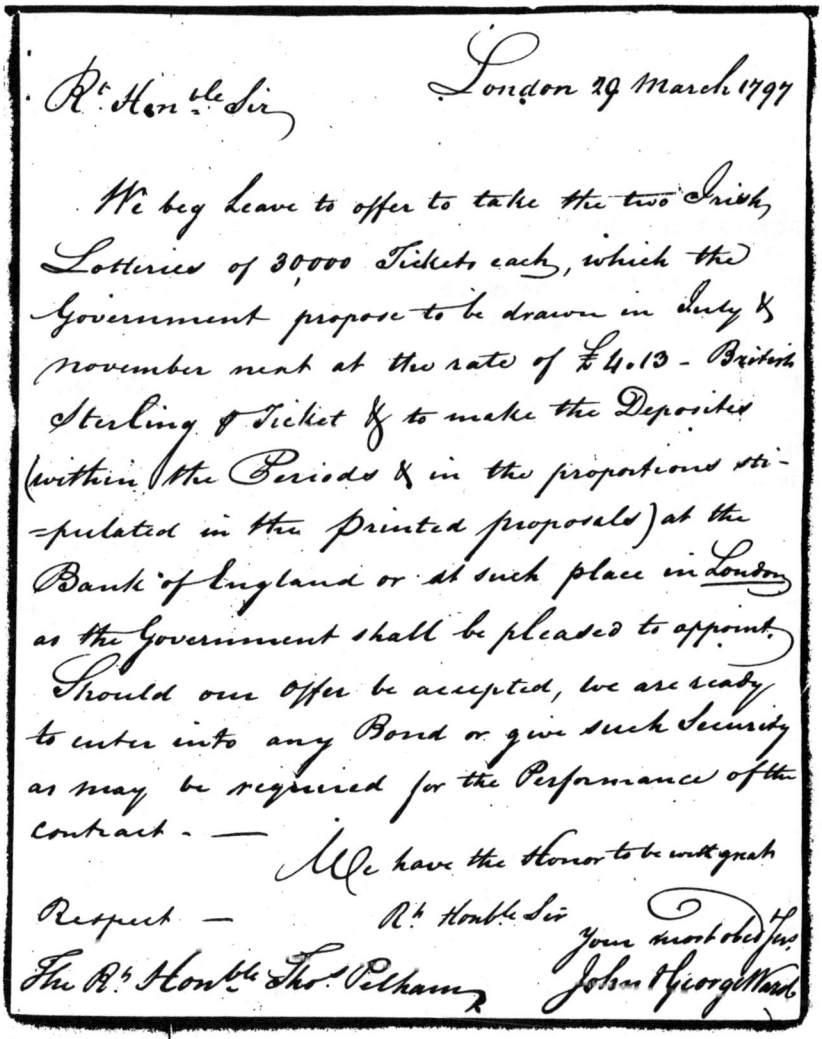

London 29 March 1797

R^t Hon^ble Sir

We beg leave to offer to take the ~~two~~ Irish Lotteries of 30,000 Tickets each, which the Government propose to be drawn in July & november next at the rate of £4.13 - British Sterling p Ticket & to make the Deposites (within the Periods & in the proportions stipulated in the printed proposals) at the Bank of England or at such place in London as the Government shall be pleased to appoint.

Should our Offer be accepted, we are ready to enter into any Bond or give such Security as may be required for the Performance of the contract. —

We have the Honor to be with great Respect — R^t Honble Sir Your most obed^t hu^ble

The R^t Hon^ble Tho^s Pelham — John & George Ward

*Fig. 1: A Proposal for the 1797 Lottery*

stupendous undertaking" as the conversion of over a million pounds of debentures to a lower interest rate basis and undertake the associated three lotteries, the number of bidders for the lotteries of 1787-89 was "much diminished". The contractors in the episode appear to have been "four private persons, and these men of no very great consequence, for two of them are clerks in the post office, the third a notary public, and the fourth some obscure individual".[40] Despite their alleged humble background they carried out the "stupendous undertaking" successfully, correctly estimating the likely premium, and that the demand for tickets was sufficient to absorb the supply. In the later lotteries the main bidding interest seems to have come from London, the 1792 lottery, for example, going to the house of Nesbitt & Stewart, while the 1797 lottery was granted to John and George Ward (see illustration 1), the bankers Roberts, Curtis & Were giving "security for the due performance of the engagement".[41] The lottery of 1800 was given to Cope & Co., who offered £7 2s. 10d. per ticket, the unsuccessful bids coming from Luke White, £7 2s. 6d., Bish & Co., £6 18s. 6d., and Frank & Co., £6 15s. 2d.[42]

The task of issuing lottery tickets, supervising lottery offices and arranging the draw was placed in the hands of seven managers and directors, all appointed by the Lord Lieutenant — the Commissioners for the Lottery. Their duties included "preparing and delivering out tickets, and to oversee the drawing of lots".[43] They were required to meet periodically at "the Royal Exchange in the City of Dublin, or at some public office or place for the execution of the powers and trust" reposed in them by "An Act for Establishing a Lottery", 19 & 20 Geo. 3, c. 5, which had been introduced into the House of Commons by John Foster.

Seven Commissioners were duly appointed, namely, Theophilus Thompson, Thomas Penrose, Peter Terrill, William Alexander, Henry Gore Sankey, Theophilus Bolton, and Marmaduke Cramer (each at the salary of £200 a year), and the last four served for all the Irish lotteries. The Secretary to the Commissioners was Christopher Deey, later joined by Robert Deey, and it was from their office in Crampton Court that the Commission did its work. In addition to the Assistant Secretary, Hill Wilson, there were ten clerks to help with the running of the lottery. Three of the Commissioners were responsible for certifying outstanding prizes in former lotteries, while from 1795 two commissioners acted as Controllers of Lottery Offices and Lottery Officekeepers, with the versatile Robert Deey serving as Inspector. After the theft of tickets from the wheels during one of the draws, the managers, with much protesting, were required in 1793 to enter into a "recognizance with two sureties in 1,000l. before a baron, conditioned for true discharge of trust".[44]

The first task of the Commissioners was the preparation of lottery tickets and for this the legislation gave precise instructions. Briefly, they were directed to have books of tickets printed and numbered arithmetically; in

1785 one Gilbert Bethel was thanked for "extraordinary trouble in numbering the tickets in oil ink with a steel pen, after the English method". The books of tickets with three columns (the outermost one was for sale, the other two were duplicates) were delivered to the officers of the Treasury who on selling a ticket would sign it, while the buyer could also sign the corresponding ticket left in the book. The books were then returned to the managers who were directed to cut out the middle portion which was "rolled up" (by women employed for "rolling and sewing tickets") and "made fast" in their presence and that of such "contributors or adventurers" as cared to attend. They were then locked up in a box (marked [A]), which was placed inside another box with "five locks and keys" and kept, secured by their seals, by the managers until the draw. The innermost column of the tickets remained as books for the purposes of detecting mistakes or frauds.

A second set of books was also prepared for the same total number of tickets and these contained the blanks and the prizes. Again, they were rolled up and fastened, put in another box (marked [B]) and kept in the prescribed manner. The fortunate tickets indicated the size of the prizes, for example, in the 1780 lottery there were two prizes of £10,000, two of £5,000, five of £2,000 etc, down to 13,600 of £10, in all a total of 14,065 prizes; the rest of the tickets, 27,935, were blanks. All the business of cutting, rolling, boxing and sealing was to be done six days before the draw and the public were notified of this so that, if they wished, they could observe the whole affair.

Tickets sold by the Treasury could be paid for in one sum, or by an initial deposit with instalments on specific dates; if payment was made in advance subscribers were entitled to a small discount. Presumably contractors also sold tickets on the basis of full payment, or a deposit with later instalments. In the main, the purchasers were lottery office keepers who then sold fractions of tickets in the form of shares or chances ($\frac{1}{2}$, $\frac{1}{4}$, $\frac{1}{8}$, or $\frac{1}{16}$), thereby attracting a greater number of buyers. Splitting the tickets enabled them to charge "prices which represented a considerable advance on the price paid for whole tickets".

Every office which was opened in order to deal in lottery tickets, Irish or British, had to be duly licensed by the Commissioners of the Lottery. There was a duty of £20 to be paid and this increased to £100 in 1787. To prevent the proliferation of small offices an act of 1787 (27 Geo. 3, c. 29) stipulated that a licence was needed where less than ten shares at a time were disposed of, and further, the Commissioners would not grant a licence unless 100 Irish lottery tickets (later raised to 200) for dividing into shares was deposited with them.

Greater financial restraints followed in 1793 which had the intention of making the laws "for the regulation of offices for the sale of lottery tickets more effectual". Lottery office keepers were now required, on or before November 1st in the year for which they were licensed, to deposit "in the

Bank of Ireland, the sum of five hundred pounds — money or government securities, for each and every licence", and the security remained at the Bank for a month after the licence expired provided no prosecution had been brought against the licensee.[45] The licence granted set out the place where business was to take place and authorized the licensee to put up near the front door of his office a sign indicating that he was duly "licensed to deal in Lottery Tickets". Applications were submitted to the offices of Christopher Deey, Secretary to the Commissioners, in Crampton Court and licences were granted to such "persons as shall appear to ....[the Commissioners] .....properly qualified".

In response to the provisions of the 1780 Act some dozen lottery office keepers in Dublin were licensed by the Commissioners to deal in State Lottery tickets. Several of them had already been dealing in Irish lotteries for some years, and among the most active were Christopher and Robert Deey, Luke White, John Magee, Isaac Colles, T. Walker, William Henry Whitestone, James Williams and Caleb Jenkin. Several of these were also booksellers. In 1785 sixteen licences were taken out, with one for Cork; all the Dublin offices were in the vicinity of Dame Street. In the early 1790s there was roughly the same number, with two offices in Limerick and one in Belfast, which was kept by William Magee. Eight licences were withdrawn in 1793 when a "number of informations were lodged before the Commissioners of the Lottery" against certain lottery office keepers for dealing in illegal insurances.[46] By October 1799 there were fourteen Dublin dealers and one had a branch in Cork. Only Henry Walker appears to have been a lottery office keeper for the entire period, and only one other, James Potts, stayed in the business into the 1790s indicating a fairly short term involvement on the part of most dealers. This may have been because they made a lot of money quickly (Luke White reputedly made a fortune from it), or the imposition of large deposits in the early 1790s may have prompted some not to continue.[47]

Lottery office profits came from buying a large block of tickets and dividing them into smaller units for sale to a much wider public at prices which often went to a premium. Tickets could, however, be a "very fluctuating article" as the Chancellor observed in 1788, "and he knew it to be a fact that within three weeks of the drawing of the last lottery there was a variation of twenty shillings in the price of tickets".[48] Since the practice of sub-dividing tickets into shares or chances had been "attended with many frauds in Great Britain" the procedure to be followed was carefully set out in the various lottery acts. From the outset a limit was set on the number of shares created on each ticket. Accordingly, dealers were directed not to sell divisions "in any smaller share or proportion than one sixteenth part or share only", which gave a nominal share value of 6s. 3d. on the usual £5 lottery ticket.[49] Such a share entitled the holder to a proportion of any prize drawn by that ticket — "the bearer will be entitled to the proportion of such beneficial chance as shall belong to the ticket numbered as above, according to the scheme printed on the back thereof". Tickets which were divided had to be deposited in an appointed office in Dublin and left there until ten days after the draw. Every share in a ticket had to be stamped with "some flourish or device" and signed by the licensed dealer, while the public were warned against buying shares which had not been properly stamped or signed. A record was kept of all deposited tickets and how they had been divided, which was open to public inspection for a small fee. Originally this was done at the offices of Christopher and Robert Deey in Crampton Court, but was later undertaken by J. Norris Thompson, John Exshaw and James Gibbons.

The drawing of the lottery took quite a time, about 30 days, and was an occasion of considerable public interest. According to one, somewhat hostile, observer, it debauched "the morals of the people.... rendering them utterly unfit for their various occupations in life, at least, during the time of the drawing".[50] The procedure used in all the lotteries, with some minor amendments, was set out in the act authorising the first Irish State lottery of 1780. On the day fixed for the start of the draw the manager had to take the boxes containing the tickets to a place appointed by the chief governor. The first lottery was drawn in the Music Hall, Fishamble Street (which years earlier witnessed a far more noble musical premier). It moved to the Little Theatre in Capel Street in 1782, but returned in 1799 to Fishamble Street, this time to another hall. While the act asserted that the ticket boxes should be taken out of their sealed containers and well shaken, this necessary preliminary was performed by the adoption of drums or wheels modelled on those used in London. They were "about 6 feet in diameter and 12 or 18 inches thick" with "convenient openings in the side for putting in the hand to draw them", and they were "suspended on their centres in a manner very convenient for shaking or mixing them".[51]

When the tickets were well mixed the managers directed "some one indifferent and fit person" to take out one ticket from the wheel containing the numbered tickets, and the "one other indifferent and fit person" to take a ticket from the second wheel where the blanks and the prizes had been "promiscuously put" and well mingled. Immediately both tickets were opened and the number and its fate read aloud. The "indifferent and fit persons" were selected from boys of the Hibernian and Bluecoat School, and the announcing was done by some half dozen "proclaimers". Unsuccessful numbers along with their blanks were filed together, while the fortunate tickets with their respective prizes were first recorded by a clerk, then signed by two managers and filed. At the end of each days drawing the wheels were duly locked and the draw adjourned till the next day, and so it went on, except on Sundays, until all the prizes had been won.

The numbers and prizes of the fortunate tickets were published and if a dispute arose the matter was settled by the managers. Fortunate ticket holders were issued with certificates which "entitled him or them to receive value for the same at His Majesty's Treasury".[52] Those who were not prepared to wait several months for their winnings could discount their lottery prizes. For example, in 1780 the Bank of Ireland empowered its Daily Committee to "Discount Lottery Prizes for the present year accompanied by the slips of the Commissioners of the Lottery attested by the Notary of the Bank in the usual way, together with the notes or notes of responsible persons to guarantee the same being the actual prizes set forth".[53]

Without doubt the practice which gave rise to most criticism and led to several attempts at regulation or prohibition, was the device of insuring lottery tickets. Generally such insurance consisted of paying a small wager for the promise of the payment of a large sum if any given number was drawn on a certain day, whether it was a blank or a prize.[54] The premiums paid were small in order to attract the widest clientele, while the sums paid out ran into several hundred pounds. Insurances were taken up by those who had bought lottery tickets and by a great many who had not but who wanted to gamble on each day's draw of the lottery. Since access to the draw was open it was an easy matter to obtain the numbers of the drawn tickets and all the licensed lottery office keepers, and others, offered insurances. Indeed, the licensed keepers held that "the Emolument derived from the bare sale of Tickets in Ireland is extremely inconsiderable", and they needed to "engage in the business of the Lottery generally" to make a living.[55] As in England the offer of insurance involving relatively small sums, brought

> ...the opportunity of Gaming...within the reach of the lowest and poorest of the labouring classes, and continued from day to day with new incitments, either of confidence or desperation; in so much that the Drawing of the licensed Lottery is rendered, by this illegal and nefarious appendage, a Public Auction of the Comforts, the Industry, and the Morals of the Poor. The bane of the sober frugality and diligence of the lower ranks which in former years continued during six weeks to poison the very sources of public virtue and happiness, will in the present year, [1797]..... be allowed to assert its pernicious influence during twice that period, in consequence of a second Lottery.

The eloquent language of this memorial from the "Association for discountenacing Vice and Promoting the Practice of Religion and Virtue" to the Lord Lieutenant may well have been one sided, but even the Chancellor of the Irish Exchequer, Sir John Parnell, a staunch supporter of the lottery , admitted that this "nefarious appendage" was a most "abominable species of gambling and swindling".[56]

In addition to criticism of the social effects of insurances, the Treasury had its own anxieties about the diversion of money from the lottery. It was soon realised that the legislation setting up the lottery was "insufficient to prevent the frauds committed, and the evils occasioned by persons, who grafting schemes, under the denomination of policies, upon English and Irish state lotteries, and by insuring chances, and by a variety of other devices have not only introduced a pernicious spirit of gambling among the lower classes of people but injured the sale of tickets in the English and Irish state lotteries".[57] To remove such competition an act of 1782 declared "any wager relating to the drawing of any ticket or tickets" to be illegal, with offenders liable to a fine of £100. To the disappointment of the Castle it had no effect and insurance continued unabated.

Another measure was tried in 1787 when legislation sought to channel insurance through the licensed lottery offices and so bring some revenue to the Treasury. To this end a levy of four pence was put on "every piece of skin or vellum or parchment, or piece of sheet of paper, on which there shall be engrossed or written... any insurance of a lottery ticket". The act also set out what the policy of insurance was to contain and charged the officers appointed to stamp such documents to do so only for persons lawfully authorised to insure lottery tickets, that is, the licensed lottery office keepers who had paid their licence fee.[58] Such minor restraints, however, were quite insufficient to curb the excesses of insurance and resort was made to more legislation in 1791 when "An Act to regulate the Insurance of Lottery Tickets" appeared on the statute book.[59]

This act required a licence of £150 to insure lottery tickets, and in addition, that £1,000 should be lodged with the Bank of Ireland until three months after the licence expired, along with a bond for £1,000 with two or more sureties. A further impediment followed in 1792 in the form of a provision that no person was to "make any policy of insurance upon any lottery ticket" unless the ticket had been shown at the time of issuing the promise.[60] Despite their restrictive tone these acts had little effect mainly because the bulk of the insurance business was conducted by "unlicensed persons in obscure and undiscovered places".

Prohibition was finally tried in 1793 with "an Act to prevent Insurance of Lottery Tickets". It declared that "no person or persons shall insure for, or against the drawing of any ticket or tickets in any Irish or British Lottery". Offenders were liable to a fine of £100, while licensed lottery office keepers would lose their licences, a penalty invoked on eight of them in December 1793.[61] The Chancellor was particularly hopeful that prohibition would succeed and that "this would help the sale of the lottery, for the money heretofore thrown away on insurance would now be expended in purchasing tickets".[62] Unfortunately his optimism was illfounded. Yet another remedy was tried by seeking to prevent knowledge of the numbers drawn becoming known to unlicensed dealers. It was stipulated that "no person shall attend at the place of drawing tickets....for the purpose of taking down the numbers as the same shall be drawn....unless by special consent, direction and appropriation of the managers of the lottery".[63]

For all the diligent exertions of the government, legislative and otherwise, insurance remained an inseparable part of the lottery. Around 1800, and the last of the separate state lotteries in Ireland, it was "as extensive as ever" being offered in "private houses in different streets where policies of insurance are issued to a very great amount".[64] Presumably it was carried out in Dublin along much the same lines as reported by the Inspector of Lottery Offices to a Committee of the English House of Commons in 1792,

> One mode is in Houses or Rooms, which are taken and kept, many of them throughout the whole year, for that Purpose — These places are generally marked by a large number upon the Windows, or a Green Curtain or Blind... At the Door commonly stands a Man with an Alarum Bell; and when any Person comes, who he suspects of an Intention to interrupt them, he rings this Bell, and the Doors are then fastened, and the Persons escape over the Tops of the Houses, or the Back Walls....; the other Mode...is thus effected. Hundreds of People are sent every Day, as well as from the Licensed and unlicensed Offices, from House to House, and from Public House to Public House, to collect such Insurances or Bets, which some do to a very large amount for which they in general receive a Commission of Six or Seven percent.[65]

From 1802 onwards the problem was greatly reduced in London by confining the drawing of the lottery to eight days rather than taking several weeks.

# NOTES

1.  "Progress of the Funded Debt in Ireland from 1716 to 1787", History of the Earlier Years of the Funded Debt from 1694-1786, B.P.P., 1898, Vol. LII.
2.  Bank of Ireland, Minutes of the Court of Directors, September 2 1794.
3.  "Progress of the Funded Debt in Ireland...", op.cit., p. 34.
4.  The Parliamentary Register, or Histories of the Proceedings and Debates in the House of Commons of Ireland, Vol. 17, 1797, p. 432.
5.  37 Geo. III, c. 54, s. 8; An Act to enable the Proprietors of Debentures issued by Government, to convert them into stock, transferable at the Bank of Ireland.
6.  Bank of Ireland, Minutes, op.cit., July 25 1797. In October 1797 the Bank of Ireland held IR£105,900 of debentures which were consolidated into stock; Minutes, October 17 1797.

7.  The procedure used by the Bank of Ireland in 1794 was as follows: "That receipts agreeable to the custom of the Bank of England, and to the form now laid before the Bank, be given from the transferor to the acceptor of Bank Stock and witnessed by the Transfer Clerk. That the Transfer Clerk do immediately witness to the signature of the Transferor and after to that of an acceptor and that the dividend on any stock shall not be paid until the stock has been accepted"; Bank of Ireland, Minutes, op.cit., September 2 1794.

8.  Bank of Ireland, Minutes, op. cit., September 26, October 3 1797.

9.  Bank of Ireland, Minutes, op. cit., July 13, August 12 1797. Mr Brabazon Stafford was appointed at a salary of IR£150 a year.

10. For full details see "The Debt of Ireland – Funded in Ireland", Report of the Proceedings of the Commissioners of the National Debt from 1786-1890, B.P.P., 1890-91, Vol. XLVIII, pp. 140-53.

11. 34 Geo. 3, c. 4, s. 31.

12. "Funded Debt of Ireland in Terminable Annuities, 1775 to 1817", History of the...Funded Debt..., op.cit., p. 49.

13. Quoted by Henry Parnell, *Financial Reform*, (1830), pp. 283-84.

14. William Pitt's use of tontines may have been prompted by the Irish success and by the attractions of life annuities which avoided increasing the redeemable capital of the national debt. The 1789 tontine was for a loan of £1,002,500 but the contractors failed to complete the subscription on the original terms. Over half the subscribers became dissatisfied with the scheme and were given long annuities in exchange for their shares in the tontine. But in order to keep faith with those who stayed with the original offer the Treasury was empowered to nominate other lives for the shares exchanged — the 'Government Nominees' who were mostly "persons in public station and therefore not likely to be lost sight of through life"; "Accounts Relating to the Public Income and Expenditure of Great Britain and Ireland", B.P.P., 1868-69, Vol. 35, Accounts and Papers (2), pp. 572-73.

15. The respective classes became extinct in 1823, 1851 and 1863, the three survivors being over 90.

16. There was no legal authority for such leniency merely the action of Boldero's.

17. 15 & 16 Geo. III, c. 2, s. 2. The last survivor died in 1866, aged 93.

18. The last survivor died in 1870, aged 94, and received one half years payment at the rate of £15,839, p.a. for the original £100 subscribed.

19. 13 & 14 Geo. III, c. 5, s. 6.

20. Edward Gale Boldero told the 1811 Committee on Irish Tontine Annuities; "We allotted an office for the purpose of paying these annuities in consideration of having a long time been the Agents and the Bankers, and also upon the consideration of its being some honour to us to pay an annuity of that sort"; Appendix to Second Report, p. 9. The office was run by two clerks, William Carr and an assistant.

21. Income tax (property tax) was apparently deducted and paid to Rogerson Cotter's account who then paid it into the Bank of England. Foreign subscribers were also paid net of tax, but their agents could reclaim the tax from the tax office.

22. William Carr told the Tontine Committee; "I send an account of the deaths in the beginning of June and December, and of the forfeitures to Mr. Standish in Ireland, who makes up the accounts in Ireland and we receive instructions every half year, what to pay each individual in each class".

23. The statutory penalty of £20 was not "inflicted upon any person who has neglected to give notice of the death of his nominee"; 2nd Report from the Committee on Irish Tontine Annuities, p. 4.

24. 49 Geo. II, c. 104. This was a short act to remedy the defects of previous acts designed to "more effectually prevent....all traitorous correspondence with, or aid or assistance being given to His Majesty's Enemies".

25. The Committee on the Irish Tontines suggested that individual certificates for each nominee should be introduced but this met with strong and successful opposition from the Geneva subscribers, who held about £90,000 of the issue; "....when the number of such certificates, as well as the expenses of public notaries, registry, postage of letters, and the effect of the variations in the exchange are taken into consideration, it will appear how much an annuity of £7 10s. will be reduced"; Appendix, 1813 Report, p. 16.

26. Committee on Irish Tontine Annuities, 2nd Report, Appendix 9, pp. 30-32, gives the correspondence between the Irish Treasury, Puget & Bainbridge, Cotter and Boldero's.

27. For details of the several loans raised with the aid of lotteries, see "Accounts relating to the Public Income and Expenditure....", op. cit., pp. 482-85. See also J. Ashton, *A History of English Lotteries*, (1893); R.D. Richards, "The Lottery in English Government Finance", *Economic History*, Vol. 3, 1934.

28. ibid., p. 485.

29. English lotteries increased in size from about £650,000 in 1785 to over £1.0mn in the early 1800s. The net profit on the lottery — the amount raised less prizes (generally £500,000 at the end of the century), discounts for prompt payment of subscriptions, and management expenses — ranged from about £140,000 to over £300,000. Full details are given in the "Accounts Relating to the Public Income...", op. cit., p. 488.

30. *Parliamentary Register*, op. cit., Vol. 13, 1793, p. 85. For details of early private lotteries in Ireland from 1568 to 1780 see C. L'Estrange Ewen, *Lotteries and Sweepstakes*, (1932), pp. 324-337. Private lotteries were outlawed when State Lotteries appeared.

31. 19 & 20 Geo 3, c. 5, s. 9. In addition £200 was given to the owner of the first ticket drawn on the first five days of the draw, and to keep up the excitement, £1,000 to the owner of the last ticket drawn.

32. *Parliamentary Register*, op. cit., Vol. 9, 1789, p. 161.

33. *Parliamentary Register*, op. cit., Vol. 8, 1788, pp. 153, 157. The estimated profit of the lotteries of 1788-89 was put at IR£140,000. Against this was the capital lost on the interest reduction on IR£900,000 from 4% to 3½%, involving £90,000.

34. These figures accord with the statement in the Irish *Commons Journal*, Vol. XXIX, p. ccxxiii, that for the 1790 lottery the Treasury "received from the contractors £80,250, and for the 1791 lottery £86,583 6s. 8d".

35. After separate Irish Lotteries had ended one third of the profits of English Lotteries was allocated to the Irish Exchequer, a procedure which lasted until the amalgamation of the two departments in 1816; see "Accounts Relating to the Public Income....", op. cit., p. 488.

36. One Irish member of parliament, a strong opponent of lotteries, claimed that the Chancellor had acknowledged that "all lotteries antecedent to the last [1787] have been corruptly disposed of"; *Parliamentary Register*, op. cit., Vol. 8, 1788, p. 160. The change from an open to a closed one using contractors was also made in London at the same time.

37. ibid., Vol. II, 1791, p. 127.

38. Notice of "Irish Lottery or Lotteries to be drawn in the year 1801", State Paper Office, S. 102/1.

39. *Parliamentary Register*, op. cit., Vol. 8, 1788, p. 88.

40. ibid, Vol. 8, 1788, p. 158.

41. *Faulkner's Dublin Journal*, March 6 1792; quoted by L.M. Cullen, *Anglo-Irish Trade 1660-1800*, (1968), p. 186; S.P.O., O.P. 31/2.

42. Ewen, op. cit., p. 344.

43. They continued with the work of supervising lottery offices and selling English lottery tickets after separate Irish lotteries ended. To help the situation of the many clerks in the Lottery Office, when Irish Lotteries stopped, they were paid their salaries for life. A suggestion in 1806 to end this 'pension' prompted a petition to the Castle pointing out that it would cause great hardship since many of the clerks had been employed "from the commencement of Lotteries in this Kingdom, a period of twenty seven years"; S.P.O. 215/5.

44. 33 Geo. 3, c. 18, s. 30, 32. Six numbers were missing and it appears "that a Robbery of the Wheel had been effected by an entrance thro' the roof of the House, and the use of false Keys, notwithstanding that a military Guard had been placed at each of the outer Doors"; S.P.O., O.P. 1/11. The Secretary, Assistant Secretary and clerks had to give sureties ranging from £1,000 to £200.

45. Legislation encouraged the public to report offences by granting "one moiety" of the penalty imposed to the informer, the other to the King.

46. Details are given in *Journals of the House of Commons of the Kingdom of Ireland*, Vol. XVI, 1795-96, p. cxlvi.

47. To be certain of getting their money back the lottery office keeper needed a letter from three of the Commissioners certifying that he had not had any prosecution brought against him, nor had he incurred any penalty or forfeiture in the latest Irish State Lottery; Bank of Ireland, Minutes of the Court, May 20 1794.

48. Irish *Commons Journals*, op. cit., Vol. 8, 1788, p. 160.

49. 29 & 30 Geo. 3, c. 31, s. 12. In England the smallest fraction allowed (by 28 Geo. 3, c. 21) was one sixteenth, but generally the lottery tickets were £10 nominal, so that each share was 12s. 6d. The cheaper Irish shares were criticised by opponents of the lottery since they "might be purchased by every journeyman, mechanic, and servant"; *Parliamentary Register*, op. cit., Vol. 8, 1788, p. 154.

50. *Parliamentary Register*, op. cit., Vol. 7, 1787, p. 106.

51. Quoted by Richards, op. cit., p. 71 from *The Lottery Displayed* (1771). William Deey obtained drawings of the London wheels and a set was made by Messrs Barber of Dublin. In 1788 brasshoops were put on the wheels to help preserve them; Irish *Commons Journals*, op. cit., Vol 28, p. cccxiii.

52. Between 1782-1801 the total of unclaimed lottery prizes stood at £24,548; a small sum compared with the total prize money paid out.

53. Bank of Ireland, Minutes of the Court of Directors, November 24 1789. The Bank's willingness to do this was apparently attributable to Theophilus Clements who wanted to increase the popularity of the lottery; see F.G. Hall, *The Bank of Ireland 1783-1946*, (1949). In March 1790 it was prepared to purchase Lottery Certificates at a discount of 4%. About this time it discounted lottery prizes for Mr. Crosthwait, Mr. Geoff, Jonathan Rogers, and lent money to Robert Shaw with "Lottery prizes as collateral security".

54. For a detailed account of insurances, see Ewen, op. cit., pp. 255-60.

55. Memorial to Castle, 1801, S.P.O. 90/102/2.

56. S.P.O., O.P. 79/1; *Parliamentary Register*, op. cit., Vol. 13, 1793, p. 85.

57. Preamble to 21 & 22 Geo. 3, c. 38.

58. 27 Geo. 3, c. 29, s. 1, 9, 10.

59. 31 Geo. 3, c. 20, s. 1.

60.    32 Geo. 3, c. 11.
61.    33 Geo. 3, c. 18, s. 22-24.
62.    *Parliamentary Register*, op. cit., Vol. 13, 1793, p. 85.
63.    35 Geo. 3, c. 35, s. 2; An Act for Amending the Laws for the Regulation of Lottery Offices and for preventing the Insurance of Lottery Tickets.
64.    S.P.O. 102/3.
65.    *Journal of The House of Commons* (London), May 21 1792, p. 809. Booksellers apparently sold large numbers of "Numerical Books" which were used "by Clerks to the Lottery Offices, and by Deputy Insurers for Taking Numbers in Private Houses, but more particularly in Public Houses and Coffee Houses". For a detailed description of the state of the English Lottery around 1808, see First and Second Reports from the Committee on the Laws relating to Lotteries, B.P.P., 1808, Vol. 11. There is little reference to Ireland in the Reports, or in the evidence presented.

# CHAPTER 3

# SUPPLY, DEMAND AND THE MARKET

Loan debentures were issued, before 1793, on the basis of an open subscription at the Treasury in Dublin Castle. Following the announcement of the terms, decided from 1783 onwards after consultation with the Governor and Company of the Bank of Ireland, subscriptions were invited for debentures at par, and the interest was payable every six months. For every £100 subscribed a debenture was issued, paid in full at the time of issue. The subscriber, however, could take up his allotment in several instalments stretching over a few months.

The coming of war and the increased scale of borrowing soon rendered this leisurely method of issue unsuitable. In a fluctuating market it became more difficult to fix terms, and with the big issues it was administratively difficult to deal with a large mass of applications within a short period. Also, the authorities needed greater certainty that the sums required would be available to them within a reasonable time. Thus, to ease the problem of fixing terms and to transfer the administrative burdens elsewhere, plus providing a guarantee that the funds would be available, the government, from 1793-94, made use of the contractor system very much on the lines that William Pitt had developed in London.[1]

With the exception of an open loan in the difficult financial conditions of 1797 all the major Irish loans in Dublin, and the separate loans made in London but funded in Ireland, were made with the use of contractors. The open loan of 1797 arose as John Foster, Speaker of the House of Commons put it, since "all hope of a close or Contractor Loan even for the small sum of 700,000*l.* is at an end"; it was possible to raise IR£400,000 through a contractor, Luke White. As to the open loan John Foster correctly warned that "there is nobody here so sanguine upon the subject.....as to look for any supply from it either considerable or speedy". The Bank of Ireland and the London Treasury were called on to help.[2]

In the case of the closed loans, prior to the Treasury announcement of the "ultimate public arrangement of the scheme of a loan", a conference was "loosely had with the moneyed men in Dublin — such preliminary conference is always usual". In the experience of Isaac Cory, Chancellor in 1799, it was not always an agreeable meeting since occasionally "the proceedings of the Gentlemen in Dublin on Loan business was attended with a degree of unprovoked rudeness towards me in my official capacity without example".[3] Proposals for the loan were then printed and sent out to all the banks in Dublin and also to the "houses of Boldero, Puget, Nesbitt and other persons.....in London", and the scheme of the loan was "read to the monied people, called together for that purpose" at the Castle.[4] Prior to the bidding when all the parties were assembled in the Chief Secretary's Chamber they were "called upon for their Bonds, in order to ascertain whether the securities proposed are sufficient". The security of bidders from England was vetted by John Puget, London agent of the Bank of Ireland, and they were thus "relieved from the inconvenience of looking for Sureties in Dublin where perhaps they might not easily obtain them on short notice".[5]

As soon as all the sealed proposals were "delivered in at the Table, each proposal will be taken down in writing distinctly in the order in which they are opened, till the whole are taken down". Where a short term annuity was part of the offer the bidding was on that, the loan being given to the contractor who accepted the least annuity in addition to the capital offered. For example, the 1796 loan of IR£640,000, on 5% debentures with an annuity of $1\frac{1}{4}$% for 15 years, was awarded to Robert Shaw, who valued the annuity at seven years purchase giving a price of £89 for the debentures.[6] Similarly, where a loan was offered with Treasury bills it was awarded to the contractor prepared to take the smallest difference in Treasury bills between £100 capital and the stock. For example, the loan of IR£200,000 on 5% debentures in 1799 was given to Luke White who was prepared to take £24 15s. in Treasury bills, the loan price then being £75 5s.[7] Finally, if the loan scheme involved the offer of two classes of stock "the proposal offering the largest proportional value in money for one hundred pounds of stock for which the proposal is made, will be accepted". If offers were submitted in both descriptions of stock reference was made to a table of the proportional value of the stocks; if the highest offers for the two stocks should be of equal value the scheme of the loan expressed a preference for one over the other. An example of this type of scheme was the 1802 loan of IR£1,625,000 offered in either 3% or $3\frac{1}{2}$% stock where the contractors preferred the $3\frac{1}{2}$% stock, the best offer of £91 15s. 11d. for £100 of $3\frac{1}{2}$% coming from the group of Bogle French, Borrowes, Canning.[8]

After the loan had been alloted the bonds of the unsuccessful bidders were returned to them. The successful contractor then placed his deposit, usually ten per cent of the loan with the Bank of Ireland but this sum was not credited to the Teller of the Exchequer until a resolution of the House of Commons had been passed sanctioning the terms of the loan. Such a large sum of money would either be borrowed from a bank, which with the Irish system of a long term deposit (see below) would be prohibitive, or more likely the contractor and those supporting him would obtain funds by selling stock — a "preparation of funds by several classes of people necessarily produces a fall in the stocks". Such a fall may, on occasions, have removed some of the benefits of competition claimed by the supporters of the contractor system.[9]

Before the introduction of inscribed stock in 1797 the general practice with Irish loans was to issue debentures ('heavy stock') against each instalment, but to withhold debentures to the value of the deposit until the last instalment had been paid. The purpose of this practice was for the deposit "to remain as security for making good the subsequent payments". With inscribed stock the procedure was to issue receipts "according to the manner practiced in Great Britain". If the purchaser wanted scrip receipts for his payments these were prepared for such sums as the contractor wanted, the receipts not exceeding three in number for each £1,000. None of the receipts issued (the scrip) could be converted into stock until all the instalments had been paid. The contractor could take part scrip and part debenture, although that was likely to lead to delays.

The practice of issuing scrip was deemed to have certain advantages over that of issuing heavy debentures. For the government it offered better security as to the completion of the contract because the scrip could not be converted into stock until all the payments had been made.[10] With debenture issues, as practiced in Ireland, only the deposit remained as security for the unpaid instalments since with each payment the corresponding amount of fully paid debentures were issued. For the subcribers to the loan the receipts were seen as "promising a more ready sale than heavy stock would command"; the scrip for the initial deposit could be used as security for a bank loan ("which by the Practice of Ireland was locked up in the Treasury"). Further, the money for the successive instalments could be borrowed by lodging the receipts with a bank.[11] If holders of scrip suddenly found themselves with funds they could convert them into stock at any time on payment of the outstanding instalments. Similarly, if an investor had money "to receive at a future day" he could purchase the scrip. Such considerations as keeping the "first 10% in Action, and the facility afforded of holding the light stock or speculating in the funds as he may find most advantageous" were thought to be sufficient to recommend the use of receipts to the subscribers.[12] In Dublin, however, easily transferable debentures remained in favour for some time.

Several London financial houses and financiers took an active part in the floatation of Irish loans. The list of proposals for the loan of 1802 (the only complete one available) identifies most of the parties involved. Five groups submitted offers for the loan, their security having been approved by John Puget. They were,

1. Andrew Jordain, Charles Flower, and Charles Horneyold (a partner in the banking house of Roberts, Curtis, Were & Co., who had taken the Irish loan of 1796 for IR£325,000; their offer was submitted jointly with that of B. Shaw and T.R -----).
2. Nathaniel Bogle French, Walter Borrowes, Henry Canning, Charles Pole, and Nathaniel Johnston. (Bogle French and Walter Borrowes had taken a loan of IR£1.5mn in 1800).
3. John Atkins, Abraham Atkins, Robert Williams, Senior, Robert Williams, Junior, and Thomas Collier.
4. James Dashwood, John Agnew, George Peacock, William Wood, Joshua Reeve and John Green.
5. John Scott, Christopher Idle, Charles Boldero, Stephen Lushington, Edward Gale Boldero, Henry Lushington, Robert Albion Cox and William Merle. (This group represented the banking houses of Boldero and Cox, Merle & Co.).[13]

Among local contractors who bid for the 1802 loan was the Dublin firm of Gibbons & Williams, public notaries and stockbrokers. James Gibbons was the public notary to the Bank of Ireland, and the firm were agents for a number of country banks and the Northern Banking Company. At the beginning of 1835 they went bankrupt, but Richard Williams continued as a stockbroker.[14] Other Dublin firms who submitted proposals for loans in the 1790s were the banking houses of J.C. Beresford & Co. and Messers La Touche. Prominent local financiers who successfully bid for loans were Luke White and Robert Shaw.

Luke White is reported to have made his fortune in the lottery business, receiving a good start when he found a lottery ticket in a book he bought, and it won £20,000 for him. In 1797 he was the only bidder for the Irish loan "having stood forward to lend money to the Government in times of Difficulty, Rebellion and Invasion", and later in 1799 he again successfully contracted for a loan. He repeated his success in 1800 offering to take a Treasury bill at £9 15s. with each debenture, compared with an offer of £11 19s. from Bogle French & Borrowes, the loan being for IR£1.5mn. He completed the customary deposit but soon after, in the words of his Petition to the Irish House of Commons, "as had been heretofore usual in such Cases", he made an "Application to the Governor of the Bank of Ireland for their Assistance, and was much surprised they would not, as usual, grant him the Accommodation he required of them".[15] The Lord Lieutenant supported his application for an advance from the Bank, so as to hasten the process of taking a loan, but despite the appeal the Court of the Bank, "having taken into their most serious and respectful consideration His Excellency's the Lord Lieutenant's hope that the Bank would advance to the Contractors of the late loan of £1.5m the sum of £525,000 on a deposit of government securities", replied that they "regret exceedingly that they cannot comply therewith".[16] With Luke White's inability to complete the payments he forfeited the deposit money and a larger loan was offered to Bogle French & Borrowes, which the latter arranged with the Chancellor of the Exchequer (Isaac Cory), the premium on the Treasury bills being £15 9s. The interest on the debentures was thus 5.9% compared to 5.5% on Luke White's original offer.[17]

The loan of IR£800,000 given to Robert Shaw in April 1796 provides an example of one which went wrong in difficult market conditions.[18] He was the sole proprietor of the loan but it appears that no "security was ever demanded or entered into". The deposit of IR£100,000 was paid, and the next two instalments of IR£120,000 followed in May and June, about which time Robert Shaw died, but his son continued to make the payments, "without complaint or much difficulty", until November. By that time IR£560,000 had been paid. Between the time the debentures were first delivered and October some IR£300,000 were sold, the price falling from 96 to 87½, the average price being about 91; the purchase price had been 89. After the announcement of a further loan in October, of IR£300,000, the price fell from 87½ to 79 in January 1797 and in this period IR£100,000 was sold at an average price of 82, well below the purchase price. Even before the announcement of the October loan it had become increasingly difficult to sell stock due to the "great scarcity of money for some months past", which had been "unquestionably owing to the difference in price between our Debentures in Ireland and those transferable at the Bank of England, these being at least 10% in favour of the purchaser of the latter which has caused.......a large and constant drain of money from this country which but for the great depression of the Irish stock in England would naturally have been invested here".[19] Prospects of another loan merely depressed the market, while those with money to invest kept out of the market awaiting the fall in price. The old loan sold very slowly indeed and the appearance of the French fleet off the coast of Ireland in December put an entire stop to the sales, at any price. Finally, when the conditions of the new loan were announced in January 1797 they gave a considerable advantage to the contractors involved; it was some 25% more advantageous to new subscribers than the old loan.[20]

Faced with such competition Robert Shaw, junior, informed the Lord Lieutenant that he could not "contend against such a loan, or to attempt to dispose of his stock", and was therefore not able to complete the three remaining instalments on the loan. There was certainly no prospect that the Bank of Ireland would lend further sums to allow the full payments to be made. The IR£80,000 November instalment had been paid by discounting a note at the Bank of Ireland at 51 days, the Bank taking government debentures as collateral, but after that the Bank declined to lend.[21] Robert Shaw complained that the new loan had been brought forward before the existing loan contract had expired, and pointed to the departure from the custom followed in London of giving preference to the contractor of the preceding loan if a new one was made before the final instalment of the old had been paid.[22] With 5% debentures falling to around 73 in February, and destined to go even lower, and with little prospect of Robert Shaw being able to fulfil his father's contract he was relieved of the obligation to complete the loan; IR£640,000 out of IR£800,000 had been taken up but the operation had left the contractor with a substantial loss.[23]

As to the demand for newly issued government stock and the distribution of holdings of the outstanding debt, very little is known. At the end of the eighteenth century people with money to invest tended either to buy land, put it out on mortgage, or had it "laid out in securities", either Irish or British. Money would tend to go into securities if the land market was depressed, or if mortgage rates were low, while money would be taken out of the security market if land prices were rising or if mortgage rates rose.[24] When it came to investment in securities investors had the choice of putting money into British or Irish Funds. Investment in the former involved the risks attendant upon the conversion of the currency, and other inconveniences, while British yields tended to be about 1% lower than those in Dublin, but London offered a much larger and more developed market. English investors may well have been tempted to buy Irish debentures given the yield advantage, but it was not until the closing years of the nineties that they had a discernible market to deal in, not perhaps with the ease of operating in London but which afforded greater market facilities than formerly. It seems likely, however, that the main interest of English money in Ireland lay in the land market, with government debt as an occasional short term retreat. English investment in Irish debt increased after the interest was made payable at the Bank of England which meant that they did not have to contend with the inconvenience of the exchanges, while the loans of 1795 and 1796 were also made transferable at the Bank of England, with the added attraction that for every one hundred pounds 'British money' subscribed interest was paid at the rate of five pounds 'British money'.[25]

The only parts of the Irish debt about which detailed information on subscribers is available are the three tontine loans of the 1770s and the open loan of 1797. As to the bulk of the debt, in the form of debentures, it is reasonable to surmise that they were fairly widely held within Ireland by the landed aristocracy, while commercial interests in Dublin and the larger towns no doubt also held them for income purpose and for use as collateral. Certainly the banks held debentures as a reserve and were prepared to accept them as loan security. What quantities they had, however, is not known. By way of contrast, the tontine loans, by virtue of the way they operated, have left considerable information about the original subscribers.

While tontine annuities were not comparable to perpetual annuities they provide some indication of the nature of the demand for government securities at this time. For the three tontines (1773, 1775 and 1777) only about 15% was subscribed for in Ireland (see Appendix 2 for detailed figures), of which over a half came from Dublin.[26] This involved, for the first two tontines, just over a hundred subscribers, while the third had nearly 230. The bulk of the subscription for the 1773 and 1775 issues came from Britain, 79% and 73% of the total respectively. London and the surrounding counties dominated the list, taking 58% of the 1773 tontine and 41% of the next; the British provincial interest perked up from 20% to 32%. This left about IR£20,000 from Europe in each case. The 1777 tontine however, presents a marked contrast. While Irish participants took about 17% of the issue the British contribution fell to 42%, but the European subscription amounted to 41% of the total, most of the money (IR£100,000 out of IR£123,000) coming from Geneva and Berne.

Continental interest, largely Swiss, in the Irish tontines stemmed from the activities of the house of Peter Thellusson & Co. Swiss subscribers were attracted by the $7\frac{1}{2}$% yield and, of course, the prospects of the gain from survivorship of their nominees. The other important inducement was the willingness of the Irish Treasury, following negotiations with Thellusson & Co., to accept a collective certificate for the nominees prepared by the latter in its capacity as agents for the subscribers. The banking house of Pasavant & Co. of Geneva acted for two clubs who invested in the tontine, one on fifty lives, the other on sixty four lives. Another Geneva banking house, Lullin, Masbore, Aubert & Co., acted as agents for individual proprietors on single lives.

Figures of individual holdings in the three tontines showed that most were below IR£500; the percentage of holdings under that figure was 81% in 1773, 91% in 1775 and 90% in 1777.[27] Indeed, well over half the holdings were under IR£200, assuming that there were very few 'clubs' of the Genevese style. Thus, only a few holdings were in excess of IR£1,000; 10% in 1773, 3% in 1775 and 6% in 1777. There were only two really very large investments, judging by the list of nominees; IR£12,000 in 1775 and IR£17,400 in 1773. The former sum was linked to the lives of the six children of Sir Edward Deering, the latter on the sons of George III — the subscriber may have had royal connections, but more likely the nominees were selected for their public prominence. Less fortunate royal nominees were Marie Antoinette and Louis XVI.

Several Dublin financial interests subscribed to the tontines, among them David La Touche, whose eleven children were given as nominees for one subscription, while his bank acted as agents for subscriptions to the 1777 issue. Among others were William Gleadowe Newcomen, Robert Shaw, Jeremiah D'Olier and Christopher and Robert Deey. Cork banking circles were represented by Charles Leslie, Robert Keller, and W. William Hewitt. Other prominent subscribers were Henry Theophilus Clements, Henry Hobart, Clotworthy Rowley, Edmond Pery, William Brownlow, John Ponsonby, Edward Sneyd and Riggs Faulkner. London financial circles were also well represented. Among the bankers were Henry Boldero, Coutts, Thomas Croft and Ebenezer Blackwell (of Croft, Blackwell, Roberts & Croft), Robert Herries (Herries, Roberts & Co.), Richard Stone and James Martin (Martin & Co.), Benjamin Barnett (Bland, Barnett & Hoare), and Thomas Sommers Cocks (Biddulph, Cocks & Co.). From the ranks of London brokers were Benjamin Vaughan, Griffith Jones, Thomas Horne and Abraham De Mattos Mocatta.

The other loan which provides details of the nature of the demand for Irish securities is the open loan of 1797. This loan, however, was for Treasury bills not debentures, which may have attracted a different class of investor. Subscribers were offered IR£100 Treasury bills, carrying a rate of 6% (the coupon rate up to that time was around 5%), on a payment of IR£92, payable in several instalments. By February 1798 IR£207,000 had been received, representing a nominal value of IR£225,000 out of the authorized issue of IR£300,000 (the hope was to raise IR£800,000).[28] The offer attracted 503 subscribers, and based on the nominal values, just over 70% of the subscriptions were for sums of IR£200 or less, with a further 12% accounted for by sums between IR£300 and IR£500, both these figures accounting for 28% of the total money subscribed.

The rest of the money came from a variety of large subscriptions. There were 47 subscriptions of IR£1,000 or more, among them large sums from three bishops, while other notable investors were Robert Shaw, several Irish peers, the Sergeant-at-Arms, and two generals. The London agents of the Bank of Ireland, Puget & Bainbridge, took IR£3,000. But the most interesting of the large subscriptions came from corporate bodies set up by the government, many in receipt of annual grants from the House of Commons, and these agencies were persuaded to part with their funds for a short time to the Treasury — a form of official underwriting. Seven such bodies were involved (the Ordnance, IR£15,000(nominal); Board of First Fruits, IR£5,250; House of Industry, IR£3,700; Lottery Commissioners, IR£2,900; Non-Conformist Ministers, IR£3,000; Commissioners for Wide Streets, IR£13,000; and Commissioners of the Revenue, IR£4,400, and between them they subscribed IR£44,390, one fifth of the loan.

A significant demand for Irish securities also came from the government itself through the practice of buying-in debt. This was done on an occasional basis or more regularly with the proceeds of a formally constituted Sinking Fund. As early as 1783 John Foster proposed applying budget surpluses for the purchase of debt, and the government was constantly reminded that "the moment you begin to pay off the principal your funds will certainly rise".[29] However, the setting up of a Sinking Fund was delayed until 1797 when its introduction was prompted by the need to borrow in London and also by mounting concern about the growth of the total debt. When £1.5mn was borrowed in London in February 1797 a Sinking Fund of 1% of the capital was established "for the extinction of the debt". The Chancellor of the Exchequer was worried "that the interest of so large a sum sent annually out of the country would be a drain which must tend to exhaust it"; the Sinking Fund provision would lessen this burden.[30] A few months later the decision was taken to set up a general fund for the entire debt, a move which found favour with William Pitt in London, while the Chancellor, Sir John Parnell, found "by conversing with monied men that nothing will more raise our credit or facilitate our future loans".[31]

In March 1797 a Committee of the Whole House quickly produced proposals for a Sinking Fund for the Redemption of the National Debt, a scheme modelled on the English one set up by Pitt in 1786. The Committee concluded that "in order to make a lasting Provision for the Maintenance of public Credit, it has now become necessary to form a permanent Plan for the Reduction of the said Debt and for the more effectually preventing the Accumulation of Debt hereafter in consequence of any future Loans".[32] The money to operate the Sinking Fund came from an annual grant from the Treasury, issued quarterly, from interest on annuities and redeemed debt held by the Fund, along with a sum equivalent to 1% per annum on any new loans made in Ireland. The Act laid down that such funds were to be applied by the Commissioners to buy stock below par, unless otherwise directed by future legislation, and to purchase "such principal sums, and capital stock, on three days at least, in every week" at certain periods in every quarter.[33] Such predictability, it was felt in some quarters, might serve to push up prices, but the official view was that large operations in the public funds should be carried out in an open manner. Debt funded in Great Britain would be covered by allocating a portion of the funds to the English Commissioners for the Reduction of the National Debt, the money being periodically remitted from the Irish to the English Exchequer.

The Commissioners charged with the responsibility of exercising such powers were the The Speaker, the Chancellor of the Exchequer, the Chief Secretary to the Lord Lieutenant, the Accountant General of the Revenue, and the Governor of the Bank of Ireland, while the Bank was to act as banker to the Fund. Jeremiah Vickers was appointed Secretary to the Commissioners, and in June 1797 the Castle notified the Bank of Ireland "that we have nominated and appointed Mr. Robert Deey, our Broker, to make the purchases of public debt and annuities on our account for the use of the public and for the purposes of an Act passed this Session of Parliament". Shortly afterwards the Bank was instructed "to issue and pay over to Mr. Robert Deey the sum of £1,300 13s. 7d. weekly until further orders for the purposes of the said Act".[34]

The Commissioners began their operations in July 1797 and by the end of the first year had bought IR£47,200 of 5% debentures for an outlay of IR£33,647 in 84 separate purchases at prices ranging from 75 in July to 66 at the year end, an average bargain of IR£400. About half the purchases were in the IR£400 to IR£600 range, the smallest was about IR£25, and the largest for IR£1,700. The Sinking Fund Broker was obviously prepared to take up stock in whatever size offers came onto the market.[35] There can be little doubt that these regular purchases provided a useful support to market prices, especially as the volume of spending by the Commissioners rose to over IR£350,000 by 1801.

The gradual increase in the amount of stock put out by the government, and its acquisition by the investing public, created conditions which sooner or later would lead to the appearance of some sort of dealing activity. But while stockbroking as a distinct role did not emerge until the early 1790s it seems reasonably certain that in the preceding decade various people were prepared to act in some capacity for intending sellers of government securities, or for those with a desire to acquire them. The most likely persons to have taken on broking in government securities were public notaries who were involved in financial dealings, particularly with bills of exchange and the procedures for protesting those in default. To offer their services as agents, dealing in debentures, would have been an easy extension of their expertise. For example, in 1790, when the Bank of Ireland made an issue of new stock to its shareholders, IR£38,750 was not taken up and the Bank ordered that the loan "be sold by the Notary Public of the Bank at market price".[36] Dublin newspapers of the period carried offers for the sale or purchase of government debentures, while a member stated in the House of Commons "that the receipts of notaries public could be produced......which proved the prices of the stocks to have been full as high as those stated in the printed documents which he had in his pocket".[37]

During the rising market of 1793, when 5% debentures stood above par, several of those acting in a broking capacity formed, on July 1st, a 'Voluntary Association'. During the 1849 Commission of Enquiry into the Stock Exchange the formation was described thus — "a body of gentlemen associated themselves in Dublin for the purpose of carrying on dealings in Stock".[38] They probably met in the brokers offices, which for the most part were located in and around Crampton Court, just below the Castle, described as the unofficial 'Change' of Dublin.[39] The Voluntary Association was probably formed for reasons of convenience associated with dealing rather than for any restrictive purposes with regard to membership or commissions. Judging by the membership of the formally constituted Stock Exchange of 1799, it seems likely that the leading half dozen brokers behind the Voluntary Association were John Ashenhurst, Robert Deey, Hugh Cumming, James Finlay, James Gibbons and John Robinson, while the following people may also have been involved, namely Gilbert Bethel, Benjamin Disrael, John Hawkins and John Williams. For a period of about six months a list of prices, under the heading 'The Stock Exchange', appeared in the Dublin papers, the stocks involved being debentures and a few local Dublin bonds, along with local canal stocks.[40] While the Voluntary Association may have lasted longer than the six months indicated by the appearance of the list of prices, it would almost certainly have lapsed in the depressed market conditions which prevailed from the start of 1796 to the middle of 1798, during which time 5% debentures fell from around 95 to 65.

From the depressed conditions of mid 1798 the price of debentures rose sharply during the ensuing year and a half so that by the close of 1799 5% debentures had recovered from the low of 65 to over 90. This rise was closely associated with the great increase in the quantity of money following on the suspension of cash payments by the Bank of Ireland in March of 1797. In this bullish market it is probable that, in addition to the established brokers with the earlier Voluntary Association, new entrants were attracted into the business. By this time there was more stock about, while in the uncertain conditions of war, complicated by internal Rebellion, investors may have been increasingly drawn to securities, deserting the other investment alternatives of the land market and lending on mortgage. Opportunities for new entrants may also have occurred if the established brokers levied high commissions, or if their dealing practices were regarded as suspect, in that perhaps they had taken advantage of clients by dealing on their own account. Possibly in the interests of maintaining an orderly market, which would be more conducive to absorbing the constant stream of new offerings, the Treasury and banking circles were moved to bring in legislation in parliament to remedy some of the deficiencies of the existing arrangements.

Towards the end of April 1799 John Claudius Beresford and the Chancellor of the Exchequer, the Hon. Isaac Cory, presented a bill to the House of Commons "for the better Regulation of Stock Brokers". During its second reading clauses were proposed for the regulation of the sale of stock, and it was later re-introduced in its amended form by J. C. Beresford and Sir William Gleadowe Newcomen, a leading Dublin banker. It received its third reading on May 9th, the Lords then agreed to it without amendment, and the Royal Assent was given on June 1st.

The intention of "An Act for the better Regulation of Stock Brokers", 39 Geo.3, c. 60, was set out in the preamble,

> Whereas the establishing of regulations by which proper persons only will be permitted to act as stockbrokers, for the selling and buying of government stock, and government securities, and by which the prices at which such stock and securities shall be bought and sold, shall be known to the sellers and buyers of such stocks and securities, will be beneficial to the proprietors and purchasers of

such stock and securities, wherefore be it enacted by the King's
most excellent Majesty, by and with the advice and consent of the
lords spiritual and temporal, and commons in this present
parliament assembled, and by the authority of the same, That from
and after the twenty-fourth day of June, one thousand seven
hundred and ninety-nine, a stock exchange shall be established in
the city of Dublin, at such convenient place, and subject to such
rules and regulations as shall be approved of by the lords of his
Majesty's treasury.......

Under its provisions no person was to "act in the capacity of a stockbroker in
the selling or buying of any government stock, or government securities on
commission" without a licence from the Lords of the Treasury who would
issue them only to persons they thought fit to be stockbrokers. Persons who
acted as brokers in government securities without a licence were subject to a
fine of IR£500. Licensed brokers were to enter into a bond "in the penalty
of two thousand pounds for himself, and two securities of five hundred
pounds each, conditioned, that he will not.....buy or sell such stock or
securities for himself or on his own account, when employed by any person
not being a broker, to purchase or sell such stock or securities". The
provision was designed to resolve the conflict of interest which might arise
where a broker acted as an agent and principal in relation to his clients; he
was to act only in a single capacity for them. He was also directed to keep a
full record of all his transactions — "that he will keep a book to contain
entries of all such stock and securities as shall be sold and bought by him,
describing the names of the persons to whom he shall sell such stock and
securities, and the amounts of every sale to every person, and the price at
which the same shall be sold". Should the Lords of the Treasury find "to
their satisfaction that any person to whom any such licence shall be granted
is unfit to be licensed" then they would annul the licence.

In addition to the obligation to record their business dealings fully,
brokers were required to render to the person for whom they sold securities
"an account in writing, signed with his name, of the quantity of such stock
or government securities so sold, to whom the same was sold, and the true
rate of purchase or price paid for the same", while he was also to enter these
particulars in his own books which were to be open to inspection by the
client. Failure to comply in these matters, or a false account of the price at
which securities were sold or bought would lead to a fine, and disqualification
"from ever after acting as a stock-broker in this Kingdom".

Section VI of the Act laid down that for buying and selling government
stocks the broker could charge "a fee at the rate of two shillings and six
pence for each hundred pounds of stock or securities, and no more, for
brokerage or commission". A licensed broker who received "directly or
indirectly, any money or other reward or thing" above the maximum rate

was liable to a fine of IR£100.

In accordance with the legislation the Lord's Commissioners of the Treasury duly announced in the Dublin Gazette on September 3 1799 that they had "for the present appointed the Stock Exchange to be held in the Room hired for that purpose by the Stockbrokers, at the Old Exchange Coffee House, until a place of Meeting shall be prepared at the Commercial Buildings....as a Stock Exchange for the use of All Persons who may resort thereto for the purposes of buying or selling; but by the said Act no person can buy or sell on Commission unless he be licensed by their Lordships". On November 1st "their Lordships" made it known that the Stock Exchange would "be held in future from Two to Three O'clock, at the Commercial Buildings".[41] Its business was to be regulated by the following short rules — the market would open each day at the times stated, all bargains were to be settled by 1.0 p.m. the next day, all purchases for the Sinking Fund were to be transferred the same day and no interest for the following day was to be charged, and prices or business done before or after the fixed times were not to constitute market prices.[42]

Thirteen persons took out licences in 1799. Ten of these were public notaries, namely, John Ashenhurst, Robert Deey, Samuel Bruce, Hugh Cumming, James Finlay, James Gibbons, Samuel John Pittar, Edward Shannon, Timothy Turner and John Robinson. Their meetings were held in the "Great Rere Room over the Coffee Room" in the Commercial Buildings. James Finlay was Secretary, with John Ashenhurst as President.[43]

# NOTES

1. In London, prior to the adoption in 1784 by Pitt of sealed tenders from rival syndicates, interested subscribers met at the Bank of England to indicate how much of the loan they were prepared to accept and to agree on the terms. As the number of applicants increased difficulties arose with the allotment and the negotiations. The closed subscription then developed out of this system: for a detailed account see J.E.D. Binney, *British Public Finance and Administration 1774-92*, (1958), pp. 100-104.

2. The Lord Lieutenant informed the House of Commons that initial attempts to raise IR£3,395,000 on the terms suggested had failed — "I am sorry to inform you that it is found after the most diligent endeavours exerted for the Purpose, that the sum intended to be raised cannot be obtained according to the terms thereof". The Committee of Ways and Means then reported that IR£400,000 would be raised on debentures issued at 63, and IR£300,000 on Treasury Bills issued at 92, carrying 6% interest (the Open Loan), the rest of the money needed coming from the Bank of Ireland and the Treasury in London. The Chancellor defended the action in the Commons — "These terms bad as they were for the Government were made necessary....by the

situation of the two countries; the other terms which had been offered the monied men had not thought proper to accept"; *Journals of the Irish House of Commons*, Vol. XVII, Part I, p. 122, Part 2, Appendix Dclxxxvii; *The Parliamentary Register, or Histories and Debates of the House of Commons of Ireland*, 1797, Vol. 17, March 13, p. 469.

3. State Paper Office, Letter from Isaac Cory, 1799.

4. S.P.O., Letter from Sir John Parnell, December 1799.

5. In the bidding for the 1802 loan there were five London lists each of which John Puget considered as "providing ample security, along with the Deposit of £50,000"; S.P.O., O.P. 121/4/9.

6. S.P.O., O.P. 22/19/4.

7. *Freeman's Journal*, May 4 1799. The other offers were £73 3s. 6d. from J.C. Beresford & Co., and £71 15s. from La Touche.

8. S.P.O., 121/4/10. The lowest offer was for £85 3s. 4d. per £100 of stock.

9. S.P.O., O.P. 22/22/20, letter from Walter Boyd. Petitioners to the House of Commons regarding the negotiation for the loan in 1795 stated — "relying... on a fair Competition being allowed in offering to make the Loan to the Public, they have been induced to prepare large sums of Money, ready to be applied to the use of the Public, should the Offer, made on their Part, have been found the most advantageous"; *Irish Commons Journals*, 1795-96, Vol. 51, p. 150.

10. It was felt that after the third payment there was little risk of default; the sum liable to risk diminished, whilst the security on the remaining sum continued in the same proportion; S.P.O., O.P. 121/4/7; O.P. 121/4/9.

11. This method of financing the operation certainly found favour in London; "The practice of making advances upon certain instalments of the Public Loans, on the security of the receipts, is a considerable recommendation to the Subscribers, and enables the government to contract for Loans on terms somewhat more advantageous than could be done if that facility were not afforded"; Second Report from the Committee on the Bank of England, B.P.P., 1807, (108), Vol. 2, p. 84.

12. S.P.O., O.P. 121/4/9. "Remarks on the Proceedings for the bidding according to the usual mode".

13. ibid. Details of the London houses appear in F.G. Hilton Price, *A Handbook of London Bankers*, (1876). Walter Boyd had tendered for the 1795 Irish loan; see Report Respecting the Negotiation for the Loan, *House of Commons Journals*, (London), Vol. 51, 1796, p. 333.

14. G. L. Barrow, *The Emergence of the Irish Banking System 1820-45*, (1975), p. 108.

15. Petition of Luke White to the Irish House of Commons, *Irish Commons Journal*, Vol. XIX, Part I, 1800, pp. 277-80.

16. Bank of Ireland, Minutes of the Court of Directors, May 19 1800.

17. Messrs Bogle French & Borrowes were prepared to allow Luke White to come in with them thus enabling him to retrieve his IR£75,000 deposit money but the government were not agreeable to this course, and hence the petition to the House of Commons requesting the return of his deposit; Petition of Luke White....op. cit., p. 278.

18. Robert Shaw had successfully taken the 1794 loan, for £500,000, payable at the Bank of England, and he transmitted "at least half of it in specie" to Dublin; Third Report from Committee of Secrecy on the Outstanding Demands of the Bank (1797), reprinted in B.P.P., 1826, Vol. 3, Appendix 2, p. 85. Before his financial career he was a prosperous flour miller in Kilkenny and did a large discount business tied in with his trading. He acted as a

Commissioner for receiving subscriptions to the capital of the Bank of Ireland in 1783. At the time of his death he was a director of the Bank; F.G. Hall, *The Bank of Ireland 1783-1946*, (1949), p. 504.

19. S.P.O., O.P. 22/19/1. He was, however, supported by various 'parties', among them Samuel Dick (Governor of the Bank of Ireland, 1797-99).

20. S.P.O., O.P. 22/23. Letter from Samuel Dick.

21. S.P.O., O.P. 22/23.

22. This principle was discussed by the 1796 Committee on the Loan in London, and Pitt supported the practice of not overlapping the loans — "....it was not usual for any application to be made for payment on a new loan till the former had been completed"; *Hansard*, 1795, p. 561.

23. In a letter to the Chief Secretary in December 1796 Sir John Parnell expressed the view that contractors ought to be forced to complete their payments — "the parties have acquired large fortunes from former loans — are they always to benefit", adding with a touch of malice, "I do not think Mr. Dick has any pretence for not making good his payment — Government security is saleable tho' perhaps attended with loss"; S.P.O., O.P. 22/22/5-7.

24. Increased rents demanded by land owners at least down to the 1790s meant that for the financier land had become a competitive field for investment, adding to the existing choices of securities or commercial loans; D. Large. "The Wealth of the Great Irish Landowners 1750-1815", *Irish Historical Studies*, Vol. 15, p. 30.

25. 35 Geo. 3, c. 6, s. XII.

26. A list of subscribers to the 1777 tontine, in the Journals of the House of Commons for 1779, gives IR£85,000 as the sum of which deposits were all made in Dublin, while Peter Thellusson & Co., was responsible for IR£190,000, out of which a deposit for IR£109,527 was made in London, the rest in Dublin, leaving IR£25,000, for which deposits were all made in London. While a large amount of deposits were made in Dublin it seems reasonable to suppose (from the detailed lists of nominees) that the subscribers would either nominate themselves, or someone nearby who they could easily keep account of. An analysis of the 1777 Tontine also appears in C. Gautier, "Un Investissement Genevois: La Tontine d'Irelande de 1777", *Bulletin de la Société d'histoire et d'archéologie de Genève*, tome X, 1951. See also R. M. Jennings and A. P. Trout, "The Irish Tontine (1777) and Fifty Genevans..." *Journal of European Economic History*, Vol. 12, 1983.

27. The figure for 1777 may be a little on the high side given that there were two clubs. A separate list of subscribers (see note 26 above) indicates that there were 243 subscribers for IR£110,000 and that for this portion of the tontine subscriptions of up to £500 accounted for 81% of the number of subscribers.

28. *Irish Commons Journals*, 1797, Vol. XVII, Part 2, Appendix Dliv-Dlxvi.

29. *Parliamentary Register*, op. cit., 1783, Vol. 3, p. 197; 1788, Vol. 8, p. 159.

30. ibid., 1797, Vol. 17, p. 321.

31. S.P.O., O.P. 22/22/4.

32. *Irish Commons Journal*, 1797, Vol. XVII, p. 77.

33. Between 1798-1817 the total income of the Sinking Fund was £18.8 mn, £11.4mn coming from provisions linked to new loans, £5.3mn of interest from redeemed debt, with the remainder coming from the quarterly issues from the Exchequer; Accounts Relating to the Public Income and Expenditure of Great Britain and Ireland, B.P.P., 1868-69, Vol. 35, Appendix No. 6, pp. 284-85.

34. Bank of Ireland, Minutes of the Court of Directors, July 3 1797. Robert Deey received from the government an annual allowance of IR£100 for his services.

He was also Secretary to the Royal Exchange Insurance Co. and a Director of the Royal Canal Co. He died in 1812. William Deey died in 1829.

35.    *Irish Commons Journal*, 1797, Vol. XVII, Part 2, Appendix Dcxciv-Dcciv.

36.    Bank of Ireland, Minutes of the Court of Directors, December 4 1790.

37.    *Parliamentary Register*, op. cit., 1789, Vol. 9, p. 228.

38.    'Stock Exchange Enquiry', *Freeman's Journal*, July 6 1849.

39.    Dublin Merchants found Crampton Court a convenient place to meet and make bargains and they only left this alley reluctantly even when proper buildings were provided for them; Stock Exchange files.

40.    The list ran in *Freeman's Journal* from July 23 to December 14.

41.    *Dublin Gazette*, September 3, November 1 1799.

42.    These requirements may simply have formalized the practices of the Voluntary Association.

43.    The Public Notaries formed in 1802 a society called "The Society of Regularly Bred Practising Public Notaries", with John Ashenhurst as President and John Robertson as Secretary. With these two officials, Robert Deey and John Barber acted as Examiners. Person eligible for admission "must be of approved Integrity, unblemished Reputation, have served regular apprenticeships to regularly bred practising Public Notaries and have undergone a proper Examination of three Members, previous to obtaining a Faculty". In 1811 there were 14 members, 11 of whom were also licensed brokers on the Stock Exchange.

CHAPTER 4

# ORGANISATION

From the modest number of thirteen brokers licensed to deal in government securities by the Commissioners of the Treasury in 1799, the membership of the Stock Exchange increased to 24 by 1806 and to 31 by 1820, a period when the size of the Irish debt expanded considerably. In the succeeding years the membership contracted to 25 by 1836, but it recovered in the mid 1840s under the stimulus of the railway share boom, although the membership by 1845 only stood at about 30, probably because of the appearance of rival stock exchanges dealing in railway shares. With the collapse of the boom and the ensuing period of consolidation the membership stabilized at about 30 in the mid century. By 1869 it had increased somewhat, to 42, greater business coming from the gradual spread of joint stock companies, but it was the active period of company formation in the last two decades of the century which brought a substantial gain in membership, reaching 85 in 1900, and 88 by 1914. The same stimulus lay behind the formation of the Cork Stock Exchange in 1886 with ten members, while the surge of local company formations in the nineties was accompanied by the admission of seven new members, making a total membership of 24 in 1900. In the inter-war years the membership of the Dublin Stock Exchange remained in the range of 82 to 96, the latter peak occurring in 1929-30. In Cork the membership fell to 11 by 1918, well below the 1903 peak.[1]

The rules stipulated that the "Society should consist of brokers duly admitted and licensed", but the floor of the Stock Exchange in the Great Rere Room of the Commercial Buildings was also open to the clerks of brokers and to the public. The Lords of the Treasury, in sanctioning the arrangements for the market to be held in the Commercial Buildings, had announced the setting up of "a Stock Exchange for the Use of All Persons who may resort thereto for the Purpose of buying or selling; but by the said Act no person can buy or sell on Commission unless he be licensed by their Lordships". The admission of the public for a "trifling fee" was regarded as likely to "afford considerable Security to the public".[2] Such visitors, however, were apparently not allowed to mingle freely with the brokers but remained "outside the bar", from where they could summon a broker to give an order, with commission, and where they probably dealt amongst themselves using the market's prices. According to the first printed Rule Book of 1822, "Visitors" could be admitted if they paid an annual subscription of one guinea (by the time of the 1846 edition of the rule book it was two guineas), while "every other stranger on coming into the Stock Exchange should pay 10d. to the porter at the door, who is thereby authorised and directed to demand and receive the same, otherwise to refuse admission"; the fee had been reduced to 6d. by 1834.[3]

In addition to the brokers and the public, brokers' clerks were also admitted to the Stock Exchange. While the rules stressed the desirability of business being done by the brokers it was permissible for clerks to deal for them but only "in the absence of his employer in the Stock Exchange". To employ a clerk in this capacity a member applied to the Committee for permission and agreed to "perform and fulfil" all bargains made on his behalf; the annual subscription for a clerk was fixed in 1822 at £4. There were probably only a few authorized clerks throughout the nineteenth century. Clerks not authorized to deal, but indentured to members, could also be admitted to the market. In the 1860s, however, the Committee sought to discourage the practice of "paid clerks in Brokers offices endeavouring to come into the Room", while later, in 1897, it was decided that each firm could only have one clerk or an apprentice in the Room during business hours.[4] On the floor of the Cork Stock Exchange authorized clerks were allowed to do business provided their names had been publicly displayed in the market.[5]

While the early versions of the rules and regulations were drawn up to take "advantage of the experience and information supplied by the wider sphere of operation in London", there was no class of jobbers present on the Dublin floor. However, as the 1849 Commission of Enquiry observed, the absence of such a class meant that "the stockbroker in this country unites, perhaps necessarily, something of the character of dealer with that of broker — characters which, if it were practicable it would be desirable to keep distinct".[6] The amount of business available was far too limited to enable persons to engage exclusively and profitably in the role of dealers or jobbers. Even so, brokers did do something in the nature of jobbing activity but it was purely in order to complete client's bargains. George Symes, of the partnership of Bruce & Symes, told the 1849 Commission of Enquiry that his firm "occasionally sold stock of his own to clients in broken sums, but only for the purpose of squaring accounts" and that he had "known this to have been done to the extent of 200*l.*; it is never done except from necessity". Similar testimony came from one Mr. Du Bedat, a clerk for fourteen years with Boyle, Low, Pim & Co., who said that "he had never known more than 300*l.* to have been transferred by the firm to their own clients at any one time".[7]

Orders for the sale or purchase of securities would be received by members during the morning and up until the opening of the market, but all were not taken to the floor of the Exchange. Before doing that they compared the orders for sales and purchases and where possible matched one against the other, the balance going to the market. In September 1799 the Lords of the Treasury had directed that the Market should open at noon and continue until 1.0 pm, but it was amended in November from 2.0 until 3.0pm. Within a few years the time of opening had settled at 2.45, closing at 3.15, and this was still the time of business in 1849 when the President of the Stock Exchange, Alexander Boyle, reported to the Commission of Enquiry that the market commenced at 2.45 "and was over generally in a quarter of an hour".[8]

One dealing session seems to have operated throughout the nineteenth century (in the 1870s it was open from 1.30 until 2.15), while up till about 1900 the market was also held on Saturdays.[9] After the suspension of normal business hours with the outbreak of war in August 1914, the market resumed with two dealing sessions at noon and at 2.15. By contrast, the Cork Stock Exchange had two business hours from its commencement, from 11 until 11.30, and at 3 o'clock; at the end of dealing a "Hammer terminating business was struck".[10]

Dealings in the Stock Exchange were made *viva voce* between brokers during the prescribed business hours. To facilitate orderly transactions the early rules clearly stipulated that "no *two* or *more* Partners of any Firm or Copartnership shall be allowed to act at the same time in the buying, selling or negotiating any Stock or Securities on the Stock Exchange".[11] It would appear that during these early years there was no formal calling over of the list with the bargains being completed in each stock as it was called, but rather dealings were probably done in more than one stock at a time. Such an informal manner of proceeding no doubt worked reasonably well given the size of the membership and the short list of stocks. Unfortunately the Rule Books are silent on precise changes in the dealing mechanism but it appears that by the 1890s the market was conducted with a formal call over (and it may well have done so for some years before this) since by this time both the list and membership were considerably larger.[12] The advantage of the call over, by concentrating business within a short space of time, was that the maximum number of bids and offers for stock were brought to the market, and accordingly the price arrived at was more likely to be within narrower margins than that which would be realised by more periodic dealings. It was a procedure suited to local stocks which lacked the large turnover of the shares of big companies, or which pertained in government stocks. What it did lack was continuity of dealing facilities, but this was to some extent overcome by "out of hours" dealing based on the official prices.

As to the precise nature of the arrangement of members for dealing purposes in the Great Rere Room of the Commercial Buildings little is known, except that they congregated for dealing inside "the bar" while "visitors" were kept outside it. When the market moved to its new premises in Anglesea Street it was arranged that the Brokers were seated in a circle in the centre of the floor, while in 1897 the seating plan was altered somewhat to correspond with that used in the Manchester Stock Exchange. To preserve the formality of the call over procedure the members were periodically admonished for "moving about the Room and so interfere with business".[13] Such was the Committee's concern over the matter in 1894 that the President was authorized to fine members "on the spot" if they interfered with the course of business during the calling over of the list. Clerks, on the other hand, were discouraged from sitting down. Fines were also used on the Cork Stock Exchange in order to induce members to attend the market promptly to facilitate business but the sanction was ended in 1897 because the Registrar had difficulty in collecting the money.[14]

As an aid in dealing activity it was laid down that unless a specific sum was named, offers for sale or purchase should be considered as binding for a minimum marketable quantity. The early rules of 1822 and 1834 specified marketable lots only in the case of government stocks, the provisions asserting that "all offers for sale or purchase of Government stock, in which no specific sum is mentioned, shall be considered as for £500 stock"; it remained at this figure until reduced to £200 in the inter-war years. With the advent of joint stock companies and shares deliverable by deed of transfer, marketable quantities for them were set out separately. In their case an offer to buy or sell a number of shares or stock at a price named "shall be binding as to any part thereof that may be a marketable quantity; and an offer to buy or sell Shares or Stock, when no number or amount is named, shall be binding to the extent of five shares, if in value under £200, or a number not exceeding in value that sum or to the amount of £200 Stock".[15] Similar values were indicated for bearer securities of foreign governments and companies.

From its early days and, certainly from around 1820, the Stock Exchange employed a clerk, The Registrar, who according to the 1822 edition of the Rule Book had to be "present in the Stock Exchange room at, or immediately before three O'clock every day, (Sundays excepted), and to attend there without interruption during the public meeting for business, and keep an exact record of the prices at which the several Stocks and Securities shall be bought and sold". Thus, if any transaction was made which required a new quotation, it was to be "immediately announced audibly" to the Registrar who then reported it to the Room, "in a loud and audible voice", so that "Brokers may distinctly know the quotations and the state of the Market". The duty of the Registrar in keeping an exact record of each days business and prices was seen as ensuring that the public would have in the "official records a most ample means of detecting every transaction that took place, entered in such a way as to put the strongest and most obvious check on the conduct of every individual member of the body that could well be conceived or devised".[16] From this information the Official List was then compiled. The only prices which the Registrar was to use for the daily quotations were those made between the members during the prescribed hours of business. This was in full conformity with the direction of the Treasury in 1799 that the "prices of business done previous to or after the hour of the Stock Exchange shall not be considered market prices".[17] It was not until 1912 that blackboards were installed in the Room for the purpose of recording prices during business hours.

The movement of prices and the closing prices of the day were recorded in the Daily List, published from the early years of the Stock Exchange "under the authority of the Committee". The prices given were generally for marketable quantities, the sizes of which were set out in the rules, and the aim was to provide a list of prices which had been made regularly in the open market. No quotations were allowed for exchanges of stock, or if there had been any "unusual consideration or inducement connected with such a sale". Prices of odd or small lots could, however, be inserted with the consent of the President and accompanied by "distinguishing marks". Brokers were also allowed to insert a nominal price, again subject to the discretion of the President, but if they did so they could be asked to deal at it for a quotable amount up to the close of business hours. This concession was seen as a means of encouraging offers.

In the early years the Committee were conscious not only of the expense involved in putting out the Daily List but also that it was very imperfect, "and that insufficient information was communicated by it to the general public".[18] Since deals were done off the floor and in brokers offices (a member could request a quotation from such deals if no one objected), it could not be a comprehensive record of price movements. So as to attempt to remedy this somewhat the Committee made several changes in the latter half of the century designed to produce a list which reflected not only the prices of stocks officially quoted but also, under a section called "other Business Done", the prices of companies not officially quoted. Dealings in these unquoted securities were not allowed until after the list of quoted stocks had been called over. Companies whose shares were seldom, if ever, dealt in for several months were eventually taken out of the list. Prices made in other markets for Irish shares were only marked with the permission of the President. After the introduction of account dealings in the 1840s the Daily List carried two columns for business done, one for cash, the other for the account. This practice ended during the First World War. With the increase in business toward the end of the century the Committee put out a Weekly List as a summary of the week's business.

From its formation, in 1886, The Cork Stock Exchange put out a Daily List which recorded "the fair price then existing" as made openly on the floor of the market. In its early years the List also carried details of offers to buy and sell securities, while deals in unlisted stocks were given under a "Remarks" title. Prior to a revision of the list in 1902 quotations were recorded not only of Cork dealings, but in addition of bargains done by the members with Dublin in both quoted and unquoted stocks; after the change the latter was discontinued. Periodically, the content of the List was reviewed, leading to the removal of securities with very infrequent dealings and the inclusion of more active ones. With local stocks, however, there was a reluctance to take out a quotation since Cork was usually the only listing, while if the Committee decided to insert others it meant foregoing a fee from the Company. The detailed work of compiling the list was, as in Dublin, undertaken by the Registrar. For the first three years one of the members performed such duties, but from 1890 onwards a paid official was employed.[19]

After a sale of government stock had taken place the broker was directed by the provisions of the 1799 Act to give the seller a docket of sale setting out the name of the seller, the quantity of stock, the "true rate of purchase or price", and "to whom the same was sold". In practice, during the early years of the century, the account rendered to the seller did not disclose the name of the purchaser since it was common practice to have the stock transferred into the broker's name with a transfer later to the purchaser.[20] This procedure was found to be convenient where several purchasers were involved in a transaction, and in cases where, to round off lots, brokers bought and sold fractional sums to make up the precise amount requested by their clients. Ostensibly, this constituted a degree of jobbing, but the practice of squaring accounts in this way was more a matter of convenience than a major activity on the part of brokers. The Commission of Enquiry in 1849 noted the practice, and that it was contrary to the spirit and intention of the 1799 Act, but concluded that no "practical mischief" had been done. It recommended no change in brokers' practices but such transfers probably became less frequent with the introduction of the account system in the 1840s.

Since, in the period before the 1845 railway boom, the bulk of the business of the Stock Exchange was in government stocks, the early rules and regulations covered only such dealing. Cash settlements were the order of the day, with members being urged to complete all bargains with the "utmost possible despatch". As directed by the Lord Commissioners of the Treasury in 1799, "All bargains made...shall be completed by payment of the value to the hour of One O'clock the following day", while all purchases for the Sinking Fund were to be "transferred the same day".[21] Such brief rules served well enough at the outset but with the growth of dealings more elaborate rules were drawn up in the 1820s and 1830s. In the case of government stocks and debentures, and Bank of Ireland stocks, delivery was to be before 1.0 on the following day, and if not delivered by 1.30 the purchaser could delay payment until the next day, while, if it was not delivered by 2.0 then the purchaser would either cancel the bargain or buy-in the stock in the market to remedy "the default at the cost of the Seller".[22] Payment for stock delivered was to be made before 2.0 and "it shall be *imperative* on Brokers to use every exertion to make their payments *at as early an hour as possible*; and if any flagrant neglect of this Rule occur, it shall be referred to the Room for their adjudication". If payment was not made before 2.0 the defaulter had to pay an additional day's interest, while if payment had not been made by 3 o'clock he was liable to a fine of 2s. 6d. per cent on the amount of stock, or the seller could opt to cancel the bargain on notice in writing.[23] The defaulter was also liable for any loss on the resale of the stock. Later, buying-in and selling-out was made publicly and officially on the Stock Exchange by the Secretary, or by a broker nominated by the aggrieved party.

During the 1840s cash dealings were supplemented by dealing for a specified day, that is, a time bargain fixed for the convenience of both buyer and seller. In this case the stock was to be delivered before 1 o'clock on the agreed day, which entitled the seller to prompt payment. If the stock was not delivered it could be bought-in on the same day without notice, the broker causing the default bearing any loss arising. Account periods for settlement of deals in government stocks also seems to have been introduced at this time. These followed the English pattern of mid-month dates for a four week account, and members were restricted from entering into bargains for a period beyond the current or next account. On the day before Account Day the buying broker was required to pass a ticket to the seller indicating the consideration and the name into which the stock was to be transferred; in 1860 the Committee decided that the furnishing of names in government stocks should take place two days before Account Day so as to leave one clear day to make arrangements. At the outset it appears to have been the practice of members to meet in the Stock Exchange Room at 10 o'clock on the morning of Account Day, and "make such arrangements amongst themselves as will limit the number of transfers of stocks and hereby avoiding all that may appear unnecessary".[24] This informal approach, however, still resulted in many unnecessary transfers, and to deal with the problem it was agreed, in 1853, that

...brokers should meet after 'Change on the day previous to the Account, each prepared with a statement of the amount of stock he is entitled to receive or has contracted to transfer and then pass slips, with their initials attached thereto from hand to hand according to arrangement between the parties so as to reduce as much as possible the number of transfers, but no broker shall be required to make any alteration in transfers on the morning of the Account Day. That upon such transfers being made the parties receiving the stock shall on delivery of the Certificate pay for such stock at even price to be fixed by a member of the Committee on the Account Day and the small balances to be settled on the following day.[25]

This system, using a making-up price and leaving differences to be settled between the several parties who had dealt in a stock, was widely used on the English provincial exchanges.

In the case of cash dealings in company securities the buyer had to issue a ticket to the selling broker not later than 12 o'clock on the third business day after the sale, and if this was not done the seller could, after due notice, have the stock sold out. The seller was required to deliver the shares, or the transfer deed duly executed, within ten days from the receipt of the ticket, and if this was not done the buyer could have the shares bought-in, after due notice, on the Stock Exchange. With the increase in the frequency of dealing in shares such procedures were obviously cumbersome and in October 1850 the Committee decided to adopt account days for settling transactions in the stocks and shares of joint stock and other public companies.[26] At the outset the Committee fixed the name and settlement days, but they later adopted the same account days as London in order to facilitate inter-market settlements. If no time was specified for a bargain it was then assumed to be for the existing account, while no bargains were allowed beyond the current or the next account period.

Settlement arrangements were designed to minimise the transfer of both stock and money so that the initial seller and the ultimate buyer in the account period came together, while those who had dealt in the stock as intermediaries were only involved in receiving or paying the differences between the buying and selling prices. Such procedures were in widespread use by the mid-century and were adopted by the Cork Stock Exchange from its formation. On name day, later called ticket day, the buyer for the Account who was to take up the securities would issue a ticket before noon giving his own name, "the amount or denomination of the Stock or Security to be transferred; the name of the transferee in full; the consideration money, date of issue, and the name of the member to whom the ticket is issued". Each intermediate seller would then, in succession, as he received the ticket endorse on it the name of his seller. Finally, the ultimate seller obtained from the issuer of the ticket the "address and description of the transferee". Where tickets had to be split to accommodate small lots a special procedure applied.

On name days the passing of tickets started at 10 o'clock, while tickets could be left at the office of the seller up till 11 o'clock. To facilitate the general activity every member, or an "efficient clerk on his behalf", who had dealings for the Account was required to attend at the Stock Exchange between 11 o'clock and 12 o'clock for the purpose of passing tickets; at one time absentees were fined a shilling. From the 1880s names for mining shares were passed on the day before the ordinary name day. Thus, on Account Day, the differences on accounts were payable and the delivery of stock sold for the Account took place against payment.

If the person selling shares had not received a ticket indicating the name of the ultimate buyer by 1 o'clock on name day he could arrange to have the securities sold out, while if a buyer found that securities were not delivered within a stipulated time he could have the securities bought-in, the offending parties being held responsible for any losses so produced. The buying-in and selling-out was done by the Secretary, at regular rates of brokerage, at the opening of the market; from about 1900 this procedure was moved to the close of business.[27]

With the increase in the volume of business in the last two decades of the century, the Committee introduced a Clearing Room Meeting on name day so as to make formal arrangements for clearing "in such securities as the Committee may from time to time order". Members, or their representatives, who had to issue, receive or pass tickets in the selected securities, were required to attend. They also had to supply the Secretary with a Clearing Sheet giving the transactions open in each security. With the aid of these sheets it was possible to put selling and buying brokers together in the most convenient form for the direct delivery of stock which thereby released the original contracting parties. On Account Day, every buyer or seller paid or received the difference between the making-up price and the contract price, and in due course all delivery of the securities included in the Clearing took place between the parties put together at the making-up price. These special prices were fixed by the Secretary on the day before Name Day "by taking the approximate average price of the two previous days", and all making-up was done at these fixed prices.[28] The making-up prices were also used to enable clients to continue a transaction into the next account. These arrangements had to be completed on Contango Day, the day before Name Day. Since all bargains had to be closed at the end of the Account it was necessary, for example, for a buyer, who wanted to postpone taking up stock or selling it, to close his position and then re-open it for the next account, a manoeuvre accomplished at the making-up price.

In the matter of commissions paid by the public the Dublin Stock Exchange was unique among contemporary markets in that it had statutory authority for its charges. Clause VI of the 1799 Act stated quite plainly that it was lawful for every licensed broker "to demand and take from every person for whom he shall sell....stock or securities, and from every person to whom he shall sell the same, a fee at the rate of two shillings and sixpence for each one hundred pounds of such stock or securities, and no more, for brokerage or commission". Anyone who charged more was liable to a fine of £100.

A maximum commission scale was quite common on English provincial exchanges, but competition among brokers usually meant that the rates levied were below the prescribed levels, which ultimately prompted the adoption of minimum scales to limit the severity of competition. In Dublin's case, the maximum of one eighth per cent on government stock imposed by the 1799 Act, had by resolutions passed in April 1824 become a minimum, not only for government stock but also for other securities; "That no Broker shall execute any business in the buying and selling of Government Stock, or other Securities, for a less rate of Brokerage, than that allowed *by law*, namely 2s. 6d. per cent". However, the commission rules allowed concessions for certain kinds of transactions. Where an exchange of stock took place only one commission was charged; stocks bought for speculation, so declared at the time, were eligible for "free closing" if done within two months, a leeway reduced to forty days in 1846 and to an Account period later; bona fide transactions for export or import (see Chapter 7) could be done at half commission; and finally, for principals who habitually dealt with a broker, the rules asserted that "from friendship, charity, or consideration of loss by speculation, Brokers are at liberty to relinquish the *whole*, but not *part* of their Brokerage on such transactions".[29] Such generosity was later confined to cases of charity.

In practice, the above commission scales applied predominantly to dealings in government securities, but with the advent of railway shares in the mid forties the Committee of the Stock Exchange found it necessary to recommend scales appropriate to shares of much smaller denomination and infinitely greater risk. Accordingly, the rates charged were appreciably above the general $\frac{1}{8}\%$ levied on government stocks. Two scales of charges were used, one for scrip, the other for fully paid shares. Reflecting the greater risk attached to handling railway scrip the Committee imposed a scale of 6d. on scrip of less than £2 10s., 1s. for that between £2 10s. and £5, and 1s. 3d. for scrip over £5; a fee of about 1%. Shares transferable by deed with the value of £15 or more were done at $\frac{1}{4}\%$, with low value shares commanding a rate of nearly $\frac{1}{2}\%$. These rates were adopted in September 1846, when the share market was particularly depressed and they were regarded as reasonable given the level of share prices.[30] It would appear that higher rates were charged at the height of the boom but no record exists of the precise scale. In a revision of the scales in 1861 somewhat similar levels were applied; shares under £2 each cost $1\frac{1}{4}\%$; from £2 to £15, nearly $\frac{1}{2}\%$; £15 to £50 at $\frac{1}{4}\%$; over £50 at $\frac{1}{4}\%$ on the consideration money. The members were instructed that these "Commissions must in every instance to be charged in full".[31]

To accommodate the growth in the industrial share market and the greater diversity of share values which this produced, a further revision of the commission scale took place in 1873. For securities transferable by deed, those under £2 in value were done at $1\frac{1}{4}$%, followed by falling percentages in £5 stages up to £25, with shares over this value bearing a rate of $\frac{1}{2}$% on the consideration money. Government funds continued at $\frac{1}{8}$% with $\frac{1}{4}$% on Bank of Ireland stock.[32] A similar scale, with an accompanying restriction on rebates, was adopted by the Cork Stock Exchange in 1886.[33]

By 1914 further amendments had been made to the commission rules, in 1905 and 1913. The main changes reflected the growth in the volume of business in industrial shares and particularly shares of low value. As a result there were five steps in the scale for shares under £2, starting with a charge of $\frac{1}{2}$d. per share for shares of less than 2s. Twelve steps applied to shares up to the value of £25, thereafter with $\frac{1}{2}$% on the consideration money. But to deal with the difficulty that the charge on small lots might not prove remunerative, the Committee introduced a minimum commission for small bargains. Thus, all transactions of less than £100 in value were to be at 10s., those under £20 to pay 5s. The Cork Stock Exchange, faced with an increase in the number of small local company floatations, initially decided in the mid-nineties to charge the commission stipulated in the rules, but in 1897 it decided to allow members to charge reduced commissions on small round lots in order not to discourage trading.[34]

The only concessions, apart from charity cases, permitted by the commission rules were for members of other stock exchanges, while "recognized" stockbrokers in other towns in Ireland (all such persons having been notified to the Committee) were charged half commission. Unlike some of the British exchanges, Dublin did not divide with other professions who brought business to it. The principal feeders granted such a concession in Britain were the banks, and it appears that despite the rules some Dublin brokers copied the mainland practice. Certainly, members reported as doing business for the banks at half commission were censured by the Committee in the mid-1870s, the guilty parties alleging that they were not the sole offenders.[35] Where such a departure from the rules persisted, the Committee, some years later, threatened to invoke the sanction that the Rule Book had been duly approved by the Lord Lieutenant and that they were "not at liberty to countenance this practice".[36] Finally, to clarify the position, in 1913, the Committee adopted a rule which asserted that if a member did business "at a less rate than that established by the Society for the time being, it shall be the duty of the Committee to report same to the Lord Lieutenant, and with his sanction such member shall be subject to a fine of £50 for the first offence, and on the second offence to expulsion from the Room".[37] Cork members were subject to a fine of £20 for the first offence and similarly with expulsion on the second, but the Committee could not threaten members with the displeasure of the Castle.

Local investors who wanted to deal in stocks or shares quoted on another market could either employ a broker on that market, ask a bank to deal for them, or use a Dublin broker. To provide such a service the members of the Exchange had developed trading links with brokers in all the main markets, particularly London, which had the most active dealings in most, but not all, industrial shares. Where orders flowed in both directions it was possible, at the end of the account period, simply to settle the balance of the fortnight's transactions, this being the practice in both Dublin and Cork in their dealings with other markets. This agency business, the main link between the various markets up to the 1870s, was conducted on what was referred to as a free trade basis, that is, no precise indication was given in the rules as to the amount of rebate to be extended to agents in other markets. In the case of Dublin, the appropriate regulation simply stated that "members are authorised to divide Commission with Members of other Stock and Shares Exchanges". This free trade basis lasted until 1912 when London introduced its minimum commission rules and brokers there were required to charge outside brokers from other markets half commission.

From the 1870s onwards the agency link between markets was supplemented by the development of shunting activity, a process which involved frequent buying and selling between markets on the basis of differences in share prices. Shunting, in the pre-1914 period, took place mainly in the home railway share market, along with some U.S. and foreign railway lines, and in the shares of large companies which were by then household names, such as J. & P. Coats, Guinness, Imperial Tobacco, Lever Bros., Dunlop, and the leading banks of the day. Successful arbitrage, based on price differences, needed rapid communication and this was made possible by the introduction of the telegraph in the 1870s, later supplemented by the gradual adoption of the telephone. Based on the knowledge of prices in other markets a shunter, in response to local demand for shares, could pick them up at a lower price elsewhere, or alternatively he could buy up shares locally to sell in another market where the price was marginally higher. Their operations thus helped to smooth out price differences, and in the process rendered local investors a useful price information service. Although sometimes referred to as "speculators acting in lieu of jobbers" they differed from London jobbers in several important respects. They did not act as wholesalers of shares for a full account period, but were "daylight" traders closing their positions at the end of the day. Normally, they tended to take what business was going and did not seek out orders, neither did they confine their activity to a particular range of shares. Up until 1908-09 shunters in Dublin, as in other British provincial markets, had direct access to London jobbers and were able to deal at 'net' prices, coupled with the added attraction that the jobbers guaranteed transactions. The London brokers were not prepared to do this. General shunting activity, and the added bonus of direct access to the London jobbing facility, thus greatly supplemented the local dealing mechanism and provided an up to date price service.[38]

This activity was greatly restricted, in so far as London was concerned, by the decision of the London Stock Exchange to institute single capacity operation in 1908, when the members were required to opt for either jobbing or broking activity. Coupled with this separation was the intention to abolish shunting activity involving London jobbers. Under the new rules a broker could not carry on the business of a dealer, and it followed that a jobber could not deal with a non-member. However, for a time outside links were not entirely severed since shunting deals continued by passing bargains through a broker at nominal commission rates, the accommodating London brokers being appropriately dubbed "dummy brokers". The London minimum commission rules of 1912, introduced with much controversy, closed this loophole. As well as a minimum scale for the public, the new rules also prescribed a minimum scale for inter-market dealing involving London. It was half the clients scale.[39] Provincial shunting, of course, continued, while a modified form of shunting developed between the provincial exchanges and London in the inter-war years. This was based on the services of specialist London brokers, but they were obliged to charge the stipulated commission. The decision of the Dublin Committee, in 1914, to levy half the client scale for dealing with members of other exchanges, which meant abandoning free trade, reduced the scope for its shunting activity in later years. On provincial markets in Britain, dealing facilities in the thirties were greatly supplemented by the jobbing network of Nicholson's of Sheffield, but there is no record that this enterprising firm had a direct link to the Dublin floor; it did have one to Belfast (see Chapter 12.).[40]

Unlike many other stock exchanges it would appear that Dublin was not greatly troubled by competition from outside brokers once the episode of the rival exchanges during the railway era was over. Brokers in Dublin all seemed to belong to the Stock Exchange and given the importance of dealings in government securities, which required a licence, viable outside dealing would have been a little difficulty. The few brokers who operated in the other main towns, apart from Cork which after 1886 had its own Stock Exchange, were allowed a share of the commission provided they were recognised by the Dublin Committee. As their numbers grew, however, with the growth of the industrial share market at the close of the century, Dublin passed a rule in 1896 whereby provincial brokers, in towns without a local stock exchange, would not be recognised unless they registered with the Committee and paid an annual fee. In May 1899 23 such brokers were registered. After the 1914 changes in the Dublin commission rules, outside brokers were only remitted half the clients scale. In its early rules Cork ordered its members not to do business with any other broker in the city, a policy which persisted for many years, and they later adopted a rule that they would only deal with outside brokers if they operated where there was no local exchange. In 1939 both exchanges fell in with the proposals from the Council of Associated Stock Exchanges of charging full commission to outside brokers operating within the postal area of an Associated Stock Exchange.[41]

The normal working of the Dublin Stock Exchange was suspended on two major occasions and one lesser event, the major disruptions being the two World Wars, the small interruption the financial crisis of 1931. The latter merely involved a fairly brief closure, in line with what happened in London, in September 1931, account dealings being suspended until November with the adoption of the London rules on cash dealings.[42]

With the outbreak of war, in 1914, Dublin closed immediately London announced its decision to do so on July 31st, while the settlement of the July account was postponed due to the closure of the banks under the emergency measures introduced. In order to alleviate the financial difficulties of the general business community, the government extended the Bank Holiday period, and hastily put through parliament the Postponement of Payment Act which postponed most commercial payments for one month, including stock exchange transactions.[43] While the moratorium suspended the need to pay for securities, the Dublin Committee nevertheless urged the members to make every endeavour to settle all outstanding bargains. A few days later the Committee ruled that all transactions made had to be settled in cash, and that no make-up prices would be fixed.

On September 14 the Committee of the London Stock Exchange announced a list of recommended minimum prices (based on July 30) for some 800 trustee securities, a move designed to protect both the members and the public from the possible collapse of prices due to bad war news. In response to this action the Dublin Committee felt that "as the hands of our Members are practically tied by this resolution, we do not consider it necessary to adopt a similar resolution". They therefore accepted the minimum prices for trustee securities since it was felt that while the pressure of local sales of government stock might not have been large, it might have disturbed the minimum fixed in London. However, like the other exchanges outside London, Dublin brokers continued to negotiate daily prices in local securities. Following the closure of the market on July 31 dealings were conducted in brokers' offices, on the street, and on the steps of the Stock Exchange, and while a request from 33 members that the Room should be opened unofficially was refused in September, the Committee relented in October "with the advent of the cold weather", and the members were allowed to use the Room, the session being wholly unofficial, no record of prices was kept, nor was the Registrar in attendance.[44] What little business was done, was all for cash. It was confined to necessary transactions by trustees and executors and "even in these cases dealings are difficult and matters of negotiation".[45]

While some semblance of dealing was restored relatively quickly there remained the more intractable problem of loans, for the purposes of speculation, obtained against the security of stock. In order to ascertain the state of this indebtedness, with a view to obtaining government assistance, the members of all stock exchanges were requested in October to supply details of the loans they had against stock. London's borrowing against stock amounted to £81mn, with £11mn for all other markets. Dublin's share of the latter total was very modest; owing to Dublin banks, with margin, £294,507; to firms or individuals, with margin £28,615, with a small sum of £3,650 from the latter group, without margin. At the end of October the Government announced proposals to deal with the problem of account to account loans. The Dublin Committee promptly decided to adopt the scheme, the most important provision being the banks' agreement not to press for repayment, while other lenders could obtain some measure of relief by way of advances from the Bank of England. With this difficulty out of the way the authorities slowly moved, with lengthy debate among all interested financial parties, to arrange for the re-opening of the stock exchanges. In agreeing to the assistance on outstanding loans, the stock exchanges had given an undertaking to the Treasury that they would not re-open without official approval and on conditions laid down for them. In all this, the Treasury was aware that most stock exchanges had already opened for unofficial cash dealings, and it had no desire to interfere with these temporary expedients. Among the conditions for official opening were the following — minimum prices would be retained for the moment, all bargains for cash, any new issues needed Treasury approval, no arbitrage business was to occur, all securities dealt in must have been in the physical possession of a U.K. resident since September 14 1914, and brokers had to obtain a written declaration from clients that they were not dealing directly or indirectly on behalf of enemy aliens. On these conditions London re-opened on December 4, with Dublin doing so on December 11.

One clause in the Treasury regulations proved quite inappropriate to the workings of all markets outside London, and hinted at the ignorance of Whitehall as to financial practices elsewhere in the country. The clause asserted that "No member will be allowed to bid or offer stock openly on the market". The President explained Dublin's position with great care to the Treasury, pointing out that business was transacted between members without the assistance of a jobber. The regulation was accordingly amended so that no member "will be allowed to bid or offer stock openly in the market in such a manner as to defeat the object of safeguarding the market against forced realisation of securities and against operations for the purposes of depressing prices". A further provision of the temporary regulations which caused difficulty was that "every bargain, whether in quoted or unquoted securities must be marked and officially recorded", with full particulars of the transactions furnished on the same day. Members, however, found that this was not always possible, and accordingly adopted the practice followed in other markets of allowing transactions to stand on the Marking Board "with a query mark", but they were not inserted in the Official List until the appropriate particulars had been supplied on the following day.[46]

While Dublin, along with other stock exchanges, had acquiesced in the need for minimum prices, the continuation of the restraint well into 1915 merely served to heighten its unpopularity. This arose since business was increasingly restricted by outdated valuations, based on July 1914, and also it was keenly felt that outside organizations were in no way bound by them. Accordingly, in October 1915, Dublin supported the Council of Associated Stock Exchanges in pressing for the revision or the removal of minimum prices. Such pleas went unheeded and relaxation came only gradually, largely when dictated by the government's borrowing needs, the final removal and return to free prices being delayed until July 1916. Thereafter, the Stock Exchange settled down to a reduced volume of business, its communications seriously depleted by the loss of the direct wire to London, and investment interest gravitating towards government securities and armament shares.[47]

An immediate return to normal working of the Stock Exchange did not take place with the ending of hostilities in 1918. In the prevailing post-war uncertainties, and the heavy fall in prices during 1919-20, very few members were interested in restoring non-cash dealing, while the authorities were concerned that the pre-war position should be resolved before they agreed to the resumption of account dealing.[48] Dublin's view was clearly expressed in August 1921 in a reply to an enquiry from the Council of Associated Stock Exchanges on the prospects of resuming normal operations. The Committee was against such a resumption, a view confirmed by the entire Room. But with more stable markets in 1922, and after detailed discussions with the authorities, the London Stock Exchange decided to resume fortnightly settlements as from May 22. Gilt edged dealings, however, would be for cash, and indeed have been so ever since. Dublin and Cork decided to do likewise, the Dublin Committee ordering the Name Room to be cleared out and made ready for use.

Although the Irish Free State remained neutral in the Second World War the experience of the Stock Exchange was very similar to that of some twenty years earlier, and it also mirrored developments in the British stock exchanges. A foretaste of the coming crisis was seen in 1938 when London fixed minimum prices for gilt edged securities, but in Dublin the Department of Finance informed the Stock Exchange Committee that it was not necessary to fix minimum levels for Irish government stocks.[49] When war was imminent, towards the end of August 1939, Dublin followed London in adopting minimum prices in British funds, that is, those quoted in the Official List on August 23. When London announced closure on September 1, Dublin, after consultations with the Department of Finance, suspended dealings and requested the members to meet in the Room on the following day. It was decided to adopt war regulations, and the Stock Exchange remained closed until the Irish Banks re-opened, business being restricted to Irish securities. The pending settlement was postponed and the afternoon session was suspended while London remained closed. Later, when London re-opened, the time of the afternoon dealing was altered several times to fit in with changes in London opening hours. On September 5 the Room decided that all bargains would be for cash . When London re-opened on September 7 dealings resumed in all securities. However, after discussions with the Department of Finance, minimum prices were adopted on September 11 for certain Irish government securities; the three National Loans outstanding, the 4% Conversion Loan, the Financial Agreement Loan and Land Bonds.[50]

Throughout the war business continued on this restricted basis, the market having to adjust to unavoidable difficulties, notably the greatly reduced telephone and telegraphic facilities. To protect the validity of the Official List it was decided in 1941 that the quotation of prices for business done in other markets should only take place with the consent of the President, and that only business transacted on the day of quotation was to be marked.[51] In 1942, to provide a better record, the date of the bargain was inserted alongside the relevant price in the List. In the extraordinary conditions of the time even small transactions tended to produce disproportionate changes in prices.

It took rather a long time to restore normal trading facilities after the war ended. This was largely due to suspicion in official circles in London as to the dangers of allowing an early resumption of speculative facilities. Even before the war finished the Stock Exchange had been urging an early return to normal working, but they had to wait until December 1946 for the restoration of fortnightly settlements, but without carry over facilities and free closing. These were delayed until 1949.[52]

# NOTES

1. Dublin and Cork local directories; Stock Exchange Minutes.
2. *Dublin Gazette*, 1799, p. 491; see also *Report of the Commission of Enquiry into the Management of the Dublin Stock Exchange*, 1849, (1870), p. 8.
3. *Laws, Rules and Regulations for the Stock Exchange, Dublin*, (1822 Edition), pp. 6-7.
4. Dublin Stock Exchange, Minutes of the Committee for General Purposes, January 31 1860, December 23 1897.
5. Cork Stock Exchange, Minutes of the Committee for General Purposes; Rules, 1886.
6. Report of the Commission of Enquiry, op. cit., p. 16.

7.   Commission of Enquiry, 1849, Minutes, *Freeman's Journal*, July 9 1849.

8.   The Commissioners in their Report felt that since the Treasury instructions in 1799 had stipulated an hour, then in their view, "it would result to public convenience if it were now continued open for at least that length of time"; *Report*, op. cit., p. 14.

9.   From 1913 until 1914 the Room was open on Saturdays for the "convenience of members"; Dublin Stock Exchange, Minutes, October 1913.

10.  Cork Stock Exchange, Minutes, 1886-87. For a short while after its start the dealing times were about half an hour later.

11.  Dublin Stock Exchange, 1834 Rule Book.

12.  Dublin Stock Exchange, Minutes, December 4 1894.

13.  ibid., July 3 1883, December 1894.

14.  Cork Stock Exchange, Minutes, September 18 1897.

15.  Dublin Stock Exchange, 1897 Rule Book, p. 24.

16.  Commission of Enquiry, 1849, Minutes, op. cit., July 9 1849.

17.  *Dublin Gazette*, November 1 1799.

18.  Dublin Stock Exchange, Minutes, April 24 1847.

19.  J. J. Mahoney served in this capacity from 1911 to 1927: Cork Stock Exchange, Minutes.

20.  A London broker, Charles Hill, stated in evidence to the 1849 Commission of Enquiry that in London "it would be considered very irregular for a stockbroker to sell stock of his own to his client, or to have the stock transferred in his own name, afterwards to be re-transferred or delivered"; *Freeman's Journal*, July 6-9, 1849. No doubt such transfers did occur.

21.  *Dublin Gazette*, November 1 1799.

22.  Dublin Stock Exchange, 1822 Rule Book, p. 7.

23.  Dublin Stock Exchange, 1834 Rule Book, p. 11.

24.  Dublin Stock Exchange, Minutes, December 5 1851.

25.  ibid., February 21 1853. For details of practices in Britain see W.A. Thomas, *The Provincial Stock Exchanges*, (1973), pp. 81-84.

26.  Dublin Stock Exchange, Minutes, October 22, 30 1850.

27.  Dublin Stock Exchange, 1879, 1905 Rule Books.

28.  Dublin Stock Exchange, 1879 Rule Book. A similar arrangement operated on the Birmingham Stock Exchange; see Thomas, op. cit., p. 84.

29.  Dublin Stock Exchange, Rule Book, 1834, pp. 7-8.

30.  Dublin Stock Exchange, Minutes, September 24 1846.

31.  ibid., December 31 1861.

32.  Dublin Stock Exchange, 1879 Rule Book, p. 43.

33.  The Cork Committee decided, in December 1887, that members would be at liberty to divide brokerage with solicitors and bankers if requested to do so, but there is no confirmation of this; Minutes, December 12 1887.

34.  Cork Stock Exchange, Minutes, December 23 1896, October 4 1897, November 15 1898.

35.  Dublin Stock Exchange, Minutes, June 16 1876.

36.  ibid., October 21 1879.

37.  ibid., February 20 1813.

38.  For a detailed description of the shunting network, see Thomas, op. cit., pp. 88-89.

39.  For details of the controversy and negotiations between London and the Council of Associated Stock Exchanges, see ibid., pp. 200-205.

40.  ibid., pp. 237-39.

41.  ibid., pp. 214-215.

42.  Dublin Stock Exchange, Minutes, September 21, October 1 1931.

43. For a detailed account of these events see E.V. Morgan and W.A. Thomas, *The Stock Exchange: Its History and Functions*, (1962), pp. 217-23; for provincial experience see Thomas, op. cit., pp. 228-35.
44. Dublin Stock Exchange, Minutes, September 8, 17, October 29 1914.
45. *The Economist*, November 28 1914, p. 946.
46. Dublin Stock Exchange, Minutes, January 5, 14 1915.
47. Presumably the experience and the reactions of the Cork Stock Exchange were very similar, but regrettably, there is a gap in the minutes of the Exchange for the period covering the outbreak of war.
48. In 1921 the authorities requested to know the exact state of the pre-war position; the Dublin minutes do not give the answer sent. Earlier, in 1920, Cork told the Council of Associated Stock Exchanges that its pre-war account still open was "practically nil"; Cork Stock Exchange, Minutes, May 10 1920.
49. Dublin Stock Exchange, Minutes, September 27 1938.
50. ibid., August 24 to September 11 1939. After the 'Phoney War' period the Committee instructed the Secretary to formulate plans for air raid precautions.
51. ibid., March 31 1941.
52. ibid., February 22 1948. It would appear that little use was made of London carryover facilities by Irish investors when they bought sterling securities in the pre-war years; "It used to be done, but the practice is practically dead now. I do not suppose there are half a dozen cases": *Banking Commission*, 1938, Minutes, Q. 2948.

CHAPTER 5

# DOMESTIC MATTERS

The "Act for the better Regulation of Stockbrokers" of 1799 laid down that
no person was to serve as a stockbroker, in the buying and selling of
government securities on commission, without a licence from two or more
Commissioners of the Treasury. The Commissioners were directed to issue
licences only to those regarded "as a proper person to be licensed". Also,
before a licence was given the applicant had to enter into a "bond to His
Majesty in the penalty of two thousand Pounds for himself and Two
Sureties of Five Hundred Pounds each", conditional on the broker not
dealing on his own account when employed by the public to buy and sell
securities.[1] The Act did not specify any particular qualification for
admission to the Stock Exchange, or that the granting of a licence required
membership there. The licences thus granted at the outset, in 1799, were
issued without reference to the existing body of brokers, the minute book of
the Treasury stating that "the following persons being approved of by my
Lords as proper to act as stockbrokers under the Act of last session...and the
necessary security being entered into a licence was issued accordingly".[2]
That the Treasury did not apparently seek testimony as to the proper
standing of these brokers is not surprising since they included in their
number such experienced practitioners as Robert Deey, broker to the
National Debt Commissioners among other official duties, and James
Gibbons, Notary Public to the Bank of Ireland since 1785 and broker to the
Bank since July 1792. James Gibbons was appointed notary to the Bank
because two officials, Hill Wilson and Thomas Williams, could not obtain
the necessary legal qualification due to "the opposition of certain Notaries
of this City".[3]

Persons licensed by the Treasury in the next few years seem to have undergone varying degrees of recommendation. Licences issued in 1805, 1807 and 1808 called on the testimony of "respectable merchants", but two issued in 1811 dispensed with such evidence. By 1818, however, the practice seems to have developed of applicants not only providing recommendations from respected merchants but also seeking the approval of established stockbrokers. It is possible that this change arose from the transfer of the power to grant licences from the Lord Commissioners of the Treasury to the Lord Lieutenant under the provisions of the Consolidated Fund Act 1816 which abolished the Irish Treasury.[4]

The following memorial (reproduced overleaf) from Charles Tisdall, College Green, Dublin, dated December 14 1815, to the Lord Lieutenant, Earl Talbot, illustrates the procedure followed until the changes introduced by the 1849 Commission of Enquiry into the Management of the Stock Exchange. It stated that Charles Tisdall,

> .......is Agent to an opulent Banking House of Belfast and was confidentially employed in the House of Croker Darling & Co. of this City until the dissolution of that firm where he acquired a general Knowledge of business, and having many wealthy and respectable Connexions, he humbly solicits to be allowed a Licence to act as a Stockbroker on the Stock Exchange of Dublin.
>
> Memorialist begs leave most respectfully to refer to the annexed Certificates of Merchants as to his eligibility and proper conduct.
>
> Your Memorialist will pray.

Fifteen merchants supported his application, and they were prepared to "certify that we are acquainted with Mr. Charles Tisdall of College Green and conceive him to be a fit and proper person to act as a Stock Broker in Dublin, having the best opinion of his abilities and integrity". Three brokers also added their signatures to the document, presumably on behalf of the Stock Exchange, namely Samuel Bruce, R. Williams and Henry Lanauze, and testified somewhat less enthusiastically than the merchants that they had "no objection to Mr. Charles Tisdall obtaining a Licence to act as a Stock Broker, as we are of opinion he is a very fit and proper person".[5]

In 1822 the Stock Exchange published its first code of "Laws, Rules, and Regulations", among them those governing the admission of members. They declared that any person intending to be a stockbroker should apply by letter to the President, proposing himself to be balloted for as a member "previous to his applying for the necessary licence" (all the early rules spoke of "Brokers duly admitted and licensed"). The President then gave the members a week's notice of the ballot, which was held on a Saturday, and should there be one black bean in three in the draw then it meant exclusion (a quorum of fifteen members was needed in the rules set out in the 1834 edition of the Rule Book). Unsuccessful applicants had to wait a year for

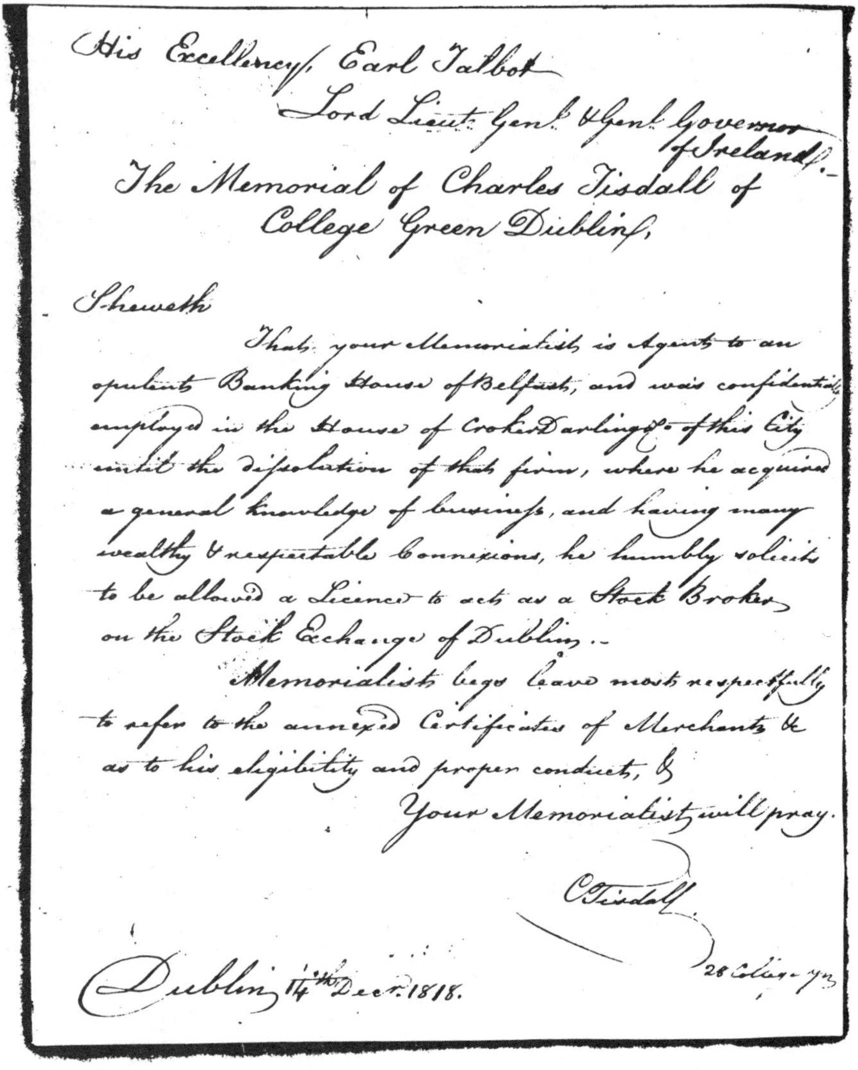

*Fig. 2: Charles Tisdall's Memorial to the Lord Lieutenant for a broker's licence, 1815*

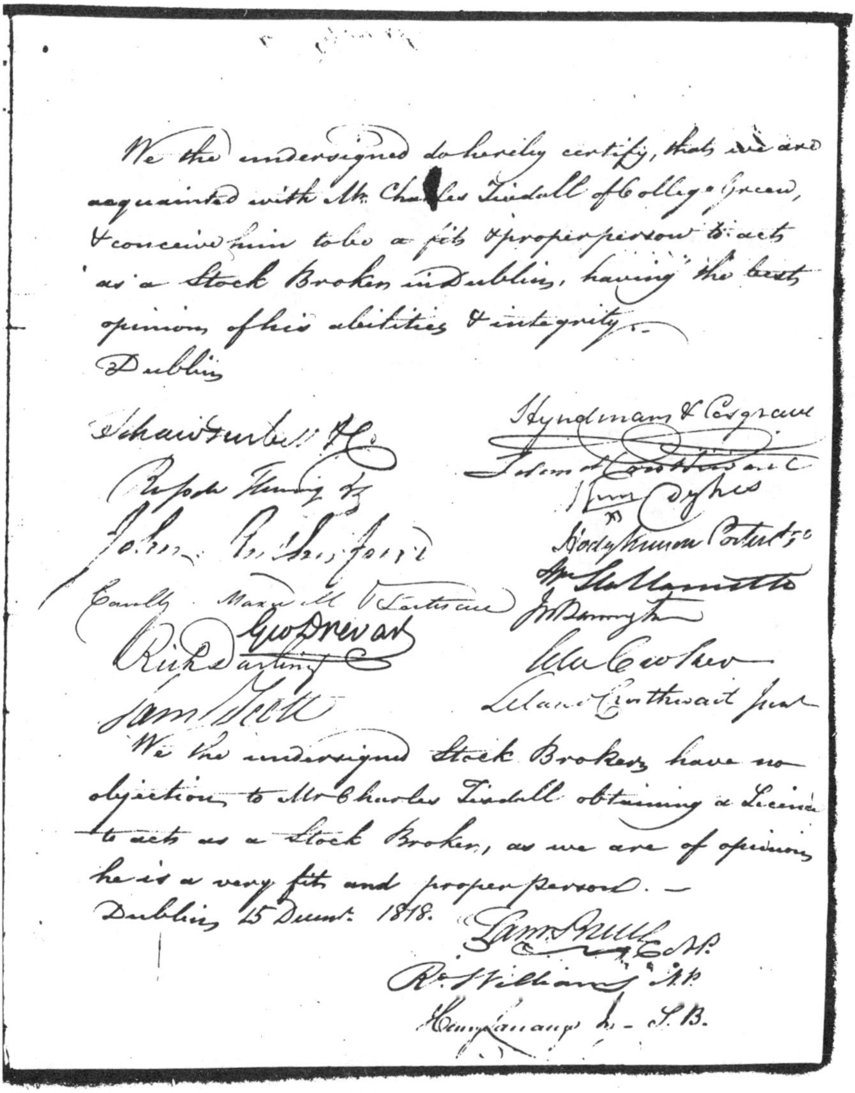

*Fig. 3: The "Certificate of Merchants" supporting Charles Tisdall's application*

another ballot. Successful applicants on obtaining their licence, paid an entrance fee of five guineas. Further requirements were added to the admission procedure as set out in the 1834 Rule Book. Applicants were required to declare if they were or intended to be in partnership with anyone, while discharged bankrupts were deemed ineligible, although this exclusion was later qualified by allowing previously insolvent applicants if they had been discharged for two years. A particularly demanding requirement was that no applicant "having been in the employment of a Stock Broker, shall be eligible to be balloted for, as a Member, unless he shall have served as an apprenticed or indentured Clerk to a Stock Broker, for the term of five years, and the indenture or article of apprenticeship be exhibited to the Committee, and registered by them in their Book of Proceedings, at least within one month from the date of the article". The requirement was further elaborated by 1846 so as to require the broker to issue a certificate affirming that the indentured clerk had served him "for the full term of five years, faithfully, correctly and diligently". However, as a relief, such entrants no longer had to endure the "ordeal of the ballot".[6] Finally, the 1834 version of the rules stipulated that a successful candidate should receive from the Committee "a Certificate of Eligibility to become a Stockbroker", which presumably would enable him to obtain a licence from the Lord Lieutenant. Before being allowed to act as a broker in the market the licence had to be shown to the Committee. The entrance fee by 1834 was 20 guineas.

Anticipating that some problems might be looming over the rules, the "Stock Exchange Society" amplified, and in some cases added to, the existing body of regulations. On membership they included a provision that applicants engaged in trade would be ineligible and set out more fully the procedure for obtaining a licence.[7] A candidate duly balloted for and approved would receive from the Committee a Certificate of Eligibility which confirmed that he had been "approved of as a fit Person to be admitted to be a Member of the said Society, and that in their opinion and judgement he is a fit and proper person to obtain a licence, pursuant to the Statute in that case made and provided, to act as a Stock Broker".[8] Stockbrokers were required to be duly admitted and licensed. The new rule book was agreed to by the Stock Exchange in April 1846 and in 1847 submitted for the approval of the Lord Lieutenant, as directed by the relevant statutes, 39 Geo. 3, c. 60 and 56 Geo. 3, c. 98. In seeking official blessing the Stock Exchange stressed that they had "for the better and more satisfactory Security of the Public and the greater provision and regularity of the negotiation of the important matters entrusted to them revised and reconsidered the Rules of the Stock Exchange, and have endeavoured to make them so far conform with the Rules of the London Stock Exchange as the nature of their business would permit".[9] A deputation from the Stock Exchange met the Chief Secretary to discuss the proposed rules, but apparently the necessary assent was not given because of criticism levied against the Stock Exchange by a group of outside brokers who were greatly annoyed at having been refused admission during 1845 and 1846.[10]

In 1845 three stock exchanges appeared in Dublin to rival the established market, and in July several members of the Royal Exchange Sharebrokers' Association submitted applications to join the Stock Exchange, but they were all rejected. Six of the candidates, "Messers Wisdom, Stephens, Clarke, Fayle, Bennett and Campbell" were rejected on the grounds that they were "engaged in trade and liable to the operation of the Bankruptcy Laws". Another, William Du Bedat, the vice-chairman of the rival association, had served for thirteen years as a clerk in the offices of Messers Boyle, Low, Pim & Co., but since he had not been an indentured apprentice for the required number of years he was excluded by the rules. But the basic reason for the refusal, as the 1849 Commission of Enquiry diplomatically put it, was that "the members of the Stock Exchange may have been influenced in their rejection of Messers Stephens, Du Bedat, and the other applicants of 1846, by the fact of their being members of the Royal Exchange Sharebrokers' Association"; membership of a rival exchange would certainly exclude them from London or one of the English provincial exchanges.

Greatly displeased with their treatment at the hands of the Stock Exchange the outside brokers took their cause to London, petitioning the House of Commons in April 1846, pleading,

> ....that a grievous monopoly exists in Ireland in the selling and buying of Government Stock and Government Securities, to the great injury of the Petitioners, to the manifest restraint of trade, and to the prejudice of the public, and all who have business to transact in the public stocks and funds; that the whole business of selling and buying Government Stocks and Funds in Ireland is vested in 18 firms self elected, who claim to exercise such power on the 1st June 1799, and intituled "An Act for the better Regulation of Stockbrokers"; and under colour and pretence of which Act the said 18 firms, exercising the trade and business of Sharebrokers in Dublin, claim and exercise the absolute, exclusive and uncontrolled power of admitting and rejecting whom they please to act as Stockbrokers in Ireland; and praying the House to take the circumstances therein into consideration, and to repeal the said Act, as imposing a restraint on trade.....

After a discreet delay of two weeks the President of the Stock Exchange submitted a counter petition expressing regret and surprise at the action of the outside brokers in coming to the Commons, and pointedly described them as "certain persons trading in the city of Dublin, as merchants and shopkeepers, and who have lately acted as a self constituted body in the character of brokers for the sale and purchase of Railway and other similar shares, in Dublin". He urged the House of Commons to reject their claims and not to alter the law affecting stockbroking in Ireland. The Commons merely ordered both petitions to "lie on the Table".[11]

Obtaining no satisfaction at Westminster the Royal Exchange Sharebrokers turned to the Lord Lieutenant, noting their lack of progress, and setting out "serious allegations against the Stock Exchange Society". The Stock Exchange requested its solicitor to draft a reply to the allegations and it was duly dispatched to the Castle. A few months later the Stock Exchange Committee submitted their revised rules for the approval of the Lord Lieutenant. An enquiry from the Castle, in January 1849, asking whether the Stock Exchange still objected to certain persons being given a licence brought the reply that the Committee had acted as prescribed by the new rules. In response the Castle authorities said they had been given to understand that the outside brokers who applied no longer had other "mercantile interests outside stockbroking", and further, that in previous cases the rule regarding apprentices had not been "invariably" acted on, several members being admitted in that manner. Dissatisfied with the uncertainty of the position the Lord Lieutenant and the Chief Secretary appointed a Commission "for the purpose of enquiry into the manner in which the Stock Exchange Society has been conducted".

The Commission was authorised to,

> ....examine into the Rules and Regulations of the Society and of the mode of transacting business with reference to the sale and purchase of Government Stock, having regard to the provisions of 39 Geo. 3, c. 60 and to report whether the existing Rules and Regulations have operated in a manner prejudicial to the interests of the public, or oppressively as regards individuals, especially in reference to the non-admission of applicants to be members of the Stock Exchange, and generally what alterations (if any) in the existing Rules and Regulations of the Stock Exchange are considered necessary more especially with regard to the admission of members.[12]

The members of the Commission, which was to sit in the Castle, were Henry Baldwin, Thomas Crosthwait, John McDonnell, George Roe and Thomas Wilson. Henry Baldwin was the Castle's law adviser, while the others were leading figures of finance and commerce in Dublin. The Stock Exchange promised its full co-operation. The Commission met on April 5th but adjourned until the 13th without doing any business, when counsel for the Royal Exchange Sharebrokers objected to the composition of the Commission on the grounds that three of them, Thomas Wilson, Thomas

Crosthwait and George Roe, had signed the Stock Exchange petition to the Commons opposing the repeal of the 1799 Act. Faced with such a protest the three concerned, "feeling a delicacy upon the present, declined to act", and the Lord Lieutenant was left to find alternatives.[13] He appointed Alexander Parker, Valentine O'B. O'Connor and George Pim. The Commission held its first meeting on July 5 1849 and proceeded to take evidence over three days. The Stock Exchange and the Royal Exchange Sharebrokers were represented by their respective counsel and solicitors.

On the first day the Commission heard long statements from the counsels and the remainder of the time was given to hearing evidence from a London broker, one Charles Hill of the firm of Hull, Fawcett & Hill, Alexander Boyle, President of the Dublin Stock Exchange, Robert Gray, a Dublin banker, and George Symes of Dublin brokers, Bruce & Symes. Most of the evidence centred on the admission procedure and the reasons for the rejection of the applicants from the Royal Exchange Sharebrokers' Association. The other main issue raised was the dealing practice in gilt edged securities and whether or not brokers sometimes sold their own holdings to clients rather than deal purely for commission as stipulated by the 1799 Act.[14]

On gilt edged dealings the Commissoners noted that when a docket was issued by the broker to a seller, the name of the buyer did not appear on it as required by the 1799 Act, but they concluded that no "practical mischief resulted from the omissions". The transfer of stock into the name of the broker and later by him to a client violated the provisions set out in 1799, but again the Commissioners accepted that it was generally done to facilitate dealings and for "public convenience, and not for the private profit of the brokers". Apart from the thorny issue of admission, the Commissioners formed the opinion that "the rules have been generally adhered to, that the books required by the statute have been kept by the brokers, that the registry has been properly conducted, and these, with the 11th rule extending admission to all persons to the Exchange during business hours on payment of a trifling fee, afford considerable security to the public".[15]

The Commission reserved its censure to the rules governing admission. These were "all strongly objected to as inconsistent with the Act of Geo. 111 and as virtually transferring the right to license Brokers from the Lord Lieutenant to the Stock Exchange and as tending to limit the number of brokers, and preserve a monopoly to the existing body and their con-nexions". To remedy the position the Commission recommended that in the first instance an application should be made directly to the Lord Lieutenant, and then the Stock Exchange could raise objections or give their support. The applicant should supply the Lord Lieutenant with evidence as to his character and general fitness to be granted a licence and suggested that suitable signatories of such a certificate might be the Lord Mayor, the Governor of the Bank of Ireland, the President or the Vice-President of the

Chamber of Commerce, and the President of the Stock Exchange. In order to implement the new procedure suitable changes were made to the Stock Exchange rules. New members now became "duly licensed and admitted", with the rules clearly stating that every person "who has obtained from the Lord Lieutenant a licence to act as a Government Stock Broker", on paying the entrance fee, and who was not disqualified by the rules, would be admitted. Applicants had to give the President ten days notice of their intention to apply to the Castle for a licence, such a notice then to be posted in the Stock Exchange. If a member knew of any reason, based on the rules, which would disqualify the applicant this should be conveyed to the President for relaying to the Castle. After ten days or so the members would resolve whether to support the application while the old style ballot was dropped, and for successful applicants the President would sign a letter of recommendation to the Lord Lieutenant who would proceed to issue a licence.[16] The letter of recommendation also seems to have been signed by some of the public figures suggested by the Commission. The arrangements appear to have worked quite smoothly since between 1850 and 1884 only on two occasions did the Castle grant licences against the recommendation of the Stock Exchange; presumably such persons were then admitted as members. Some irritation remained, however, at having such an external reference and in the early 1870s the Committee expressed concern at the recent "disunited action between the authorities who are parties to the admission of members" and concluded that the "present....mode of admission is invidious and anomalous, such as no other Society would tolerate".[17]

With the formation of Seorstat Éireann in 1922 the power to grant licences passed to the newly formed Department of Finance. In 1923 some delay was experienced in the issue of licences by the Department, which in the circumstances was understandable, so the members decided to admit a few new entrants to the full privileges of membership pending their issue by the authorities. These, when they came had the added interest that they were in Gaelic (see illustration 5 on p. 85), which produced some consternation when they were exhibited in the market for all to see.[18]

To match the increasing diversity and extent of business the Stock Exchange Committee introduced into its rules, as presented in the 1879 edition, certain financial requirements for new entrants which were on the lines of those widely used in the provincial exchanges of Britain.[19] An applicant for admission was required to furnish the Committee not only with the names of "two solvent and respectable persons" who were prepared to give security for him to the sum of £1,000 each for three years, but the applicant also had to satisfy the Committee that he owned not less than £2,000 which was "immediately available for the conduct of his business".[20] To regulate the level of entry, and to strengthen the financial position of entrants during times of increased business activity, periodic revisions were made to the amounts required. By the turn of the century candidates for admission were required not only to have £2,000 available for the conduct of business, but also to deposit £1,000 in cash or securities, with the Committee for three years, a figure increased to £2,000, and the duration to five years, in 1925.[21]

Another financial hurdle for new entrants was the entrance fee, which over the years was altered to accord with the general prosperity of the business. From a modest five guineas in 1822 it rose to twenty in 1834 and to 50 in 1846, a figure which brought internal criticism and a reduction to a mere £10. However, by 1879, it had climbed back up to a hundred guineas and to 250 in 1890. By the turn of the century it had become 500 guineas and a thousand in 1925. Concessions were granted to indentured clerks with a certain period of service in a broker's office; generally if they had completed at least three years service they were only charged about a third of the entrance fee, the broker testifying that the clerk involved had "served regularly in his office during the term of his indenture". The perennial financial burden for all was the annual subscription whose proceeds went to meet the operating expenses of the organisation. From seven guineas in 1834 it rose to twenty in 1879 and remained at this level until 1920 when it was increased to fifty for members who had joined after 1913 but kept at the old level for those admitted before then. Such a long period of stability was testimony of the buoyancy of other sources of income for most of these years, the money coming largely from quotation fees.

As on other exchanges the Cork Stock Exchange also balloted for the admission of new members. In the prosperous conditions of the mid 1890s consideration was given to limiting membership by imposing a ceiling or else by putting up the entrance fee. In the event the Committee raised the fee to 100 guineas, but later reduced it. Similar sort of requirements to Dublin were adopted by way of sureties, while members could not enter into partnership with non-members, and they were also required to have "offices in Cork and convenient for the Exchange".[22]

From early days brokers employed clerks to assist in the running of offices, attending to correspondence and keeping the necessary ledgers. They were also able to use them to deal on their behalf in the market but various restrictions were imposed on this concession. Members generally felt it was "very desirable that the business of the Stock Exchange shall be done by the Brokers in person and not by clerks", and accordingly the rules required members, who wanted a clerk to deal for them periodically, to seek the permission of the Committee. In 1834 the Committee decided to charge a fee of four guineas for authorised clerks, and a member had to agree to honour all bargains made on his behalf. Such permission was generally given on the clear understanding that the clerks would act only in "the absence of his employer" from the Stock Exchange. As far as the records show there were very few authorised clerks during the nineteenth century.

*By the Lord Lieutenant-General and*

*General Governor of Ireland.*

*We having approved of Mr.* **Hubert Briscoe**
———————————————— *of the City of Dublin, as a*
*proper person to be licensed to act as a Stockbroker*
*in buying and selling Government Stock and Govern-*
*ment Securities on Commission, and he having given*
*the security required by law to entitle him to such*
*Licence, We do hereby license and empower the said*
    **Hubert Briscoe**
*to act as a Stockbroker in buying and selling Government*
*Stock and Government Securities on Commission.*

*Given at His Majesty's Castle of Dublin*
*the* **27** *day of* **September** *1913*
*By His Excellency's Command,*

*Licence to*
    Mr. *Hubert Briscoe*
    *to act as a Stockbroker.*

Fig. 4: *A Broker's Licence, 1913*

# SⱯORSⱵⱯⱵ  ÉIREⱯNN.

## AN ROINN AIRGID

Dinim-se, Earnán de Blaghd     an tAire Airgid

i Saorstát Eireann, tar éis dom   Seán Aodh Mac Liaim, 36, Faitche

, an Choláiste, Baile Atha Cliath

do cheadú mar dhuine ceart chun a bheith ceadúnaithe chun gníomhú mar Bhrócaer Stuic i gceannach agus i ndíol Stuic Rialtais agus Urrúsanna Rialtais ar coimisiún, dinim, leis seo, ceadúnas agus comhacht do thabhairt do   Sheán Aodh Mac Liaim     san chun gníomhú mar Bhrócaer Stuic i gceannach agus i ndíol Stuic Rialtais agus Urrúsanna Rialtais ar coimisiún, agus tá seisean   tar éis an t-urrús san do thabhairt uaidh is gá do réir dlí do dhaoine gur mian leo bheith ceadúnaithe amhlaidh do thabhairt uatha.

*Earnán de Blaghd*

Aire Airgid

Dáta: an 14adh lá de Mhi na Nodlag 19 25.

*Fig. 5: A Broker's Licence, 1925*

Restrictions were later imposed on the number of clerks a firm was allowed to have on the floor, the Committee having decided in 1860 that it was undesirable to encourage "the practice of paid clerks in Brokers Offices" coming to the Room. Indeed, in 1897, it adopted a rule stating that each firm was only to have one clerk or an apprentice in the market during business sessions.[23] In addition to paid clerks brokers also employed indentured clerks who were bound to their employer generally for a term of five years, for a fixed fee, so as to learn the business of stockbroking.[24] Such clerks were allowed in the market in the early years but only to attend upon the broker.

In 1925 the Committee of the Stock Exchange was faced with an unusual, and for the time, somewhat delicate request. An application for admission was received from Dona May Irene Keogh. When it was proposed that the admission of a woman member should be put to the vote of the members, the counsel to the Stock Exchange advised that "the Body were not legally entitled to refuse to admit to membership a Lady applicant on the grounds that she is a woman". Denied such a straight forward choice the matter was set aside for a short time, but later the Committee interviewed the applicant and was satisfied as to her "fitness and means"; one of her sureties was the then Minister of Agriculture, Patrick Hogan. She was duly admitted and the President gave the usual recommendation to the Department of Finance to issue a licence. To prevent future doubts a note was added to the rules to the effect that "any words which import the masculine gender shall be understood also to indicate the feminine gender wherever the context so permits".[25]

From its early years the general affairs of the Stock Exchange were directed by a Committee consisting of the President and six members, all elected annually, with an honorary secretary and treasurer drawn from among them. The President presided over the daily business meeting of the market and at committee meetings.[26] By the time of the 1879 Rule Book a Vice-President was also elected annually. Apart from two periods in the 1860s and 1870s the office of President was an annual one, although a few members did occupy it on two or more occasions. The first exception was from 1860-69 when Alexander Boyle occupied the Presidency in response to the generally expressed view of the members in 1860 that there should be a "more permanent Chairman of the Society".[27] This was, of course, the practice on most British provincial exchanges, which may have prompted the temporary change. There was certainly no great changes afoot in the Dublin market which called for the greater continuity of a more permanent leadership. While R. H. Boyle held the Presidency from 1874-79, for the move to the new building, thereafter annual incumbents prevailed. As to who held the office during the years 1800-35 little is known. Dublin Directories give Richard Williams as President from 1835-45, and the first holder of the office was probably John Talbot Ashenhurst, 33 Dame Street.

The Committee at the outset consisted of seven members but was

**This Indenture** witnesseth that George Brooke Symes of Mount Druid Killiney Co Dublin doth put himself Apprentice to George Symes of 37 Dame Street Dublin, Stockbroker. to learn his business, and after the manner of an apprentice to serve from the date hereof for the full end and term of three years. During which term the said Apprentice his master faithfully shall serve, his secrets keep, his lawful commands everywhere gladly do. He shall do no damage to his said Master nor see it done by others but to the best of his power shall let and forthwith give notice to his said Master of the same. He shall not waste the goods of his said Master, nor lend them unlawfully to any, and shall neither buy nor sell without his Masters license and in all respects behave himself as a good and faithful Apprentice ought to do, during the whole of the said term.

And the said George Symes in consideration of the faithful services of the said George Brooke Symes will instruct the said George Brooke Symes in his business as a Stockbroker which he now useth, after the best manner in way that he can or will cause him to be so instructed.

And for the true performance of all and every the covenants and agreements herein contained, each of the said parties bindeth himself to the other by these presents. In witness whereof the said parties to these presents have hereunto set their Hands and Seal this first day of January in the year of our Lord one thousand eight hundred and ninety six.

Signed

Fig. 6: An Apprenticed Clerk's Indenture, 1876

increased to nine by 1846. Although annually elected, the members achieved some continuity of service since in practice the rules provided for two members to retire by rotation each year. To ensure that they had adequate experience of share dealing and related matters those seeking election needed to have been members of the Stock Exchange for at least five years. While no doubt its work in the early years covered a wide range of problems, the rules only guided its deliberations when arbitrating disputes between members. In the 1840s all such disputes were submitted to the Committee who then heard evidence from both parties and its decision was final.[28]

Up until the 1890s the resolutions arrived at by the Committee could not be put into force until they had been confirmed by the "Society at large", unless they related to by-laws on Official Quotations, the settlement of a dispute between members, or other routine business. But as the range and volume of work handled by the Committee increased it became apparent that frequent reference to the general body of members was becoming impractical, and very time consuming, so that from around 1900 the sanction of the members was only sought for major changes in the rules. Also, in line with the growth of business, and its greater complexity, the powers and duties of the Committee were set out in much greater detail in the 1905 edition of the Rule Book. Among the duties laid down were the general supervision of the Stock Exchange, the appointment of the "Secretary, Assistants and Servants", fixing dates for carry over days, special name days, settling days, buying-in days, etc., the admission of members, the declaration of defaulters, the management of the funds of the Stock Exchange, and so forth. Special meetings of the Society could be summoned by the President, two members of the Committee, or through a written request from seven or more members, but such meetings could only discuss the subject referred to in the requisition.[29]

Another important administrative change, closely linked to the above developments, was the amalgamation in 1902 of the office of Registrar with the post of honorary Secretary. The growth in membership, the increasing number of company quotations and the detailed work often involved, more inter-market discussion and communication culminating in the formation of the Council of Associated Stock Exchanges of which Dublin was a founder member and active participant, all this and more, greatly taxed the resources of an honorary position. To resolve the problem the Committee decided to appoint "a clerk, to be called the Secretary" whose duties included those previously done by the Registrar and also the administration of the newly formed Secretary's Department. The work taken over from the Registrar's position included the keeping of a "true and exact record of the proceedings of each day" and from such information the preparation of the share list with all the detailed particulars about share dividends, payment of calls, closing of transfer books, etc., which it increasingly carried. The

Secretary was to be present at the daily call over sessions, and to attend in the Name Room on Name Day. His department also had the responsibility for Certification of Transfers where the number of shares on a certificate did not correspond to the number sold, the Secretary then forwarding the certificate to the office of the company and certifying on the transfer deed that it constituted a valid delivery of stock. In addition, he was expected to be something of a librarian keeping "as far as practicable, a record of Law Cases, etc., bearing upon Stock Exchange business", and on the same lines also to file copies of company prospectuses, reports and accounts. A most important task was to attend at meetings of the Committee, "keeping proper minutes of the proceedings and conducting correspondence connected therewith".[30]

Unlike many of the English provincial markets the Dublin Stock Exchange has not led a particularly roving existence. For its first few meetings it met, at the direction of the Lords of the Treasury, in the Old Exchange Coffee House, but in November 1799 their Lordships agreed to the market moving to the newly constructed Commercial Buildings [Plate 1] where it remained until 1878. Located on the north side of Dame Street the building was put up by a company of merchants, drawn largely from the membership of the Ouzel Galley Society, expressly for the purpose of transacting branches of business for which the traditional location of the Royal Exchange was found to be inconvenient.[31] Financed by an issue of 350 shares, construction started in 1796 and in January 1798 the company was incorporated by Royal Charter and opened for business in 1799. Annually, the shareholders elected a Committee of Directors, fifteen in number, to manage its affairs and in the early years they included such influential business names as Leland Crosthwait, Samuel Dick, Nathaniel Hone and Joshua Pim. The Secretary to the company was Thomas Daniel who for twenty years was also Secretary to the Stock Exchange. This elegant building (now partially reconstructed by the Central Bank of Ireland) contained a central hall, a fine library and reading room, a spacious court lined by the offices of brokers, insurance and other agents, and with an entrance from Cope Street. The Stock Exchange held its meetings in the "Great Rere Room" which was just above a large coffee room.

By the early 1870s the Stock Exchange felt that the "Rere Room" was "in many respects very inconvenient" and started looking for more suitable premises. After several years of searching they eventually found a place in Anglesea Street in 1876, and to a design provided by Messers Miller & Symes, architects, one Mr. Meyer built the present Stock Exchange building at a cost of £15,000. The money came from the sale of investments and by the issue of debentures to the members under a trust deed.[32] On January 1878 the brokers held their first meeting in the new building and according to one report they marched round from the Commercial Buildings to Anglesea Street led by a brass band. However, *The Irish Times* reported a less flamboyant inauguration; "Yesterday, the commodious and handsome building in Anglesea Street....opened for the transaction of business. There was no ceremony whatever observed in connection with the opening but the President of the Chamber, Mr. Richard Boyle, and a large number of brokers celebrated the event by an informal luncheon. About a quarter before 2.0 upwards of forty brokers assembled in the new hall and seated in a circle in the centre of the apartment, books in hand, proceeded with the usual clamour with the financial work of the day".[33] In addition to the market and the related offices the building contained office accommodation for rental, but due to the somewhat depressed state of trade at the time the Committee were not able immediately to find tenants.[34] In 1895 the Society decided to convert itself into a limited liability company (largely for legal reasons) with an allocation of shares among the members, each receiving 108 £1 shares, fully paid, making a total capital of £12,000.[35] The company, Dublin Stock Exchange Limited, was registered on April 30 1895.

While the preliminary meetings of the Cork Stock Exchange, in October 1886, were held at 59 and 74 South Mall, the first home of the market was a back room at number 75. However, in January 1890 they were ordered to leave and they gladly accepted an offer of a room from the Irish Temperance League at number 81. By 1895, with the "body increasing in number" they sought new premises, looking for a "front room in a good position on the South Mall, affording opportunities for suitable advertising of the Stock Exchange on its frontage".[36] In March 1896 they moved to a first floor room at 86 South Mall as tenants of the Cork Turkish Bath Co. They moved again in 1928, this time to a back office in Goodall's premises.

Dealing activity on the floor of the Exchange depended on the flow of orders from customers to brokers, delivered verbally or by mail, and on the latest prices of securities which were dealt in not only in Dublin but also in other markets, particularly the prices of stocks whose main markets were in London or other provincial markets. Shares or stocks which "took their rise" locally depended on the flow of local buying and selling orders, but brokers were not keen to deal in more widely quoted stocks without the most recent information on prices in the main markets, especially London. Early reports of London prices depended on the frequency, and more important in winter on the regularity of the mail delivery, and with the resulting spasmodic level of information price discrepancies between markets in the same securities were inevitable, reflecting local buying and selling activity. The first significant improvement in communications between markets took place with the introduction of telegraphic facilities around 1850. Manchester and Liverpool markets were receiving mid-day and closing London prices by this time from the Electric Telegraph Company, and it appears likely that early in the 1850s Dublin also received similar information but from the rival company, the Magnetic Telegraph Company.[37]

Normally this kind of price service was provided for a fixed annual rental. In 1854, however, the Committee decided to discontinue the Magnetic Telegraph prices, but two years later a London price service, three times a day, was reinstated.[38] But regularity and promptness, which would make such a service extremely valuable, were not always present. Complaints were widespread and frequent. For example, in 1873, the Committee complained about the very unsatisfactory state of the telegraphic service, which by 1870 had been taken over by the Post Office, and to emphasize its disquiet it sent a deputation.[39]

Despite lapses the telegraph service was in extensive use by the 1870s, not only for transmitting price information but also for giving orders to agents in other markets. Shunting activity, of course, relied greatly on this kind of speedy communication to take advantage of price differences between markets. In the mid 1870s the College Green office handled over 5,000 messages a week.[40] To bring the facility closer to the market the Committee decided in 1881 to petition (with support from London brokers) for a full telegraph service in the new building, operating from a room on the top floor, with a direct stock wire to the London Stock Exchange. The petition to the Post Master General pointed to the

....disadvantages under which they labour in consequence of there being no special wire for the transmission of telegraphic messages between the London and the Dublin Stock Exchanges. The result is that messages can be sent more expeditiously from London to Dublin and vice versa through Liverpool and Manchester than direct and business is consequently diverted from its natural channels to the great detriment of all concerned. The time now occupied by a message from the London Stock Exchange to the office in College Green in Dublin is about 40 minutes and the delivery to Brokers offices within 300 yards of that office takes frequently 13 minutes more, making the entire delay nearly an hour. The amount paid annually for messages is very considerable and the returns would be very much increased by the establishment of a direct wire.[41]

Before installing the latest equipment the Post Office wanted a guarantee that business would generate an income of £1,200 a year; the Committee accepted the condition. In the first year of operation the value of business fell short of the target by about a quarter, but with more active markets in later years receipts to the Post Office improved. As the volume of business increased the telegraph operations room was enlarged in 1891; it was connected to the market floor by a shoot. Even with a special wire to London complaints about delays were frequent, both from Dublin and Cork. The Post Office's characteristic response, especially during winter months, was that "rough and stormy weather is responsible for many interruptions to telegraph wires, and wet weather, mist or fog by lowering the insulation of wires and causing thereby a loss of electrical efficiency also impairs telegraph communication".[42] On the outbreak of war in 1914 the Stock Exchange lost its through wire to London, but the service was resumed after the war and the wire was finally taken out in 1946.

As on other stock exchanges the use of the telephone for communicating between brokers offices and the market, and for linking Dublin with other markets, was a very gradual process. While the telephone had been reluctantly introduced into the Manchester and Liverpool exchanges in the 1880s, only to be little used, telephone boxes were not installed in the Dublin market until 1897 but again the main use was for local calls, long distance communication being done by the telegraph.[43] By the outbreak of war in 1914, however, there were signs that the telephone was beginning to replace the telegraph as the most important inter-market link, its progress aided by technical improvements and the continued frustration of delayed cables. Wartime restrictions finally put paid to the telegraph as a major channel of stock exchange business and after 1918 the telephone took over. Members' dependence on it was evident in that they quickly became sensitive to increases in telephone charges imposed by the Post Office, and they argued strongly in 1921 that as a result business would be greatly reduced. Cork, in 1927, decided not to install a phone in the market due to the small amount of business done at the time and the expense involved. In 1929 Dublin had eleven lines into the market. Irritation about cost was replaced in the 1930s by mounting concern about access to trunk line facilities and the opportunities this provided to outside interests to obtain direct access to market floors and giving them up to date knowledge of current prices. This thorny issue was not one which greatly affected Dublin but as a member of the Council of Associated Stock Exchanges it adopted, in 1941, restrictions agreed to by the Council and the London Stock Exchange prohibiting direct telephone links with outside brokers declared by London to be non-member jobbers.[44]

A basic requirement of stock exchange dealing is that bargains must be completed. The early rules, therefore, imposed on members, "in order to preserve entire the credit and reputation of the Members", a duty not to accept a composition of debt due to them from another member without the consent of the Committee, with the additional stricture that "it shall be also considered imperative on Members generally, to declare within one week to the Committee such fact or circumstance, leaving them to deal with the information for the protection of the Society at large, in such a manner as will best accomplish that object". A broker whose credit failed was thus no longer considered to be a member of the Society "having been declared a defaulter on the Stock Exchange".[45]

These general clauses for default were later replaced by somewhat more specific provisions. The 1879 Rule Book provided for the public declaration of a member in default, and added that cessation of membership would arise from default on the stock exchange or to the public. An application would then be made to the Lord Lieutenant to annul a defaulter's licence. To settle outstanding claims against a defaulting broker there appear to have been informal arrangements to draw, in the first instance, if it still applied, on the surety money, and then the available resources of his estate. Later, when the volume of account dealing was considerably greater, these procedures were more fully set out in the rules.

By the turn of the century the procedure for dealing with defaulters ran along the following lines. A member who could not fulfil his obligations, on the Stock Exchange or to the public, was publicly declared a defaulter on the direction of the President or any two members of the Committee. Following this step the Secretary fixed prices at which all open accounts with the defaulting member should be closed. One or more members were then appointed to act as Assignees or Inspectors of the Estate of the defaulter, and it was their duty "to obtain from such member his original books of account and a statement of the sums owing to and by him; to attend meetings of creditors; to summon such member before such meetings; to enter into strict examination of every account; to investigate any bargains suspected to have been affected at unfair prices, and to manage the estate in conformity with the Rules, Regulations and Usages of the Exchange".[46] A difficult case could prove a trying and time consuming labour. However, the Assignees could enlist the aid of an accountant, and when a balance sheet of the final position had been obtained, the Committee would declare a dividend to be paid. The claims of the public against the estate were considered if allowed by the Assignee, but any surety money available could only be used to discharge debts due on the Stock Exchange.

Prompted by the uncertainties of the period a sub-committee was set up in 1941 to devise a scheme to protect members against losses arising from such defaults. The proposed Mutual Guarantee Fund involved an initial subscription of £20 per member, with £10 a year thereafter, and would be available to meet claims from members, the payment to each one not to exceed 75% of individual losses, subject to the total available at the time of the default. But strong objections were made to the compulsory nature of the scheme, the basis of subscription, and it was also argued that the time was not right for such an innovation. However, most of the members were prepared to adopt a voluntary scheme and they were left to administer it themselves. By the early fifties some 50 members participated in the voluntary fund. In 1953 it was decided to set up a compulsory guarantee fund, and the resulting Mutual Protection Fund operated from May 1954.[47] Modelled on the voluntary scheme, with somewhat lower subscriptions, it could be supplemented by a call on members of up to £100. By 1960 the fund stood at £2,600 and at the time of forming the Irish Stock Exchange in

1971 it amounted to £9,800.

It was not until 1950 that the London Stock Exchange set up a Compensation Fund to make "ex gratia" payments to the public who suffered loss due to a broker's default. Prompted by that example, and more so by the general acceptance of the principle of having such protection for the public, several members of the Council of Associated Stock Exchanges embarked on similar measures. By October 1959 six provincial exchanges had earmarked funds for that purpose, while another four had schemes under active consideration.[48] In November Dublin set up a sub-committee to consider the setting up of a Compensation Fund for non-members and in March 1962 its proposals were accepted by the membership. The fund, built up from annual subscriptions and the allocation of certain revenues linked with entrance fees, together with the resulting investment income, was to be used for the purpose of "making 'ex gratia' payments to members of the Public who suffer loss resulting from the failure of any Member of the Dublin Stock Exchange to meet his obligations". At the time of joining the unified Stock Exchange in 1973 the Compensation Fund was around £24,500. After that Irish investors had the benefit of the protection afforded by the very large central fund of The Stock Exchange.

Membership of the Stock Exchange, and a broker's licence, was granted to individuals, not to firms. While single broker firms predominate in the early years, partnerships later became common. They afforded greater capital resources, shared burdens of work and they displayed greater longevity than one man concerns.

The Dublin firm with the oldest associations is Stokes & Kelly, Bruce, Symes & Wilson. Samuel Bruce, of 37 Dame Street, was a Public Notary, one of the first licence holders and a founder member of the Stock Exchange in 1799. He was also Secretary to the Commercial Insurance Company. From the sparse records available it appears that his son, Halliday Bruce, joined the Stock Exchange in 1819 and they traded as Samuel & Halliday Bruce. By 1836 Halliday Bruce had been joined by George Symes, who acted as Secretary to the Stock Exchange for some years, the firm, Bruce & Symes being located at 42 Dame Street. George Symes was a member of the Stock Exchange for several decades. In the eighteen nineties the name of the firm changed to Bruce, Symes & Williams, once again based at 37 Dame Street. A later change rendered the firm as Bruce, Symes & Wilson. The firm of Stokes & Kelly dates back to the inter-war years.

The origins of Bloxham, Toole, O'Donnell can also be found in the early years of the last century. Patrick Curtis joined the Stock Exchange in 1826, and he too acted as Secretary to an insurance company, the Hibernian Fire & Life Assurance Co. of Dublin. About 1836 he took John Power into partnership, trading as Curtis & Power. However, by 1847 John Power had been replaced by Thomas Woodlock and the partnership, Curtis & Woodlock, lasted until Patrick Curtis died in 1871. James O'Donnell then joined Thomas Woodlock, and later in 1877 the firm became O'Donnell & Fitzgerald when William Fitzgerald joined as a partner. In the 1970s O'Donnell & Fitzgerald merged with Bloxham, Toole & Co. whose origins go back to Henry C. Bloxham, a member of the Stock Exchange in 1880.

Henry James Dudgeon joined the Stock Exchange in 1850 after giving up his insurance and law business. His father, James Dudgeon, had been in business at 113 Grafton Street as an insurance broker and agent to the County Fire Office Ltd. of London since about 1832. In 1873 Henry James Dudgeon was joined by Henry Dudgeon, to be followed later by Hume Dudgeon in 1887, and Herbert Dudgeon in 1897. In 1874 Henry James Dudgeon was appointed as one of the brokers to the High Court of Chancery in Ireland, and in 1888 as a broker to the Court of the Irish Land Commission.

The firm of Goodbody & Webb was set up in 1874 by Robert Goodbody with offices at 43 Dame Street. Two years later Jonathan Goodbody was admitted as a partner and the business moved to 50 Dame Street. Shortly afterwards Robert Goodbody left for New York where he set up the successful business of Goodbody & Co., taken over some years ago by Merrill Lynch. In 1887 Jonathan Goodbody took into partnership C.F. Allen and Theodore Richard Webb, but the former left shortly afterwards while Theodore Webb remained until his retirement in 1912, when Albert Webb joined the firm. William Woodcock Goodbody became a partner in 1895 but he died in 1905. Jonathan Goodbody, who joined the Exchange in 1876, retired from the firm after over fifty years service in 1928 but he remained a member until his death in 1944, an association with the Stock Exchange lasting for 68 years. His son, Denis Goodbody, who joined the firm in 1913, remained a member of the Stock Exchange until 1971, while his son Donald Carter Goodbody entered the firm in 1948. In 1976 Goodbody & Webb merged with Wilkinson & Faulkner to form Goodbody & Wilkinson. Recently, in January 1985, the firm merged with Dudgeon to become Goodbody Dudgeon.

Another firm with roots in the 1870s is Maguire, McCann, Morrison & Co. which can be traced back to McCann & Naish established by James McCann and Richard Naish. A few years later Lawrence A. Waldron became a member of the Stock Exchange, trading as a L.A. Waldron & Co. He was a director of Dublin United Tramways and many other local companies, as well as being a member of parliament. He died in 1925, leaving as a memorial of an elegant period the splendid panelled offices at 10 Anglesea Street. T.V. Murphy joined the firm in 1924 and is now one of the senior stockbrokers in The Stock Exchange. The firm amalgamated in 1969 with M. Dillon & Son, which was started in the late 1880s by Michael Dillon, to form Dillon & Waldron. Moore, Gamble, Carnegie & Co. could also be traced back to the 1890s when Moore & Gamble and J.D. Carnegie started. The firm was dissolved in March 1985.

Cork's oldest business also dates from this period when Walter Morrogh commenced dealing. For a short time the firm traded as Morrogh & O'Callaghan but when M. S. O'Callaghan left Walter Morrogh took into partnership his brother Robert. Dominic C. Morrogh joined the firm in 1920, becoming a partner in 1928 and he continues to be active in the business to the present day. P. B. Pearson joined in 1947, and in 1960, continuing the long family tradition, Alexander Dominic Morrogh became a partner.

Moving into the present century the firm of Butler & Briscoe was established in 1913 by Herbert Briscoe and J. P. Butler. In 1924, the then senior partner was appointed the Government Broker, a position he held until his death in 1957. He was succeeded by Desmond Butler. In 1966 Brendan Briscoe became Government Broker, and on his death in 1982, the present senior partner, Kenneth Beaton, assumed the office.

# NOTES

1. No bonds were apparently enforced and an amending act of 1868, "The Stockbrokers (Ireland) Act", decreed that such bonds were not to be registered or redocketed until a breach of the original conditions had taken place.
2. Report of the Commission of Enquiry into the Management of the Dublin Stock Exchange, 1849, (1870), pp. 19-20.
3. The duties of the Notary Public to the Bank of Ireland were to attend at the Bank every evening to receive bills presented in the morning but which remained unpaid, and that "he demands payment of all such bills before the hour of eight o'clock in the evening and if not paid protest all foreign bills on the day they become payable sending the protest the same evening to the latest endorser and holding the bill...". Bank of Ireland, Minutes of the Court, August 8 1783.
4. 56 Geo. 3, c. 98, s. 15.
5. State Paper Office, O.P. 498/13.
6. Dublin Stock Exchange, 1834, 1846 Rule Books.
7. Rule 16 of the 1846 Rule Book asserted that if an applicant "be himself, or on his own behalf, engaged, or in any way concerned *directly* or *indirectly*, as Co-partner with any person or persons, in carrying on any *Manufacturing Trading, or Commercial business, or any employment which in the opinion of The Committee, shall be incompatible with the regular, legitimate, and proper business of the Stock Exchange, or by which, in the opinion of the Committee, any other or further risk may be incurred, he shall not be deemed eligible as a Member of the Stock Exchange.*"
8. Dublin Stock Exchange, 1846 Rule Book, Rule 21, p. 14.
9. Dublin Stock Exchange, Minutes, August 25 1847.
10. Dublin Stock Exchange, Minutes, November 16 1847.
11. House of Commons, *Journals*, April 21, May 4 1846-47, pp. 527, 627.

12. Dublin Stock Exchange, Minutes, January 19 1849.
13. Dublin Stock Exchange, Minutes, March 1849.
14. The complete evidence appears in *Freeman's Journal*, July 6-9 1849.
15. Report of the Commission of Enquiry, op.cit., pp. 15, 18-19.
16. Dublin Stock Exchange, 1879 Rule Book.
17. Dublin Stock Exchange, Minutes, May 6 1871.
18. Dublin Stock Exchange, Minutes, February 1 1923, July 7 1925.
19. For details of these see W.A. Thomas, *The Provincial Stock Exchanges*, (1973), pp. 95-6.
20. Dublin Stock Exchange, 1879 Rule Book. The 1799 Act laid down that brokers needed two sureties of £500 but this requirement was not specifically incorporated into the Stock Exchange rules until 1879 and presumably could not be called on by the Stock Exchange Committee for compensation purposes.
21. Dublin Stock Exchange, 1905, 1928 Rule Books.
22. Cork Stock Exchange, Minutes, January 22 1896, April 22 1914, February 3 1916.
23. Dublin Stock Exchange, Minutes, January 31 1860, December 23 1897.
24. In 1848 this fee was £100. The practice may well have carried over from the legal background of many of the early stockbrokers.
25. Dublin Stock Exchange, Minutes, May 18 1925, October 29 1925. Miss Keogh resigned in July 1939.
26. To reinforce the President's authority during business sessions he could impose a fine of a guinea on a member guilty of "improper conduct, or of disorder, or irregularity"; 1905 Rule Book.
27. Dublin Stock Exchange, Minutes, April 28 1860.
28. Dublin Stock Exchange, 1846 Rule Book.
29. Dublin Stock Exchange, 1905 Rule Book.
30. ibid., pp. 33-36.
31. The most recent account of this arbitration society is in L.M. Cullen, *Princes and Pirates: The Dublin Chamber of Commerce 1783-1983*, (1983), Chapter 2. Among the members of the Ouzel Galley Society were several brokers, notably Christopher and Robert Deey (Secretary at one time; he was made an honorary member in 1798), Samuel Bruce and John Williams. See also G.A. Little, *Ouzel Galley*, (1953); and *The Ouzel Galley, Rules and Regulations*, (1859).
32. Dublin Stock Exchange, Minutes, May 6 1871, May 4 1878, December 21 1878.
33. *The Irish Tatler*, February 1960, pp.11-13; it gives the quote from *The Irish Times*.
34. Dublin Stock Exchange, Minutes, May 3 1880.
35. Dublin Stock Exchange, Minutes, January 8 1895.
36. Cork Stock Exchange, Minutes, January 5 1895.
37. For details of British usage see Thomas, op. cit., pp. 102-04.
38. Dublin Stock Exchange, Minutes, September 16 1854, March 22 1856.
39. Dublin Stock Exchange, Minutes, November 23 1873.
40. *Select Committee on the Post Office*, B.P.P., 1876, XIII, p.262.
41. Dublin Stock Exchange, Minutes, October 1881.
42. Dublin Stock Exchange, Minutes, December 7 1880, October 31 1883, June 21 1912.
43. Dublin Stock Exchange, Minutes, October 20 1897, November 17 1904.
44. Dublin members had no teleprinters or private lines to a non-member jobber, that is, they had no link with Nicholson's of Sheffield. For the controversy

about private wires in the 1930s see Thomas, op. cit., pp. 222-23; see also Chapter 12.

45. Dublin Stock Exchange, 1834 Rule Book, pp. 4, 8. Defaulters were only readmitted after the lapse of a year from obtaining a certificate of bankruptcy.
46. Dublin Stock Exchange, 1905 Rule Book, pp. 83-90.
47. Dublin Stock Exchange, Minutes, July 7, September 15, 24 1941, September 18, November 17 1953.
48. Council of Associated Stock Exchanges, Minutes, October 31 1959.

# CHAPTER 6

# IRISH RAILWAY SHARES

It was the successful completion of the Liverpool and Manchester Railway, followed by its profitable operation, which stimulated investment interest in English railways. In the wake of the sober emulation of this line, which took the form of projected routes between large cities, came the speculative boom of 1836 when, fuelled by the optimism of investors and the eagerness of promoters, some £46mn of capital was authorized for railway construction. In the boom the prospects of capital gain considerably widened the ranks of the investing public, with "blind capital" coming forward from rich and poor artisans alike. The inevitable collapse left few viable promotions. Its legacy to investors, apart from painful losses, included a certain whetting of their appetite for participating in share dealing, and to cater for their needs Lancashire found itself after the boom with two stock exchanges, at Liverpool and Manchester, which were formed to meet the needs of local investors. The ensuing lull lasted until 1844, by which time a combination of cheap money and a revival of trade again stimulated interest in railway promotion. In 1844 parliament approved forty eight railway acts, in 1845 another 120, and 272 in 1846, involving a nominal capital of over £200mn; several hundred more schemes never got that far. Investment interest was greatly stimulated, leading to a doubling of the general level of railway share prices, while the speculative stocks, the "light stocks", advanced infinitely more in price. Early provincial interest was joined by that of London, which then increased to supplant it as the main financial support for railway schemes. While London had its own market, the needs of provincial investors were now catered for by a stock exchange in every major city. The ensuing fall in share prices in 1847-49 was a magnified repetition of the previous collapse, but after the speculative frenzy had evaporated the

99

construction of several thousand miles of track went ahead providing Britain with its main rail network. Ireland did not remain aloof from these developments. The construction of railways and the investment interest they aroused mirrored much that was taking place across the water.

Ireland's first flirtation with railway schemes occurred in 1825, but it was the completion, in 1834, and successful operation of the Dublin & Kingstown line, superbly managed by James Pim, Junior, "the father of Irish railways", which marked the quiet beginnings of the railway era. In the 1836 speculation many schemes were put forward involving an authorized capital of some £2.5mn, but only two reached the construction stage, and as in Britain interest lapsed until the upsurge of 1845-46 when £20mn of capital was authorized. Up to that time railway promotion and investment had produced about sixty miles of track; by 1859 the figure had swelled to 700, and by the late 1860s not far short of 2,000 miles had been constructed, operated by seventeen companies. Irish and British savings over a short span of years flowed into a great many schemes to produce ultimately a comprehensive railway network; indeed, investment and speculative interest probably forged one which exceeded the transport needs of the country.

The 1825 flutter of railway promotion was a short lived and largely abortive affair. Five schemes appeared but only one ever came to anything, and even then the line was not opened until 1854, some thirty years after the scheme received parliamentary sanction.[1] A much shorter period between sanction and completion was displayed by the Dublin & Kingstown Railway, the first successful Irish railway. Parliamentary approval was obtained in 1831 and the six mile line opened for traffic in December 1834. The main "projector of that work" was James Pim, Junior, a member of the stockbroking firm of Boyle, Low, Pim & Co. He was treasurer to the line from its formation and for many years he "devoted nearly the whole of his life and attention to its general management".[2] When the scheme was first launched "public opinion was most unfavourable" and it was only by the support of a limited circle of commercial and financial friends that the subscription list was completed. Among them were some of James Pim's Stock Exchange colleagues, namely George Symes(for £1,000), Henry J. Williams (£2,000), Francis Low, Richard Williams and Alexander Boyle (£5,000 each). The public subscribed £112,000, but the company also had to obtain a loan of £37,000 from the Commissioners of Public Works. The shares first appeared in the Dublin Stock Exchange list in March 1833 at £25½.

Interest in railway investment revived in 1835 and in the ensuing euphoria 26 projects were put before the public, while parliament authorized nearly £3.0mn of capital for Irish lines during 1836-37. However, of the five schemes sanctioned, only two, the Dublin & Drogheda and the Ulster Railway, managed to attract money from disenchanted investors after the collapse of the share boom in the summer of 1836. With a depressed share market (prices fell by about threequarters from the June peak) and higher interest rates in the money market, most schemes remained in abeyance. After November there were no railway quotations at all in the Dublin list, except of course an occasional price for the Dublin & Kingstown Railway. Investment prospects were further clouded by political intervention prompted by the unseemly competition as to who should build the line from Dublin to Drogheda. The struggle between alternative schemes, a feature of several railway projects, led the government to set up the Drummond Commission to inquire into the "most advantageous lines of railways in Ireland", an alternative to the unplanned schemes characteristic of the 1836 boom. The reports, which appeared in 1837-38, recommended a considerable degree of state intervention and control, but little came of its deliberations.[3] Railway construction was thus left largely to the dictates of the private market. But while the views of the Drummond Commission may have instilled some caution into promoters, it was the state of the money market which really caused delays in the raising of capital and in the progress of actual building. An example of this was the experience of the Dublin & Drogheda line. When it was promoted in February 1836 the initiators planned to get two-thirds of the capital from the government but the "mania" for shares led to a flood of applications, and deluged with private capital they saw no need to seek government aid. As the market retreated from its June peak difficulties arose in getting in calls on shares which led the promoters to put the scheme into abeyance. With the gradual recovery of the share market, and easier money market conditions in 1838, the promoters found themselves able to sign the first contracts for building.[4]

As trade recovered and the condition of the money market eased in the early forties, the investment climate in both England and Ireland improved greatly. The general picture was that throughout 1843 railway share prices rose slowly and by the end of 1844 they were about 30% above their mid-1843 levels. On the Dublin Stock Exchange the shares of the Dublin & Kingstown stood at 105 in January 1843, increased to 118 by the end of the year, and reached 195 by November 1844; the shares of the Dublin & Drogheda rose by about a third during 1844. With the prospect of easier money in sight promoters began launching their schemes and investors, healed from the financial wounds of 1836-37, were once again eager to reap some quick capital gains. The scale of the Irish railway boom was smaller than that which took place in Britain, but for all that, it had its own intensity and character.

The share boom reached its peak, as recorded by a well known index, in July 1845 when prices were about 65% above their level in the autumn of 1843.[5] They then fell by about a fifth by the year end, and over the next two years the decline continued at a gradual pace reaching the pre-boom level in

the spring of 1848; in terms of the share index (June 1840=100) they went
from 98.8 in October 1843 to 167.9 in July 1845, and back to 100.2 in March
1848. This picture of the market, however, is based on the prices of well
established railway lines and does not adequately reflect the intensity of
speculation found in the shares of newly promoted schemes, both from the
standpoint of the volatility and range of price changes, and in the volume of
dealings (see below).

In the period 1844-46 over a hundred Irish schemes were mooted, but
only seventeen of the twenty eight authorized had begun building by 1850.
The effect of all this on the list of the Dublin Stock Exchange was dramatic.
In January 1844 it carried three railways, the Dublin & Kingstown, Dublin
& Drogheda, and the Dublin & Kilkenny. The surge in 1844 produced a
further eight quotations, among them the Great Southern & Western,
Waterford & Limerick, and the Irish Great Western. But by January 1846
the Dublin list had expanded to 54 railway companies and railway share
dealings dominated the floor of the Stock Exchange, as it was to do for
several years.

Railway shares reached the public through two main channels. The most
sure way, from the standpoint of securing a complete and impressive
subscription list, was by private placing of shares among the influential
connections of the promoters. In the case of the early railways shares were
placed among commercial interests in Dublin, while English funds were
similarly obtained predominantly from Lancashire subscribers who had a
clear eye for future commercial benefit arising from improved railway
communication within Ireland. In the 1844-46 promotions London
displaced Lancashire as the main external contributor, much of it again
coming from business interests with Irish links. The placing of Irish shares
among English capitalists was undertaken by local brokers, for example, in
the provinces Joseph Boyce and George Carr, Glasgow and Manchester
stockbrokers, directed local investors into the shares of the Great Southern
& Western, of which their fathers were directors.[6] London money was
pointed towards Irish projects by such influential brokers as Lawrence,
Pierce and Cazenove. This method of soliciting capital was not dependent
on the unpredictable reaction of unknown "applicants in answer to public
advertisements" but it could secure for a railway "at the outset a respectable
constituency".[7]

The wider "constituency" of shareholders was reached by extensive
advertising in local and national newspapers. Investors were invited to
subscribe for shares through the agency of brokers, solicitors, banks or
directly from the company itself. Among Dublin brokers who received
applications were Bruce & Symes, Richard Williams, Henry Lanauze, and
Labertouche & Co. Generally speaking this method worked well where
investors knew that influential interests had already pledged their support
for a line, or when prevailing euphoria for shares was such that investors,

large and small, would subscribe for anything that was put before them. There were instances of both types of behaviour in the 1844-45 boom. Among early offerings, Great Western & Southern only took off with the public when it was known that a large slice of the capital had been taken up by London financial interests, while in the floatations of the boom months in the middle of 1845 applications flooded in from investors with little or no regard as to whether an issue had been underwritten by, perhaps, more prudent institutional participation.[8]

Speculative activity, from both monied and less well off persons, was greatly facilitated by the nature of the capital offered by the companies. The nominal value of the shares of most Irish lines (at least those that made it to the Stock Exchange list) were mainly in the £20, £25 or £50 class, with only two being under and two over those levels. But in practice the sums paid on the shares were considerably less than this, making them for the most part shares of low value, more amenable to a wide variety of investors. Shares in the more established lines tended to have about a quarter of the capital paid up, but the newer companies only had 10% or less paid up, thus providing the market with a wide array of £1 and £2 shares, the so called "light stocks" of the share market. For the most part speculation occurred in the scrip of shares, that is, the provisional certificate issued after the payment of the deposit and the first instalment.

Further opportunities for speculative dealings arose with letters of allotment which could be traded in without a deposit being paid. However, there is no record of large scale dealings in such letters outside London, but they probably did take place since it is most unlikely that the opportunity would have been entirely ignored.[9] Even where deposits had been paid, speculative trading took place in deposit receipts since companies took some time to issue scrip. The need to obtain the approval of the Board of Trade further stimulated speculative activity since the railways given its blessing quickly advanced to a premium, while the lengthy procedure of procuring parliamentary authority added more uncertainty; "The great Speculation is when Parties are seeking their Act of Parliament; and it is very remarkable that last year [1845] those shares were all at a great Premium, and there was great anxiety as to the Progress of the Bills, and the Shares rose in Value as the Bill advanced through Parliament".[10]

The movement of Irish railway share prices probably followed that portrayed by the index based on London prices. From 1842 onwards prices climbed from around 80 (1840=100) to reach a peak of 168 in July 1845. This general upward movement was also found in the English provincial markets, and the prices of the few established Irish lines over the period displayed the same trend. When the boom got underway speculation took place largely in the 'investment stocks', that is, lines which had some sort of dividend record, but by April interest shifted to the new lines with hectic dealing in their scrip. The rapid expansion of the Dublin list of scrip shares reflected the vogue, which was also evident in the frequent markings of price changes. Some examples will serve to illustrate the degree of price movements. At the peak of the boom speculation centred on the "light stocks", generally with about £2 10s. paid. The Belfast & Ballymena rose from $3\frac{1}{4}$ in January 1845 to $8\frac{3}{4}$ in June; the Cork & Bandon from $2\frac{3}{4}$ to $8\frac{3}{4}$; Dundalk & Enniskillen from $2\frac{1}{2}$ to $4\frac{3}{4}$; most of the "light stocks" doubled in price.

Where Irish shares were dealt in on other markets prices tended to be fairly close to those ruling in Dublin. This arose since all the markets were linked by a correspondent network which ensured that if prices in other markets were not known before the day's dealings were through they would certainly be available for the next day's call over, subject to the usual transport uncertainties of the time. Liverpool, which had quite a large section of Irish lines in its 1845 List, quoted prices which were quite close to Dublin; in the case of six lines prices over the year 1845 were within $\frac{1}{4}$ to $\frac{1}{2}$ of each other for the two markets, and for the high value stocks, like the Dublin & Drogheda, the difference was about 1%. Larger differences no doubt did occur as chronicled by the *Irish Railway Gazette* in July 1845. It noted that "sad complaints" had been received from investors who had done business in Liverpool and London; "Some of our correspondents say they were induced to purchase Irish shares in those markets at a lower rate than they could be had for at the time in Dublin; but months elapsed before they obtained their scrip", by which time they found that it was "considerably under the price for which it was purchased". The *Railway Gazette* concluded that "this lax state of things is only part of the 'account' system which has not yet found its way into Ireland, nor is it likely it will"; on that score it was to be disappointed.[11]

The reaction when it came was both prolonged and severe. The collapse took place in the autumn, although prices had started to move back from the July peak during August and September. Persistent railway calls, seasonal pressures for funds, and the higher interest rates in November, all served to produce a reversal of expectations and once sellers appeared on a large scale to take their profits, the downward trend was quickly accelerated by general loss cutting activity. The tide of speculation turned away from scrip shares leaving most schemes with merely nominal quotations. By the end of the year many stood at par or at a small discount.

According to contemporary reports railway speculation in Dublin was seen as going ahead too fast even in December 1844, the market displaying "a degree of diseased activity, which is certainly, in many respects, alarming".[12] Into the New Year the Dublin Stock Exchange reported to the *Railway Gazette* that the market was, in its view, "good and presented a healthy appearance with the promise of continued activity and briskness in all descriptions of stock".[13] By the Spring, however, casualties were beginning to appear, and market observers were of the view that "railway scrip shares have in many instances risen to a most unnatural price". In July there was a run on all new projects, "more of the scrip being transferred the first week or second than for months afterwards". But already everyone was not profiting from the activity; some "parties in Dublin have suffered heavy losses that they have been forced to retreat". By November markets were in a panic. The *Railway Gazette* asserted that "We are no doubt in a crisis. What we all along feared would be the case when a panic set in, has proved correct — the good have been confounded with the bad and both have suffered. The prices of our best stocks have fallen and timid holders increase the evil by the flooding of the market when there are no buyers".[14] Undoubtedly it was the small speculators who lost most since they came into the market as prices neared their peak. Professional speculators having engineered prices upwards were getting out of the market leaving the less well informed small investor to reap the impending losses. Pierce Mahoney, solicitor to the Dublin & Kingstown, viewed the process as follows — "Persons connected with the Stock Exchange bargained that they would give their Influence and Power to any Scheme on getting a certain Quantity of Shares, Three or Four thousand sometimes; that done, they went into the Market, and managed it so as to raise the Shares to a Premium, and the minor class of Speculators became the buyers in retail from those parties".[15] By the end of the year business was down greatly from the summer peak, and Dublin brokers, perhaps smarting from having done too much scrip business, were reported as concentrating on "safe business" and looking increasingly "to the stability of their clients".

The extent of share dealing activity in 1845 is clearly indicated by the contemporary accounts quoted above, but it is also confirmed by the emergence in Dublin of three markets to compete with the long established Stock Exchange. On a smaller scale local markets were also set up in Belfast and in Cork, where an organized Stock Exchange was formed. The appearance of rival markets was not unique to Dublin, they also featured in the share boom activity of Liverpool, Manchester and Leeds.

Three factors may account for such rival markets in Dublin. First, the volume of business may have been too large to be serviced by the existing institutional arrangements; second, established brokers may have charged too much for their services thus encouraging competition; and third, there may have been dissatisfaction with the conduct of some existing brokers in that they may have assisted price rises by share manipulation. On the first point it is only possible to conjecture that in the hectic atmosphere of 1845, and the great increase in the number and activity of investors, the twenty or so established brokers could hardly have served all investors with equal promptness and attention. As to commission levels, the charge levied by the Stock Exchange on railway scrip in the range of £1 to £2 was of the order of 1s. 3d., rising to 2s. 6d. in July, which on a percentage basis was quite a high fee. On the final point of the manipulation of prices against the interests of clients, there are only the complaints which appeared in the local press, which may have been prompted more by frustration at lost opportunities or painful losses than by genuine evidence of price manipulation. One irate shareholder, urging the establishment of a rival institution to frustrate the "gorged appetite of the 20 insatiable brokers of this city", claimed that the "Brokers of Dublin have dealt more on their own account in the share market than the whole community so that it is impossible for any person to deal through them without suffering a certain loss and yielding to them, over and above their brokerage a large and sure profit".[16]

The first rival market made its appearance at the height of share speculation in July 1845. At a meeting attended by some 24 people on July 12, with John Croker in the chair, it was resolved that "the present extent and daily increase of Joint Stock Companies loudly call for additional facilities for the purchase and sale in Dublin of Railway.....etc., and all other Shares", and looking to the "advantages derived by the English Public from the establishment of the Share Associations in London, Liverpool and elsewhere" it was therefore desirable to form a similar body in Dublin to be called the Dublin Royal Exchange Stock & Sharebrokers' Association.[17] The rules were based on those of Liverpool, the main attraction for investors being a charge of 1s. for all scrip dealings and members were precluded from dealing on personal account. To conduct business the members met daily at the Royal Exchange (later they seem to have moved to the Commercial Buildings), and they "received at their respective offices orders for the purchase and sale of Railway, Assurance, Bank, Mining and other shares". A share list was published in the local press for a time. The organisation was presided over by a committee of nine, with Joseph Jones Stephens, chairman, William George Du Bedat, vice chairman and Thomas Howard Wilson, secretary. In 1846 the Association had 33 members drawn from a range of ancillary and other activities; four were listed in local directories as sharebrokers, there were six insurance and bank agents, six merchants, two wine merchants, and the rest went unrecorded. With the slump in business over the next few years their number fell to eleven by 1850, when the Association seems to have lapsed. Its attempt to end the monopoly of the Dublin Stock Exchange in dealings in government securities, with a petition to the Commons to repeal 39 George III, c. 60, was unsuccessful, while some of its members failed to gain admission to the Stock Exchange which induced the Castle to set up the 1849 Commission of Enquiry into the Stock Exchange (see Chapter 5).

The City of Dublin Merchants' Stock and Sharebrokers' Association was formed at a meeting held on September 15 1845 with the Lord Mayor elect of Dublin, Alderman John Keshan, in the chair. Its formation was brought about by the "continued increase in Joint Stock Companies", which rendered "indispensable additional facilities in Dublin for the Purchase and Sale of Railway, Bank, Mining, Canal, Insurance and other shares", while the advantages derived from the numerous provincial markets in England also lent support to the move. Rules were adopted based on London, Liverpool and Dublin, the proceedings of the Association being supervised by a Committee drawn from the membership. The chairman was Richard O'Gorman (a director of the Hibernian Bank, bankers to the Association), with Edward Fox and James Kirwan as honorary secretaries. As with the Royal Exchange Association the leading feature of the rules was the fixed commission of 1s. for scrip shares and the prohibition on members dealing on their own account, a rule designed to "secure to the Public the fullest confidence". To enhance public acceptance a little more "no time shall be lost in providing the necessary accommodation for the admission of the Public into the Rooms of Meeting".[18] The Exchange opened for business on September 23 at the Royal Exchange and for some months its share list appeared in the local papers.

Although there was strong aldermanic and banking patronage at its formation, the twenty seven or so members were predominantly people who appear (on the evidence of their entry in the 1845 Dublin Directory) to have added share dealing to their existing commercial activities at an earlier date, forming a group of outside brokers who may well have operated informally for some time prior to the creation of the new market. The interest of the Hibernian Bank in their activity probably arose from its direct links with railway company formation and the allotment of shares. This particular share market does not appear to have survived for long after the autumn collapse in 1845, most likely ceasing by early 1847.

To complete the trinity of rivals the New Stock Exchange made its appearance sometime in November 1845.[19] Why this group of about twenty aspiring brokers should set up yet another organisation to cater for the needs of the Dublin share dealing public is not entirely clear. No doubt they sought to obtain a slice of the boom business, and they may have felt that the other markets display of openness in executing transactions was not entirely effective. To this end they declared that the New Stock Exchange transacted "the public business.....in the presence of all parties who chose by the payment of a small fee [6d. a day] to gain admission, at a reduced scale of charge on sales, on the plan of short settlements, and registering on cheque cards all sales at the moment made, to which the broker cannot afterwards have access; whilst it affords the public an opportunity of investigating the reality of all transactions, [and] the buyer or seller is advised by the secretary the business his broker has done for him".[20] Like the other markets, prices were supplied to the local papers. The membership appears to have added broking to a miscellaneous range of occupations, the most prominent group being shopkeepers; J. C. Egan, a tea and wine merchant was secretary. At the outset the market was held at the Royal Exchange, later moving to the Commercial Buildings. By late 1846 the membership had fallen to around sixteen, and the New Stock Exchange probably went out of existence some months later.

Interest in railway shares also seems to have been sufficient in the south of the country to lead to the emergence of several brokers in the City of Cork. In the allotment of shares railway companies always tended to treat local applicants favourably so as to ensure goodwill towards the project, while the considerable land and trade wealth in and around the City was no doubt attracted towards the prospects of gains from share operations. By early 1845 at least two local brokers were advertising their facilities in the local press; William Connell indicated that "every description of public Securities are Purchased and Sold without difficulty or delay at his Established Stock Debenture and Railway Share Office, No. 80 South Mall", and John Rourke & Son, insurance agent, informed the public that he had made arrangements "with Brokers of the highest respectability for the sale and purchase of Shares in the various Markets in the Kingdom, from whom we daily receive Advices and Share Lists, which may be seen, and all Information had on application to our office".[21]

By October 1845 the level of activity in railway shares had induced a further handful of insurance agents and solicitors to add sharebroking to their list of services, and they were sufficiently numerous to justify the setting up of the City of Cork Stock and Sharebrokers' Association, with offices in the local Commercial Buildings.[22] Their aim was to "facilitate the purchase and sale of Railway and other shares". For the conduct of business they modelled their rules on those of Liverpool, and in line with the several Dublin markets they resolved that "to secure the full confidence of the Public, no member shall purchase or sell shares on his own personal account, and if any complaint should arise, and on the same being made in writing to the Secretary, it shall be investigated and reported on by a Committee of the Society who are authorized and have full power to examine such Brokers' books to satisfy the complainants of the correctness or otherwise of the transaction".[23] The charge for scrip shares was 1s. per share. The members met daily at the Commercial Buildings to transact business and they received orders at their respective offices; no mention was made of admitting the public to the market. Thomas Exham was chairman, and W. H. Townsend, secretary. Presumably the Association survived into 1846-47 but later lapsed with the shrinking of the railway share market.[24]

To cater for the investing needs of shareholders and speculators in the Belfast area a few brokers emerged briefly for the boom period, but only one continued to service local investment interest through to the end of the century. Four people appear to have been active as brokers in this period; Jackson S. Stevenson, Josias Cunningham, Tobias and Theobald Bushell. In the autumn of 1844 Jackson Stevenson was supplying regular bulletins on the state of the local share market to the *Irish Railway Gazette*, the market improving from being "very languid and little or nothing doing" at that time, to one with a "firm appearance with a tendency to advance" by

December. The upturn had been transformed into a "lively market" by the spring with, as elsewhere, "a good deal doing in scrip", but it was not to last. In July interest in scrip was beginning to wane, with another broker, Josias Cunningham, who supplied regular reports to *The Economist*, stating that "New stocks are very inactive, and neglected.....buyers are not so keen to meet sellers".[25] The inactivity continued throughout August, with a brief resurgence in the first week of September when Josias Cunningham observed that the "Belfast Share Market is certainly livelier but we cannot yet speak of it as active". As share business faded so the weekly reports no longer appeared in the national press.

Of the total investment in Irish railways between 1831 and 1852 it has been estimated that about 80% came from private investors, both within and outside Ireland, while the other fifth came from government sources and private financial interests.[26] In the case of private investment, of the estimated total of £8.7mn involved, Ireland contributed roughly £4.4mn and England £4.3mn; the Irish contribution is thus quite appreciable and larger than the impression frequently conveyed by contemporary and later writers. Looking at individual lines the proportion of Irish funds varies quite markedly. The early lines for example, the Dublin & Kingstown and the Ulster lines, found over 90% of their money in Ireland, but the Dublin & Drogheda managed to attract only half its capital from Ireland. Of the major 1845 boom companies which raised over £100,000 capital, seven obtained more than half their funds from Irish investors, and the other six had to rely on English investors for the bulk of their capital.

Irish interest in the pioneer line, the Dublin & Kingstown, was particularly lukewarm, indeed, the project was apparently "derided by the Dublin monied class". Its success, as noted already, was largely due to the efforts of James Pim and the financial support he obtained from a close circle of commercial interests. Several members of the Stock Exchange (see above), in addition to James Pim, put up a total of £17,000, a quarter of the promised capital as indicated by the original subscription list.[27] This help, along with a government loan which induced some English participation, ensured that the project did not have to wait until the more ebullient investment climate of 1836. When the Dublin & Drogheda and the Ulster lines came along later Irish interest, as reflected in the subscription contracts, had certainly improved indicating a willingness to take 57% and 66% of the capital respectively.[28] In the 1845-46 floatations Irish participation varied greatly between the numerous lines put before the investor, ranging from 75% to a mere 2% for the Londonderry and Coleraine. In the case of ten lines, however, initial local participation, as viewed from the subscription contract, was less than half of the capital requested by the companies. Even so local contributions made an impressive total and represented, where information is available for twelve lines which appeared in 1845, a promise of about £2.4mn in funds, and a cash outlay in that year (assuming 10% deposit) on scrip shares of around £250,000, with later calls, and for 1846 lines a promise of nearly £1.0mn, and further cash outlay of about £100,000, again with later calls.

As railway lines prospered and share prices rose, local investors increasingly bought into companies thereby swelling domestic holdings of Irish railway shares. One example will suffice to illustrate the pattern, that of the largest and most important company, the Great Southern & Western Railway. In 1844-45 the percentage of its capital held in Ireland was only 35%, but as the dividend prospects improved in the 1850s the proportion rose to 73%.[29] Such a general pattern of later buying-in prompted the view that in the case of investment Irish interests held back at the outset and allowed English capital for the most part to bear the initial risk. Once the lines and the shares had proved themselves then the non-mercantile class bought them as safe investments, their early distrust stemming perhaps not so much from the novelty of railways, which was real enough, but to the uncertainty surrounding investment in Irish enterprises. This view was certainly canvassed by the *Irish Railway Gazette* in 1847, when it held "that we are not without money in this country to sustain our own legitimate enterprises, but rather it is that we lack self reliance — we are too timid about investing capital...and that all our great companies have been sustained in their early stages by English capitalists; yet afterwards, when they have proved remunerative, and their shares have commanded premiums, Irishmen have become purchasers".[30] In mitigation of this view of Irish investors as "timid" participants in the boom it can be pointed out that 1845 saw an unprecedented volume of speculative activity in Dublin, and lesser ones elsewhere, when people from diverse income groups were drawn into dealing activity, as testified by the existence of four exchanges involving the services of over a hundred brokers to meet their varying needs. While few of the brokers survived the share slump, for a time there must have been sufficient activity to support such a degree of specialisation. Plainly, Irish investors like those elsewhere could not altogether resist the prospect of some capital gain. A certain degree of hesitancy on their part, however, was understandable. Given the capital intensive nature of railways it would have involved Irish investors in a major change in asset holdings in a very short space of time had they supplied a much larger fraction of the initial capital. Assuming that those who had wealth held it predominantly in land, mortgages or government securities, then for them to take on a large proportion of equity, about which they had no great experience, was clearly not a most obvious substitution. However, once the dividend record of lines was seen to be reasonably stable, railway shares gained mounting acceptance and a change in the composition of investment holdings followed.

English interest in Irish railways can be traced to the shares of the Dublin & Kingstown line taken up before 1835 by investors in Liverpool, Lancashire, Birmingham and London. But in the case of large scale early

English participation Lancashire clearly dominated the scene, as it did with English railways, the investors of the Liverpool and Manchester areas putting up six times the amount London supplied; all but £4,500 of the total of £252,000 of British funds to the Dublin & Drogheda came from Lancashire.[31] However, in the boom of 1845 London money dominated the westward flow of capital but even so provincial interest had not entirely waned. George Carr, a Manchester stockbroker, guided his clients into the shares of the Great Southern & Western Railway.[32] At the height of the 1845 boom the Liverpool Stock Exchange list carried quotations (not all active) for nearly forty Irish shares, while Manchester had about half that number.

English suspicion of investing in Ireland seems to have been overcome by the attractions of railways rather than any change of heart about the general nature of the country for investment purposes. Some funds, no doubt, could not resist the speculative possibilities of railway shares, especially in the 1844-45 boom period, but the bulk of the funds which came from the commercial and financial interests had more long term motives in mind. Lancashire had close links with the east of Ireland and the spread of Irish railways brought prospects of greater trade from the opening up of new markets. The directors of some of the major English railway lines with links to Ireland took a keen interest in Irish developments since they saw the prospect of increased traffic and associated higher dividends. London financial concerns saw added business arising from its role as an important financial centre for rural Ireland. The two most active banks in rural Ireland, the National and the Provincial, had their headquarters in London, and they also dealt with such matters as calls and dividends on shares. Political considerations may also have had some sway since Sir Robert Peel seemed anxious to divert English capital away from continental ventures towards Irish railways.[33]

When the volume of business on the Stock Exchange collapsed in 1845 and share prices remained depressed for several years afterwards (the general index of share prices drifted downwards until 1850) it meant for the market a considerable reduction in turnover and income, and the disappearance from broking activity of many short term recruits. For railway companies it produced a rise in the cost of capital and much greater problems in terms of its availability. Faced with a falling share market, and widespread difficulty in getting shareholders to meet their calls, companies resorted to several expedients to meet their capital needs to enable them to complete their construction programme. The device which impinged most closely on the Stock Exchange was the extensive resort to preference shares. In the period 1849-52 over £1.0mn of preference capital was put out by Irish railway companies and this was reflected in a separate section in the Stock Exchange list of 37 preference shares, whose denominations ranged from £5 to £100, but predominantly they were under £25 and mostly carrying a coupon of 5%. By 1862 the Dublin list contained 33 preference shares from 18 railway companies with a total paid value of £4.8mn (an average per preference issue of £144,000). The market was dominated by £1.3mn preference of the Great Southern & Western, and alongside were seven other issues of over £200,000. By 1872 a further £1.0mn had been added to the preference section. Railway ordinary shareholders viewed them with some displeasure since they conferred on newcomers into the companies a prior claim on dividends, and sometimes other advantages, and all this after they had assumed the initial risk. Companies in less strained financial positions also issued them to finance extensions and undertake consolidations. Debentures, with a further prior claim on railway income, also featured in capital structures in the difficult circumstances of the construction years. Many were issued to contractors, as security for loans to banks, and in order to enable companies to repay government loans. By the early 1870s the Dublin list contained thirteen debentures, mostly at 4% to 5%, with a total value of £1.6mn. The largest issue was that of the Great Southern & Western with £438,000, followed by £384,000 from the Midland Great Western, and £242,000 from the Irish North Western.

By the mid sixties the bulk of the main routes had been constructed with two thousand miles in operation. In the next fifteen years a few more hundred standard gauge miles were added. More remote parts of the country, however, had to wait until the surge in light railway construction in the 1880s before obtaining the full benefits of improved communications. Under the provisions of the Tramways Act 1883, and two later enactments in 1889 and 1896, some six hundred miles of narrow gauge and standard gauge line was built to serve as feeder networks from more remote agricultural and fishing areas to the main lines. They were constructed at a total cost of around £6.0mn, half of which came from public funds and the rest from share capital, the interest on this element of subscribed capital being guaranteed by the baronies through which the lines ran. The purpose of such guarantee was to tempt private capital into those investments and while initially it did have some success, a great deal of capital eventually had to come from public funds.[34] These railways, built to carry lighter loads and with lower construction costs than standard lines, never achieved their aims since the projected traffic did not materialise. They suffered from heavy initial expenses, had indifferent management, and many were built on too substantial a scale. Some of the baronially guaranteed shares featured in the Dublin list, and no doubt many others changed hands on the market.

Urban tramways produced some more activity for inclusion in the Dublin list. The largest of the Irish tramways were the Belfast Street Tramways Co. (incorporated in 1872, operating 18 miles) and the Dublin United Tramways (incorporated in 1881 following the amalgamation of three companies — Dublin Tramways, North Dublin Street Tramways, and Central Tramways, operating 32 miles). In 1896 they had called-up capitals of £206,000 and £624,000 respectively, and were also listed in Glasgow,

Liverpool and London. Along with these two companies the Dublin list also carried quotations for twelve British companies operating in the major cities.

The railway share market constituted an important part of the Dublin list up until the First World War. Railway shares and stocks were generally looked upon as fair investments, the dividend levels being quite stable. For example, the Great Southern & Western Railway regularly paid around 4½% in the 1880s and some 5% a decade later, which compares favourably with the prevailing yield on government stocks. Such a stable dividend record has been ascribed more to low labour costs than to high tariffs, but even so the accusation was levied against the railways that the level of their prices hampered the development of the industry.[35]

As a result of the experience of state control of the railways during the First World War, and the need to repair the railway system after considerable damage suffered in the Civil War, which was paid for by the government, the decision was made to amalgamate the lines within the Free State into one company. At the time there were 46 railway companies in Ireland, under 28 different managements, with a total capital of around £47mn; some were prosperous, others not, and there were the precarious light railways of the south and west. The Railways Act of 1924 amalgamated 26 companies, which operated exclusively in the Free State, into the Great Southern Railway Company with a capital of £26mn. It was hoped that unified direction would produce commercial success. However, high costs (labour costs had risen sharply during the war) and increasing road competition served to produce mounting losses. The experience was reflected in the price of the company's shares on the market. Within a year of formation the price of the ordinary stock halved from £38. To attempt to ease the financial burden the capital was written down in 1933 to £11.6mn, but the market in railway shares virtually froze and the ordinary stock stood as low as £13.

Persistent financial and management problems throughout the inter-war years finally resulted in the partial nationalisation of the railway network, under the terms of the 1944 Transport Act, and the formation of Córas Iompair Éireann. It acquired the undertakings of the Great Southern Railway and the Dublin United Tramways Company. The capital was made up of £9.8mn of 3% debenture stock issued in exchange for the securities of the absorbed companies, with capital and interest guaranteed by the government, along with £3.5mn of common stock which had a limit of 6% on its dividend level.[36] These securities were quoted in Dublin and Cork. But its experience was no happier than its predecessors. Within two years the value of its shares had been halved on the Dublin market. Mounting costs, deteriorating equipment and crippling competition from road haulage finally led to state ownership in 1950. In this change of organisation the Grand Canal Company was amalgamated with Córas Iompair Éireann, compensation to the stock and shareholders taking the form of 2½% and 3% Transport Stock.

# NOTES

1.  R.D.C. Black, *Economic Thought and the Irish Question 1817-1870*, (1960). This was the Waterford-Limerick line.
2.  Select Committee on the Amending of Railway Acts as to Audit of Accounts, B.P.P., 1849-50, p. 493, evidence of James Pim.
3.  For a description of the background and the contents of the Reports, see Black, op. cit., pp. 190-94.
4.  J. Lee, "The Provision of Capital for Early Irish Railways 1830-53", *Irish Historical Studies*, Vol. XV1, 1968-69, pp. 37-39.
5.  The index is that given in A.D. Gayer, W.W. Rostow and A.J. Schwarz, *The Growth and Fluctuation of the British Economy 1790-1850*, (1953), Vol. 1, p. 437. The index (June 1840=100) is based on railway shares quoted in London. A detailed description of its construction is given in A.D. Gayer, A. Jacobson and I. Finkelstein, "British Share Prices 1811-1850", *Review of Economic Statistics*, 1940-41, pp. 78-93.
6.  For details see Lee, op. cit., pp. 42-43.
7.  ibid., p. 47.
8.  ibid., p. 46.
9.  Some speculation along these lines may have prompted the Dublin Committee to resolve in September 1845 not to recognize transactions in unallotted shares or in new companies which had not issued scrip. The prohibition was designed to limit "sales....made for the 'coming out'"; *Irish Railway Gazette*, September 8 1845.
10. Evidence of P. Mahony, who had a long association with Irish railways as solicitor to the Dublin & Kingstown, to the House of Lords Select Committee on the Management of Railroads, H. C. 1846, (489), X111, Q. 417.
11. *Irish Railway Gazette*, July 4 1845.
12. ibid., December 2 1844.
13. ibid., February 10 1845.
14. ibid., November 10 1845.
15. Evidence of Pierce Mahoney, op. cit., Q. 418.
16. *Irish Railway Gazette*, July 21 1845.
17. ibid., July 28 1845.
18. ibid., September 22 1845.
19. A little earlier one C. Bennett, auctioneer, valuer and estate agent, advertised in the *Irish Railway Gazette* that "at the instance of several influential Share Proprietors, he has been induced to appropriate a portion of his establishment as a SHARE MARKET, for the conduct of Sales by Auction of Shares of every description, where both Buyer and Seller can superintend their own business. Publicity is given in the daily papers of the respective shares intended for sale, free of any expense". He held his market at 14 Dame Street on Monday, Wednesday and Friday from 11 until 12.00. It may well have been the precursor of the New Stock Exchange since Bennett was a member of that market; *Irish Railway Gazette*, November 10 1845.

20.    ibid., February 9 1846. An exchange working on similar lines was set up in Liverpool at the same time; it was equally short lived.

21.    *Cork Examiner*, April 28 1845.

22.    The following were listed as brokers in Cork in November 1845; J.J. Barry, John Rourke & Son, Richard Exham & Sons, T.R. Evans, Kennedy & Harvey, James Morgan, W.H. Townsend and A.N. Meade.

23.    *Irish Railway Gazette*, November 3 1845.

24.    A Stock Exchange was again formed in the City in 1886 in response to the next wave of joint stock company formation (see Chapter 8).

25.    *The Economist*, July 19, 26 1845.

26.    The figures used in this section are drawn from the authoritative work of Dr. J. Lee, "The Provision of Capital for Early Irish Railways, 1830-53", op. cit., pp. 40-41. Dr. Lee's estimates are based on subscription contacts which have several drawbacks: normally they covered only 75% of the capital; rapid turnover of shareholders put many out of date before they were deposited; and they were often filled up at the last minute by artificial means: for a full account see J. Lee, "An Economic History of Early Irish Railways", M. A. Thesis, University College, Dublin, 1965.

27.    List of Subscribers to the proposed Railway from Dublin to Kingstown, House of Lords Record Office.

28.    The Dublin & Drogheda faced extinction in 1839 and was only saved by a loan from the brokers, Labertouche & Stafford; *Irish Railway Gazette*, March 2 1846, p. 255 (quoted by Lee, op. cit., p. 52).

29.    Lee, op. cit., pp. 48-49.

30.    *Irish Railway Gazette*, February 1 1847, p. 122.

31.    Lee, op. cit., p. 42. Both the Dublin & Kingstown and Dublin & Drogheda lines were listed on the Liverpool Stock Exchange in 1836-37.

32.    ibid., pp. 43-44.

33.    ibid., p. 46.

34.    For a detailed account see J.C. Conroy, *A History of Railways in Ireland*, (1928), pp. 246-53, 266-73, 300-01.

35.    It was difficult in several cases to reduce tariffs due to the serious losses made by the lines whose capital was subject to a baronial guarantee; see Conroy, op. cit., p. 319.

36.    For full details of these developments see J. Meenan, *The Irish Economy since 1922*, (1970), pp. 158-62. When the terms of the transfer of Great Southern capital to the new public corporation were announced in 1944 there was considerable speculation in Great Southern issues. Its guaranteed stock rose by some 20%, the debenture stock by around 25%; "Allegations have been made that large fortunes were made by persons possessing confidential information.....and a judicial tribunal has been appointed to investigate these accusations": *The Economist*, January 22 1944, p. 108.

# CHAPTER 7

# GOVERNMENT AND OTHER FIXED INTEREST STOCKS

When the Union of Great Britain and Ireland came into effect on January 1 1801 the funded public debt of Great Britain stood at £420.3mn, nominal value, while the funded debt of Ireland was a modest £26.8mn, with about a half funded in Ireland in Irish currency, the other funded in Great Britain. Although the debt of Ireland had greatly increased since 1793 it was still comparatively small at the Union and it was felt that an amalgamation of the debts would have been unfair to Ireland, while equal taxation would have been an impossible imposition. "Such....is the disproportion of debts of the two Kingdoms to each other at the present", Lord Castlereagh commented in 1800, "that a common system for the present is impossible, nor could any system of equivalent be applied for equalising their contribution. It is therefore necessary that the debts of the two countries should be kept distinct, and, of course, that their taxation should be separate and proportionate".[1]

To allay fears that the Union might lead to heavier taxes in Ireland, and to recognise the favourable debt position of Ireland relative to that of Great Britain, Section 7 of the Act of Union (39 & 40 Geo. III, c. 67) contained complicated financial provisions. It set out that the interest and sinking funds of the debts already incurred were to be separately defrayed by each country. Such items were to constitute the first charge on Irish revenues to the consolidated fund, while the remainder would meet Ireland's contribution to the joint expenditure of the two Kingdoms. During the next twenty years both countries were to contribute towards the expenditure of the United Kingdom in the proportion of 15 to 2. At the end of that time, unless equal taxation had been introduced in the meantime, the respective proportions would be reassessed to reflect the prevailing resources of the two economies. The respective contributions were to be raised by taxes in each country, but no article was to be taxed more heavily in Ireland than was the case in Britain. If any surplus was left after meeting the charges set out then it was to be used for specific purposes. Also, it was stated that all debt incurred after the Union for the service of the United Kingdom was considered a joint debt, with the charge borne by the two countries in the proportions of their respective contributions. The proportion of 15 to 2 was arrived at by averaging the proportions of the average annual value of imports and exports of the two countries, and that of the average annual value of dutiable articles consumed.

Article 7 further provided that if the separate debts should be liquidated, or if the values of the debts should be in the same proportion to each other as the respective contributions to the joint expenditure (15 to 2), then parliament could decide to defray all the United Kingdom's expenses indiscriminately by levying taxes overall subject to any abatements which might seem reasonable. This would then permit the merging of the two Exchequers and of the national debts. Both Castlereagh and Pitt expected that the debts would be merged because they saw the required relationship of 15 to 2 being attained by a reduction in the size of the English debt. John Foster and Henry Grattan were not so optimistic at the time of the Union, fearing, rightly as it turned out, that the Irish debt would increase greatly and with it the burden of taxation.[2]

The experience of the next fifteen years vindicated Irish fears. Enormous war expenditure produced a rise in the joint expenditure, for which both countries were liable, from £31.5mn in 1802 to a peak of £89.9mn in 1815, which thereby increased Ireland's contribution of $2/17$ under the Treaty, from £4.3mn to £9.8mn respectively. Such was the burden in the last years of the war that Ireland ran into arrears with its contributions. In the period 1802-17 the total expenditure of Ireland amounted to £159.7mn, £96.7mn of which represented Ireland's contribution under the Treaty. Against this total expenditure revenue amounted to £77.8mn, leaving a large deficiency of £81.9mn.[3] Without a crushing increase in taxation (which came largely from customs, excise and stamp duties) there was no way of meeting expenditure needs save by resort to borrowing. As Sir John Foster put it to the House of Commons in 1810, "heavy" as the loans were it was more expedient to resort to them "than under existing circumstances to load a country like Ireland with so great an amount of new taxes".[4] Since the great part of the expenditure of Great Britain was met by taxation her debt increased by about two-thirds, but that of Ireland quadrupled; the debt charge of Great Britain went up by about 90%, that of Ireland increased fivefold.

By the issue of loans funded in Ireland the Irish Treasury raised a total of IR£17,018,283 between 1801 and 1815, with an additional IR£1.5mn from the Bank of Ireland. Market borrowing was largely derived from nine large loans, ranging in size from a million to the largest of around three million in 1815. Against IR£17.0mn of loans, capital of IR£19.4mn was issued most of it in the form of 3½% stock and debentures, the rest in 5% stock and debentures. The loan of 1804, for IR£1.25mn, was raised at 5.6%, a rate the Irish Chancellor regarded as very satisfactory and within 1% of the prevailing market price of 90 for 5% stock.[5] Pleased as the Chancellor may have been with the success of that issue an attempt to obtain local funds in 1805 failed since the contractors for the loan wanted around 7½%. To fill the gap a separate loan of £1.5mn was raised in London at 6¾%. An offer of IR£2.0mn a year later met with a little more success, but in the end the Treasury had to request help from the Bank of Ireland by way of special loans to subscribers to enable them to pay calls in arrears, such loans being secured against the scrip.[6] During the next few years, with the exception of 1807 and 1810, loans were successfully contracted in Dublin, although the 1812 loan did require some assistance from the Bank of Ireland. Of the IR£2.0mn hoped for the market supplied IR£1.5mn after strenuous efforts and several extensions of the closing date for subscriptions. To make up the deficiency the Bank of Ireland agreed to provide IR£500,000 against the issue of Treasury bills.[7] In 1807 and 1810 loans were offered in Dublin, in line with the policy of raising as much as possible there, the Irish Chancellor being "anxious that it [the loan] should be made payable at the Bank of Ireland, for the purpose of obviating the inconvenience that were felt from the Irish government, they being obliged to draw upon this country for the money". However, on both occasions the terms offered by the bidders for the loans "were higher than the government thought themselves justified in closing with".[8] The last separate loan raised in Ireland was the IR£3.0mn raised in 1814, obtained on what were regarded as satisfactory terms of 5½%, well below the 6¼% which the loans of 1812 and 1813 had cost.[9]

The great bulk of the borrowing needed to cover the overall deficit came from loans funded in Britain, the loans being part of much larger annual loans raised by the government in London. In all, between 1801 and 1816, fifteen loans were raised in this way ranging in size from £2.0mn at the outset to £9.0mn, making a total of £56.7mn. In addition £4.4mn was borrowed by three smaller separate loans for Ireland in London. Against the money raised capital to the total of £103.2mn was issued, mostly in 3% Consols and Reduced 3%.[10]

Since Irish borrowing had been so much more rapid than that of Great Britain, the proportion cited in 1801 as constituting grounds for amalgamating the two national debts had in fact been reached by 1811. A Committee of the House of Commons reported that "the actual value, estimated according to the current prices of the public funds of that day, was in the proportion of nearly two to fifteen", and that there was little variation in it.[11] However, nothing was done and the Committee continued with its deliberations until 1815 when they again reported on the respective values of the two debts. They pointed to the proportion of 2 to 13, considerably in excess of the Act of Union figure. The Committee concluded that for Ireland to attempt to continue to pay a fixed proportion towards expenditure would serve no practical purpose, particularly "since that proportion had rapidly carried the debt of Ireland from a state of relative inferiority into a growing excess".[12] Prompted by the Committee's dilatory reminder Mr. Vasey Fitzgerald, the Irish Chancellor, moved a bill in the Commons to effect the amalgamation of the two Exchequers, and it received the Royal Assent in July 1816.[13] Thus, on January 5 1817, all revenues in the two countries were consolidated into a general fund to be indiscriminately applied to the various heads of expenditure for the United Kingdom generally. Also, the office of Chancellor of Exchequer for Ireland and the Irish Treasury Board were abolished, but complete uniformity was a little delayed. The difference of currency remained until 1826 (with the passing of 6 Geo. IV, c. 79), but the 1816 legislation had provided that all accounts were to be kept in British currency, an imposition achieved by reducing Irish currency figures by one-thirteenth; the view was that "the difference of currency was attended with considerable inconvenience". In practice the full transfer of Irish business to London did not take place until 1836-37.

The 1816 Act also did away with the National Debt Commissioners for Ireland, and duly unified the debts of the two countries. However, due to the different currencies the accounts relating to the Irish debt were kept distinct for some time while the separate application of the Sinking Fund in Dublin continued until 1829, when the whole of it was made to apply to Britain only. Also, for some time after 1826, Irish stocks continued to be quoted in Irish currency. During its period of operation, from 1797 to 1817, the Irish Commissioners for the Reduction of Debt had redeemed £8.1mn of debt, taking in mostly $3\frac{1}{2}\%$ annuities, involving expenditure of £6.4mn, while they had also redeemed £19.0mn of Irish debt funded in Great Britain in roughly equal amounts of 3% annuities and Reduced 3%, involving a total expenditure of £11.8mn. Thus, at the time of the amalgamation the consolidated debt of the United Kingdom was £800mn, the Irish portion of this being £83.9mn of debt funded in Great Britain and £23.4mn funded in Ireland.

Shortly after the consolidation of the debts facilities were provided which enabled stockholders to transfer their holdings from the transfer books of the Bank of England to certain other stocks transferable at the Bank of Ireland. The granting of these facilities probably arose from a desire to offer a convenient means for Irish stockholders to draw their dividends in Dublin, but such mutual transfer facilities later produced wider benefits by way of enabling arbitrage operations to take place between the London and Dublin markets, affording means of making payments in London or Dublin, and also providing a mechanism so as to influence the exchanges between the two capitals. Indeed, this last consideration had led John Puget to advocate a scheme for importing stock to the 1804 Irish Currency Committee; it would have lessened the amount of Irish debt held in London thus reducing the amount of money that needed to be remitted to London across the exchanges to meet interest payments.[14]

Transfers from England to Ireland were authorized by an act passed in 1817, 57 Geo. 3, c. 79. It permitted transfers in 3% Consols, 4% Consols, 5% 1797 stock and 5% Irish, payable in London. Due to the difference in British and Irish currency (£100 sterling to £108 6s. 8d. Irish) the legislation set out specific terms of transfer. For the above stocks they were as follows; £100 of 3% Consols were transferable into IR£92 17s. 2d. of 3½% Irish stock, £100 of 4% Consols into IR£86 13s. 4d. of 5% Irish, and £100 of 5% 1797 stock, or £100 Irish 5% payable in London into IR£108 6s. 8d.[15] In the following year further provision was made in 58 Geo. 3, c. 23 to enable holders of newly created 3½% stock to have their holdings transferred into similar annuities payable at the Bank of Ireland, at the rate of £100 for IR£108 6s. 8d. Further pieces of legislation, 58 Geo. 3, c. 80 in 1818, and 3 Geo. IV, c. 17 in 1822, between them amended and extended the scope of transfers from England to Ireland.[16]

Considerable use was made of these new facilities during 1818 and 1819 with over £5mn of stock being transferred to Ireland; for the yearly totals of transfers for these and later years see Appendix 5. This large inflow may have been partly due to the desire of stockholders to transfer onto the Dublin register for reasons of convenience, but the bulk of the transfers were probably motivated by the higher prices of stock ruling in Dublin which produced profitable opportunities for arbitrage operations. As Thomas Bainbridge reported to a House of Lords Committee in 1819, "The Act enables the Proprietors of certain English stock to transfer it at Par by which individuals were encouraged to make Purchases here, [London] as the Price of Stock in Ireland was always higher than here".[17]

It was not until July 1821 that holders of certain stocks in Ireland were accorded facilities to transfer them to England, while the legislation (1 & 2 Geo. IV, c. 73) also contained the restriction that not less than £1,000 stock should be transferred at one time. The Act remained in force for three years. Again, the terms of transfer reflected the differences in the currencies; for example, IR£100 3½% annuities for £80 16s. of 4% Consols, and IR£100 5% annuities and debentures for £92 6s. 6d. of Navy 5%.[18] However, only comparatively small sums were transferred under these provisions, some IR£10,500 in 1821 and IR£20,400 in 1822, while no transfers were recorded in 1823.

Since the provisions made by the above acts were found to be "highly beneficial and that an amount of capital exceeding £8,000,000 British Currency had been transferred from Great Britain to Ireland, and a certain amount of Stock from Ireland to England", the separate pieces of legislation were repealed and duly consolidated in 1824 by 5 Geo. IV, c. 53. Now holders of 3% stock in Britain could transfer into Irish 3% stock while holders of 3½% and 4% could also transfer into Irish stocks with the same nominal rate, all transfers to be done at £100 for IR£108 6s. 8d. After the assimilation of the currency, from January 5 1826, all transfers took place in sterling. Where dividends were payable at different times in England and Ireland it was arranged (in the case of 3½% and 4% stock) that the Bank of Ireland should ensure that dividends were received on a half yearly basis. Apart from minor amendments in 1861-62, the 1824 provisions served to regulate transfers of stock until the various legislation was consolidated by the National Debt Act of 1870 (33 & 34 Vict. c.71).

To accommodate the needs of stockholders the legislation provided that,

> there shall constantly be kept in the Office of the .....Accountant General of the....Bank of Ireland for the time being, within the City of Dublin a Book or Books wherein all Assignments or Transfers of the said several Capitalists etc....shall be entered and registered; which entries shall be conceived in proper Words for that Purpose, and shall be assigned by the Parties making such Assignments or Transfers or if any such Party or Parties be absent, by his, her or their Attorney or Attorneys thereunto lawfully authorized by writing under his, her or their Hands or Seals to be attested by Two or more Creditable Witnesses; and that the person or persons to whom such Transfers or Transfers shall be made, shall respectively underwrite his or her, or their Acceptance thereof; and that no other method or assigning or transferring the said stock....shall be good and available in Law.[19]

To get stock inscribed into the books of the Bank of Ireland an investor, after buying in London, would instruct his broker there (who would usually have power of attorney from him) to arrange with the Bank of England for a transfer. After receiving such an application the Bank of England would transfer the stock to the National Debt Commissioners, the statutory notification to the Commissioners taking the following form,

> I, Robert Alexander, Junior, of Sackville Street, Dublin, Banker, this 23rd day of January in the year 1818 do assign and transfer £1,000 of my interest and share in the Joint Stock of Three per Cent Annuities...unto...The Commissioners for the Reduction of the National Debt of Great Britain pursuant to Act 57 Geo. 3, c. 79.[20]

The Bank of England would then issue a certificate to the Bank of Ireland to write the appropriate amount of stock into its transfer books in the name of the stockholders. Up until 1861, however, such transfers could not take place (for several weeks) at various times of the year since the books of the Bank of England were periodically "shut" for dividend payments to be made.

When Irish investors bought stock in London payment could be made in several ways. They could do so by obtaining in Ireland a bill due on London, obtain a draft on bank funds in London, or procure Bank of England notes in Dublin. Thomas Wilson, a director and former Governor of the Bank of Ireland, noted in this connection in 1841, "We frequently observe a considerable demand for English money, or for bills of Exchange upon England".[21] Conversely, English buyers of stock in Dublin could pay with bills due for payment in Dublin, with Bank of England notes or post bills which could be exchanged on the local money market for Bank of England notes, or by obtaining a draft on the Bank of Ireland by payment into its account at the Bank of England. When Dublin brokers or Irish stockholders made a sale in London they generally took back "the produce of Stock in Bank of England notes and post bills". Large sales of transferred stock in London often resulted in the notes or post bills obtained pressing on "the Dublin market to such an extent that the notes would be at a discount and money would become scarce in Dublin".[22]

The mutual transfer of stock between England and Ireland provided several benefits to the financial system. One ready use was for the transmission of money in that stock could be bought in one place and transferred to another for sale, and provided it was done speedily price changes would be relatively small. More significant was the means it afforded for maintaining the relative stability of the monetary positions of the two countries. In the case of an imbalance in the monetary circulation, an excess of money supply in Dublin ("that money has been full") would lead to a fall in interest rates and a rise in stock prices above those of London. Investors would then buy stock in London for transfer to and sale in Dublin. As funds left Ireland to pay for the stock the monetary circulation would fall, that is, stock would be substituted for cash. On the other hand, if money was relatively scarce in Dublin ("a want of circulation"), with high interest rates and lower stock prices, then stock would be bought in Dublin for sale in London. In this case there would be a substitution of cash for stock in Dublin, thus relieving the monetary pressure. By the 1830s James Pim was of the view that the tendency towards an equalisation of the value of money had "been very manifest since we were allowed to import and export government stock equally; it has equalised the value of those securities with us; we have the English market at our command for the sale of stock; thus the value of money is gradually nearly assimilated".[23]

Other benefits arose to the stability of the exchanges. If the balance of payments was in favour of Ireland, the pound in Ireland would tend to go to a premium, interest rates would fall and stock prices rise. This would lead to the importing of stock and an outflow of funds. That is, the surplus of exports would be matched by an import of stock, while the exchange rate would be restored to a stable level by the movement of money out of Ireland. Or, as the versatile James Pim described the mechanism in 1835, "In as much as the amount of the exports has considerably exceeded the amount of imports, the balance is then to be made up in a great degree by the importation of Government securities".[24] If there was a balance of payments deficit the exchanges would turn against Ireland, interest rates would rise, and the fall in the price of stocks associated with the decrease in monetary circulation, arising from the need to pay for the excess of imports over exports, would lead to an import of funds to buy stock for transfer to London. The import of capital would tend to appreciate the exchange and the export or sale of stock represented the counterpart of the deficit on the balance of payments.[25]

All the above adjustments involved considerable arbitrage operations arising from differences in prices for the same stocks on the London and Dublin markets. Arbitrage would become profitable if the price differences exceeded the commission costs, which were fairly modest. In the case of "Stock bought for Export, or sold on Import" a reduced rate of brokerage was allowed from 1824 onwards, so that the cost in Dublin was $\frac{1}{16}$%. Where an investor instructed his broker to get stock from London a further commission would be payable there of $\frac{1}{16}$%, making a total of $\frac{1}{8}$%. Generally speaking purchases for sale in London, or imports for sale in Dublin, cost the Irish investor about $\frac{1}{8}$%. If he elected to use two brokers independently the London broker would presumably charge him full commission of $\frac{1}{8}$%, making a total cost of $\frac{3}{16}$%. Where brokers themselves indulged in such operations their only cost was the London commission, which at half the normal rate would only involve an expense of $\frac{1}{16}$%, enabling them to indulge in such switches on slim price differences. In addition to cost the other consideration was the uncertainty arising from delays in communication. In the 1820s it frequently took five or six days to communicate between London and Dublin which allowed prices to change considerably from the moment an investor decided to make a transfer and the time when it was actually executed. By the 1860s delays in communication had been greatly reduced, one day being the standard time for links between the two capitals.[26]

Differences in prices between London and Dublin could on occasions be quite large. Robert Murray of the Provincial Bank of Ireland referred to instances in the 1840s when differences went as high as 1%, caused by large forced sales of stock on the Dublin market; "the money market in Dublin is so limited that no transaction which would involve 20,000*l.* could be arranged upon any one day".[27] Smaller selling pressure in Dublin would lead to differences of $\frac{1}{4}$% to $\frac{1}{2}$% between the markets, whereas generally there would be a difference between markets which would not exceed the commission level of ⅛%. However, to discern the presence of opportunities for arbitrage between the two markets it was not sufficient merely to compare the quoted prices since these were on a different basis. In London market prices included accrued interest but in Dublin stock was sold without interest which was charged for separately. Thus, before obtaining the pure price differences London prices had to be rendered less the accrued dividend. It was not until April 1889 that the Dublin Stock Exchange adopted the London practice of quoting prices for fixed interest stocks inclusive of accrued interest.[28]

In the long span of years from 1817 to 1890 £85.2mn of stock was transferred from England to Ireland, while between 1821 and 1890 £75.5mn of stock was transferred from Ireland to England. Such transfers involved thousands of separate transactions but very few records of all this activity have managed to survive. The ones that are still available relate only to transfers from England to Ireland and the generalisations presented below are drawn from the surviving transfer records at the Bank of England.[29] It was stated earlier that one use of the transfer facilities was to assist in the movement of money between the two countries. The records of the transfers of Consols 3% between 1818 and 1824 certainly indicate that this took place. For example, in 1818 representatives of the Treasury in Dublin arranged to transfer nearly £10,000 of stock (the stock being bought in London for resale in Dublin to provide the Treasury there with funds), the nine transfers being in the names of Thomas Higginbottom, Rowland Price and R. Pim. Similar operations were conducted by the militia to obtain funds for payments in Dublin. In 1818 Nathaniel Low, paymaster to the Roscommon Militia, brought over in nineteen transfers, ranging in amounts from £700 to £5,000 (nominal value), a total of £47,700 of stock.

By far the largest sums transferred were for the Bank of Ireland, the transactions appearing in the register under the names of the Bank's directors. These were either stocks which had been held in London as part of the Bank's investments, or stock bought with a view to transferring it to Dublin for sale on the Stock Exchange. Up until 1824 the investments of the Bank were in Irish stocks, estimated at about £3.3mn in 1822. From 1824, the Bank placed part of its London funds in longer term stocks, rather than holding all its reserves there in short term Exchequer bills. Indeed, in October 1825 the Bank started a policy of selling in Dublin to obtain funds to buy stock in London. But the Bank also from the 1820s onwards, transferred stocks from London to Dublin, either drawing down their London holdings or buying stock for transfer. For example, in 1825, when prices were lower in London, the Bank experienced considerable pressure for drafts on London to buy stock. Accordingly it exchanged some £200,000 of Exchequer bills for 3½% stock for transfer to Dublin for sale on the Stock Exchange.[30] In the same year the transfer records of 3% Consols indicate that in February £1.1mn was transferred to Dublin in the names of

Nathaniel Hone (immediate past Governor), Hugh Trevor (Governor) and Leland Crosthwait (director), while later in the year Hugh Trevor, John Leland Maquay (Deputy Governor), and Leland Crosthwait arranged the transfer of £400,000, to be followed by £220,000 in 1826. In the ensuing decade the Bank undertook very large transfers of stock from London to Dublin, presumably as part of the management of its investments and to aid its general monetary operations. As Thomas Wilson, a former Governor of the Bank stated to a select Committee in 1841, "the sales and purchase of government securities....are made solely for exchange purposes and not with a view to profit". If the Bank wished to get in notes rapidly "we generally throw our stock upon the Dublin market", while if the circulation was regarded as too small "it could be increased by our becoming the purchaser of Government funds and thereby giving the country a sufficient circulation".[31] By the 1870s and 1880s the transfers were of the order of £500,000, the investments of the Bank at this time standing in the region of £5.5mn. Presumably such transfers to Dublin were mainly for selling purposes.

Another category of large transfers were those made by Dublin firms acting as agents for banks in Dublin and in other parts of Ireland. Among such agents were Solomon Watson, Dublin agent of Gordon's Bank of Belfast, and later for the Belfast Banking Co., and Robert Law, a partner in Law's Bank and a Governor of the Bank of Ireland from 1840-42. Another prominent Dublin merchant and agent who transferred stock to Dublin was Joseph Pim, Ushers Island, agent for Newport's Bank, Waterford and Riall's Bank of Clonmel. The largest transfer by an agent in the early years was the sum of £70,000 by Richard Williams of Gibbons & Williams, agents to several country banks and for the Northern Banking Co., public notaries, and, of course, members of the Stock Exchange. Two bankers whose names appear on the transfer records were Robert La Touche, of La Touche's Bank (the Bank kept funds in London and this may have been simply a method of transfer), and the other was H. Guinness of Guinness & Mahon of College Green, Dublin. Most of the transactions of the above were in sums of under £20,000.

As well as Gibbons & Williams other Dublin stockbrokers participated in the stock transfer business. According to a witness before the 1849 Stock Exchange Enquiry "it was perfectly true that some of the stockbrokers imported to a very considerable extent on their own account; but that a very large amount of stock came to them from England on account of their clients — in fact that a large proportion of the stock imported into this Country was imported in the name of the brokers on account of their customers". An outside bill discounter, Robert Gray, told the 1849 Commission that "the import and export of stock by some of the brokers has become quite a trade; by watching the markets in England the broker could traffic in stock to his own advantage, anyone who commands stock can influence the market", but he could not confirm whether or not they sold such stock to their own clients. This, of course, they were debarred from doing by the rules and on the evidence of George Symes (of Bruce & Symes) to the 1849 Commission breaches of the rule were few and expressly for the purpose of making up the required amounts — "It is not the practice of stockbrokers to sell their own stock to their customer when employed by them to buy; [he had] imported stock very largely;.....[and] occasionally sold stock of his own to clients in broken sums but only for the purpose of squaring accounts;.....this to have done to the extent of £200; it is never done except from necessity".[32] The same view was expressed by Alexander Boyle, President of the Stock Exchange at the time, and by James Pim. However, brokers did buy stocks from clients for transmission to England when large sums came onto the market which could not easily be absorbed. For example, in the 1840s, when on one occasion £50,000 of stock was offered for sale by order of the Court of Chancery the "Dublin Market would not take off that 50,000l., in ordinary circumstances in 10 or 14 days; the brokers would purchase as much of the stock as they could command and....they would export it;....they would realise the stock here [London] and take back Bank of England post bills or Bank of England notes".[33] Among brokers who appear on the transfer records were D. Charles Roose, Henry Lanauze, Junior, Rowland Price, and Patrick Curtis.

Individuals also figured prominently in the transfer records. Whether they transferred stock to Ireland for speculative reasons or for personal convenience it is not possible to tell, but doubtless some would have been alert to the profitable opportunities present in the market. The sums ranged from a few hundred to several thousand pounds. While most transfers were for persons in Dublin a goodly sprinkling of provincial ones appeared from time to time. There were also a few transfers by executors and solicitors linked no doubt to the business of settling estates. Very substantial transfers appeared in the 1840s for Quintin Dick (son of Samuel Dick), member of parliament, involving seven transfers amounting to £175,000 of stock. The only other rival to this total was a transfer in 1863 by George James, Earl of Egmont, of £134,000. It is, however, noticeable in the transfer records for the 1860s onwards, that transfers were more or less all in names of London stockbrokers, the transactions ranging from £5,000 to £15,000. What might be described as occasional non-financial transfers were associated with the estates of deceased persons. It could be that Irish clients simply employed London brokers much more often, but it might also suggest that smaller price differentials due to improved communications, coupled with a wider range of alternative investments outlets, led arbitrage activity to devolve largely into the hands of professionals.

The volume of stock transferred from England to Ireland and from Ireland to England during the years 1847 to 1863 is given in the accompanying graph. The early 'boom' in stock transfers to Ireland reflects not only the higher prices then ruling in Dublin but also the opportunity afforded to transfer stock for the convenience of collecting dividends in Dublin rather than having to remit them from London. The 1825-26 inflow is in no small part attributable to a large import of stock by the Bank of Ireland (see above). A feature of the graph is the large net inflow of stock during most of the 1840s, motivated probably by many considerations including price differentials, a desire to repatriate assets to acquire alternative investments, or a need for cash. Around £7.3mn was transferred to Ireland between 1842-48. The graph also suggests that quite a large body of stock was moving from one centre to another in response to changing price differentials. When prices were higher in Dublin than London stock would move to Dublin for sale and the proceeds either repatriated or held locally temporarily; if prices then fell in Dublin relative to London stock would be bought and transferred to London for sale, and the cycle would then repeat itself. Since the prices of stocks were not determined solely by those influences the net transfers to London and Dublin would not repeat themselves neatly, but at some points there are indications that this kind of continuous arbitrage was taking place. For example, in the 1820s the net inflow to Ireland changes to a small net outflow, and in the mid 1830s a large net outflow from Ireland is later reversed to become a large net inflow, while a similar sequence of events appears in the early 1850s and again some years later.

*Chart 1: Transfers of stock between England and Ireland, 1820-1860*

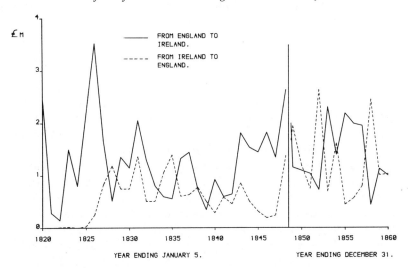

Over the period 1818-47 some £40.8mn of stock was transferred to Ireland compared with an export of stock of only £16.2mn, while for the ensuing period, 1848-63, a further £21.1mn was imported with £22.7mn exported. In terms of capital stock held in Ireland this, in 1847, amounted to £37.2mn (excluding a debt of £2.6mn due to the Bank of Ireland), while by 1863 the sum was £38.1mn. In the case of the 1847 figure it was mostly in the form of 3½% stock, later converted to 3%, and this constituted the bulk of the unredeemed marketable capital held in Ireland in the 1860s.[34] However, this represented the high point of holdings of government stock in Ireland. Over the next few decades the amount dwindled gradually to about £24mn in 1890, falling to around £18mn in 1905; there was, in addition, some £23mn of Land Bonds issued as compensation stock but very little of this was on the Bank of Ireland register (these totals do not include gilt edged stocks held in bearer form). The main reason for this disinvestmnent from gilt edged is not difficult to discern; the low yield on government stocks for most of this period led investors to put their money into more rewarding outlets such as industrial and commercial companies, particularly in the 1890s, while in earlier years the attractions of foreign bonds and shares had not escaped Irish investors (see below).

Dealings in government stock on the Dublin market were, of course, conducted on a broker to broker basis and the normal size of a bargain was probably in the region of £500 to £2,000 (a marketable quantity was deemed to be £500). Certainly no large bargains could be conducted quickly; "no transaction which could involve £20,000 could be arranged upon one day".[35] If bargains of a very large order appeared, from the courts or the banks, then they could only be completed over a long period of time. It was estimated in the 1840s that it took two weeks to realise the sale of £50,000 of stock.[36] In the absence of any London style jobbers, sellers had to wait until buyers came along and it would take a while for a sufficient number of small orders to materialise to absorb a large sale. However, the thinness of the Dublin market was greatly relieved by the availability of the transfer facility since stock could easily be moved to London for sale (or purchase) on a larger and more absorptive market. As James Pim viewed the position in 1835, "If we get an order from the Court of Chancery or others to sell a large sum of stock which could not be affected in our market without reducing the price, we have the power of transferring that stock at once to London and having it sold there".[37] Such transfers may not always have fully answered local needs if the conversion of English into Irish bank notes later caused difficulties. Nevertheless, allowing for such secondary problems, the London market was available as an extension to the local market in cases of overwhelming need. As James Pim testified to the 1838 Select Committee, "we have the English market at our command for the sale of stock".[38]

Prior to the 1840s all dealings in government stock were for cash. To assist members in meeting their obligations they appear, in the 1830s and 1840s, to have lent money amongst each other on the security of government stock, bank stock or other stock dealt in on the Stock Exchange. The stock given as security for these short term loans ("for a definite time") was transferred into the lenders name, and for "the general protection of the Members" the rules stipulated that it was "expedient to define the surplus security of Stock to be delivered on Collateral Loan Transactions". It was deemed that 2% was adequate to cover the lender, but if the market value fell during the period of the loan then the borrower was obliged to provide additional security of the same stock. If the price of stock appreciated the lender was directed to return the appropriate amount of stock which would re-establish the required 2% cover margin.[39] Presumably with the introduction of the account system for settling transactions in the mid-1840s such loans became less necessary and the rules relating to them do not appear in later editions of the Stock Exchange rule books.

Commission on transactions in government stock remained at the level of $\frac{1}{8}$%, fixed by the 1799 Act, 39 Geo. 3, c. 60, for well over a century until it was altered under the terms of another act of parliament, 8 & 9 Geo. 5, c. 46, in 1918. When the London Stock Exchange raised its commission on gilt edged from $\frac{1}{8}$% to $\frac{3}{16}$% in 1918 Dublin decided to do the same. However, while commissions on all securities other than government stocks could be changed with the approval of the Lord Lieutenant, the commission on government stocks was fixed by statute. To adopt the new rate therefore required the troublesome resort to further legislation. Following approaches to the Castle, and interviews with the Solicitor General, a bill was introduced into the House of Commons which repealed Section 6 of the 1799 Act.[40] Section 2 of the short 8 & 9 Geo. 5, Stockbrokers (Ireland) Act provided that the "maximum rate of fees which may be charged by a licensed stockbroker in Ireland for brokerage or commission on the sale or purchase of any Government Stock or securities may be fixed by rules made by the Dublin Stock Exchange and approved by the Lord Lieutenant, and any maximum rate which may from time to time be fixed by rules so made and approved, shall be substituted for the maximum rate specified in Section 6 of an Act passed in the Parliament of Ireland in the thirtyninth year of the reign of King George the Third".[41] In 1920 the Stock Exchange again followed London and raised its commission on government stock, other than Consols, to $\frac{1}{4}$%.

Holdings of stock in Ireland, along with the subscriptions of Irish investors to the stocks issued by the British government to finance the First World War, brought the total of stock registered with the Bank of Ireland in 1922 to around £106mn. However, in June of that year, six months after the signing of the Anglo-Irish Treaty which paved the way for the formation of Seorstat Éireann in December, the Treasury informed the newly set up Department of Finance, and the Bank of Ireland, of their intention "at an early date to seek parliamentary authority for the discontinuance of the register of British Government Stock at present maintained at the Bank of Ireland in Dublin, and for the establishment of a register at the principal office of that Bank in Belfast".[42] The Treasury's action, which lacked both sensitivity and timing, was prompted by a legal rather than a practical difficulty. As it saw the position the British government could not allow the management of part of its internal debt "to be in the hands of those over whom, after the establishment of the Irish Free State, they would cease to have any control". However, the Treasury was prepared to concede that "in practice there might be no difficulty", but added scrupulously, "in law the Bank of Ireland would be entirely outside the control of His Majesty's Government".[43]

The prospect of the Bank of Ireland Transfer Office closing caused considerably anxiety to the Stock Exchange. The President, Richard Pim, and the Committee swiftly drew up a memorandum on the matter and dispatched it to the Minister of Finance, Michael Collins. Pointing to the significance of the local register, they argued that withdrawal of the facility would be a "great loss....not only to our own Body but to the investing and trading public, Solicitors, Bankers and other businessmen throughout the South of Ireland....which will seriously cripple dealings on our Exchange and transfer the market almost entirely to London or Belfast". The memorandum also noted (to the embarrassment of London) that large subscriptions had been made in Ireland to wartime British loans and that these had come forward mainly due to the convenience of local transfer, adding pointedly that the "withdrawal of this Register will be a direct contradiction of the terms of the various prospectuses".[44]

All the main financial interests in Dublin rallied to support the Minister of Finance and the Bank of Ireland in bringing pressure to bear on the Treasury in London. A deputation of representatives from the Bank of Ireland, the Incorporated Law Society and the Stock Exchange called on the Chancellor of the Exchequer and under considerable pressure the Treasury agreed to a compromise solution although apparently "it was only after personal representation made by the Governor General that the decision already taken to remove the register from Dublin was cancelled". The visit of the Governor General to London to discuss the matter with Mr. Bonar Law was in response to a direct appeal from the Stock Exchange.[45] The Treasury conceded that only holdings of stockholders in Northern Ireland, if they were agreeable, would be transferred to the new Belfast register. Just over £6.5mn was later transferred to the Belfast register, representing the accounts of over 12,000 people. Meanwhile, the Dublin register was retained for existing holdings but no further stock issues would be added to it. Subsequent attempts to get the Treasury to make concessions on this point failed. For example, in 1929, a conversion stock was offered for 5% War Loan for which Irish holdings were registered in Dublin but the Treasury declined to extend that convenience to the new offer.[46] The arrangements arrived at in February 1923 lasted to the present day, with the procedures employed by the Bank of Ireland being brought into line in 1964 with those governing the United Kingdom national debt. During this long period the amount of stock on the Dublin register fell from £97mn in 1923 to £17.5mn in 1977, mostly the dismal 3½% War Loan; for a few years during the last war the total rose from £49mn to £67mn, reflecting transfers from London and switches into gilt edged from far more risky investments.

Irish investors did not confine their investment horizons to the British Isles. During the third quarter of the century the London market was dominated by a flood of foreign issues from governments and railways, and Irish interest in such offerings was reflected in the inclusion of several securities in the Dublin list. By 1871 the loans of over a dozen governments were listed, among them the loans of Argentina, Mexico, Peru, Spain, Turkey, Egypt, France, Russia and the United States; by 1885 a further eight countries had appeared, along with the stocks of seventeen railway companies, the most important being those in the U.S. and Canada. All these securities continued to be represented in the list up to the First World War.

Among the colonial stocks listed from early in the 1860s were Indian loans raised in London. These were accorded a special place in the Dublin list since the main ones were transferable at the Bank of Ireland. This arose from officials of the India Office approaching the Bank in 1861 to inquire whether it would be prepared to act as registrar for Indian sterling stocks held by Irish residents on the terms which applied to the Bank of England register. The Bank directors duly agreed and the new stock registers operated from 1862.[47] At this time the Stock Exchange listed 5% and 4% India Stock, and Indian stocks continued to feature in the list until after the last war. The amount on the Irish register increased from £2.7mn in 1896 to £6.1mn in 1911. During the inter-war period the total remained at around £3.4mn, mostly of 3½% India Stock, but by 1948 the amount dwindled to a mere £100,000. The bulk of Indian sterling loans were either repaid by the Indian government or acquired by the British Treasury under the wartime policy of acquiring overseas securities.

The other important group of fixed interest stocks were those issued by the Corporation of the City of Dublin. Numerous city obligations had been dealt in right from the start of the Stock Exchange, indeed, they were listed in the local papers in the 1780s. These early stocks took the form of debentures issued to finance municipal improvements, such as, Pipe Water Debentures, Paving Debentures, Wide Street Debentures, and those issued by the Ballast Office (which ran the port). Later came City of Dublin Debentures, issued in both British and Irish currency, 4% stock at £92 6s. 2d. and 6% at £100 Irish. In the middle of the century a number of mortgage bonds in bearer form appeared and the proceeds were used to finance capital projects in the city, including a waterworks, a public library, and the Cattle

Markets. The amounts involved ranged from a few thousand in the case of the public library to £86,000 of Cattle Market Bonds. By 1889 there were nine bonds outstanding with a total value of £158,000.

The terms of the Dublin Corporation Loan Act 1889 gave the Corporation powers to consolidate its existing loans. To do this the Corporation in 1889 invited tenders for an issue of £500,000, at a minimum price of par. The average obtained was a "fraction over par". Holders of the stock could have it transferred by inscription at the Munster and Leinster Bank. A further tranche of the stock was offered in 1890. Not only did this serve to consolidate the debt of the Corporation and reduce the overall interest charge on it, but it also greatly improved its marketability. A large uniform stock was eminently more suitable to the market's needs than the previous numerous small issues. By 1914 the total debt outstanding had risen to a modest £1.7mn, some £300,000 having been paid off through the Sinking Fund procedure attached to the loans. The offers of stock made by Dublin Corporation in the inter-war years, on a fixed price basis, involved the Stock Exchange since the members underwrote a sizeable portion of each issue.[48] In 1939 £7.9mn of stock was quoted in the list. The quoted debt of the City in 1980 amounted to £3.7mn.

# NOTES

1.  Memorandum on the Financial Relations Between Great Britain and Ireland, Royal Commission on the Financial Relations Between Great Britain and Ireland, Appendix 1, p. 327, B.P.P., 1896, Vol. XXXIII.
2.  Earl of Dunraven, *The Finances of Ireland*, (1912), p. 77; A. P.W. Malcomson, *John Foster: The Politics of the Anglo-Irish Ascendancy*, (1978), p. 97.
3.  Ireland ran into arrears on its proportion but had made up most of the payments by 1817 leaving only £2.0mn due, which was later cancelled; Memorandum on Financial Relations, op. cit., p. 335.
4.  *Hansard*, May 30 1810.
5.  The Irish Chancellor told the Commons that when the bidding was taken in Ireland, "the price of 5 per cents, in the market in London, on that day, (a thing hardly to be accounted for), was not more than £80 10s."; *Hansard*, April 27 1804, p. 327.
6.  For full details see F.G. Hall, *The Bank of Ireland 1783-1946*, (1959), p. 113.
7.  ibid., pp. 113-14.
8.  *Hansard*, March 25 1807, May 30 1810. Loans were made in London, of £1.4mn and £1.5mn, to provide the necessary funds.
9.  *Hansard*, May 14 1813, pp. 203-4, June 20 1814, pp. 101-2.
10.  Full details are given in "Notes from 1786 to 1890, relating to the National Debt, and the duties imposed by various enactments upon the National Debt Commissioners", Report by the Secretary and Comptroller General of the Proceedings of the Commissioners for the Reduction of the National Debt

from 1786 to 1890, B.P.P., 1898 (6539), Vol. XLVIII, pp. 308, 310.

11.   *Hansard*, May 1816, p. 291.

12.   Memorandum on Financial Relations, op. cit., p. 333.

13.   56 Geo. 3, c. 98.

14.   Committee on the Circulating Paper, the Specie and the Current Coin of Ireland and also on the Exchange between that part of the United Kingdom and Great Britain, 1804, B.P.P., 1826, Vol. 461, Appendix, p. 146.

15.   Full details of all the transfer legislation is given in "Transfers of Stock Between Great Britain and Ireland", Report....of the Proceedings of the Commissioners, op. cit., pp. 254-56.

16.   ibid., pp. 254-55 for full details.

17.   Second Report from the Secret Committee Relative to the Bank, *Journals of the House of Lords*, Vol. 52, 1818-19, p. 473. Similar evidence was given by Nathaniel Sneyd, Governor of the Bank of Ireland, p. 476.

18.   "Transfers of Stock Between Great Britain and Ireland", op. cit., p. 255. One effect of transferring stock from Ireland into lower nominal amounts of stock in England was to reduce the total nominal figure of the funded debt of the United Kingdom to a small extent.

19.   5 Geo. IV, c. 53, s. 6.

20.   Bank of England, Record Office, Transfer Books of Consols 3%, Irish Transfers 1818-87.

21.   Report of the Select Committee on Banks of Issue (1841), B.P.P., Vol. 5, evidence of Thomas Wilson, Q. 2697.

22.   ibid., evidence of Robert Murray, of the Provincial Bank of Ireland, Q. 2962.

23.   Select Committee on Joint Stock Banks, B.P.P., 1837-38, (1826), Vol. 7, evidence of James Pim, Q. 389.

24.   Select Committee on Public Works (Ireland), B.P.P., 1835 (XX), Q. 1386.

25.   For a full discussion of these mechanisms see G.L. Barrow, *The Emergence of the Irish Banking System 1820–45*, (1975), pp. 47-50; "The Irish Banking System in 1845", in *Faisnéis Ráithiúil*, Banc Ceannais na hÉireann, Samhradh 1975, pp. 92-111.

26.   Dublin Stock Exchange, Minutes, April 28 1861.

27.   Report of the Select Committee on Banks of Issue, op. cit., Q. 2962. James Marshall, Secretary of the Provincial Bank of Ireland, told the Select Committee on Joint Stock Banks (B.P.P., Vol. XIV, 1837), that his bank held most of its investments in public securities in London because of the "limited nature" of the Dublin market; "we could not sell an immaterial sum without lowering the price considerably"; Q. 4403-4.

28.   Dublin Stock Exchange, Minutes, March 18 1889.

29.   The following records were looked at; Consolidated 3% Annuities, Irish Transfers 1818-87, New 3% Annuities, Irish Transfers 1859-63, 1877-88. These records are lodged at the Bank of England, Record Office.

30.   Barrow, op. cit., p. 49.

31.   Report of the Select Committee on Banks of Issue, op. cit., Q. 2804, 2850.

32.   Commission of Enquiry, 1849, Minutes, *Freeman's Journal*, July 9 1849.

33.   Report of the Select Committee on Banks of Issue, op. cit., evidence of Robert Murray, Q. 2962.

34.   Accounts relating to the Transfer of Stock etc., B.P.P., 1864(341), Vol. XXXIV, p. 395. A return of stock held on the books of the Bank of Ireland on which interest was paid in January 1852 showed a total debt of £37.9mn, which accords closely with the figures given in 'Accounts relating' cited above; see Report of the Select Committee on the Income and Property Tax, B.P.P., 1852(354), Vol. IX, p. 419.

35.    Report of the Select Committee on Banks of Issue, op. cit., evidence of Robert Murray, Q. 2962.

36.    This was Murray's estimate, but the picture was earlier highlighted by James Pim; "there is a very great difficulty in raising any large sum of money by the sale of government stock in a case of that kind — bank sales in order to realise a quantity of specie to meet engagements": Select Committee on Joint Stock Banks, B.P.P., 1837-38(626), Vol. VII, Q. 369.

37.    Select Committee on Public Works, (1835), op. cit., Q. 1368.

38.    Select Committee on Joint Stock Banks, (1838), op. cit., Q. 389.

39.    Dublin Stock Exchange, 1834 Rule Book, pp. 13-15. Brokers could also borrow short term from the banks. Robert Murray told the 1841 Select Committee; "...we lend money on three, seven and ten days' notice upon stock but we cannot always depend upon getting it back in Dublin when it is required"; Select Committee on Banks of Issue, (1841), op. cit., Q. 2960.

40.    Dublin Stock Exchange, Minutes, September 8 1918.

41.    Some concern was expressed in Belfast and Cork at the possibility that the attention focused on the 1799 Act might revive "other obsolete sections" and leave Dublin as the only Stock Exchange legally entitled to deal in government securities"; Cork Stock Exchange, Minutes, November 13 1918.

42.    Quoted by Ronan Fanning, *The Irish Department of Finance 1922-58*, (1978), p. 131.

43.    ibid., p. 132.

44.    Dublin Stock Exchange, Minutes, June 13 1922. In 1916 the Bank of Ireland handled transfers amounting to £4mn; after the war the volume of transfers was put at seven times the pre-war level; Hall, op. cit., p. 336.

45.    Fanning, op. cit., p. 645, n. 28.

46.    Dublin Stock Exchange, Minutes, November 1929. A similar refusal took place in 1924 when a conversion offer was made.

47.    Hall, op. cit., p. 269. The act confirming the arrangement was 25 & 26 Vict., c. 7.

48.    Dublin Stock Exchange, Minutes, August 28 1925, September 20 1932, November 29 1935.

# CHAPTER 8

# IRISH JOINT STOCK COMPANIES

When the Stock Exchange opened its doors in 1799 there were only three stocks, apart from the growing volume of public debt, which could be labelled as important investments. They were the Bank of Ireland, the Grand Canal and the Royal Canal. Apart from public utilities and banking, most forms of enterprise in trade and manufacture could be conducted with modest sums of capital usually available from the resources of an individual, a friend, or obtainable by mortgage. In Ireland there was also the prospect of getting funds by setting up a partnership, since in the economic liberalisation of 1782 the Irish parliament passed legislation to encourage modest combinations (see below). With the exception of some limited areas, England at the time also displayed an absence of widespread joint stocking, but there the general demand factors were reinforced by the Bubble Act of 1720 which rendered corporate bodies with transferable shares illegal unless specially authorised by parliament.[1]

Compared to most projects of the time, the issue of IR£600,000 of stock by the newly established Bank of Ireland was a mammoth undertaking; indeed it was the largest yet attempted in Ireland. In the wake of political agitation proposals for financial independence found favour in parliament, and after a short lapse of momentum legislation was passed in 1782 authorising the raising of IR£600,000 to be deposited in the Treasury in return for an annuity of IR£24,000 in lieu of interest. Public subscriptions were received by twenty eight commissioners, among them Robert Shaw, Samuel Dick and Henry Theophilus Clements. Subscriptions were in cash or 4% debentures up to a maximum of £10,000 with 25% payable on application, the rest on demand. Since the price of 4% debentures stood at around 80 all the subscription took this form; in cash terms the capital was equivalent to IR£480,000. To obtain the concession those who did not possess stock could buy them on the local market. While two years was allowed for completing the subscription, the list itself was filled quickly in the space of four months and by March 1783 all payments had been made. Seventeen subscribers took up the maximum sum allowed, most of them coming from the ranks of the collecting commissioners — men of "business and finance".

Of the 228 subscribers only 12% had applied for sums of under £500, most of the subscribers, just over 50%, taking sums of between £500 to £2,000, with a further quarter requesting amounts from £2,001 to £5,000.[2] Among the subscribers with stock trading connections were Samuel Dick, Leland Crosthwait, Robert Shaw, Christopher Deey, Caleb Jenkin and Luke White. Further additions of capital in 1791, 1797 and 1808 increased the total to IR£2.5mn, with the Bank paying a regular dividend of 10%. Bank stock stood alongside that of the government, public esteem reflected in the hefty premium it displayed. In the early 1790s it stood at about 150 with a higher yield than government stock, its virtues widely acclaimed — "Bank stock gives the best interest, and is better circumstanced than any other stock in the country, from the possessor not having charge of it".[3]

Canal building, like its successor and rival, required large capital outlays from the beginning; even so only two canals made it to the Stock Exchange list of 1800.[4] During the first half of the eighteenth century special duties were set aside to meet this need but little construction ensued, while from 1751 spending on canals was entrusted to a national body, the Corporation for Promoting and Carrying on an Inland Navigation in Ireland. It was this body which in 1756, started work on a major canal linking Dublin and Shannon, but progress was slow. To speed up matters the project was handed over to a company of "private adventurers" in 1772, all duly incorporated by act of parliament.[5] This authorised the raising of IR£150,000 by the Company of Undertakers of the Grand Canal, but when IR£100,000 was offered to the public the response was somewhat muted. They put up IR£63,000 while the sale of defaulting subscribers' shares only realised IR£14,000. In the case of the initial subscription only one subscriber had a holding in excess of £1,000 — the Corporation of Dublin with IR£10,000 of stock. Further capital issues and heavy borrowing produced, by 1796, a capital of IR£324,000 and a debt, in debentures of IR£373,800.[6]

Faced with persistent deficits and the burden of debt, the market price of Grand Canal Stock slumped from 150 in 1792 to 104 in 1796. By 1810 its capital had reached IR£572,000, alongside an awesome debt of IR£1.1mn. After the Napoleonic Wars falling trade and no dividend for several years drove the shares even lower, and to alleviate the financial plight of the company loan holders accepted reduced interest in 1817, while in 1848 a major capital reorganisation took place with consolidation of the stock and the loan. Over the next thirty years the Canal managed a regular but small dividend, and by 1884 the stock price had fallen to 33. Further borrowing was authorised by the Grand Canal Act of 1894, which also provided for the division of the stock into £10 ordinary and preference shares. The advent of road transport brought more damaging competition, falling dividends, and finally in 1950 the canal was merged with Córas Iompair Éireann, the shareholders receiving £702,500 compensation in government stock. It had paid its best dividends in wartime, around 5%, but in the long intervals of peace its trade was never sufficient to sustain the large capital and debt incurred during construction and as a result the shares never excited the Stock Exchange floor.

The Royal Canal, which ran a little to the north of the Grand Canal, also connected Dublin to Shannon. Apparently it was the outcome of a quarrel among the directors of the Grand Canal, the offended party seeking vengeance through a rival waterway. It proved a troublesome and costly reprisal.[7] In 1789 petitions were presented to the Irish House of Commons who obliged with a charter and a grant of IR£66,000, the subscribers to the project having put up IR134,000. The grant took the form of an issue of 4% debentures to the company who then had the task of selling them to raise money. In the event they only raised IR£60,240, and the debentures not taken up were sold by "public cant". The stock was bought by 185 people, in amounts ranging from £100 to £2,000; among names connected with stock dealing activities were Christopher and Robert Deey, along with other prominent financiers such as William Gleadowe Newcomen and Nathaniel Low.[8] The stock featured in the local share list and later in the official list of the Stock Exchange.

Assistance continued to flow from the public purse and such was the company's plight in 1796 that a Committee of the Commons investigated the position only to provide yet more help. But sales of debentures in 1797 and 1799 produced only a fraction of the nominal sums granted; in 1797 3,000 debentures were sold at IR£33 6s.8d, while 7,000 were sold in 1799 at IR£40. By 1810 its debt had reached £862,000 but two years later a parliamentary enquiry finally recommended that the company should forfeit its Charter, the construction of the canal being completed by the Director General of Inland Navigation. After completion in 1817 it was handed over to the New Royal Canal Company, the original shareholders getting £40 of new stock for every £100 of old. Relieved of its large debt it was able over the next few years to show a profit and pay a dividend, but it finally yielded its independence in 1844 to the Midland Great Western Railway.[9]

The formation of the Bank of Ireland and the building of the canals indicated that large sums could be raised by public subscription but such companies had the advantage of incorporation stemming from a charter or act of parliament. Such benefits included a legal persona, assets as security for debts, members who enjoyed limited liability, transferable capital and perpetual life. In cases where the amount of money needed could not justify incorporation, a costly and cumbersome privilege, the only other way to assemble capital quickly was the simple partnership which conferred no such benefits. Indeed, the liability of the partners was unlimited — "to his last shilling and acre" — while partnership changes could lead to dissolution, and it had no means of acting as a single body in law to settle disputes.

In an effort to remove some of the disabilities, so as to encourage investment activity, John Foster introduced into the more liberal parliamentary climate of 1780 a "Bill for regulating Partnerships and promoting the Trade and Manufacturers of this Kingdom". The bill, whose provisions resembled the French *en commandite* form of partnership, got as far as the Lord Lieutenant. However, in December 1781 it was re-introduced as a "Bill to promote Trade and Manufacturers by regulating and encouraging Partnerships", and supported in the Commons by a deputation of Dublin merchants and traders who saw it as of "very great Utility and Advantage and tended to promote the Trade and Commerce of this Kingdom". The bill received the Royal Assent in July 1782.[10]

The preamble of 21 & 22 George III, c. XLVI elaborated its aims as follows,

> Whereas the increasing of the stock of money employed in trade and manufacture, must greatly promote the commerce and prosperity of this Kingdom, and many persons might be induced to subscribe sums of money to men well qualified for trade, but not of competent fortune to carry it on largely if they were allowed to abide by the profit or loss of trade for the same, and were not deemed traders on that account, or subject thereby to any further or other demands than the sums so subscribed.

To fulfil these aims the act provided that any number of persons could join together in a partnership by deed which was then registered at the Deed Office in Dublin. Such co-partnership was for the "purpose of buying and selling in the gross, or by wholesalers, or for establishing or carrying on any manufacture or business for any term not exceeding fourteen years".[11] The capital could range from a minimum of £1,000 to £50,000. Subscribers nominated one or more of their number to manage the business — the acting partner or partners — while the addition of "and Company" to the name gave the partnership its trading title. The partners who then took no part in the management were aptly styled "anonymous partners". At the time of executing the partnership they had to pay a quarter of the subscription and the remainder within a year. A balance sheet was to be drawn up every year agreed to by the acting partners and two-thirds of the anonymous, while each of the latter were entitled to half and no more of their share of the net profits for the year, the residue to go to "increase the said capital or joint stock, until the expiration of the term of their copartnership". However, the anonymous partners were not to be "subject to any contracts or engagement of.... [the] acting partner of partners, or to any loss or miscarriage which may happen in the said partnership business". While shares in the partnership could be sold, it was only with the consent of the other partners. Also, the partnership could sue or be sued by the title assumed, that is, the acting partner or partners. Some of these provisions anticipated later company law and conferred on small concerns many of the benefits enjoyed by more elaborate incorporated bodies; in effect they were private limited companies.[12]

There was no great rush of registrations at the Dublin Deed Office after 1782. From 1782 to 1800 registrations averaged six a year, ranging from 2 in 1782 to 13 in 1792, a total of 125. This involved £342,865 of capital, £112,098 of which came from the active partners. The average capital per partnership was £2,742. Most had only one active partner, with two or three anonymous partners. This suggests that the characteristic partnership was a closely organised affair with each partner putting up about £800; in fact the average capital for active partners was £795, and £838 for the anonymous members.[13] The paucity of registrations in the 1780s may have been due to reluctance to adopt the new legal framework, and also perhaps because of hostility to limited liability, while the even smaller use after 1792 reflected the problems of trade and industry in a war economy, compounded by the troubled years of 1797-1798.

Political stability after the Act of Union, the boom in trade due to the removal of restrictions with Britain and monetary expansion, all seemed to produce a marked increase in the number of partnerships registered at the Deed Office. Over the years 1801-15 registrations averaged 16 a year, the peak being 26 in 1802. In all £1.2mn of capital was put up, making an average partnership of £5,017, substantially larger than the pre-1800 level. The ratio of active to anonymous partners remained much the same at 1 to 2, but in line with the higher capitalisation both increased the size of their contribution to £1,613 for active partners and £1,429 for the anonymous ones.

The peacetime recession produced a decline in the number of registrations, but even when trade and investment recovered no great use was made of this form of partnership, registrations being around four per year during 1816 to 1844. They were also smaller than their wartime counterparts, the average being £3,915, the active partners putting up £1,134 and the anonymous partners £1,017. From 1844 onwards the joint stock form became more easily available but without the protection of limited liability. The neglect of the partnership form after 1815 may have stemmed from the relatively short life it allowed for an organisation, while the ceiling of £50,000 on capitalisation was a little out of date by the 1820s. Also, the legal requirements imposed by the act led to an unwillingness to resort to it. In evidence to the 1854 Mercantile Law Commission a Belfast manufacturer asserted that "its provisions are so loose and have been interpreted so illiberally by our Courts of Law that no lawyer would advise his client to

take advantage of the Act". In practice the courts tended to "lean against...
the privilege of the anonymous partners", while the "almost insuperable
difficulty of avoiding liability", deterred persons from entering into
partnerships under its provisions.[14] On a financial level it was also claimed
that the provision whereby only a half of the share of the net profits due to
the dormant partners could be distributed meant that capital would stay in
the business whether needed or not.[15]

The first boom in company promotion after the war came in 1824-25
following a prolonged period of recession. In 1824 monetary ease, rising
prices and improved trade induced a large flood of company promotion in
England. The boom reached its peak in late 1824 and early 1825, and
according to its famous chronicler, Henry English, it gave rise to 624
companies involving a nominal capital of £372mn, but many of these never
opened a subscription list. In the ensuing crash most companies folded with
127 surviving, having collected £15mn of paid up capital. In the euphoria of
the boom, the government, unable to distinguish the good from the bad,
repealed the Bubble Act of 1720 which had rendered all incorporated
companies, and dealings in their shares, illegal. Henry English's compilation
was concerned solely with London and excluded "many provincial
companies, and others founded in Scotland and Ireland".[16]

While Ireland witnessed no such wild profusion of floatations, and there
was no meticulous chronicler to hand, the period saw the promotion of
several companies which later appeared in the Stock Exchange list and they
made a substantial addition to the number of corporate bodies in the county.
During the boom 13 companies were floated involving a nominal capital of
about £10mn with around £2.75mn paid up.[17] The effect of this minor
promotion boom was to produce by 1830 an enlarged miscellaneous section
in the Dublin share list with two gas companies (United General Gas, Oil
Gas), four mining companies (Mining Corporation of Ireland, Royal Irish,
Hibernian Mine, Imperial Mine), four insurance companies (National
Insurance, Irish Patriotic, Royal Irish, St. Patrick — only the first two
survived for any time), and two important joint stock banks, the Provincial
Bank and the Hibernian Bank.[18]

The Hibernian Bank, formed in March 1824 under Catholic patronage
and encouraged by Dublin merchants, was generally welcomed as a rival to
the Bank of Ireland, but of course, it had no note issue powers. Established
as a common law partnership by an act of parliament it could sue and be
sued in the name of the chief officer. A capital issue of £1.0mn, in £100
shares with £25 paid, obtained good support in Dublin along with £225,000
from the main commercial centres in the south, but this fell short by
£100,000 of the £800,000 needed to make the provisions of the act effective.
An issue of £100,000 on the London Stock Exchange produced the
deficiency and with a full subscription the Deed of Settlement was signed in
April 1825 by 1063 members, Irish subscribers taking up 6,750 shares and

English investors 3,250. To promote greater Irish ownership the shares could be transferred from London to Dublin but not back, and by 1846 all but 10 of the 500 shareholders were resident in Ireland.[19]

The Provincial Bank was set up by Irish interests in London to provide the south with banking facilities; and it also issued notes by operating outside the 50 mile preserve of the Bank of Ireland. Based on Scottish joint stock banking lines it was run by a board of directors in London led by Thomas Joplin. With a capital of £2.0mn, in £100 shares and £25 paid, it was floated in London and Dublin but the bulk of the original subscribers were located in England. At its formation there were 414 English shareholders and 275 Irish, mostly in Dublin. Irish holdings were generally smaller than those in London, there being only five in excess of 200 shares compared with forty five in London. However, by 1846 of 900 shareholders about three fifths had Irish addresses.[20]

The above examples point to the existence, certainly in and around Dublin, of a body of fairly wealthy individuals prepared to invest in local joint stock enterprises. Some indication of their identity is provided by the list of subscribers to the shares of the Commercial Insurance Company which enlarged its capital in 1824. Formed by a deed of partnership in 1799 and with a capital of £100,000 in 200 shares of £500 with £100 paid, the 1824 increase took the capital to £500,000 on the basis of four new shares for one of old. The capital was held by 95 shareholders, all but a dozen coming from Dublin. In terms of holdings 41 had five shares each, 24 had 10 shares, 10 had 15 shares, and 20 had 20 shares. Merchants certainly predominated — 56 in all with most of the Dublin names represented — Pim, Law, Orr, O'Connor, Roe, Sneyd, Crosthwait, Ferries, Harness, Kinahan, McDonnell and McCall. Next as a group came gentlemen, widows and spinsters (15), the tail being taken up by three shopkeepers, a druggist, brewer, banker, watchmaker, tobacconist and one Public Notary, Halliday Bruce of the Stock Exchange.[21] There is little doubt that many of these held shares in several local companies, indeed quite a number of the merchants were directors of several enterprises.

Apart from the appearance of some railways (see chapter 6) the 1835 boom also saw the second wave of Irish Joint stock bank promotions, but only two figured in the Stock Exchange daily list.[22] The National Bank was promoted in London in June 1834 with the help of Daniel O'Connell. Of the total capital of £1.6mn, divided between the main company and the branch offices, £412,000 was called up. Although at the outset most of the support came from London, gradually, English holdings were acquired by Irish investors, the local or branch shares being extinguished.[23] The other enduring product of the boom was the Royal Bank of Ireland based in Dublin which took over Shaw's Bank in Foster Place.[24] While the proprietary were about equally divided between London and Dublin most of the large shareholders were English, holding shares "taken under the spirit of the share mania". But within ten years or so very few of the 480 members were from Britain.[25]

One company, which appeared in the share list in 1827, attracted lasting attention due to its contribution to the debate on company law. The City of Dublin Steam Packet Company was formed in September 1823 as a co-partnership under the provisions of the 1782 legislation, with a capital of £24,000 and with the object of trading between Dublin and Liverpool and other ports. Two vessels were built and "trading became so considerable, that an increase of capital from time to time took place... by subscription from merchants and manufacturers in Dublin, Liverpool, Leeds, Manchester, Cork, Belfast and other manufacturing towns", bringing the capital in 1828 to £218,000 and the company's fleet to sixteen vessels. However, this increase in capital took the company out of the protection of the 1782 act, denying the anonymous partners their limited liability. A new deed was then drawn up consistent with the enlarged capital and the partnership was to last for 99 years. To afford some protection to the co-partners the company obtained an act in 1828 so that it could sue and be sued in its own name.[26] Further legislation in 1833 enabled the company to raise more capital but the request induced several petitions to the Commons opposing an extension of its activities.[27] The Company went to the Commons again in 1836 seeking yet more capital and also incorporation so as to obtain limited liability for its members.

Numerous petitions against conferring such privileges flowed to the Commons; there were only two in favour, from Dublin and Belfast merchants. The third reading of the bill took place in April 1836 and generated a diversity of views on the desirability of limited liability. The supporters argued that, particularly in Ireland where "there was little capital and much room for the extension of it", limited liability was "under proper guards and on fitting occasions, a very useful principal of legislation because it promoted concentration of capital for great public purposes not otherwise practicable".[28] The opponents, who won the day, supported the arguments voiced by Sir Henry Parnell, the member for Dundee, who opposed such "exclusive and peculiar privileges", suggesting that they discouraged the employment of capital; "a private adventurer could not go into competition with a company managed on the principle of non-liability. The business of a company, the partners in which were not liable for loss beyond a certain amount, was never conducted upon the true principles of trade and commerce". He also claimed that the adoption of such a principle "in the formation of trading companies had been attended with bad effect both in Ireland and France".[29] However, during the debate the President of the Board of Trade, Mr. Poulett Thompson, indicated his wish to remedy the unsatisfactory state of the law and that a measure would come from the government "which would comprehend partnerships of less than six individuals and Joint Stock Companies" and which would decide the "question generally". The outcome of the debate was the postponement of the bill for a few months and the end result was an Act (6 & 7 William IV, c. 6) which authorised the company to apply a portion of its funds for the construction of new vessels. But there was no limited liability for the shareholders and a further twenty years elapsed before it became generally available. However, within a decade a general measure relating to company regulation and registration reached the Statute Book.

The repeal of the Bubble Act and the difficulty of obtaining the privileges of incorporation meant that companies, apart from railways and some public utilities formed before the 1844 Act, were left to the procedures of the common law. In an attempt to apply a partial remedy to some of the problems, illustrated by the City of Dublin Steam Packet Co., parliament passed the Trading Companies Act in 1834 whereby the Board of Trade could grant companies the right to sue and be sued in the names of their officers, but an onerous condition was that the liability of shareholders continued for three years after the sale of shares. Later, in 1837, the Chartered Companies Act granted certain corporate rights to unincorporated companies, among them the right to sue and the regulation of the liability of individual members "to such extent only per share as shall be declared and limited", but liability ceased on transfer. However, the above privileges were only granted sparingly mainly from the fear that it might lead to charges of giving unfair competitive advantage to some companies compared to unincorporated companies operating under partnership law. Between 1837 and 1854 only eight Irish companies received charters, while one was refused.[30]

The decisive step came in 1844 after the Report of the Select Committee chaired by W. E. Gladstone which was set up after a series of disturbing frauds. The Companies Act of 1844 (7 & 8 Victoria, c. 100) defined a joint stock company as "Every partnership which at its formation, or by subsequent Admission...shall consist of more than Twenty five Members" or "Every partnership whereof the capital is divided or agreed to be divided into shares, and so as to be transferable without the express consent of all the copartners".[31] Unlimited liability applied and did so for three years after the transfer of shares. The office of Registrar of Companies was set up to provide for the registration of all new companies and some old ones. Incorporation was obtained in two stages; a provisional one which legalised the company for promotion purposes, and the second ("complete") which incorporated the company for carrying on business. For this the deed of settlement had to be signed by at least a quarter of the subscribers, both by shares and number. Dealings in shares before completing registration was prohibited since many companies had earlier foundered on scrip jobbing speculation with the calls not completed and the deed of settlement unsigned, but in practice the penalties imposed by the Act proved inadequate to eradicate such profitable manipulation. To assist in the formation of companies in Ireland the act authorised the Committee of Privy Council for Trade to appoint an Assistant Registrar in Dublin. The Dublin office was opened in November 1844 with Ponsonby Arthur Moore as Assistant Registrar; he was succeeded in 1845 by George Crawford.

The Act also ordered a census of existing companies, except banking, and the results for Ireland gave 47 companies in September 1844; gas and water 9, railway 8, coastal shipping 7, public utilities and works 6, lead and copper mines 6, and miscellaneous 11. Ten of these companies appeared in the Stock Exchange list which is a reasonable proportion of all companies in existence. Under the Act 46 Irish companies were 'completely' formed between 1844 and 1856. Gas and water undertakings were the most prolific with 28, followed at some distance by 7 mines, with the remaining 11 companies spread between diverse activities.[32] In the British case there was a large number of provisional registrations which never got further and no doubt the Dublin Office also saw instances of companies where the resolve of promoters weakened and the appetite of investors waned. How many there were is not recorded.[33]

The great omission from the 1844 legislation was the granting of limited liability on incorporation. Considerable debate surrounded the matter at the time but the arguments for and against had been rehearsed by Irish members of the House of Commons when they discussed the City of Dublin Steam Packet Co. bill years earlier. However, in 1855 the supporters of limited liability won the day and the Limited Liability Act (18 & 19 Victoria, c. 133) conferred the privilege on companies registered under the provisions of the 1844 act, provided the company had 25 shareholders with 75% of the capital subscribed and a least 15% paid up.[34] Little use was made of the legislation in Ireland during the months it operated. Only three companies registered under its provisions, all gas companies with small capitals.[35]

A far more permissive piece of legislation followed in 1856 after criticism by the Committee on Insurance Associations of the registration procedure of the 1844 act. The 1856 Joint Stock Companies Act (19 & 20 Victoria, c. 476) allowed seven or more persons to obtain limited liability by placing with the Registrar of Companies a memorandum of association giving the name and objects of the company and the fact that it was limited; most of the prudent provisions of the earlier legislation were swept aside and all that remained was a "measure of publicity".[36] The Companies Act of 1862 (25 & 26 Victoria, c. 89) merely modified existing company law.

For many decades the view had been expressed that the "backward condition of Ireland is mainly to be attributed to the want of capital". The new legislation at least provided enterprising persons with easy access (sometimes too easy) to the privileges of incorporation, while for the cautious investor it brought the protection of limiting his liability. During the next fifty years some 2,850 companies were registered in Ireland under the company acts, all but a few limited companies. They had a total nominal share capital of £109.6mn with a called up capital in the region of £55mn. Not all these companies survived, indeed, the overall loss was relatively high. By 1855, of the 861 companies formed 420 were still on the register; by 1897 976 remained from 1,894 formations, and by 1906 1,387 companies survived out of 2,854 formations. Overall, at various dates, about half the companies formed had gone out of existence either by insolvency, voluntary liquidation or merger. Compared to English experience this was quite a good rate of survival; those for England in the years given above ranged from 35% to 42%.[37] The superior survival record of Irish companies was probably due to their local origin and acceptability since many were simply conversions of existing private businesses. In addition, relatively fewer Irish promotions were to be found in such volatile activities as finance, land and mining, shipbuilding or specialised engineering, to say nothing of foreign railways. Indeed, towards the end of the century, while the range of limited liability company formation had increased there was a discernible preponderance of companies in the supply of consumption goods, the distributive trades and the service industries.

At the outset the impact of limited company formation on the Dublin Stock Exchange list was relatively small. Taking the 1862 list, the paid up value of Irish commercial and industrial companies amounted to just over £4.0mn; 32 quoted securities from 29 companies consisting of nine steam shipping companies, eight mines and twelve assorted companies. Some, of course, had been on the list for many years and two of them, the City of Dublin Steam Packet Co. and the Grand Canal accounted for £1.25mn. By 1881 the quoted capital had risen to £5.3mn (36 securities) and a further decade produced a rise to £7.25mn (47 securities), while adding on Arthur Guinness would boost the total to £10.9mn (Guinness was registered in London but naturally was also quoted in Dublin). It was, however, company formation in the early and middle 1890s which brought the great enlargement of the Dublin list to 78 companies involving 129 securities and paid up value of £17.2 mn in 1897. In rough terms this represented nearly half the total paid up capital of all companies on the Irish register at the time, but only eight per cent of companies by number. It meant that most of the large companies were quoted in Dublin, and several were also to be quoted on the Belfast and Cork Stock Exchanges (see below). Additional promotions before 1914 brought the total to 91 companies with a paid up value of £19.3mn (165 securities).

As in Britain a great many of the companies formed under the 1862 act were little more than small partnerships seeking the protection of limited liability. Usually they had small capitals and displayed a marked degree of similarity between the number of shareholders and the signatories of the articles of association. The "limiting" of private partnerships was also evident in the objects stated by new companies which invariably were cast in terms of "purchasing and carrying on". Relatively few of the companies formed were thus large enough in terms of paid up capital, or had sufficient numbers of shareholders, to justify a stock exchange quotation. As a result the number of quoted companies in Dublin only increased from 29 to 35 between 1862 and 1889.

In the years immediately after the 1856 act the formation of limited companies centred on public utilities in the form of no less than 39 gas companies during 1856-62, but their average nominal capital was a modest £7,300 which was nowhere adequate to merit a stock exchange quotation. The two gas companies which did appear in the Dublin list of 1862 came from much earlier years; the United Gas Company from about 1830 and the Alliance and Consumer Gas Co. of 1845. The next most active category was that of hotels, restaurants and markets with 18 formations, again with small capitals; the largest in 1859 was the Dublin Exhibition Palace and Winter Garden Co. with over 500 shareholders and a paid up capital of £17,000. Coastal shipping featured twelve "limiteds" with somewhat larger capitals giving an average nominal level of £23,000. The largest, which had existed before 1856 in other forms, found their way on to the Stock Exchange list; the Drogheda Steam Packet Co. (paid up capital in 1886 of £133,000 and 348 shareholders) and the Dundalk Steam Packet Co. (£131,000; 422). Irish mine formation was equally prominent, twelve companies in all with an average nominal capital of £15,500. Several of these made up the mining section of the Dublin list in 1862, among them the Wicklow Copper Co. (registered in 1858 with a paid up capital of £25,000 and 336 shareholders), the Connorree Mining Co. (1859; £49,910; 438) in County Wicklow, the Carysfort Mining Co. (1859; £29,000; 223) and the Castlewood United Mining Co. (1859; £5,760; 68).[38] The other active area of limitation was newspapers (10 companies) but none made it to the Stock exchange list of 1862; they had an average nominal capital of only £3,100.[39]

The period 1863-66 in England was noted by a general mania for company formation with a marked emphasis on finance, banking, insurance and hotels; it all came to an abrupt end on Black Friday, May 10 1866, with the failure of Overend, Gurney & Co. Enthusiasm for joint stock companies also spread to Ireland, albeit on a more modest level. In the boom year 1865 43 companies were registered; there had been 34 in 1864, and 37 followed in 1866 most of them in the early months. During 1863-66 half a dozen mines were joined by a similar number of quarries, while coastal shipping produced another ten companies, and there were seventeen small gas companies. Heightened activity was also very discernible in three areas, that of finance, hotels and the like, and the linen and flax industry of Ulster.

Thirteen finance companies were registered during 1863-66 involving a total nominal capital of £1.5mn, an average per company of £112,500. Five appeared in 1864, four the next year, and one just before the 1866 crash. While six had nominal capitals of £20,000 or less, some of the others were more substantial concerns. The Belfast and Provincial Building and

Investment Co., formed in May 1864, had a nominal capital of £100,000 in 4,000 shares of £25 each, but with only £2 10s. paid on 2,000 its subscribed capital, from 197 people, was a very humble affair indeed. In July came the National Investment Co., based in Cork, with a nominal capital of £200,000 in £10 shares but it was wound up shortly afterwards. It then reappeared under the name Munster Bank Limited, with a nominal capital of £500,000 in £10 shares, £2 10s. paid and from its 287 shareholders, mostly Cork people, it raised an impressive £74,077. For many years it was a successful bank with its shares actively traded on the Dublin market, at one time reaching £10. But in 1885, due to the fraudulent appropriation of funds by its directors which led to a run on the bank, it was forced to close its doors.[40] In contrast to several other banks registered under the 1862 act, the Munster Bank conferred limited liability on its shareholders, albeit not altogether effective due to the low paid up state of the shares. The largest finance company, at least in nominal terms, was formed in November 1865, the National Building and Land Investment Co. of Dublin with a nominal capital of £1.0mn in £10 shares. Finally, some weeks before the crash the Royal Land Building and Investment Co. of Belfast was registered with a nominal capital of £100,000 in £10 shares; little else seems known about it.

The general object of these companies was that of "lending and borrowing money, dealing in land and tenements, and securities, receiving moneys on deposit, granting letters of credit and transacting [the] business of bankers".[41] Obtaining deposits for the purpose of speculative investment usually led to insolvency, and it is more than likely that these Irish incursions into this sphere ended up in failure and loss. Also, they typically left a large part of their capital uncalled, thereby giving shareholders only sham limited liability. In some cases they seemed to set out to attract the small investor by adopting the device of making calls payable in monthly instalments. It was introduced by the Metropolitan Loan Company of Dublin in 1862; it was not used by other types of concerns. None of these finance enterprises made it to the Dublin list.

Also absent from the Stock Exchange list were the crop of newly formed hotels and similar public venues, some inspired by temperance principles, which appeared during 1863-66. Seventeen issues, with a total nominal capital of £133,000, gave a very modest average capital of £7,800, hardly the makings of a viable quotation. The largest issue, £20,000 by the Gresham Hotel of Cork in 1865, was in the 1880s, to be quoted on the newly formed Cork Stock Exchange.

Much larger companies flowed from the limitation of the flax industry. While Lancashire saw a flood of "Oldham Limiteds" in the early 1870s, many flax spinning and weaving companies took this step in 1864-66. Nine companies were registered in 1864, ten in 1865 and thirteen in 1866; £31mn of nominal capital, with an average of £97,000. The early limiteds were involved in flax production in several parts of the country but they were generally small. The later formations were in the spinning and weaving section, concentrated around Belfast, and had much large capitalisations. Indeed, six of the companies were of adequate size to be quoted in the list of the Belfast Stock Exchange when it was formed in 1895.[42] They had capitals ranging from £100,000 to £500,000; for example, the York Street Flax Spinning Co., registered in 1864, had a nominal capital of £500,000, with £100,000 paid up, and 112 shareholders, and the Ulster Spinning Co. had a nominal capital of £500,000, paid up £213,150, from 104 shareholders. As was the general practice of the time most companies had shares of large denominations, £50 being the most popular but only about a quarter was paid up. The market for shares centred on Belfast where about four brokers served the needs of local investors.

In the four years after the Overend, Gurney failure company registrations ran at about fifteen a year, well down on the boom level. The only activity which maintained a steady flow of companies was local gas but these usually only had capitals of a few thousand pounds. However, during the lull there were some notable incorporations among the banks, beginning with the Belfast Bank in 1865, followed by others over the next four years. The Belfast Banking Co. (established 1827) was incorporated in December 1865 with a nominal capital of £1.0mn, £250,000 paid up (£25 paid on £100 shares) from the 302 shareholders. In September 1866 the Northern Banking Co. (established 1824) followed, again with a nominal capital of £1.0mn, with £300,000 paid up from its 272 shareholders. The third Belfast bank, the Ulster Banking Co. (established 1836), obtained incorporation in October 1867, with a nominal capital of £1.2mn, of which £183,000 was paid up, but in £10 shares with a quarter paid, from 522 shareholders. Two Dublin banks, the Royal Bank (formed 1836) and the Hibernian (1825) took similar steps in 1868 and 1869. The Royal Bank had a nominal capital of £1.5mn and £300,000 paid up (£10 on its £50 shares) from 1,339 shareholders. The Hibernian called up £375,000 of its £1.5mn nominal capital (£20 on its £100 shares) from the 986 shareholders. Essentially all the above were conversions of large partnerships to the joint stock form which, of course, brought the benefits of incorporation, but they did not claim the protection of limited liability until the salutary lesson of the City of Glasgow Bank collapse in 1878. The two Dublin banks took this step in 1881, followed by the northern banks in 1883. However, at the time of their limitation, while the paid up portion had increased somewhat, they still had a very large uncalled element in their shares which left the shareholders with the possibility of a hefty demand should failure occur. Despite this prospect bank shares were widely held, each of the banks having about two thousand shareholders with an average shareholding in the region of £150-£200.[43]

While England enjoyed a promotion boom in iron and steel companies in the early 1870s, followed swiftly by another in cotton, Ireland, lacking opportunities in these directions, witnessed a spurt of promotions in the general area of transport and distribution, in the food and beverage industries, with money lenders reappearing following a lull after the 1866 crash. In the brief spell 1871-72 fifteen shipping companies were registered with an average nominal capital of £365,000. Three were large enough to merit inclusion in Stock Exchange lists; the Dublin and Glasgow Steam Packet Co. Ltd. (registered 1871, paid up capital £90,000 and 150 shareholders) and two Cork shipping lines, the City of Cork Steam Packet Co. Ltd. (1871; £200,000; 154 shareholders), and the Cork Steam Ship Co. Co. Ltd. (1872; £225,920; 91 shareholders) — both these appeared in the Cork Stock Exchange list from 1886.

In the next few years breweries and distilleries came to the fore with nine registrations which produced an average nominal capital of £76,000. Following earlier reforms of the excise duties and technical advances it had become a large scale industry needing considerable capital and the limited company form provided a suitable means of procuring such funds.[44] Among the largest was the Dublin Distillery Co. Ltd., registered in 1872 with a nominal capital of £100,000 and which amalgamated in 1889 with the old Dublin distilleries, William Jameson & Co. and George Roe & Co. to form the Dublin Distillers Company Ltd., quoted in Dublin and London. Other large Dublin distillers which also appeared at this time were Irish Whisky Distillery Co. Ltd.,(1872), the Athlone Distillery Co. Ltd., (1873), and the Dublin & Chapelizod Distillery Co. Ltd., (1873). The first two companies had acquired existing concerns, the latter proceeded to erect a distillery. The other important formation of the period was in Belfast, Dunville & Co., formed in 1879 with a paid up capital of £500,000.

A closely related activity, hotels, restaurants, clubs, coffee taverns and the like, dominated the decade in terms of numbers of registrations with 36 in all during 1870-79, but for the most part they had small capitals, the average being £12,000. Some had a distinctive temperance intent such as the Cork Total Abstinence Club, or a little less stern the Dublin Coffee Tavern Co. whose object was "carrying on public houses (without intoxicating drinks) fitted up in the style of gin palaces". During 1875-76 Irish fancies, like the English, turned to roller skating rinks, with four in Dublin and one in Belfast. They all had small capitals but even so one of the Dublin quartet sought a Stock Exchange quotation only to be refused on that count.[45]

With rising share prices in the early seventies, and fading memories, the investing public were again invited to take an interest in money lending companies. During 1870-75 fifteen were registered with an average nominal capital of £20,000. The largest, by nominal capital, was the National Discount Co. of Ireland with £100,000 but although it could field 115 shareholders its paid up capital was a mere £8,765. After this brief surge such offerings only appear very occasionally until the 1897 revival.

Less speculative and more substantial arrivals in the seventies were the warehousing companies set up to cater for the growing needs of the distribution industry in the main cities and ports, while the development of centralised bonding of whiskey added a further demand for such facilities. Between 1871-79 thirty warehouse companies were registered with an average nominal capital of £98,000. The years 1873 and 1877 produced the biggest crops, five and eight respectively. For the most part they were Dublin concerns reflecting its dominant role as a port, communication and commercial centre, with a few formations in Belfast, Limerick and Cork. Several were quoted in the Stock Exchange list. Among the Dublin warehouses quoted in 1881 were Arnott & Co. (paid up capital of £150,040), John Arnott & Co., a Belfast company (£60,000), McBirney & Co. (£57,880), Pim Bros (£210,000), Cannock & Co., of Limerick (£106,250), Merchants Warehousing Co. (£37,500), and McSwiney & Co. (£75,000).

While Irish investors, like many others, were attracted by the offerings of foreign mining and land companies which appeared in the early 1880s, none of these concerns were registered in Ireland. In other areas, however, Irish registrations did follow certain trends evident in England. The first effective single ship formation appeared in Liverpool in 1878, followed by a flood in 1882-83. The first Irish counterpart was registered in 1882, the Sirian Star Steam Co. of Belfast with a paid up capital of £1,600 and eight shareholders. A further fifty four companies appeared in the period up to 1893.[46] Most of these had paid up capitals ranging from £1,500 to £3,000, a few reached four figures, while their shares varied from £10 to £250 but £100 was the commonest; a few reflected the time honoured division of a ship's capital into sixty fourths. The average shareholding was probably in the region of £200 to £300, with about 10 to 30 shareholders per ship. Most of the registrations originated in Belfast, with a few from Dublin and Antrim. The main motive for incorporation arose from the advantage of limited liability in meeting damages from collisions, whether in home or more distant waters.[47] Needless to say companies with such small capitals and few shareholders had no place in the Stock Exchange list but it seems likely that brokers may well have been employed in the transfer of "ship" shares.

Figures of company registrations for the early 1880s were greatly inflated by the multitude of light railway and tramway formations which followed the legislation giving financial assistance in the form of a baronial guarantee to cover dividend payments (see chapter 6). Seventy promotions were registered in 1883 involving a nominal capital of over £7.0mn, and 1884-85 saw another 20 with £1.5mn nominal capital. Since most of these had small paid up capitals few of them merited a Stock Exchange quotation; the Dublin list for 1889 had quotations for nine lines with baronial guarantees. While the tramway section of the list was somewhat larger, consisting not only of local lines but also British and Latin American companies, the number of Irish lines was small.[48] Dublin United Tramways, after its consolidation of 1896, dominated the Irish section with a quoted capital of £920,000 in 1897, followed by Cork Electric Tramways (£353,000), Belfast

Street Tramways (£306,000), Dublin and Lucan Electric Railway Co. (£58,700), Dublin and Blessington Steam Tramway (£57,100), and the Clontarf & Hill of Howth Tramroad Co (£50,000).

Two activities characterised by small capitals, hotels, clubs etc. and farming, produced a spurt of limitations in the 1880s, and while these brought no direct benefit to the Stock Exchange they produced gains for their own industries. The services registrations may well have been encouraged by the gradual recovery from the Great Depression, but apparently many sought incorporation for reasons of legal expediency; the Registrar of Joint Stock Companies maintained that due to a recent court case (1886) "there was no power to recover unless they registered these clubs, whereupon a number of them came in".[49] Such cautionary motives were absent from the incorporation of several creameries. That arose from the need to resist Danish incursions on the English butter market. In 1886 and 1889 alone 19 creameries were registered, mostly in the south eastern counties, all with very modest capitals of about £1,000 and 20 to 50 shareholders holding £1 shares.[50]

The increase in company promotion was not confined to the capital city. Further south in Cork there had appeared by the mid 1880s a sufficient number of local companies, which together with local interest in national companies, justified the setting up of a local stock exchange with members drawn from the increasing number of local brokers. Since the passing of the Companies Acts over 100 companies had been formed in the Cork area but most of these were very small, essentially private companies with no need of stock exchange facilities. However, with the local railways, gas companies (Cork, Skibbereen, Waterford), the Munster and Leinster Bank, together with the national concerns in which local investors obviously had an interest, and the 20 or so recently formed miscellaneous industrial and commercial companies, there was by the mid-1880s a local share list of some 30 Cork companies and a further 30 national companies with strong local participation (see illustration 7 overleaf).

To cater for the dealing needs of local investors there were fourteen broking concerns operating in Cork by 1886, mostly of recent formation; none had bridged the forty years from the short lived railway Stock Exchange (see Chapter 6). In October a group met at 74 South Mall, with J. H. Carroll in the chair and Edward Hayes as secretary, and decided to set up a stock exchange. A Committee of five was duly elected, accommodation was obtained in a back room on the second floor of 74 South Mall, and the market opened for business on December 1 1886 with ten member firms.[51] Suitable rules and regulations were selected from the Dublin and British rule books and adapted to meet local conditions. Initially the market opened from 12.0 till 12.30 but this was later altered to conform to the general British practice of a morning and afternoon dealing session. A share list was published with an additional feature in that it contained details of shares

# CORK STOCK EXCHANGE,

No. 318.

## DAILY PRICE LIST.

NOTICE. Members of the Stock Exchange are not allowed to advertise for business purposes. Brokers or Agents who advertise are not in any way connected with the Stock Exchange.

Published by authority of the Committee.

**WEDNESDAY, JANUARY 4th, 1888.**

MEMBERS.

ALLEN, F. W., 53, South Mall.
BEALE, ALFRED, 81, South Mall.
BELTON, R. W., 78, South Mall.
CARROLL, JOSEPH H.
CARROLL, THEODORE F.,
CARROLL, JOSEPH H., jun., } (J. H. Carroll & Sons.) 80, South Mall.

CLARKE, W. P., 10, Marlboro' Street.
HAYES, EDWARD (E. Hayes & Sons), 59, South Mall.
MORROGH, WALTER, 74, South Mall.
ROBINSON, R. S. O.,
ROBINSON, A. C., } (R. & A. Robinson), 31, South Mall.

TOWNSEND, H.,
TOWNSEND, R.,
BEAMISH, W. H., } (H. & R. Townsend), 18, South Mall.

| Amount | Paid. | NAME. | Last Two Dividends. | When Payable. | When Ex. Divd. | Prev. Price. | To-day's Price. |
|---|---|---|---|---|---|---|---|
| | | **Government Funds.** | | | | | |
| 100 | all | 3 Per Cent. Consols ... | ... | 5 Jan Jul | ... | 102 | |
| 100 | all | 3 Per Cent. Stock—New ... | ... | 5 Apl Oct | ... | 101⅛ | |
| 100 | all | India Stock, 4 per Cent. ... | ... | do. | ... | 102⅞ | |
| | | **IRISH BANKS.** | | | | | |
| 100 | all | Bank of Ireland ... | 11 11 | Feb Aug | 19 July | 281½ | 281½ |
| 20 | 5 | Hibernian limited ... | nil. 2 | do. | 12 Aug | 2 | 1 15/16 |
| 5 | 2 | Munster and Leinster limited | 3 5 | do. | do | 2⅛ | 2⅛ |
| 50 | 10 | National limited .. | 10 10 | Jan July | 28 July | 18¾ | 18¾ |
| 100 | 12½ | Provincial limited ... | 10 10 | Feb Aug | do. | 19½ | 19½ |
| 20 | 10 | Do. New limited .. | 10 10 | do. | do. | 18 | |
| 50 | 10 | Royal limited ... | 11 11 | Mch Sep | 15 Sept | 23¼ | |
| 15 | 2½ | Ulster limited .. | 18 18 | do. | do. | 9½ | |
| | | **IRISH RAILWAYS.** | | | | | |
| 50 | all | Belfast and Co. Down .. | 5 5 | Mch Sep | 12 Aug | 53¼ | |
| Stock | 100 | Belfast & Northern Counties | 2 2 | Feb Aug | do. | 88⅝ | |
| Stock | 100 | Cork and Bandon ... | 3 2½ | Mch Sep | do. | 68 | |
| 10 | all | Cork and Macroom .. | nil. nil. | Feb Aug | ... | 4⅞ | |
| 20 | all | Cork, Blackrock & Passage | 1¼ 1 | do. | 31 Aug | 5 15/16 | |
| Stock | 100 | Dublin, Wicklow & Wexford | 2 2 | Mch Sep | do. | 50½ | 50½ |
| Stock | 100 | Great Northern (Ireland) .. | 4¼ 4¼ | do. | do. | 106¾ | |
| Stock | 100 | Great Southern & Western | 4½ 4½ | do | do. | 100¼ | 100½ |
| Stock | 100 | Ilen Valley, Bar Gtd. 5% ... | 5 5 | do. | do. | 97 | |
| Stock | 100 | Midland Great Western .. | 3¾ 3¾ | Mch Sep | 15 Sep | 74¼ | 74½ |
| 50 | all | Waterford and Limerick .. | nil. 2/6 | do. | 25 Aug | 12 | |
| | | **Railway Preference.** | | | | | |
| 100 | all | Belfast & Northern Counties | 4 ⅌ ct. | ... | 12 Aug | 99¼ | |
| Stock | 100 | Cork and Bandon ... | 5½ „ | ... | 31 Aug | ... | |
| Stock | 100 | Do. .. | 4 „ | ... | do. | ... | |
| 10 | all | Do. Bantry Bar Gtd. ... | 5 „ | ... | do. | 8 13/16 | |
| 10 | all | Do. Clonakilty do. ... | 5 „ | ... | do. | ... | |
| Stock | 100 | Do. Kinsale Gtd. .. | 4 „ | ... | do. | .. | |
| Stock | 100 | Do. West Cork do ... | 4 „ | ... | do. | ... | |
| 10 | all | Cork and Macroom ... | 5 „ | ... | ... | 6¾ | |
| Stock | 100 | Dublin, Wicklow & Wexford | 6 „ | ... | 31 Aug | 142 | |
| Stock | 100 | Great Northern (Ireland) .. | 4 „ | ... | do. | 107 | |
| Stock | 100 | Great Southern and Western | 4 „ | ... | do. | 109 | |
| Stock | 100 | Midland Great Western .. | 5 „ | ... | 15 Sept | 122 | |
| Stock | 100 | Do. .. | 4 „ | ... | do. | 102 | |
| Stock | 100 | Waterford and Limerick .. | 4 „ | ... | 31 Aug | 76½ | |
| 50 | all | Do. ... | 5 „ | ... | do. | 81 | |

| Books Closed. | NAME. | Last Two Dividends. | When Payable. (Books Closed.) | When Ex. Div. | Prev. Price. | To-day's Price. |
|---|---|---|---|---|---|---|
| | **Railway Debentures.** | | | Ex. Accrued Interest. | | |
| June, Dec. | Cork and Bandon ... | 4½ ⅌ ct. | Dec. June | | 111 | |
| do. | Do. ... | 4 „ | Do. | | 101½ | |
| May, Nov. | Cork, Blackrock and Passage | 4 „ | June Dec. | | 91 | |
| June, Dec. | Cork and Macroom ... | 4 „ | Do. | | 95 | |
| 24 Jun. Dec. | Great Northern (Ireland) ... | 4 „ | Dec., June | | 112 | |
| 1 July, Jan. | Great Southern and Western | 4 „ | Jan. July | | 112 | |
| do. | Midland Great Western ... | 4½ „ | Do. | | 116 | |
| do. | Do. .. | 4 „ | Do. | | 106 | |
| 17 Jun. Dec. | Waterford and Limerick ... | 4½ „ | June Dec. | | 108 | |
| do. | Do. .. | 4 „ | Do. | | 100 | |

| Amount | Paid | NAME. | Last Two Dividends. | When Payable. | When Ex. Div. | Prev. Price. | To-day's Price. |
|---|---|---|---|---|---|---|---|
| | | **TRAMWAYS.** | | | | | |
| 10 | all | Belfast Street ltd. ... | 5 6 | Feb. Aug. | 31 Aug | 11½ | |
| 5 | all | Cork & Muskerry Light Rly. | — | — | — | 5½ | |
| 10 | all | Dublin United ltd. .. | 5½ | Feb. Aug. | 12 Aug | 10¾ | |
| 10 | 9 | Glasgow Tram & Omnibus ltd | 8½ 8½ | do. | do. | 15¼ | |
| 10 | all | Liverpool United T. & O. ltd | 5 5 | do. | do. | 9⅜ | |
| | | **GAS.** | | | | | |
| 10 | all | Alliance, Dublin ... | 10½ 10½ | April Oct. | 14 Oct. | 18¾ | 18¼ |
| 10 | all | Do. New .. | 7½ 7½ | do. | do. | 13¾ | |
| 5 | all | Cork .. | 8 8 | Feb. Aug. | 31 Aug | 7¼ | |
| 10 | all | Queenstown ... | 10 10 | Mch. Sep. | 14 Oct. | | |
| 5 | all | Skibbereen .. | 8 8 | Feb. | 31 Aug | 5½ | |
| 10 | all | Waterford ... | 10 10 | Mch. Sep. | ... | | |
| 10 | 5 | Do. C. ... | 7 7 | do. | ... | | |
| | | **MISCELLANEOUS.** | | | | | |
| 10 | all | Allsopp & Sons, Samuel, ltd. | 8 | Aug. Feb. | 12 Aug | 11⅞ | |
| 10 | all | Do. 6% Preference ... | 6 | do. | 14 July | 13 | |
| 5 | 4 | Arnott & Co., Dublin, ltd. ... | 8½ 8½ | Mch. Sep | 31 Aug | 4¼ | |
| 10 | all | A. Guinness, Son & Co., ltd. | 12 12 bonus 2°/o | 31 Aug. | do. | 27¼ | 27⅝ |
| 10 | all | Do. 6% Preference ... | 6 6 | do. | do. | 14¼ | |
| 100 | all | Do. 5% Debentures ... | 5 5 | — | ... | 118¼ | |
| 5 | 4 | Cannock & Co., Limerick, ltd. | 6 6 | Feb. Aug. | do. | 3¾ | |
| 2 | all | Citizens' River Strs. Co. ltd. | nil. | July | ... | | |
| 15 | 12 | C. C. Steam Packet Co. ltd. | 5/-, 6/ p.s. | Jan. July | 1 July | 10¼ | |
| 100 | all | Commercial Buildings, Cork | nil. | July | ... | 39 | |
| 5 | all | Cork Imp'd Dwllg's Co. ltd. | 5½ 5½ | Jan. July | 19 July | 5¼ | |
| 10 | all | Cork Steam Ship Co. ltd. ... | nil. 4 | April Oct. | ... | | |
| 5 | all | Cork Opera House ... | nil. | do. | ... | 15/- | |
| Stock | 100 | Corporation 4% Debs. ... | 4 4 | May Nov. | ... | 100¼ | |
| 5 | 4 | "Freeman's Journal," ltd. ... | | — | . | 7½ | |
| 10 | 8 | Goulding, W. & H. M. ltd.. | 7 7 | Jan. July | 1 July | 7⅜ | |
| 5 | all | Gresham Hotel ltd. ... | 5 5 | Oct. | 29 Sep. | 2¼ | |
| 100 | all | Do. 5% Debs. ... | 5 5 | Feb. Aug. | ... | | |
| 100 | all | Harbour Board, 4½% Debs. | 4½ 4½ | May Nov. | . | 100¼ | |
| 10 | all | Hotchkiss Ordnance ltd. ... | 20 | — | 12 Aug | 17¼ | |
| 6 | 5 | Levy's Jute Co. ltd. ... | 5 nil. | Mch. Sep. | ... | 3½ | |
| 6 | 5 | Sir J. Arnott & Co. (Brs.) ltd. | 8 8 | do. | 10 June | | |
| 5 | 4 | T. Lyons & Co. ltd. ... | 6 6 | do. | 12 Aug | 3¼ | |
| 5 | all | Do. fully paid ... | 6 6 | do. | do. | 4¼ | |
| 100 | all | Do. 5% Debs. .. | 5 5 | Jan. July | . | 98½ | |
| 5 | all | Thom & Co. ltd. ... | 12 | — | 31 Aug | 7 | |

## REMARKS.

Bank Stock repeated 281½; Munster and Leinster were sold for 2⅛; Hibernian fell to 1 15/16; National changed hands at 18¾; closing sellers and Provincials repeated 19½.

Macrooms were offered at 4⅞; Passages were enquired for at 6¼; Waterford and Limerick at 12; Dublin, Wicklow and Wexford repeated 50½; Great Southern and Western were done at 106½; and Midland Great Western at 74½.

In preference, Bantry are offered at 8⅞, Clonakilty at 9¼, and Macrooms at 6¾.

In Trams, Muskerry were offered at 5½.

In Gas Shares, Skibbereen are wanted at 6 and Cork at 7¼, Sellers at 7½, Queenstown were asked for; Alliance were sold at 18.

In Miscellaneous, River Steamers were offered at 3/-; and Arnott (Brewers) at 6; Steam Ships were enquired for; Improved Dwellings were asked for at 5¼, Corporation Stock were asked for at 100¼; Cork Dock Preference were offered at 25/-; Steam Packets were enquired for at 10¼; Gresham's at 2¼; Lyons' (fully paid) were offered at 4¼ and Debentures were asked for; Cannock's were asked for at 3½; Levy's were on sale at 3¼; Guinness's were done at 27⅝; Goulding's were enquired for; Harbour Board were asked for at 100¼; and Commercial Buildings were offered at 39.

Name Day, 11th January, 1888. Bank of England Rate, 4 per cent.

Account Day, 12th January, 1888. Bank of Ireland Rate 4½ per cent. Broker's Office Hours—10 to 5; Saturdays 10 to 2.

*Fig. 7: Cork Stock Exchange Daily Price List, 1888*

wanted and on offer which was designed to assist the market's usefulness for investors.

The recovery of trade and industry in the late eighties, after prolonged depression, produced a marked increase in the number of enterprises seeking incorporation, and significantly from a stock exchange standpoint, an increase in the number of large companies which could merit a quotation. Conditions at the time not only encouraged new promotions but also prompted the "limitation" of well established concerns. The expansion of trade gave good prospects of maintaining income and hence future dividends, and cheap money drove funds from trustee stocks towards more profitable outlets. Rising stock market prices certainly tempted promoters to push out companies and as usual in such circumstances investors were always willing to try their luck. From around 50 or so registrations in the mid eighties the number rose to over 90 in the early nineties, reaching 134 and 145 in 1896 and 1897 respectively. Most of these companies were concerned with meeting the needs of the two expanding urban centres of Belfast and Dublin, while several companies owed their expansion to the improvement in the export trade.[52] Thus, during the period 1890-97 more than half of the companies registered had to do with the necessities of living, that is, household goods, food and provisions, brewing and mineral waters, hotels, newspapers, warehouses, tramways and farming. The end result for the Stock Exchange list between 1888 and 1897 was the addition of 40 companies (see Appendix 6) which were shared between the various sections, that is, bakeries, drapery and trading, hotels, cycle shares, and manufacturing companies.

The smaller of this range of companies had a paid up capital of £18,000 but most of the quoted companies had larger capitals in the region of £50,000 to £100,000, with only five larger than £200,000. The majority were thus viable from a stock exchange dealing standpoint since they had a few hundred shareholders. Small share denominations, £5 predominating, encouraged wider ownership while £1 shares were used by about a quarter of the companies, usually those with smaller capitalisations. Lower share denominations, fully paid up as a rule, was in contrast to the earlier practice where the nominal value was much greater and a large proportion uncalled. Not that these companies constituted a particularly active market dominating all else (with one notable exception), rather they provided a welcome diversification away from dependence on government stocks, banks, railways and foreign stocks, and in so doing supplied a staid and proven range of general industrial investments, testimony to which is that several of them are still quoted on the Dublin market.

In the fifty or so years after the railway share boom the Dublin market had a relatively staid existence with the occasional speculative ripple coming from London. The arrival of cycle shares changed all that for a few years. The basis of the industry was laid with the invention of the safety frame in

1884, followed in 1888 by Dunlop's (a Belfast veterinary surgeon) pneumatic tyre; both of these were adopted by a few firms in the early 1890s. The first registered company to enter the field, Pneumatic Tyre and Booth's Cycle Agency, was formed in November 1889. It had a capital of £25,000 in the £1 denomination used by cycle companies, and by 1892 the shares stood at a handsome 19⅜ since the company in that year paid a dividend of well over 50%. It was, however, the "fashionable rage" for cycling in 1893 which produced the first cycle share boom and the appearance of nearly fifty companies in the cycle and tyre trade.

While Birmingham people, and London investors, did not give this "crowd of new companies a second thought", the Dublin market and Irish investors had a very merry time in the early months of 1893. *The Statist* pictured the episode as follows,

> No sooner does a company come with its £1 shares offered at par...than benevolent speculators push up the quotation to a big premium, in some cases as much as 200 or 300% in a very few hours and this inflation in patent rights must in a great many directions result in loss and disappointment.... We are given to understand that promoters whose antecedents are not altogether pleasant in regard to bringing out undertakings in London and the provinces in this country have devoted their attention to the unsophisticated Irish. This attitude to the Irish is really a *boulversement* of the old fashion cry of "no Irish need apply".[53]

Within Ireland twelve cycle and tyre companies were registered in 1893 but for the most part they were small agencies. A few, however, were sizeable concerns but only one, the "Grappler" Pneumatic Tyre & Cycle Co. Ltd., found a lasting place in the Stock Exchange list. After a lull in 1894 some dozen Irish registrations were made in 1895-96 but they were mostly small agencies in Dublin and Belfast. Only two large companies were floated, the Revolution Cycle Co. in 1896 (£44,000 capital and 197 shareholders) and the John Griffiths Cycle Corporation (nominal capital £125,000). By 1895-96 the centre of speculation had moved to Birmingham but Dublin remained a good second, with London showing a belated interest.

For most of 1893 dealing in cycle shares dominated all else on the Dublin Stock Exchange. At the outset two cycle companies were quoted in the list, Pneumatic Tyre & Booth's Cycle Agency Ltd., and Seddon's Pneumatic Co. During the year some 50 companies, local as well as English, made their appearance involving a capital of some £2.0mn. Since pound shares were widely used and there was only about 10% payable on application, with a small sum on allotment, they were undoubtedly very appealing to a wide range of investors. In the new year cycle shares showed signs that they would soon dominate daily business with steady buying from the "best

*MAY 27.*

The National Bank, Limited, Dublin, Belfast, Cork, and other branches, and Messrs. Brown, Janson, and Co., 31, Abchurch-lane, London, E.C., are authorized to receive subscriptions on behalf of the Company for the undermentioned shares.

The Subscription List will Open on Saturday, May 27, and will Close on or before Monday, May 29, for town, and the following morning for the country.

It is claimed for the "Grappler" that it can be adapted at little cost to existing forms of "pneumatic" tyres, and therefore that all pneumatic tyre manufacturers should of necessity be compelled to adopt it.

# THE "GRAPPLER" PNEUMATIC TYRE and CYCLE COMPANY, Limited.

Incorporated under the Companies Acts, 1862 to 1891, whereby the liabilities of shareholders are limited to the amount of their shares.

Share capital £75,000, divided into 75,000 shares of £1 each.

Payable 2s. 6d. per Share on application.
" 7s. 6d. " also on allotment.
" 10s. 0d. " on the 1st July, 1893.

### DIRECTORS.

WILLIAM CARTE, Esq., J.P., Military-road, Dublin, Chairman (Chairman of Dublin United Tramways Company).

Henry Vincent Jackson, Esq., J.P., 12, Merrion-square north, Dublin, (Chairman Bray Township Commissioners).

Thomas W. Pim, Esq., of Glen-house, White Abbey, Belfast, Director of the Belfast Board of the National Telephone Company.

*T. S. Frank Battersby, Esq., 45, Upper Mount-street, Dublin (Chairman Irish Cycle Company, Limited).

*Will join the Board after allotment.

Bankers—National Bank, Limited, Dublin, Belfast, Cork, and other branches ; Messrs. Brown, Janson, and Co., 31, Abchurch-lane, London, E.C.

Solicitors—Dublin : Messrs. Casey and Clay, 71, St. Andrew-street, Dublin.

Auditors—Messrs. Peterson and Son, Accountants, 1 and 2, Foster-place, Dublin.

Patent Agent—J. P. Bayly, 18, Fulham-place, Paddington, London. Secretary (pro tem.)—J. Farrell.

Offices—Dublin : 27 and 28, Clare-street, Dublin. London Branch office : 78, Gracechurch-street, London, E.C.

### PROSPECTUS.

This Company has been formed to purchase, take over, work, develop, or otherwise deal with (a) the invention of R. R. Gubbins and George Harcourt, for a new method of attachment of pneumatic tyres, covers, &c., and for the manufacture of the same, and all privileges and benefits appertaining thereto. (b) To acquire as going concerns and to work the following cycle businesses:—(1) The Irish Cycle Company, Limited, whose premises and factory are situated at Clare-street and Clare-lane, Dublin ; (2) the business of John Alexander and Company, Royal-avenue, Belfast ; (3) the business of W. R. M'Taggart, Patrick-street, Cork.

The patent rights for the Grappler attachment available for every pneumatic tyre have been applied for and will, when granted, cover

Great Britain and Ireland,          Germany,
United States of America,           France,
Austria-Hungary,                    Belgium
Canada,            Victoria,        Italy.

The patent specifications have been submitted to Mr. J. P. Bayly, Registered Patent Agent and Engineer of London, who states : "I have carefully searched the Patent Office records, so far as they relate to pneumatic tyres or their rims, and examined all specifications published up to the 22nd instant (April, 1893), but fail to find an invention like the one claimed in the above. I am of the opinion that the claims are novel and that the same are valid." The opinion of Mr. J. Fletcher Moulton, Q.C., the well-known patent authority, has also been obtained, of which the following is a copy :—" I have settled specifications and claims of Patent No. 14,913 of 1892, and am of opinion that, upon the materials before me, which I understand to be the result of a search, the claims are good and valid to protect the details of the devices to which they relate."

The Grappler can be applied to existing forms of pneumatic cycles, a feature that will be availed of not only by cyclists but by manufacturers ; and old non-detachable tyres can by this method be converted into detachable at a cost of a few shillings. The cover can be opened for repair by any person readily in half a minute, and secured again in less time than any other tyre. There is no possibility of nipping the air tube when replacing the cover, and no chance of the tyre "creeping" on the rim, and it is believed to be one of, if not the very fastest, lightest, and cheapest tyres yet invented. A great point of merit in this tyre is that it admits of the use of an almost flat rim, and therefore possesses a large cushioning area, which makes it second to no other tyre for speed, comfort, and resiliency, and on this point see testimony of experts herewith. Specimens of the new tyres and old converted ones can be seen and tested at the offices of the Company, 27 and 28, Clare-street, Dublin.

An offer has been received from a firm in France, who desire to take up the agency in that country, to purchase from the Company 9,000 pairs Grappler Tyres. It is expected that a large number of these tyres will be sold in France, if, from the success of the trade in that country, it is estimated the makers will turn out over a hundred thousand cycles this year.

Another proposal from an American house is now under consideration. The sum offered is 50,000 dollars (say £10,000) for the exclusive right to manufacture the Grappler Tyre in that country, but the

Directors have not accepted it, believing the privilege to be of much greater value.

The Irish Cycle Company, Limited, was formed in the year 1890, and acquired the business of one of the oldest cycle agencies in Dublin. This Company has acquired, as from the 30th November, 1892, the business premises, factory, and stock-in-trade of the Irish Cycle Company, Limited, and all other assets of the Company as a going concern. It will be seen that the Chairman of the Irish Cycle Company will join the Board of this Company, and the services of Mr. J. Paget Sweny (for five years) and the trained staff of that Company have been secured.

The business of Messrs. John Alexander and Co. (the well-known Cycle Agents in the North of Ireland), which this Company is to acquire, is situate in Royal-avenue, Belfast, and will be taken over as from the 17th day of May, 1893, consisting of leasehold premises, stock-in-trade, and the other assets in connexion with the business.

The concerns of Mr. W. R. M'Taggart, 18, Patrick-street, Cork, have also been acquired as from 17th May, 1893. This is the principal cycle agency in the South of Ireland, and this Company will be entitled to the interest of the said W. R. M'Taggart in the leasehold premises in which he carries on business, as well as all stock-in-trade, machinery, and plant, and other assets of the business.

Both Messrs. John Alexander and Co. and W. R. M'Taggart have agreed to represent the Company in their districts for the respective terms of five years.

Thus it will be seen that by the acquisition of these going concerns the Company can at once commence business operations and manufacture tyres, and so bring the capital into immediate and profitable employment.

This Company will sell their foreign patent rights, or grant licences for working them on royalty, or may open works or depôts in various countries, or otherwise deal with them as will be deemed best in the interests of the shareholders.

The Directors, for obvious reasons, do not disclose the exact cost of production, or publish an estimate of profits, but from the sales in Great Britain alone (without calculating on the receipts from the foreign patents or sales of tyres abroad) profits are expected to be earned sufficient to pay large and annual dividends on the Company's capital.

The price to be paid to the four Vendors respectively, for the invention, premises, stock, book debts, &c., is £46,000, payable as to £25,000 in fully-paid shares of the Company (which is the largest amount that can be taken in shares by the Vendors under the rules of the Stock Exchange), and the balance, £21,000, in cash, leaving £29,000 for working capital outside that in the businesses purchased as going concerns.

The contracts entered into have been as follows :— A contract dated 24th day of May, 1893, between Messrs. Gubbins and Harcourt (by their power of attorney) of the one part, and W. B. Gardiner, as trustee for and on behalf of the Company, of the other part. A contract dated 24th day of May, 1893, between F. Callaghan, A. F. Galwey, and J. P. Sweny, on behalf of the Irish Cycle Co. (Limited), of the one part, and W. B. Gardiner, as a trustee for and on behalf of the Company, of the other part. A contract dated 24th day of May, 1893, between John Alexander of the one part, and William H. Gardiner, as trustee for and on behalf of the Company. A contract dated 24th day of May, 1893, between W. R. M'Taggart and W. B. Gardiner, as trustee for and on behalf of the Company. A contract dated 24th May, 1893, between W. B. Gardiner, as trustee for and on behalf of the Company, and J. Paget Sweny.

In addition to the foregoing arrangements and contracts, certain trade contracts, agency contracts, and other contracts have from time to time been entered into by the vendors which it is not considered advisable to specify. Applicants for shares will be deemed to have had notice of such arrangements and contracts, and to have waived the insertion of the dates thereof and the names of the parties thereto, and to accept the above statement as a sufficient compliance with section 38 of the Companies Acts, 1867.

The Memorandum and Articles of Association, together with all the contracts set forth, and testimonials, and other documents may be inspected at the office of the Solicitors of the Company.

Machines fitted with the Grappler Tyres can be seen at the offices of the Company, 27 and 28, Clare-street ; in Belfast, at Messrs. John Alexander and Co.'s, Royal-avenue ; and in Cork, at W. R. M'Taggart's, where full particulars can be obtained.

Applications will be made in due course for a settlement and quotation on the Stock Exchanges of Dublin and London.

Prospectuses and forms of application can be obtained from the Bankers in England and Ireland, at offices of the Company, and from all Stockbrokers in Dublin, Belfast, and Cork.

Where no allotment is made the application money will be returned in full, and where the number of shares alloted is less than the number applied for, the surplus will be appropriated on account of the allotment money, and any excess returned to the applicant.

*Fig. 8: Prospectus of The "Grappler" Pneumatic Tyre & Cycle Co. Ltd., 1893*

quarters". The leading shares were Seddon's, some 2,000 shares changing hands every day, and in two weeks the price rose from 50s. to 84s. By the middle of February the price of Seddon's has reached 110s., the market closing in a "wild and buoyant" state.[54] However, a week or so later the pace of advance slackened due to profit taking and sales of shares by weak operators who could not carry over to the next account or take up stock. The postponement of the Home Rule Bill then gave a fillip to the market and the euphoria went on, Seddon subsidiaries attracting "enormous applications" and dealings proliferated in all cycle shares, old and new. In an effort to check speculative excesses the Stock Exchange Committee decided not to recognise dealings before allotment in new shares in the hope of stopping the marking of fictitious premiums designed to lure the public.[55]

The enthusiasm of investors was as great for Irish offerings as it was for English. In May the offer of shares in two Dublin companies induced a flood of applications; the 2s. share seemed irresistable. Early in May the Puncture Proof Tyre Co. issue produced applications of over £300,000 for an offered amount of £20,000. Similar interest surrounded the offer of shares in the "Grappler" Pneumatic Tyre & Cycle Co. some weeks later. It was greatly oversubscribed in Dublin alone (there was "quite a rush at the banks on Saturday morning, people awaiting their turn to hand in applications"), while the Cork branch of the National Bank reported that investors there would easily have taken the entire issue.[56] The speculative fever had obviously spread south; "it behoves Cork investors to be up and doing if they are to share in the good things yet to come".[57]

By June resistance to the more recent ventures started to appear, and in July it was reflected in heavy discounts on some of the new offers. Private fears were matched by Stock Exchange concern about the bona fide of many of the "Pneumatic and other kindred companies recently formed and about to be brought out". The Stock Exchange Committee decided that they would only consider applications for special settlements after the first balance sheet had been issued and approved by the shareholders.[58] By August the market had drifted into a "state of dullness and depression not seen for many a long day".[59] There was practically no market for cycle shares with prices for the most part being merely nominal. Prices had indeed fallen greatly; Puncture Proof fell from its issue price of £4 7s. 6d. to £1 10s., and the "Grappler" from £1 15s. to 10s.

For the Stock Exchange, cycle share speculation presented a degree of activity unequalled since the railway boom, all of which produced administrative and dealing problems. Such was the volume of turnover in the early months that the Committee decided to extend the time of dealing by fifteen minutes to allow business to be finished and also to help dealings with other exchanges which had greatly increased since cycle share trading centred largely in Dublin.[60] The very heavy dealing for the account occasionally resulted in only about a tenth of the securities to be delivered changing hands by the time stated, so "great is the crush of office work at all the leading brokers offices".[61] Four special settlements at the end of June required considerable overtime in brokers' offices "to clear the block".[62] Individual brokers found problems of arranging carryover at the end of the more speculative accounts with rates as a result being very variable. They were also active in the business of assisting in share issues, receiving applications and making requests for Special Settlements to the Committee of the Stock Exchange; few companies could aspire to a full quotation. Among Dublin brokers acting for cycle companies were Molony & Murray, Manifold & Hines and Griffin & MacDougall.

The following year, 1894, saw a welcome lull in dealing, and in the number of new companies. Those that did appear managed to show a premium on the issue price at a time when their predecessors had fallen to low levels and a few had gone into liquidation since the shareholders refused to sanction a reconstruction. Low share prices reflected the disappointing profit record of cycle and tyre companies due to the decline in sales, and the disturbing realisation that many companies with large capitals, usually heavily "watered" (inflated by mere goodwill), had little in the way of working capital.[63]

Promotions and dealing spurted in 1895 when large blocks of money came to Dublin for investment from England after the election results, but the boom really got underway in the early months of 1896 due to the increased demand for cycles. Over three hundred companies were formed (a handful of them Irish) involving a nominal capital of about £24mn. The boom carried over into 1897 but then soon died off and share prices dropped sharply. Birmingham was now the centre of share dealing but Dublin continued to take a keen interest in cycle promotion; London remained relatively aloof. At one stage, on the Dublin Market, the public in the gallery became so excited "cheering and shouting instructions to their brokers that...the police had to be sent for to clear them out and to close the gallery for some time."[64] With such activity in Dublin, and more subdued trading in Birmingham, it is not surprising that prices diverged greatly between the two centres giving ample scope for shunting activity. By the end of 1897 it was all over with prices reaching a low point, reflecting excess production in the industry, foreign competition, and the gross over capitalisation of most concerns. The forty or so cycle companies whose shares were dealt in actively in Birmingham, Dublin or London, lost half their market value in 1897; less known ones lost far more.

After the euphoria of the mid-nineties and the indulgence in cycle share speculation, Irish company registrations fell off quite markedly during the Boer War years, to recover to around a hundred a year just before 1914. However, there were no significant new entrants to the Stock Exchange list over this short period since most of the large scale firms in services, transportation and manufacturing had already been made "public". But although the years up to 1914 were essentially a period of consolidation the Stock Exchange did enjoy one last speculative fling, this time in much more distant rubber plantations.

The 1910 boom in rubber plantation shares was induced by a sharp rise in the price of rubber giving established concerns high dividends, and an opportunity for promoters to float off new companies at grossly inflated capitalisations.[65] By the spring of 1910 the dozen or so older and more reliable companies found their market value standing at twenty times its nominal sum. Alongside were numerous new ventures which had been quickly launched and whose shares stood at twenty to thirty times their face value. During April brokers and Irish investors were enjoying an "unprecedented boom" with the staff in brokers' offices working "literally night and day in executing orders and carrying through these transactions; this was the first chance investors had of making some money following the long period of business stagnation after the Boer War.[66] But such high levels could not last and once rubber prices started to slide in May, share values quickly followed with a very sharp drop in the Autumn. There was a brief outbreak of speculation in the spring of 1911 and it was used by many investors as a long awaited chance to "clear out" of a highly speculative and volatile market.

A company was not automatically admitted to the Daily List, although in the early years of limited liability all that was needed was evidence of dealings taking place in the shares. By the time the 1879 Rule Book appeared a set of requirements had been developed, modelled on those of London and other major exchanges, which were designed to ensure that there were no impediments to a continuous market in shares. Thus a new company seeking a special settlement and quotation had to satisfy the Committee of its bona fide character and that it was of "sufficient magnitude and importance" to justify such a step. More particularly the Committee wanted to examine a copy of the prospectus, the act of parliament or the articles of association, the original applications for shares, the Allotment Book, see a signed certificate giving the number of shares applied for and unconditionally alloted to the public, the amount of deposits paid, and a banker's statement to that effect. It was laid down that one half of the nominal capital should be issued and that two thirds of the amount issued should be applied for and unconditionally allotted to the public, with 10% paid on allotment (shares allotted to vendors, contractors, etc, did not count as part of the allotment). Among other requirements was the stipulation that a "member of the Stock Exchange must be authorised by the Company to give full information as to the formation of the undertaking and be able to furnish the Committee with all particulars they may require". When a company wanted only a special settlement (that is, the completion of bargains already done) the Committee was mainly concerned to ensure, before giving its authority for the enforcement of bargains, that the shares were adequately distributed, the deposits paid and no impediment existed to prevent transfers.[67] Normally companies were able to satisfy the requirements with no difficulty but in the 1890s some were refused a special settlement. One notable example was the refusal of the Committee to grant a special settlement in September 1893 to the shares of the cycle company, Stewart James Pneumatic Type Co. Ltd., since the allotment was such as to enable a "corner" to be attempted in the shares. It was only averted from closing on many speculators when the directors threw their shares on the market.[68]

From 1895 the Committee of the Cork Stock Exchange required all new companies seeking a special settlement to prove their bona fides and that the allotment of shares to the public had been suitably made, all to be put before the Committee through the agency of a member firm. Some years later in 1901, the Stock Exchange adopted Dublin requirements for special settlements and quotation, and if a company already quoted in Dublin requested a Cork listing the local requirements were waived.[69] The accusation was sometimes made that small stock exchanges granted a quotation too leniently and acceded to the wishes of companies that were too small. On the evidence available from the conduct of the Cork market in the pre-war years, they followed London requirements in almost every particular, and on occasions the Committee was prepared to take companies off the list "should sufficiently frequent dealings not take place in them".[70]

The complaint was often made in the nineteenth century that there was a shortage of capital in Ireland, which in turn contributed to the low level of development. The available evidence does not give a great deal of support to this notion. Funds flowed out of the country in the form of holdings of English government debt and foreign securities of many varieties; money was found in large amounts for the capital intensive public utility projects launched at various intervals; and, in the latter half of the century, while most of the companies registered under the Companies Acts were small and were no more than private companies with a public "shell" many large concerns were floated off, especially in the 1890s, and the Irish investor at least on this occasion did not wait to follow the lead of his English counterpart. What is apparent in this particular group of companies, as represented by those of sufficient size to merit a stock exchange quotation, was that they were largely concentrated in the service and transportation industries and in a few trades where the export market was very important, for example, biscuits and mineral waters. The notable absentees are a large number of manufacturing companies, although a few light manufacturing firms did surface as witnessed by the cycle boom. In general, however, manufacturing was but sparsely represented. This is not to say that its absence was due to a want of capital, other elements were clearly far more crucial. Proximity to a large manufacturing neighbour may account for a great deal of the reluctance of such firms to emerge in Ireland, but also the size of the local market was not sufficient to enable firms to grow to the point where significant economies of scale could be achieved and at which large sums of capital would be needed. The capital market at the end of the century served the visible needs of companies; where its contribution was small this was due not to lack of funds but to the absence of demand.

# NOTES

1. The Bubble Act, 6 George I, c. 18, did not apply in Ireland.
2. A list of subscribers is given in F.G. Hall, *The Bank of Ireland 1783-1946*, (1949), pp. 508-10.
3. *Freeman's Journal*, March 14 1793.
4. No doubt dealings in the other canal shares took place periodically but they were small concerns in comparison to the big two.
5. 11 & 12 George 3, c. 31.
6. Details of these loans are given in The Debt of Ireland – Funded in Ireland (Irish Currency), Report of the Proceedings of the Commissioners of the National Debt from 1786 to 31st March 1890, B.P.P., Vol. XLVIII, 1890-91.
7. V.T.H. & D.R. Delany, *The Canals of the South of Ireland*, (1966), p. 77.
8. Among the total, 54 took £300 each, 59 had £600, 44 took £1,000, and 14 had £2,000; Report from the Committee on a Petition from the Royal Canal Co., B.P.P., 1812-13, VI:35.
9. In 1944 the canal became part of C.I.E.
10. *Journal of the Irish House of Commons*, February 18 1782, p. 303.
11. Bankers or shops selling by retail did not come within the scope of the act.
12. In the *Report on the Law of Partnership* of 1837 (B.P.P., XLIV (303)) H. Bellenden Kerr suggested that the risks attending failure to comply with the strict and minute provisions of the 1782 act might have deterred Irish capitalists from adopting its provisions; it did not apparently deter them a great deal during 1801-15.
13. *Royal Mercantile Law Commission*, B.P.P., 1854, XXVII, Appendix, p. 299; Return from the Register of Deeds Office, Ireland.
14. ibid., p. 236; reply of the Dublin Chamber of Commerce.
15. ibid., evidence of James Kennedy, Belfast. Under the act's provisions a company could not use surplus capital to discount bills, while if it happened to "break bulk in any way", the limited partners could lose all the advantages of their position.
16. H. English, *A Complete View of the Joint Stock Companies formed during 1824 and 1825*, (1827), p. 31.
17. A list is given in Appendix No. 1, *Report of the Select Committee on Joint Stock Companies*, B.P.P., 1844, VII, pp. 612-13. Three other companies which appeared at the time were the Irish Company for Promoting Manufactures, the Irish Bogs Draining Co., and the Irish Patriotic Insurance Co. The latter was to appear in the Stock Exchange list so it obviously proved a successful floatation.
18. Most of these companies had shares of high denomination, £100 to £250, but with only 5% paid up.
19. Full details are given in G.L. Barrow, *The Emergence of the Irish Banking*

*System 1820-45*, (1975), pp. 69-71. Since it only conducted limited discounting business profits were modest, which was reflected in its share price of £19 in 1830.

20. ibid., p. 30.

21. Commercial Insurance Company; Partnership Deed 1824.

22. The Ulster Bank, also formed in February 1836, was not listed in Dublin until the 1860s. The shareholders were largely from Ulster — 90% of the initial 830, involving a total paid up capital of £204,000; see Barrow, op. cit., p. 130.

23. ibid., p. 130.

24. Its Deed of Settlement was signed in May 1836. It did not obtain an act of parliament and was in effect a large partnership with transferable shares.

25. Barrow, op. cit., p. 135.

26. 9 George IV, c. LXVII, (Local and Personal Acts).

27. Petitions against the proposed legislation came from dock and shipping interests in Belfast, Liverpool, Greenock, Glasgow and Londonderry; *House of Commons Journals*, Vol 83.

28. Speech by William Roche, *Hansard*, Vol. 32, April 1836, pp. 1,190.

29. *Hansard*, Vol. 32, p. 1,189.

30. Four of the charter companies were involved with land, peat and agriculture; others were for fishing, mining and a submarine telegraph company. The capital authorised ranged from £100,000 to £500,000; *Return of all applications for charters with limited liability*, B.P.P., 1854, LXV.

31. The provisions of the act did not apply to partnerships formed in Ireland under the Anonymous Partnerships Act of 1782.

32. H. A. Shannon, "The First Five Thousand Limited Companies and their Duration", *Economic History*, 1932, p. 420. He compiled the figures from manuscript registers at Somerset House.

33. Shannon put the failure rate for all companies which entered registration in Britain and Ireland at 50%;, ibid., p. 397.

34. H. A. Shannon, "The Coming of General Limited Liability", *Economic History*, 1932, pp. 374-78; see also P. L. Cottrell, *Industrial Finance 1830-1914*, (1979), chapter 3.

35. Castleblayney Gas Light Co. Ltd. with a paid up capital of £2,500 and 20 shareholders; Navan Gas Co. Ltd, £2,000 paid up and 41 shareholders; Kilrush Gas Co. Ltd., £1,420 paid up and 29 shareholders.

36. Some minor amendments were made to it by an Act of 1857, 20 & 21 Vict., c. 14.

37. Calculated from Return Relating to Joint Stock Companies; Companies Registered in England, B.P.P., 1907, LXXVI, 549.

38. Return Relating to Joint Stock Companies etc., IRELAND, B.P.P., 1864, LV111, 291. Other mines on the Dublin list in 1862 were Crookhaven, General Mining Co., Hibernian, and the Mining Company of Ireland, the last two dating from the 1820s.

39. *Freeman's Journal* was registered as a limited company in 1887 with a paid up capital of £33,332 and 752 shareholders.

40. See Hall, op. cit., for a full account, pp. 279-94.

41. Objects of the Belfast Discount Co. This company had a nominal capital of £20,000 in £10 shares, £5 paid up but only a quarter of the capital was issued and the £2,500 involved was held by 22 shareholders.

42. These were York Street, Edenderry, Falls Flax, Brookfield, Whiteabbey, and Island Spinning Co.

43. The number of shareholders in each bank had increased greatly between incorporation and limitation; the Belfast Banking Co. from 302 to 1,525,

Northern from 272 to 2,242, Ulster from 526 to 2,860, Royal Bank from 1,339 to 2,081, and the Hibernian from 986 to 2,202. The average shareholding in the Dublin banks halved during the period — Royal from £224 to £144; Hibernian from £380 to £227 — but that of the northern banks fell by far more — Belfast from £827 to £163, Northern from £1,102 to £135 and the Ulster from £572 to £134. For details of the formation of the three Belfast banks see Barrow, op. cit., pp. 65-68, 82-3, 129-31.

44. E.B. Maguire, *Irish Whiskey*, (1973), pp. 246-81.

45. Dublin Stock Exchange, Minutes, June 13 1876. This was the Dublin Skating Rink Co., nominal capital £12,000, paid up £9,500, but with only 17 shareholders.

46. There was a lull in 1894-95, three appeared in 1896 and none in 1897.

47. H.A. Shannon, "The Limited Companies of 1866 and 1883", *Economic History Review*, 1932-33, p. 307.

48. The overseas interests of Irish investors took in tramways in Rio de Janeiro, Saõ Paulo, Mexico, British Columbia and Argentina, as well as large English companies.

49. *Royal Commission on the Depression of Trade and Industry*, First Report, B.P.P., 1886, Vol. XXI, Q. 679.

50. L.M. Cullen, *An Economic History of Ireland since 1660*, (1972), p. 155. The number of creameries grew from about 30 in 1893 to 230 or so in 1902.

51. The firm of Carey & Buckley withdrew some weeks later, alleging that quotations had been incorrectly made. The other member firms of the Exchange were F.W. Allen, A. Beale, R.W. Belton, J.H. Carroll & Sons (J.H. Carroll, T.F. Carroll, J.H. Carroll), W.P. Clarke, E. Hayes, Walter Morrogh, R.A. Robinson (R.S.O. Robinson, A.C. Robinson) and H.R. Townsend (H. Townsend, R.Townsend, W.H. Beamish). All had offices in South Mall.

52. In Cork, companies registered between 1890-97 represented nearly 40% of all registrations since 1864; for other towns the percentages were — Waterford 40%, Derry 62%, Limerick 54%, Newry 40%, and for the rest of the country 34%.

53. *Statist*, June 3 1893, pp. 604-5.

54. *Irish Times*, February 13 1893.

55. *Irish Times*, May 10 1893.

56. *Irish Times*, May 26 1893.

57. *Finance Union*, January 14 1893.

58. Dublin Stock Exchange, Minutes, June 7 1893.

59. *Irish Times*, July 19 1893.

60. *Irish Times*, January 24 1893.

61. *Irish Times*, June 1 1893.

62. *Irish Times*, June 22 1893.

63. On the promotional techniques used by the leading company promoters, E.T. Hooley and Harry J. Lawson, see W.A. Thomas, *The Provincial Stock Exchanges*, (1973), pp. 130-31.

64. *Irish Tatler and Sketch*, February 1960, p. 43.

65. About 40 of these estates were registered in Scotland (the bulk of the others were London creations) and in 1912 they had a paid up capital of £2.2mn, with capitalisations ranging from £20,000 to £150,000. Mostly, they used £1 shares with a few companies resorting to 2s ones; Thomas, op. cit., pp. 311-12.

66. *Irish Investors Guardian*, March 1910. Even at the point of issue most of the capital was heavily watered by way of "promoters profits".

67. Such was the steady flow of applications in the 1890s that a sub-committee was set up, consisting of the Vice-President, the Secretary and the solicitor to

the Stock Exchange, to report on each application.

68.   Dublin Stock Exchange Minutes, September 5 1893; *Irish Times*, September 16 1893.

69.   When local companies sought a quotation the Committee was anxious to see the relevant documents since some of them had clauses which imposed restraints on share transfer; Cork Stock Exchange, Minutes, September 1907.

70.   Cork Stock Exchange, Minutes, May 31 1897.

# CHAPTER 9

# IRISH GOVERNMENT SECURITIES

From the small beginnings of a clandestine loan raised by the first Dáil Éireann in 1919 the national debt of the Irish Free State had reached £73mn in 1937, the marketable portion consisting of £24mn in National Loans and £27mn in Land Bonds. By 1968, when the *Report of the Committee on the Functions, Operation and Development of a Money Market in Ireland* appeared, the total nominal debt of the country stood at £750mn, with Irish government bonds accounting for £386mn and Land Bonds a further £35mn.[1] In the next decade or so the debt grew even more alarmingly, the total domestic debt reaching £2,200mn in 1975, with a further £470mn in foreign debt. Out of the total debt about £1,500mn was quoted on the Dublin Stock Exchange. By 1984 the total of Irish marketable securities had risen to £7,672mn.

Following the signing of the Anglo-Irish Treaty in December 1921 the Irish Free State came into being in December 1922. The early years of the government, formed after elections in July, proved difficult. Civil War during 1922-23 led to heavy expenditure which could not be met from taxation, forcing the government to resort to short term borrowing from the banks.[2] When this dependence became too great in the eyes of both lender and borrower, the government in 1923 made the first of its National Loans. This was to set the pattern for government financing for several decades. Throughout the twenties the government ran a modest deficit on its current account of around £1mn (despite the depression a similar level existed in the thirties), financing this in the short term through issues of saving certificates, Exchequer bills and Ways and Means Advances from the banks. As these sources built up they were then funded by a large National Loan, which usually left enough over to defray the next year's deficit. This appears to have been the pattern in the case of the loans made in 1923, 1927, 1930, 1933, 1939 and 1941. The other loans of the inter-war period, the 1935 Conversion Loan and the 1938 Financial Reconstruction Loan, were undertaken for specific financial purposes (see below).

Although the first National Loan was made in 1923 the Department of Finance had already acquired some experience in fund raising some time before this when the Dáil, formed in 1919 and not recognised by the British government, set out to obtain money to cover its expenditure since it had no means of collecting taxes. When Dáil Éireann assembled in January 1919 one of its first acts was to appoint a Minister of Finance, the holder of the post being Michael Collins. He was charged with the duty of raising revenue to meet the expenditure of the other newly formed departments and for the purpose of prosecuting the Anglo-Irish War. Michael Collins was not entirely unversed in financial matters since for about four years before 1914 he was a clerk with a London firm of stockbrokers.[3] The Dáil duly approved a loan prospectus for an issue of £250,000, in small denominations, and the new Ministry proceeded to advertise the offer widely despite the illegal nature of their activities. To evade capture Michael Collins had elaborate arrangements for concealing the work of the Ministry, while the proceeds of the loan were lodged in Dublin banks in the names of several individuals. Despite great difficulties the loan realised £370,165.[4]

The first National Loan, at 5% for a total of £10mn, was made in December 1923.[5] Earlier, in the spring, the Department of Finance thought it desirable to look at the possibility of raising money on the open market since relations between itself and the banks were gradually worsening due to the size of the government's borrowing, and the Department was anxious to proceed on orthodox financial lines by dealing with permanent deficits through long term borrowing. A successful issue, however, needed the support of the banks and the stockbrokers who were essential to the promotion of the loan and its later marketability. In April Joseph Brennan and J. J. McElligott, Secretary and Assistant Secretary of the Department of Finance, met the Committee of the Stock Exchange to discuss the prospects for an early issue of government securities. The Department suggested a loan in the region of £25mn which the Stock Exchange thought too large for the market to absorb, while it would also need large banking involvement by way of underwriting, and they also regarded a guarantee as to the principal and interest from the British government as a necessary safeguard to mollify local investors.[6] One alternative would be a London loan but the Bank of Ireland advised the Department that in the prevailing financial conditions the money market there would not regard it favourably. Despite the difficulties it was obvious that an internal loan would soon be imperative but it was decided to leave the matter until after the September elections, and the banks obliged with more short term accommodation in the meantime. With a more settled political climate after the election arrangements for a loan went ahead.

The 5% National Loan, redeemable between 1935-45 at the option of the government, was offered for public subscription in December 1923 with the Bank of Ireland acting as agent to the government. It could be held either in registered or inscribed form, transfer registers being kept in Dublin and Cork. The £10mn of stock was offered at a price of 95, with £10 on application, £20 on allotment and the rest in two instalments. It gave a yield of 5¼%, a little above comparable British stocks. The dividends, distributed in June and December, would be paid without deduction of income tax, and non-resident holders would be exempt from income tax. A commission of ¼% was allowed to bankers, stockbrokers and finance houses on allotments made on applications bearing their stamps. The stock was quoted in Dublin and Cork.

Under the direction of J.J. McElligott an extensive publicity campaign was undertaken and the issue proved a complete success. Such was the response that the application list was closed three days early, while the loan was over subscribed by some £200,000. None of the loan had to be underwritten; indeed the banks had only offered to underwrite £4mn of it if they got 2% underwriting commission. The ready response from investors delighted the Department of Finance and surprised both bankers and stockbrokers. When dealings opened on the Stock Exchange on January 7 1924 the loan rose 4 points to 99, putting it virtually on par with War Loan stock.[7]

Several elements probably contributed to the success of the loan. The higher yield, compared to that available on British gilt edged, may well have induced some switching, while the dearth of Irish trustee stocks meant that it was filling an obvious gap (Dublin Corporation stocks at the time yielded only 4¾%). It was also reported that Irish funds had been withdrawn from London due to the complexities associated with income tax and the prospects of double taxation. Further, there was an understandable disposition to support the new government, with money coming from not only a large number of small investors but also from unlikely minority interests, including the Church of Ireland and the Grand Lodge of Freemasons of Ireland. But perhaps the most powerful attraction was the generous Sinking Fund scheme. To cover interest and the Sinking Fund provision, the government set aside annually a sum equal to 7½% of the nominal amount of the loan, that is, £750,000 of which £500,000 would be for interest, and the balance of the money would be applied to the purchase of stock if the price was below or even above par. Naturally this was seen as an important source of support for the market price, indeed some commentators felt that the "arrangements for the application of the Sinking Fund contemplate that it may go above par".[8]

During the remainder of the inter-war years the Irish Free State made six more loan issues at intervals of about two to three years. The Second

National Loan (1950-60) was issued in December 1927 with a coupon of 5% and offered at 97, giving a redemption yield to 1960 of 5.2%. It was distinctive in that it was issued simultaneously at home and in New York. Of the £7mn or so raised, just over £4mn was obtained at home, while $15mn came from New York subscriptions. A register was kept in each centre and holders were entitled to transfer between them at a fixed conversion rate of $1,000 for £205 9s.8d. The Third National Loan (1950-70) followed in May 1930, for a total of £6mn, with a coupon of 4½% and issued at 93½% giving a redemption yield of 4.87%. Like its predecessor it was successfully floated.

However, the Fourth National Loan was not so fortunate since it was made in the greatly altered economic circumstances of 1933. The loan for £6mn, redeemable between 1950-70, carried a coupon of 3½% and was offered at 98 giving a redemption yield of 3.6%. It proved a disappointment for the authorities since it was only partially taken up by the public, the unsubscribed balance being absorbed by the underwriters. Investors withheld their support due to the uncertain economic conditions, but the government had also been negligent in ensuring that there was no competition from other issues at the same time. Shortly before the National Loan appeared Dublin Corporation made a loan, also at 3½% but priced at 96, thereby giving a better yield than its bigger rival. This offer also was not fully subscribed but it may well have attracted funds which otherwise might have gone to the government loan.[9]

The other loans for cash were made shortly after the outbreak of the Second World War; in December 1939 and in November 1941. The 1939 loan was in 4% Exchequer Bonds 1950-60, issued at par for the sum of £7mn. Primarily prompted by the need to raise funds to cover an existing, and most likely a future deficit, the Minister of Finance was also anxious that "any funds available for investment here should be put into this loan rather than into British war issues".[10] Despite the Minister's wishes investors, on a falling market, did not rush to take up stock, while the banks expressed unease about the possibility that the money raised would merely swell current expenditure. The public took up £4mn, partly financed by selling sterling assets, a further £1mn was taken up by the Minister on behalf of various government funds, and the balance was left to the underwriters. Considering the prevailing uncertainty the loan did reasonably well but there was a feeling that it might have done better if the London Treasury had allowed British subscriptions.[11]

In marked contrast the 1941 offer of £8mn of 3¼% National Security Loan (1956-61), issued at 99, to meet abnormal defence expenditure, was heavily oversubscribed. By this time the uncertainties of 1939 had been reduced since the country had secured neutral status. On the financial front local investors, both personal and institutional, were eagerly looking for suitable outlets for their idle cash resources. All this was reflected in the behaviour of Stock Exchange prices. Between 1938 and 1939 the major loans had fallen by about four points, but by 1941 they had recovered to their previous level. As reflected in a general index of market prices the onset of the war caused the level to fall to 98.6 from 103.2 in 1937 (1938=100), but by 1941 the return of confidence was sufficient to raise the index to 104.4.[12]

Alongside these cash loans there were two rather special issues, the 1935 Conversion Loan and the 1938 Financial Agreement Loan. One of the conditions attached to the First National Loan of 1923 was that the government could repay it at par in 1945, or exercise the option to redeem the stock at par on or after December 1 1935 on giving three months notice to all holders. When the loan was made money was relatively expensive so that by 1935 interest on the loan accounted for over 30% of interest on all debt outstanding and its sinking fund requirement took 60% of all such provision.[13] Conversion to a lower interest rate would ease the burden of financing, and produce significant savings. With government stocks, including the 5% National Loan, standing at large premiums the opportunity presented itself of putting out a replacement stock with a lower coupon rate. Accordingly, the government decided to exercise the conversion right and offered investors 4% Conversion Loan Stock (1950-70) at par; market yields stood at around 4% at the time. Holders of £7mn of the National Loan (the amount still outstanding) were thus offered conversion into an equal nominal amount of the new stock, or redemption at par. Cash subscriptions were also invited for the new stock, but in the event the offer proved so popular that very little of the total issued was available for new subscribers. Indeed, it proved necessary to return all applications for sums over £200, small investors being given preference over others. In all £6.8mn of the new stock was issued in conversion for the old and the remainder, nearly £190,00, for cash at par.[14]

The 3¾% Financial Agreement Loan (1953-58), was issued at par in May 1938 shortly after the government had agreed to pay £10mn in final settlement of financial claims to the United Kingdom. The market, however, did not have to absorb the full £10mn offered since the Minister of Finance took £4mn for various funds under his control. Even so the speed with which the total was raised pleased the Department of Finance, surprised the Bank of England, and enabled the settlement to be completed ahead of the agreed date. Since the Financial Agreement removed one of the major political disabilities of Irish loans, the offer succeeded in attracting a fair amount of British and continental interest with about one third of early applications for the loan coming from those quarters.[15]

The four National Loans made between 1923 and 1933, all to raise cash, were issued at a discount, ranging from 93½ on the third to 98 on the fourth. One advantage of this was that the sinking fund provision could be more easily applied assuming that interest rates did not fall appreciably. On the other hand, the disadvantage of a large discount and a low nominal rate was that it might prejudice any further prospects for carrying out a conversion after the optional redemption date since the loan would be less likely to go to a premium. In the event the terms of the loans gave the Department of Finance the best of both worlds. Up until 1933 the annual highs and lows for the loans ranged from small discounts to large premiums, affording some opportunity for sinking fund purchases, while the premium of about 5% on the first National Loan provided the chance to convert to a 4% stock. With the advent of cheap money in the thirties the Second and Third National Loans went to hefty premiums, the former reaching 118 in 1936, the latter 114¾ in 1937. Even the 3½% Fourth National Loan, issued in 1933, showed a 5% premium in 1936; it fell in the next few years to a discount of some 3% thus enabling sinking fund purchases to be made. Presumably these National Loans were not candidates for conversion since their terms were not as onerous as those attached to the first.

Although the First National Loan was successfully completed without the comforting safeguard of underwriting, the other loans were so insured. It was arranged by the Irish Banks Standing Committee, who in turn offered a portion of the underwriting to the Stock Exchange. For the main loans Stock Exchange participation was usually around 10% of the loan, although members and their clients were prepared to take a larger commitment with the applications coming to twice the amount on offer. In this case applications for small sums were granted in full with the larger ones being scaled down on a pro rata basis.[16]

An important feature of all the loans made in the inter-war years, and indeed later, was the provision of a sinking fund. For stockholders this meant that there would be a persistent buyer in the market, particularly if the price was below par. The prospectuses of the loans specified the sums to be set aside, usually every six months, and after deducting the amount required for the payment of interest "the balance of the sum so set aside will be carried to a Sinking Fund which will be applied during the succeeding half year to the purchase of the loan for cancellation if the price is at or under par; when the price is above par, it will be either so applied or otherwise invested for the benefit of the Sinking Fund under the control of the Minister of Finance".[17] The First National Loan carried an extremely generous sinking fund provision, which no doubt allayed some nervousness on the part of investors in taking up a loan from the newly formed State. However, the succeeding loans were not so amply provided for, the annual amounts set aside being about 1% of the loans compared with 2½% for the first.[18] By 1937 the unapplied Sinking Fund amounted to £180,000, equivalent to 0.7% of the total stock on the market; indeed in 1935 J.J. McElligott admitted that "we find it difficult to invest some of these sinking funds".[19] Their application in the market, an important influence on the price of government securities, rested with the Department of Finance and the orders were duly executed on the floor of the Stock Exchange by the

Government Broker. In 1924 the Department appointed the firm of Butler & Briscoe to act for it, initially on half commission basis but some months later the Committee of the Stock Exchange agreed to a request that they should be allowed to act as broker to the Department for a fixed payment.[20]

A sizeable portion of the marketable debt consisted of Land Bonds; in 1937 £26.7mn out of a total debt of £51.3mn.[21] Three issues were involved, namely 4½% Land Bonds, to the sum of £24.3mn and which carried a sterling guarantee as to principal and interest from the British government, and the rest in 4½% New Land Bonds issued under the Land Bond Acts of 1933 and 1934 without such a guarantee. They were created to finance the purchase of tenanted land in the "congested districts", the vendors receiving Land Bonds, while the land acquired was transferred to the Land Commission, ultimately to be vested in the tenants as owners and in return they paid an appropriate annuity.[22] Issued in denominations of £100, £10 and £1, the 4½% Land Bonds were quoted not only in Dublin and Cork but also for some years on the London Stock Exchange. This additional accolade, coupled with the sterling guarantee, made them a popular form of investment in the inter-war period and they were "always a big attraction".[23] If holders did not wish to sell them to obtain cash, the bonds were also redeemable by the operation of a half yearly sinking fund. However, for most of these years the Bonds stood at a premium, occasionally quite a large one, which could prove a frustrating experience should the holder of a registered bond find that his holding had been drawn for redemption at par.[24]

Apart from the dollar portion of the Second National Loan (estimated at around $985,000 in 1937), the other loans, and the Conversion Loan, were almost entirely held within the country, the only important exception being the banks incorporated outside the Irish Free State but who did extensive business within it. In 1937 banks held about £3.6mn of stock, compared with an estimated £4.6mn in 1934. Land Bonds, again, for the most part were held internally, although the 4½% Land Bonds, with their sterling guarantee and London quotation were held "to an appreciable extent outside". Of the total of £51.3mn of marketable securities outstanding in 1937 government departments held about £8.3mn, with a further £880,000 held by public authorities and institutions. Given the banks' holdings, this left about three quarters of marketable debt in the hands of the personal and company sectors.[25]

In the mid-thirties some £25mn of government securities (excluding Land Bonds) were quoted on the Dublin market, and also on the Cork Stock Exchange. With this fairly modest total, and given the nature of some of the holders, it was not to be expected that there would have been a very active two way market in the debt. The government held about a quarter of it and they were generally more interested in buying than selling, while personal holders were mainly motivated by income rather than capital gain, and there was little in the way of participation by financial institutions (their main holdings of stocks and dealing activity were centred in London). Indeed, the Stock Exchange representatives told the 1938 Banking Commission that the market was "wonderfully good in the circumstances, but the sum total was small". The tendency was for the market to be one way with a preponderance of sellers or buyers; when a buyer turned up there was a rush to supply him with stock, the price falling by about a point in a day, and when there might be half a dozen buyers in the market there would be no seller, the price then rising sharply to induce sales.[26] Small deals posed no great problems and were executed quickly but considerable difficulty surrounded larger amounts. A sale of £30,000 of stock could take up to a month to complete.

That the market was "not a bad [one] for government securities" was due in large measure to the activities of the Government Broker acting on behalf of the Department of Finance. Very often he was the only buyer on the market and as a general rule he was always prepared to make a price. He was certainly the main avenue whereby large blocks could be accommodated and to this end he was under instructions to inform the Department of Finance when there were "large Stocks floating about". In the case of sales on the market the not inconsiderable resources of the Sinking Funds were available to assist marketability. But the Department of Finance was also eager to encourage the growth of a two way market, where the public would be not only ready sellers but willing buyers as well. To this end they had a number of official holdings from which they sold stock so as to get "the public interested in the securities".[27] The Secretary of the Department, J.J. McElligott, told the Banking Commission that by such willingness to sell "we got large interests amongst the Free State public in our Securities". Naturally the larger the turnover on the market the more readily would it absorb any additional issues of stock. Despite these encouraging moves it remained a small market indeed compared to the London giant and the differential of $\frac{1}{2}$% to $\frac{3}{4}$% between Irish and London yields reflected the limited marketability on the Dublin floor.[28]

After the 1941 National Security Loan no issues of long term stock appeared on the market until March 1948. While Ireland remained neutral during the war there was nevertheless a sharp increase in expenditure on the army, and in the civil services, which together produced an average deficit on current account over the war years of around £2.5mn. This, coupled with restrained capital expenditure and fairly large repayments of advances from the Local Loans and other Funds, produced overall deficits of about £3.0mn for most years, with an actual surplus in 1943-44. Although savings continued to rise, and was reflected in bank deposit figures and the liabilities of other financial institutions, all of whom might well have welcomed an issue of government stock, the government saw no need to tap this growing pool in that way since it covered its deficit needs by resort to short term finance. By the end of the war small savers provided an annual inflow of over

£1.0mn which together with Ways and Means Advances and some from "other borrowing", covered the financial needs of the government for most years, indeed up to 1948. The absence of government issues meant that the Dublin capital market "has been very idle". Government stocks appreciated in value significantly over the early years of the war and despite a later lapse they closed above the pre-war level. During this time the customary gap in yields between Irish and British stocks narrowed somewhat, their improved standing no doubt reflecting the lack of alternative domestic outlets for the growing volume of savings.

It was the launching of the Public Capital Programme soon after the war which led to a considerable enlargement of the quoted debt. During the years 1947-51 government capital spending increased fourfold, along with higher current expenditure. The aim of the capital programme was to improve the economy's infrastructure, with emphasis on projects in construction, power supply, transport and communications. In terms of the consequent need for funds the government's borrowing requirement rose markedly. For example, the average overall borrowing requirement for 1946-48 was about £6.0mn, but by 1951-53 it was of the order of £28.0mn. A small part of the funds came from personal savers, and money was also used from Marshall Aid resources during 1949-51, while temporary accommodation was as ever obtained from Ways and Means Advances. But the bulk of the long term finance was covered by issues of government stock which took the form of a series of well publicised National Loans designed to absorb savings, particularly from the agricultural sector. The loans were also seen as a means of attracting funds away from external investments, and to both these ends, domestic and external, they carried attractive yields and generous sinking funds.[29] The prospect of attracting British money into the loans was greatly diminished by the ban imposed by the London Treasury on advertising overseas issues in London.[30]

The next few years saw the virtual stagnation of public expenditure, and in particular reduced capital spending, which was reflected in both the borrowing requirement and in the financing needs of the government. A deflationary fiscal policy was accompanied by a desire to switch resources away from what was seen as unproductive public investment towards more productive projects likely to contribute to growth, as later set out in the blueprint *Economic Development* in 1958. These general influences led to reduced borrowing by way of National Loans, the average for 1954-60 being only £15.0mn, with the average borrowing requirement for the period running at £28.0mn (the difference came largely from Ways and Means Advances and the re-introduction of Exchequer bills).

However, from 1959 onwards, current and capital expenditure was put on an expanding basis, the overall borrowing requirement increasing nearly fivefold between 1959 and 1968. During the early sixties aggregate demand was boosted by the high level of public sector investment, and the resulting increase in the borrowing requirement played a key role in the stimulation of the economy. Indeed to sustain such expenditures in 1965-66, when the normal channel of small savings and National Loans could not meet government requirements, not only did it resort to additional short term bank accommodation but for the first time foreign borrowing was undertaken, some £23mn in 1965-66, followed by £9mn a year later, a move which would not have been contemplated some years earlier.[31] This was at a time when the volume of finance raised by loan issues had reached a peak, nearly £90mn in the financial years 1965-67. From meeting, on average, about 50% of the borrowing requirement during 1960-62 by loan issues, the level of dependence rose to 63% in 1965-67. The obvious importance of this source of funds, and the need to resort to external borrowing clearly pointed to the significance of the bond market. As part of its policy of building up the financial system to cater more fully for domestic needs the Central Bank undertook a detailed study of the money and bond markets and this was published in 1968 as the *Report* of the *Committee on the Functions, Operation and Development of a Money Market in Ireland.*

The Money Market *Report* was able to note that within the recent past the financial system had seen an increase in the number of institutions, a development linked to the growth of the economy and in particular to the level of savings, and it observed that the financial sector was displaying signs of greater "maturity" in the sense of being less dependent on the London market than was the case ten years earlier. But there was still a considerable way to go. The leading financial institutions continued to hold the greater part of their bond portfolios in gilt edged securities. For example, the Associated Banks, grouped around the Bank of Ireland and the Allied Irish Banks, still had about threequarters of their investments in London. These had been built up over the years but the most important factor in their continued role in the asset structure of the banks was "the state of the market in this country". Before 1964 it was usually the case that deals at quoted prices could only be done up to £50,000.[32] On the other hand the banks' holdings of Irish bonds had grown somewhat from the low level of a mere 6% of investments in 1950, largely under the impetus of underwriting and some direct issues of bonds to the banks in the early sixties. A similar picture prevailed in the rest of the banking sector; in 1968 24 institutions held a modest £1.2mn of Irish bonds. Their general shyness about domestic debt reflected the view that they found the absence of an active market in government short term bonds a shortcoming in the Irish financial sector, and they therefore regarded the London market as "more attractive for this kind of investment".[33] Similar views, and practices, prevailed amongst other financial institutions.

The total of Irish government bonds (including £34.3mn of Land Bonds) outstanding in September 1968 was £420mn. Roughly 60% of stocks were in the medium to long term range, with the rest in the shorter range of 1-10 years. Of the total, Departmental Funds and the Central Bank held about 16%, the remainder was held by the public and the various domestic financial institutions. Exchanges of stocks between these holders generated a turnover of some £128mn in 1967 which represented about 30% of the total stock outstanding in the case of short term stock, and about 45% of the longer dated stock. However, the bulk of these transactions involved the Government Broker, as either buyer or seller, since there was "very little matching of requirements between the other brokers in the market". In rare cases where the Government Broker was unable to satisfy the demand for a particular issue "other brokers have obtained the required amount of the Bond from their clients".[34] In quantitative terms the prominent role of the Government Broker is clearly apparent in the figures for 1967 where he was involved in nearly 90% of the business conducted.[35]

Evidently the bond market had several deficiencies which would have to be removed if it was to serve as a major channel for institutional investment, as a significant source of funds for the government, or as a means of assisting conventional monetary control by the use of open market operations. In line with the dominance of the Government Broker the prices which ruled on the market were generally those quoted by him, and apart from short bonds all the others tended to give the same redemption yield, so greatly reducing the scope for any switching activity. As the Committee noted "the prices which prevail in the Stock Exchange are those fixed periodically by the Government Broker, acting on behalf of the Department". But in addition to price problems there were also difficulties as to volume. While the market catered reasonably satisfactorily for the investment needs of the small personal saver, the larger institutional investor found great difficulty in executing quickly large deals of around £1mn, particularly in the short and medium term stocks. Marketability would have to improve if greater institutional activity was to be encouraged; deals of about £1mn at the short end, without affecting price, would be required. To remedy some of these defects a series of measures were instituted over the succeeding years which were designed to reduce dealing costs, widen the range of securities available, increase the amounts outstanding of individual issues, and add to the resources at the disposal of the Central Bank and Departmental Funds generally so that they would be in a position not only to buy but also to sell stock, thereby helping to create a more active market.

To encourage dealing in short bonds the margins between buying and selling prices quoted by the Government Broker were reduced from $1/4$% to $1/16$% for the two shortest stocks on the market, and to $1/8$% on other stocks up to five years maturity. Even so, it meant that the stock had to be held for several days for the accrued interest to be sufficient to offset the margin if the bond was re-sold at the same middle price. The other element of cost, broker's commission, was also reduced for short stocks (up to 5 years), especially for deals of £200,000 or more.[36] Also, in 1969, the Department of

Finance allowed the Government Broker to deal in £100,000 of stock without altering the price, compared to the previous limit of £50,000; the limit was gradually raised thereafter.

With the growth in the size of the borrowing requirement from around £130mn in the early seventies to an average of £1,800mn in 1981-84, issues of stock clearly came to play an important role in meeting the government's financing needs.[37] The pace of borrowing was such, however, that while the government exploited as far as possible the supply of domestic savings through the bond market, it was also forced to rely heavily on bank and overseas funds. It would probably not have been possible to extract more funds from the bond market without an appreciable rise in rates and perhaps risking the collapse of the market. As it was, the government's needs soon rendered the traditional National Loans a very inadequate conveyer of funds.

Up until 1975 part of the funds obtained by bond issues came from the yearly National Loan. This regular autumnal feature was designed to tap small savings for national development purposes, but it was becoming apparent that the sums so raised were modest compared with overall needs, and that the proportion derived from small savings was falling as investors put more money into financial institutions and probably diversified their assets away from fixed interest securities. The Annual Report of the Central Bank for 1962 spoke hopefully of the "growth in applications for the relatively small amounts, which indicates an encouraging rise in the participation of individuals as opposed to institutional investors in the capital issue market". In the case of the National Loans made between 1957-61 some 60% of the money raised, on average, came from applications of under £10,000, and only 25% of funds came from institutional investors in the £100,000 plus category. By the early seventies this homely picture had altered markedly. Taking applications for the period 1971-75 only 23% of the funds, on average, were derived from small savers, that is applications under £10,000, while the proportion obtained from institutional sources, taken to be applications of over £100,000, was now 67%. Further difficulties arose from the increased variability of interest rates. Since the terms of a public issue had to be fixed some weeks in advance of the subscription date, interest rates could change significantly in the intervening period, thus making the offer appear as either extremely attractive, or much more serious, a bad failure. Thus, the annual National Loan made its last appearance in 1975.[38]

To improve the "breadth and depth" of the market the number of stocks was increased during the seventies, as was the amount outstanding of individual stocks. A greater variety of maturities was achieved by making several stock issues a year for both cash and conversion. Some thirty issues, involving £550mn of stock, were made between 1973 and 1981, nearly threequarters of which went initially to Departmental Funds for later sale in the market through the Government Broker. In 1970 there were six stocks in the 0-3 year range, only four of 4-10 years, and twelve in the long term ranges. By 1985 the large programme of issues had produced a greater range of choice for both personal and institutional investors, with 27 stocks of up to three years, 16 of 4-10 years and ten in the longer categories, a total of 53 stocks compared with 22 in 1970. In all this, emphasis had been placed on widening the variety available at the short end of the market, with the addition in 1981 of variable interest rate stocks as a short term haven for institutional funds.

The "depth" of the market was improved by creating large tranches of existing stocks which were placed by the Department of Finance in various funds, under the control of the Minister, and then sold to the market to meet a demand for stock and to facilitate holders of maturing stocks in re-investing redemption money. Over the period 1973-81 some £5.5bn of additional stock was created in this way, half of it in the 0-5 year range. In terms of individual stocks the average outstanding rose from a modest £22mn in 1970 to £153mn in 1985. Further, there was a marked effect on the general maturity distribution of the marketable debt. In the period 1969-73 some 50% of the debt had a maturity of ten or more years, but by 1980-81 the proportion had fallen to 45%, while at the short end, in the 0-5 year range, the proportion had increased from 25% to 44%. By 1984 it had reached 47%. The expansion of the market in short bonds reflected the growing importance attached to institutional investment and the desire of the authorities to promote general marketability in order to attract more institutional dealing, particularly bank participation.

To improve the marketability of short term stocks the Central Bank in September 1969 started dealing in stocks with under three years to maturity, and its active participation soon produced an improvement in the market's capacity for coping with large scale switching operations by financial institutions. Following this successful initiative, and after due consultations with the Department of Finance, who handled dealings in 3-5 year stocks, the Central Bank in 1974 extended its dealings to stocks of up to five years maturity. Since the Bank's portfolio of stocks was somewhat limited at the time, standing at about £58mn, it was gradually increased to permit operations in a greater variety of maturities and, of course, in larger quantities. By 1984 the Central Bank's holdings had increased to £420mn. Its market dealings in securities with less than five years to run, on the other hand, were greatly in excess of this figure. In 1974 they amounted to £400mn swelling to £2.7bn by 1978, falling back to around £2.0bn in 1980. However, in 1982, reflecting increased market activity and greater demand for short dated stock, the Bank's dealings amounted to £3.0bn. The longer end of the market was helped by the build up in the portfolio held by the various Departmental Funds under the control of the Minister of Finance. A large portion of new stock issues were initially absorbed by these Funds, as were the tranches of existing stocks. From £60mn in March 1969 Departmental Funds increased to £232mn in December 1983, but this modest increase gives no indication of the substantial movement of stock into and out of official holdings.

By 1975 the Central Bank felt that considerable progress had been made in the development of the bond market. It held a "portfolio of a number of short term government stocks, each in sufficient quantities to enable it to deal with banks in amounts large enough for their needs". Also it "actively" supported the market by fixing prices at which it was prepared to buy and sell securities, and in this improved market "deals and switches involving the banks are frequent". Further, in order to maintain a "suitable and orderly price structure" across the full range of maturities and to ensure, especially at the short end, that issues and maturities accorded with institutional needs, a close liaison was maintained with the Department of Finance.[39] Undoubtedly official fostering of the bond market produced the generally desired result.

The Money Market *Report* also drew attention to the low proportion of assets which Irish financial institutions invested in Irish government bonds, making the telling point that in relation to their domestic liabilities they ought to be significantly larger. The reasons for neglect lay in the limited home bond market and the attractions of the capacious gilt edged market in London. During the seventies, however, in response to the great improvement which took place in the marketability of domestic bonds, the position of such investments in the assets of the financial institutions altered greatly. In 1969 the Associated Banks held about £40mn of bonds, rising to £290mn in 1974, and to £1,362mn in 1983; that is, 21% of outstanding bonds. As a percentage of their assets it represented a change from 4.6% in 1967 to 12% in 1974 and then settled at the 19% level for recent years, predominantly in short term stocks. The Non-Associated Banks increased their holdings from a mere £1.8mn in 1967 to £50mn in 1974, and to £342mn in 1983, that is, from representing 1% of assets to around 6% for recent years. The largest investor of the non-bank financial institutions, the insurance sector, increased its bond holdings from £45mn in 1969 to £91mn in 1974, and to £1,070mn in 1983, which accounted for about 17% of marketable stock.[40] Building Societies also added to their bond holdings, taking them from £12mn in 1974 to £323mn in 1983; as a share of their assets this was an increase from 8% to 15%. "Other" financial institutions displayed the same appetite for bonds, their holdings going up from £84mn in 1976 to £327mn in 1983. As to all other holders, including the personal and company sectors, their ownership rose from £640mn in 1976 to £2,380mn in 1983, a sizeable 37% of all marketable bonds.[41]

A bigger and more diversified debt, coupled with greater institutional interest and nurtured by official involvement produced a considerable improvement in the activity seen in the bond market during the seventies.

The turnover of the market increased from £3.5bn in 1975 to nearly £9.0bn in 1978, falling back somewhat in the next few years under the influence of higher interest rates, to about £7.5bn a year, but with a dramatic surge to £14.6bn in 1982 under the stimulus of falling interest rates.[42] However, it was noticeable that while turnover at the short end doubled between 1975 and 1980, that of the medium to longer term stocks (5 years plus) trebled. Also, the peak year for short bond turnover was 1977 with £5.4bn, whereas for longer bonds it was two years later with a figure of £3.6bn. Both were surpassed in 1982 with £8.9bn for short bonds and £5.6bn for longer dated stock, with similar levels in 1983. It seems probable that the bigger improvement in turnover displayed by the longer term market, and its continuation into 1979, were due to greater opportunities for switching operations, arising from variable interest rates, which the now more active institutional participants were prepared to undertake. The above trends are confirmed by the appreciable rise in the ratio of turnover to stock outstanding. In 1974 this stood at 1.56, whereas by 1978 it had improved to 3.07, but it fell back to 1.79 in 1980; this sharp fall was due to a decline in turnover but there was also a sharp increase in the volume of debt outstanding. It recovered to 2.7 in 1982 with the buoyant demand for stocks, falling off a little in 1983.

Improved marketability is also reflected by the number of bargains. From just over an average of 1,300 per account in 1975, transactions in bonds rose to a peak of 2,535 in 1977 and apart from a lull in 1979 when interest rates rose sharply, activity over recent years has remained at an average of about 2,000 bargains per account. At the short end of the market the number of bargains per account rose from 468 in 1975 to 887 in 1977, it fell to 610 in 1979, but then recovered to 750 in 1980, and increased to nearly 1,100 in 1983. In the medium to long end of the market the same statistic increased from 840 in 1975 to 1,647 in 1977, it slumped to just over 1,000 in 1979 and then recovered to 1,250 in 1980-83. The change which occurred in average bargain size reflects the growth of institutional activity in the market over the period. For the bond market as a whole it rose from £107,000 in 1975 to £187,000 in 1979, but fell back a little to £160,000 in 1980, to reach £255,000 in 1982. In the case of short bonds, where institutional interest dominates, average bargain size increased from £202,000 in 1975 to £277,000 in 1977, falling to £236,000 in 1980 but then reached £330,000 in 1982, dipping to £283,000 in 1983. Average bargain size in the longer end of the market rose from £54,000 in 1975 to £136,000 in 1979, lapsing to £105,000 in 1980, but then doubled to £215,000 by 1983.

One feature of the 1960s bond market which attracted the attention of the Committee on the Money Market was that bonds of all maturities, except very short bonds, "tend to give approximately the same yield to redemption", and this uniformity of return "reduces the scope for switching between stocks".[43] However, over recent years the yield curve for Irish bonds has been far from flat. With greater interest rate movements the differential between short and long rates (0-3 years compared with 15 year bonds) has fluctuated from a maximum of over 4½% in mid 1972 to an inverse differential of over ½% in mid-1980, while throughout most recent years a 2% gap has usually existed. Also, there has been a differential of about 1% between medium term stocks (8 years) and longer term stocks (15 years). With rising interest rates the differential tends to narrow, with short rates rising more rapidly than long term rates, the gap widening again as interest rates fall with long term rates falling more slowly than those at the short end. In such a market there would therefore appear to be much greater scope for switching and speculative activity than was formerly the case, while the yield curve can now be said to reflect to a considerable extent the preferences of bond holders. Formerly, it was largely influenced by the dealing activity of the Government Broker; he has not removed his hand from the market but it is less protective than it once was.

# NOTES

1.  The Committee was established by the Central Bank of Ireland in 1967; it was chaired by Professor W.J.L. Ryan.
2.  The deficit on the current account for 1923-24 was £7.2mn and it was due largely to increases in supply services from £26.9mn to £35.4mn.
3.  He worked for the London firm of Horne & Co., Moorgate; M. Foster, *Michael Collins, The Lost Leader*, (1971), p. 30.
4.  For a full account of the formative years see Ronan Fanning, *The Irish Department of Finance 1922-58*, (1978), pp. 13-25.
5.  In addition to marketable stock the government issued, as from August 1923, 5% Compensation Stock (3½% from 1934) to owners of destroyed property. Stock rather than cash was used due to the "abnormally difficult situation". The stock was not marketable but it was redeemable from the sinking funds. By 1928 over £1.0mn had been issued, with a mere £14,500 outstanding in 1934; *Commission of Inquiry into Banking, Currency and Credit*, 1938, Report, para. 525.
6.  In the event no such guarantee was sought. Land Bonds did resort to such a guarantee. In November the Department of Finance announced that interest and redemption would be in sterling, but this would only mean something if the link with sterling was cut.
7.  Fanning, op. cit., p. 98. In the spring of 1924, after the Army Mutiny, the price of the loan fell but the quotation was successfully pegged at 97 through government purchases. When this support was withdrawn the price fell to 92 which induced nervousness in the Department of Finance as to the state of national credit; ibid., p. 118.
8.  *The Economist*, December 8 1923.
9.  *The Economist*, December 8 1923, p. 1,235. The government might well have done better had they made the issue a year earlier when stock prices rose

steadily; when it came to the market they had levelled off.

10.   Fanning, op. cit., p. 316. An additional attraction was that investors were guaranteed the right of conversion into any other government issue "during the present state of emergency or within six months of the termination thereof"; *The Economist*, December 30 1939.

11.   Fanning, op. cit., pp. 316-17.

12.   E.T. Nevin, "The Capital Stock of Irish Industry", Economic Research Institute, Paper No. 17, pp. 18-19. In 1943 the index reached 108.

13.   *Statist*, September 7 1935, p. 333.

14.   *The Economist*, November 2, 23, 30 1935.

15.   *Statist*, May 28 1938, p. 810.

16.   Dublin Stock Exchange, Minutes, May 7 1930, October 31 1935, May 20 1938.

17.   Prospectus for the 5% National Loan 1935-45, November 1923.

18.   The 2nd, 3rd, and 4th National Loans and the 4% Conversion Loan had annual sinking fund provisions of £85,000, £44,000, £67,200 and £78,400 respectively.

19.   *Banking Commission*, op.cit., 1938, Minutes of Evidence, Q. 2991.

20.   Dublin Stock Exchange, Minutes, November 25, December 12 1924.

21.   The Transfer Registers for Land Bonds were kept by the National City Bank, Dublin.

22.   Similar schemes had operated before 1914, but the government stock issued at the time had been greatly depreciated by market falls during the war; see *Banking Commission*, op. cit., 1938, Report, pp. 12-13.

23.   *Banking Commission*, op. cit., 1938, Minutes of Evidence, Q. 2955.

24.   Not all Land Bonds were registered at the National Land Bank (Land changed to City in 1927) and therefore did not participate in the draw; in 1937 £6.2mn were unregistered; *Banking Commission*, op. cit., 1938, Report, p. 318. Local insurance cover could be obtained against going into the draw.

25.   *Banking Commission*, op. cit., 1938, Report, Appendix No. 24.

26.   ibid., Minutes of Evidence, Q. 2938, 2973.

27.   ibid., Q. 2977.

28.   Average Irish yields for 1927-29 were 4.96% compared with London's 4.50%. For 1933-36 the corresponding figures were 4.05% and 3.20%; see Nevin, op. cit., p. 19.

29.   *The Economist*, September 27 1952, October 10 1953.

30.   *Statist*, September 27 1952.

31.   A sortie into the London market in 1966 for £5mn at 7½% proved a disappointment since 88% of the issue was left with the underwriters, and later the price of the stock fell from 97 to 95 to give a redemption yield of over 8%; *The Economist*, August 13 1966, p. 676.

32.   T. Garry, *The Irish Gilt Edged Market*, Unpublished Dissertation, University of Dublin, 1977, p. 7.

33.   *Committee on the Functions, Operations and Development of a Money Market in Ireland*, Report, 1968, p. 22. There was talk of having such an inquiry in 1953 but it never came to anything. However, consultations did lead to greater willingness to deal on the part of the Department; M. Moynihan, *Currency and Central Banking in Ireland 1922-1960*, (1975), pp. 311-12.

34.   *Money Market Report*, op. cit., p. 48.

35.   ibid., pp. 48-50.

36.   ibid., p. 52.

37.   As a percentage of the government's expenditure the borrowing requirement increased from some 20% in the early seventies to 30% in the 1979-81 period.

38.  *Quarterly Bulletin*, Central Bank of Ireland, 1975, p. 79.
39.  Garry, op. cit., pp. 27-30.
40.  These figures included holdings of non-Irish insurance companies. It appears to be generally understood that all insurance companies operating in the country invest some 80% or more of their assets within the State; see *Committee of Inquiry into the Insurance Industry*, Final Report, 1976, (Prl. 5330), pp. 115-17.
41.  This category includes holdings by companies, nominees, third party bank accounts, churches and schools, Courts of Justice, individuals, accounts under £5,000 and holdings by non-residents other than foreign insurance companies. The attraction for companies is that of tax free capital gain on short term liquid balances. For an excellent detailed treatment of the investment policies of the major categories of government stock holders, see Garry, op. cit., pp. 52-95.
42.  Turnover figures are available from February 1974.
43.  *Money Market Report*, op. cit., pp. 70-71. The Report also noted that no private dealers operated in the market (i.e. jobbers) and that the earlier absence of yield differentials may have been an important element in this. But even with larger differentials no jobber or dealer has emerged, the main factors militating against this being the need to have a very large capital base to do so successfully, while the institutional dominance of the market produces a tendency to periodic one way transactions.

# CHAPTER 10

★

# THE INDUSTRIAL SHARE MARKET

While the war years and their immediate aftermath were relatively profitable for Irish companies, due to rising prices and less outside competition, the effects of the ensuing recession were prolonged by the political turmoil surrounding the formation of the new State. Continued difficulties in agriculture, which accounted for some 80% of economic activity, and further trading setbacks in 1925-26, delayed recovery for a few more years. The downward slide of the economy over the period was mirrored in the performance of shares on the Dublin market. Prices fell back steadily during 1922 to 1926, the market in general losing about 20% of its value. This was in marked contrast to the movement of prices on the London Stock Exchange where over the same years they exhibited a sustained rise (see chart 2; 1926 = 100).

*Chart 2: Share Price Indices 1922-1939*

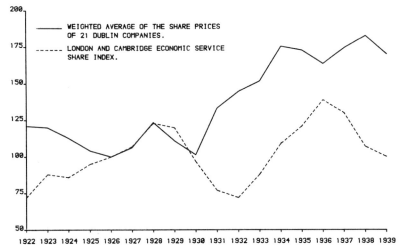

In such conditions it was not surprising that company borrowing from the capital market was negligible. With reduced output to meet the lower level of demand, industrialists were able to meet their limited financial needs for investment from savings, or failing that, by going to the banks. Had there been a strong demand for long term funds then companies could have resorted to the "usual method of sale of securities to investors". But as the 1926 Banking Commission confirmed in its Second Interim Report, they could find no evidence of a "general demand for long term credit in business".[1] What capital was available had little opportunity for a domestic outlet, and given the persistent decline in share prices there was little to attract it; there was always the alternative of external investment and during these years the attraction was considerable. For example, during the London new issue boom of 1927-28 several Dublin brokers (especially Wilson & Son, Moffat) acted as agents for London issuing houses in offering several new issues to Irish investors.

It seems that the general needs of industry were adequately catered for, sufficiently so to warrant the observation from the Banking Commission that the "business community as a whole does not feel that there is occasion for much in the way of special action designed to promote long term industrial or commercial credit". But the Commission did feel that due to the economic problems associated with the transition to the new government, some industries could encounter difficulties, while new firms seeking to grow might "struggle and thus require special credit facilities". To provide an element of protection for the markets of such companies and to ease the provision of finance three measures were taken, not all of which realised to the full the hopes of the originators.

In the early years selective protection was given to certain industries heavily dependent on the home market, and whose scale of operations were very modest. Generally, however, industrialists did not favour protectionist measures, especially for such activities as brewing and distilling, biscuit manufacture, and certain parts of agriculture. More direct assistance was rendered by the Trade Loans (Guarantee) Act of 1924. Under this legislation (amended in 1934) the government guaranteed the principal and interest of loans made to companies following a "careful survey of their application by public authority".[2] While the loans were intended to help with capital expenditure and thereby employment, in practice they were used for repaying bank debts and for reconstructing businesses which had got into difficulties. The 1924 act specifically prohibited loans for working capital purposes, a limitation lifted by the 1934 amendment. Overall the experience of direct government guarantees of company loans, which came largely from the Industrial Trust Co. and the National City Bank, was not altogether a happy one. Loans varied from £1,500 to £70,000 to firms in a range of industries, several of them enjoying tariff protection. During 1924-29 sixteen trade borrowers had loans amounting to £240,000; eight met their obligations but the other eight, with debts of £185,000, defaulted leaving the government to honour an expensive promise.[3]

Associated with the policy of giving guarantees for loans was the active promotion by the government, in association with other interests, of the Industrial Trust Company of Ireland. Since commercial banks generally did not give long term advances, which qualified for government guarantees, a specialist institution was set up to fill the gap. Registered in July 1925, it had an authorised capital of £250,000, of which £163,000 was issued with the government holding £50,000, the rest coming from banks, company directors and some "powerful American financiers with a sympathetic interest in this country". Despite the influential backing it had a short and inglorious life. "Owing to an imprudent policy in external investments" it was forced into liquidation in 1933 with "an almost total loss of the capital provided for it by the State and by private interests".[4]

While the number of company registrations for the twenties ran at about one hundred a year, they were almost all small private concerns. For the period 1922-30 only 50 public companies were registered, sixteen of which filed a prospectus, and they had an average nominal capital of £78,000. A further 34 companies filed a statement in lieu of a prospectus, with an average nominal capital of £60,000. It would seem reasonable to suppose that the paid up capital involved in such companies would have been around a half to threequarters of such figures. On the scanty evidence available it appears that only one public issue of shares took place during the entire period and that was for a small sum of £15,000. Presumably the depressed state of the market in the early twenties would partly account for the paucity of issues, but there was a recovery in share prices during 1927-28 (see chart 2), and the continuing absence of capital issues can only be explained by an adequate supply of funds from other sources, and a reluctance by both established and prospective businesses to seek long term capital given the competitive pressures felt by the manufacturing sector. In marked contrast, certain official measures taken in the early thirties sent companies scurrying to the capital market on a scale reminiscent of the 1890s.

The arrival of the Great Depression produced significant changes in industrial activity and the degree of protection afforded to it, but at least in the early stages the impact of the downturn on industry was fairly limited. While exports fell off, overall production remained at a reasonable level since most industries were geared to the domestic market. This was reflected in the performance of the share index which fell by around 20% compared to a much larger decline in the London market (see chart 2). But the deepening of the world recession by 1932, coupled with worsening economic relations with Britain, saw the emergence of a series of defensive economic measures. In particular the dispute with Britain, which lasted some six years, gave rise to a general range of protective duties and quotas which were designed to bolster the agricultural sector, and on the industrial front made the country less dependent on imports by encouraging Irish industrialisation. In general the process was seen as leading to increased industrial employment, and indeed employment and output rose, particularly in footwear, hosiery, glass and paper, metals, leather, clothing and confectionery. All this was reflected in the balance of trade with a change of emphasis from imports of finished manufactured goods to that of raw materials.[5]

In the drive towards greater manufacturing self-sufficiency the capital market had an important role to play. Not only would existing firms, wanting to expand capacity, require additional long term capital, but new firms also would need to turn to the market. Accordingly measures were introduced to facilitate the flow of funds to Irish enterprises, and to ensure that direct foreign investment did not seriously damage the prospects for Irish firms who were intended to benefit from the protection granted by the tariff wall. Also, it was seen as important to prevent the new industries from being almost exclusively owned by foreign funds and interests. Thus the Control of Manufactures Acts, 1932-34, required new manufacturing concerns to have one half of their issued capital and at least two thirds of capital with voting rights in the beneficial ownership of Irish persons, with the majority of the directors being Irish nationals. External capital and firms were not entirely excluded because provision was made for the issue of "new manufacturing licences" to such companies, and between 1932 and 1939 96 such licences were granted. In practice, however, the above provisions had no great inhibiting effect; in 1939 the Stock Exchange list contained twenty nine companies denoted as subject to the provisions of the Control of Manufactures Acts.[6] The restrictive intent of the legislation was to have much more damaging effects after the Second World War.

The power of the state, by way of conferring benefits through the tax system, was also marshalled to direct the flow of private capital into Irish industry. To induce individuals to take up shares in new companies, Section 7 of the 1932 Finance Act offered an abatement of 20% of the income tax and surtax which applied to dividends or interest on certain stocks and shares. To qualify for the relief securities had to be publicly issued (after the introduction of the legislation) by Irish companies whose business was conducted mainly within the country, and the money used for direct investment. In its first few years of operation the shares of twenty seven companies qualified for relief, involving £2.1mn of new issued nominal capital. By 1956 thirty four companies enjoyed the concession, with the qualifying capital standing at £5.3mn.[7] Whether this concession was a powerful influence in shifting demand towards Irish shares is probably debatable since other factors such as profits and price movements were more influential. Certainly, the Stock Exchange witnesses before the 1938 Banking Commission were divided in their opinion as to its effect with one suggesting that it had been important, the other that it had merely been a slight inducement.[8] In the matter of marketability of a company's shares the measure seems to have somewhat segmented the market with capital issued before 1932, and not qualifying for relief, being traded alongside the qualifying shares. This gave rise to the prospect that dealings in each category was certain to be less in volume than if the entire capital of the company had qualified for relief. Such division was finally removed in 1956 when relief was extended to shares issued before 1932.[9]

A further aid to industrialisation was the resumption in 1933 of the system of Guaranteed Trade Loans whereby the government guaranteed both principal and interest on loans obtained by companies. The record of the earlier system in the twenties (see above) was distinctly bleak, so much so as to incur severe criticism from the 1926 Banking Commission. Under the revised scheme many of the restraints operating in the 1920s had been removed, the most important of which meant that loans could now be used for working capital purposes.[10] Whereas the earlier loans had come from the Industrial Trust Company or the National City Bank, the government now reached an understanding with the commercial banks to provide the bulk of the loans. Effectively the scheme involved a state guarantee of bank accommodation for new industries and this probably meant that many of the tests usually applied to loan applications were set aside. Between 1932 and 1936 guarantees were accorded to 70 companies mostly in tariffed industries, involving £594,000 spread out in 80 loans; only half a dozen exceeded £20,000, the bulk being under £5,000.[11] Already by 1936, while only two companies had actually failed and so obliged the government to fulfil its pledge, the Minister of Industry and Commerce, Mr. John Leydon, admitted to the Banking Commission that he did not "think there is anything in the present procedure which would lead us to expect a lower ratio of liability".[12] Certainly, none of the companies provided with the safeguard made it to the Stock Exchange list, reflecting their small capitalisation and limited scale of operations.

Institutional support for developing the home capital market took the form of resurrecting the idea of an issuing house to sponsor and assist new companies which were ready to come to the market. Having failed some years earlier doubts lingered about the likelihood of success but the newly formed Industrial Credit Company, unlike its predecessor, prospered, probably for three reasons. First, it had much larger financial resources to operate with; second, the prospects for the firms it sponsored were improved by the existence of tariff protection; and third, and perhaps most significantly, the share market was exceedingly buoyant for most of the thirties, prices rising by some 70% between 1930 and 1934, and after a minor slip in 1936 they reached a peak in 1938 (see chart 2). In this generally receptive financial climate issues went reasonably well, and any stock taken in by the issuing house could profitably be sold out to the market after a suitable lapse of time.

The Industrial Credit Company was formed in 1933, following the passing of the Industrial Credit Act. It had an authorised capital of £5.0mn and the first issue of part of this, for £500,000, took place in November 1933, the public subscribing only £7,936 and the rest of the issue being taken by the Minister of Finance. A further tranche of £500,000 followed in July 1936, the bulk of this again going to the Minister of Finance. With its capital quoted on the Dublin Stock Exchange, official holdings were then sold off to the public through the open market. The main objects of the company was to act as issuing house, underwriter, lender and investor. At the time it was felt that no satisfactory organised facilities existed in Dublin to make long term industrial issues; the mechanism which had operated before the First World War had lain dormant for several years.[13] Before the industrial capital market could be successfully revived it was thought necessary to provide the appropriate institutional channels.

The first chairman of I.C.C., Mr. John P. Colbert, who guided its fortunes for nearly twenty years, felt that the prospects for developing the domestic security market were good since the securities likely to be offered to the public would have several advantages to Irish investors over English alternatives. Apart from the 20% tax abatement he suggested that "the prices of these securities on the Stock Exchange will not be subject to violent fluctuations due to extraneous causes, as they would be in the case of a big international finance centre such as London"; the price index of Irish securities suggests that there was some truth in the claim. Also, on a more defensive tack, that in a small economic unit "it will be possible more easily than in a big industrial nation both to rationalize internal competition and to act quickly if the market is threatened with flooding from abroad". Finally, "the shareholder in home industry will be able to follow more closely the fortunes of his company than would be possible in the case of an external investment".[14] In many ways the record of I.C.C. up to the war justified the optimism of its founders.

During 1934-38 I.C.C. was involved in the floatation of £4.7mn of capital; it extended loans for £978,000, gave bank guarantees for £100,000, and held share investments, linked with its operations, of £121,000. While all this was not accomplished without some problems the company made annual profits, although no dividend was paid until 1940.[15] It participated in 27 capital issues, two thirds of which took place during 1934-36, amounting to well over a million pounds a year, while the average size ranged from £291,000 in 1934 to £340,000 in 1935. Only a few were debenture stocks, the most popular issue being a combination of £1 preference shares and £1 ordinary shares, with an occasional resort to 5s. shares.

The years 1934 and 1935 were particularly active for new issues. In 1934 some £2.5mn was raised for industrial purposes, with four of the issues being for £500,000. Three of these were sponsored by I.C.C.; two were for the newly formed Irish Sugar Co., and the other for Ranks (Ireland) Ltd.

All were well supported. The pace of issuing quickened somewhat in 1935 but apart from a large issue by the Irish Sugar Co. the others were in the region of £30,000 to £150,000 and made by new companies or ones just set up to acquire existing businesses. By this time the market in new issues seemed "a little tired", with the danger that if more issues were rushed along the previous ready response (with some issues being oversubscribed ten times), would undoubtedly fade away. During the next two years the issues handled by I.C.C. were mostly small, the major exceptions being a very large issue of £750,000 for Cement Limited in 1936 and £247,000 for Salts (Ireland) Ltd. in 1937. While two of the issues made by I.C.C. were underwritten jointly with Butler & Briscoe (Ranks (Ireland) Ltd, 1934) and Guinness, Mahon & Co. (Irish Dunlop Co., 1935) the general policy was to keep a large portion of the underwriting for itself and place the balance with a "solid circle of sub-underwriters".[16] On this basis the Stock Exchange participated in the underwriting of the two large issues for the Irish Sugar Co. in 1934 and 1935.[17] While such activity did not impose a burden on I.C.C. at the outset, by 1936 it had acquired nearly £300,000 of shares on this basis, a matter which prompted cautionary words from the 1938 Banking Commission since it feared that these holdings might prove difficult to dispose of in the market, thereby threatening to turn the issuing house into an investment trust. But, in the event, a large portion of the holdings were gradually sold to the public.[18]

Stimulated by general market conditions and perhaps by the example of the officially sponsored issuing house, several other bodies participated in the revival of the new issue facility. The long established banking house of Guinness, Mahon & Co. undertook several issues and was joined for a time by three other local issuing firms, while many Dublin brokers were also very active in handling issues for industrial and commercial companies. As recorded by *The Times Issuing House Year Book* 46 industrial and commercial issues were made between 1933 and 1937; starting with three in 1933, then nine in 1934, a dozen in both 1935 and 1936, and ending with ten in 1937 (only one or two issues were made up to the outbreak of the war). In twenty of these issues brokers and local issuing houses acted alongside the Industrial Credit Company. The house of Guinness, Mahon & Co. handled four issues on its own, but the other entrants to the local new issuing fold, General Estates Trust Co. (formed in 1932), Brockhouse Nominees (1935) and North Kerry Proprietary Co. (1932), only handled five issues, all with the participation of a broker; all three had ceased to operate by about 1940. As to the stockbrokers, among those who handled one or two issues were James Keogh, Lillis & Harrington, James McCann, O'Donnell & Fitzgerald, M. Dillon & Son, Lawrence & Waldron, and Dudgeon. Kennedy & Gordon and J. & E. Davy handled three or four, the three largest issuers being Goodbody & Webb with eight, P.W. Tunney & Co. with nine, and Butler & Briscoe with seventeen, several of the issues being done in conjunction with the Industrial Credit Company.

Notwithstanding the effectiveness of the new issue machinery, the involvement of domestic investors in the provision of industrial finance depended ultimately on the quality of the subsequent market for shares on the Dublin Stock Exchange. Certainly by 1939 the breadth of the market in industrials had increased significantly. In 1933 there were 24 quoted industrial companies with a total capital in the region of £5.0mn; by 1939 the number had risen to 78 with a capital of some £9.8mn. But the marketability of individual stocks was a much more variable matter. In the case of large issues dealings were effected at "close" prices, reflecting the opinion expressed by the Stock Exchange to the 1938 Banking Commission that "it takes a company with a capital of nearly a quarter of a million to make a market that is of any consequence at all".[19] However, since the majority of the new issues made at the time were well below this size, the market in such stocks ranged from being extremely limited to moderately good. Many of the new arrivals were depicted as possessing "slow" markets; "In the case of the smaller companies, you get an order to sell shares at about the last price, then you have to wait three or four days or you may sell them at once as luck would have it, but it is possible you may have to wait".[20]

Even so, Irish investors were apparently prepared to accept the difficulties of dealing when they occurred, which from the point of view of long term holders was not a serious drawback. They were also prepared to switch out of shares quoted on the London Stock Exchange and into some of the new home offerings. Money invested in the new issues of the mid-thirties had "to a large extent been financed by the realisation of British securities", the experience of Dublin brokers being that "when a client comes to apply for these new issues he has to sell something".[21] With the larger issues, where marketability was such as not to deter investors, there were even some applications from England. By 1939 the most active markets were in the shares of the larger companies on the market, such as Carroll, Goulding, Irish Tanners, Ranks (Ireland), Salts (Ireland), Cement, and Mooney. In addition to the list of Irish companies dealings took place in several leading British ones, the Stock Exchange list containing 34 well known industrial and commercial concerns, along with nine textile firms. Indeed, the Imperial Tobacco Co. and Woolworth could justify a separate register for their Irish shareholders.

The war years saw a fall in the level of employment and output in the economy, which was reflected in a fairly quiescent share market and the virtual suspension of all industrial borrowing.[22] The share index (1936 = 100) stood at 99.4 when the war began but then fell back to 93.6 by 1941, recovering steadily afterwards to 135.5 in 1945. With peace the economy grew rapidly for a few years, sustained by a revival of protection, Marshall Aid spending and the considerable stimulus given by the Public Capital Programme which was designed to improve the social and economic infrastructure of the country. The increases which took place in output, company profits and savings, were mirrored in a gradual upward movement in share prices of about 27%. But the advance was short lived. Apart from a minor surge during the Korean War the market fell gradually over a very long period (see chart 3), the turning point coming only in 1958-59. This was in marked contrast to the London market where the long term upward trend began in 1953 with "Mr. Butler's Boom"; between 1953 and 1955 the Actuaries Index (1950 = 100) rose from 104 to 154. For most of the fifties output grew very slowly, with a fall in gross domestic product in 1956, a depressing trend caused by several bouts of restrictive policy measures, including reductions in public spending, and which was evident in the stagnation of company profits and savings. The latter fell from £15mn in 1954 to £10mn in 1957. In this lethargic economic environment there were only limited opportunities for investment, while the falling supply of company savings imposed a further brake on activity.

Once the economy secured a turning point in the closing years of the decade a long bullish market followed, share prices doubling between 1959 and 1964. Several elements contributed to this revival of fortunes. By the mid-fifties it was widely appreciated that the investment programme followed since the war, with its emphasis on infrastructure, had produced disappointing results overall. The contents of *Economic Development*, published in 1958, set out to alter that bias, and generally ushered in a period of more open development for the economy. This was also aided by the Anglo-Irish Agreement on trade of 1965. Firms were also given various fiscal incentives to help with modernisation and to increase their ability to compete effectively in external markets. The old policy of only admitting outside capital reluctantly and with considerable safeguards (which were not always effective) was abandoned and direct external investment was encouraged.[23] The general effect was an accelerated growth rate for the economy running at about 4% a year. Under the stimulus of expanding output and profits the share market climbed out of its long standing becalmed state. From a low of 36 in 1958 (1963 = 100) it reached 125 by 1964. Expansion, however, had to be halted in the middle sixties due to balance of payments problems with the familiar restraints being imposed on consumption and public expenditure.[24] In the closing years of the decade the upswing was renewed, the share market reaching a high point of 170 in 1969. But rising inflation served to produce a slower growth rate and a decline in the competitiveness of Irish firms. This proved but a temporary setback and the economy surged ahead during the 1972 -73 boom, with manufacturing output up by nearly 11% in 1973. Share prices reached the 250 level, the highest level ever recorded up till then.

As happened elsewhere the economic collapse of 1974-75 did not spare the share market. Manufacturing output rose by only 2.7% in 1974; in 1975 it fell by 6.7%. The stock market behaved likewise. From a peak of 269 in

March 1973, the index fell to 210 in January 1974 and by the end of a dismal year had slumped to 109. While the economy had lost some of its momentum before the oil crisis broke, this coupled with rising commodity prices and declining world trade pulled it downwards. But, by way of some compensation, the ensuing period of adjustment to new energy prices proved to be the foundation of a period of prosperity for the economy. During 1976-79 the gross national product rose by an impressive 20%, a performance sustained by the buoyancy of world trade, agricultural expansion from Common Market membership, and an increase in both consumer and investment expenditure, the latter helped by the public capital programme. As company profits and savings rose, the market was not slow to discount these promising trends. From the low level of 164 in 1975 the share index recovered to 392 in 1979, reaching a high point in April. The second oil crisis brought an end to the boom, while the downward drift of the economy was quickened by action taken to deal with the mounting government deficit, inflation, and the record balance of payments deficit. As a result manufacturing output in 1980 fell by about 1% (very modest indeed compared to the U. K. experience), but 1981 saw a gain of 2.9%. The share market also turned downwards, but only marginally so.

Looking at the post war years from the point of view of the use made by Irish industry of the new issue facility available in the local capital market, it is evident that up to the early seventies only moderate use was made of this channel for raising funds to further industrial expansion. Taking the figures published by the Central Bank of Ireland it appears that for the years 1952-71 some £47mn was raised for 'other concerns' (that is private sector companies), compared with £618mn for public sector purposes. Such private sector independence from the market is also revealed in the figures for the types of new issues given in the *Issuing House Year Book*. Public issues, offers for sale and rights issues, which may be seen as cash raising methods, were not much in evidence over the long span of 1946 to 1970; there were only 49 public issues for £13.3mn of funds (giving a low average of £270,000), 32 offers for sale appeared for £5.9mn (an average of £185,000), while rights issues provided a similar sort of level with 43 issues for £10.2mn (an average of £237,000). What is noticeable is that most of the issues were made during the late forties and early fifties, and that thereafter, until the early seventies, the new issue market relapses into an exceedingly dormant state. The early post war issues arose, no doubt, from the need to seek long term capital after the virtual closure of the capital market during the war years, while the reasonably buoyant state of the share market, with a reviving economy, also encouraged companies to make issues. In addition to cash raising issues, bonus issues were also in evidence, 36 issues taking place during 1947-70, for a total of £2.9mn. Such a free distribution of capital was a means of bringing nominal capital more into line with actual capital, but the main motive may well have been a desire by some companies to reward shareholders by means other than dividend increases.

Infrequent use of the capital market by companies during the fifties and sixties may probably be accounted for by several features of the financial and fiscal systems. In a period when the economy had a slow rate of growth, and was to some extent protected from external competition, the investment needs of companies could be met largely from internal funds and by looking to the banking system. Traditionally the latter had been a ready source of money, and indeed bank advances tended to occupy a more significant role in the finance of companies in Ireland than in Britain. For example, the 1956 Committee of Inquiry into Taxation on Industry reported that in the case of 83 manufacturing firms in 1953, 15% of assets was financed by bank loans, whereas the corresponding figure for British companies was only 3%.[25] More recent figures confirm the trend; industrial and service companies financed 12.5% of their assets from bank funds in 1956, falling to 9.6% in 1967.[26] It is very probable that for small companies bank finance is the most important source of outside funds.

The supply of internal funds was boosted in Ireland, as elsewhere, by the granting of generous depreciation allowances. A significant innovation in this direction was made in 1956 with the object of encouraging more investment and to stimulate export production. While the usual allowances had always been granted, initial allowances of 20% were given on investment in plant and machinery, the level increasing in later years to reach 100% in 1972. Earlier, in 1967, free depreciation had been granted for new machinery and plant located in the western part of the country. Lower levels of initial allowances were also granted to industrial buildings in 1956, the rate in 1972 standing at 20% with annual allowances of 2%. Tax relief on profits from exports was also introduced in 1956, initially granted at 50% but raised to 100% a year later, and the period of relief extended to 1970, then further extended for up to 20 years.[27] In 1981 a new relief replaced the above in that profits from sales (export or home) of goods which a company itself has manufactured can obtain relief from corporation tax so that the effective rate paid does not exceed 10%.[28] No doubt such concessions benefited output, employment and exports, and in addition improved the internal financial position of qualifying firms.

Finally, on the availability of finance from sources other than the banks or the market, the point was made in the fifties and more recently in the early seventies, that companies tended to lend to each other if they had surplus funds, the incentive for this arising from fixed rates on bank funds and the absence, certainly in the early period, of a local money market. Such inter-company loans occurred where their seasonal requirements did not overlap.[29] In the main such activity represented the sharing of liquid assets within a group of companies. This particular category of assets, for all industrial and service companies, increased from £22.5mn in 1956 to £151.6mn in 1967 and prompted the comment in *Company Taxation in*

*Ireland* (1972) that inter-company borrowing was "a feature of growing significance in the corporate sector".[30] However, it would seem most unlikely to occur between companies who are not members of the same group.

Compared with the sparse new issue activity of the sixties, the seventies saw a marked increase in the number of issues, both cash and non-cash. From a few million the cash raised increased to around £16mn a year in the 1972-73 expansion, falling back later, but recovering again to some £20mn and reaching a peak of £49mn in 1979. The 1980 recession produced a collapse to £3.3mn, then recovery to a record figure of £122.4mn in 1981 (nearly half of this total came from two issues, one for Allied Irish Banks, £31.5mn, the other for Bula Resources, £29.8mn). While some funds were raised by public issue or an offer for sale, companies also raised money by direct calls to their shareholders, that is, by rights issues. Such increased resort to the market was due to the investment needs of rapidly growing companies exceeding their internally generated funds. Also, the general competitive climate altered with entry to the European Economic Community, a change which induced firms to expand in the search for economies of scale, which could really only be obtained by a policy of increasing exports. In addition, the resort to more equity capital may have been prompted by limitations on the amount of debt financing which could be adopted, while the commercial banks — traditionally a very important source of finance — probably exerted some pressure on companies to fund their loans. On the demand side companies were well aware of the more receptive state of the equity market during the time of its sharpest rises in 1972-73 and 1976-79 (see chart 3).

*Chart 3: Irish Share Price Index*

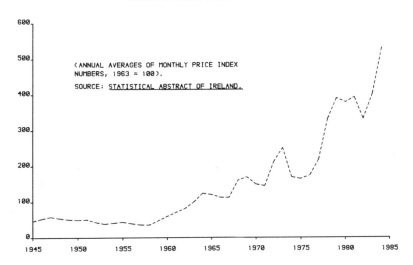

( ANNUAL AVERAGES OF MONTHLY PRICE INDEX NUMBERS, 1963 = 100).

SOURCE: STATISTICAL ABSTRACT OF IRELAND.

Non-cash issues similarly increased in frequency at this time. These were mainly capitalisation issues (bonus issues) and issues of shares associated with acquisitions of other companies, that is, merger activity. In the period 1973-74 eleven capitalisations were made for a total of £11.0mn, while a further 35 issues appeared between 1976-79 to the value of £46.0mn.[31] In such cases companies sought to bring their nominal capital more into line with actual capital, and some may have been prompted by the need to remove the temptation of large reserves in relation to the existing quoted equity. During 1970-80 *The Times New Issuing House Year Book* gave 63 issues associated with mergers, the amount involved being £77.6mn; most of this activity was handled by brokers, half the issues and nine tenths of the volume of stock. Company expansion by acquisition has been fashionable at various periods, and it certainly does provide a quick route to a larger market presence, the benefits of economies of scale being more easily acquired this way than by painstaking growth. Most of the leading Irish companies acquired subsidiaries by this process during these years, among them Waterford, Smurfit, Irish Distillers, Carroll, T.M.G. Group, and Doreen Holdings.

When a company wants to make a large issue of shares which is likely to have a wide appeal among investors, the appropriate method is either a public issue or an offer for sale. Essentially the procedures to be followed are very much the same, the important difference is that with a public issue the issuing house or broker acts as an agent for the company, whereas with an offer for sale the shares are bought from the company by the issuing house or broker and then sold to the market. Both procedures involve compliance with the same Stock Exchange regulations regarding capital structure and financial reporting, and they present the same kind of marketing problems to the issuing house and broker.[32] Two basic ones arise, that of fixing the price of the share (there is only one case of a tender issue, back in 1964), and ensuring a full subscription within a fairly short space of time. After a detailed look at a company's financial position and its future prospects, the issuing house or broker will fix the price in relation to the general market level and the price of comparable shares, giving a slight competitive edge in the process. In all this the expertise of the broker will be invaluable to the issuing house in gauging the response of the market. The listing requirements of the Stock Exchange require full publicity of the offer and of the relevant financial information, which serves not only to enable investors to evaluate the offer but also to advertise it as widely as possible. To ensure that the company gets its funds the issue is underwritten, the usual practice being to sub-underwrite it with local institutional investors and others. In Dublin there are about thirty institutions involved, drawn mainly from the pension funds, life and general insurance offices, and foreign and merchant banks. But whereas several public issues and offers for sale were made in the immediate post war years, and in the mid-sixties, over recent years there have been virtually none. If companies need cash they tend to resort to rights issues; during 1971-81 there were 37 bringing in an impressive £204mn. Where existing shareholders are prepared to put up further capital this is a very much cheaper method than either of the above.

For smaller issues, with limited public interest, the most suitable method is that of a placing. Here the shares are placed with the various institutional and other clients of the issuing house or broker.[33] Since the procedure is a less public one it does not require a full prospectus with all the accompanying expense, merely more limited press statements. In cases where a company wishes to obtain a quotation for shares which are already widely held by 100 or more shareholders, then the method used is a stock exchange introduction. To facilitate dealings a certain number of shares are made available in the market. Again only limited publicity is involved. While this was a popular method in the immediate post-war years it was little used in the fifties, but over recent years there has been a sprinkling of introductions on the market.

The costs of making an issue of securities varies with the nature of each individual issue and the complications which may be attached to it. In general terms the cost of placing £2.0mn would be around £50,000 to £75,000, while an offer for sale of the same amount would be of the order of £75,000 to £100,000; that is about 3% for a placing and 4½% for an offer for sale. The costs involved do not fall appreciably for a smaller issue, the percentage costs rising accordingly. With a placing the main expenses are fees to solicitors and accountants, limited advertising, and the fees payable to the merchant bank and the broker to the issue, the latter normally being in the region of 1 to 1½% of the amount placed. An offer for sale, however, involves much more publicity, considerable handling costs with applications and allotments, and underwriting, all of which greatly enlarge the costs. For underwriting the issuing house would take ½%, with a further 1¼% for the sub-underwriters, while the broker to the issue would get a fee in the region of ½% of the issue. An essential part of the service rendered by the broker would be advice on the state of the market and the pricing of the issue, and he would also act as the point of contact between the merchant bank and the Stock Exchange committee dealing with the application for a quotation.

Institutional facilities for handling new issues improved greatly in the post-war period, particularly from the mid-sixties onwards. In the early post-war years merchant banking services were supplied by the Industrial Credit Company, the banking house of Guinness, Mahon & Co., and for a short time by two companies formed in 1947. They were Hibernian Industrial and General Investment Co. and Tokenhouse Securities (Ireland) Ltd., the former having strong links with the Stock Exchange.[34] In response to the growth of the economy and a more encouraging stock market, with its bouts of takeovers in the middle and late sixties, several merchant banks entered the field, among them Hill Samuel (1964), Ansbacher, Hodge,

Lombard, Charterhouse (in Cork), Northern Bank Finance (all in 1969) and Fitzwilliam Securities Ltd. (1971). None of these were particularly busy in the new issue field. However, two concerns set up about the same time, subsidiaries of the main banking groups, did become very active as issuing houses. They were the Investment Bank of Ireland and the Allied Irish Investment Bank.

Very few of the issues made during recent years were handled solely by a merchant bank, most were done jointly with a stockbroker. Dublin brokers, along with W. & R. Morrogh of Cork, have of course long been involved in this kind of work. Butler & Briscoe not only acted as brokers to government issues but for industrial ones as well. The other firms who were most active in the early post-war years were Goodbody & Webb (now Goodbody, Dudgeon), O'Brien & Toole, Dudgeon & Sons, and J. & E. Davy. In addition about a dozen other firms at some time handled new issues, ranging from a single issue to half a dozen during the years 1946-56.[35] In the resurgence of new issues from the mid-sixties onwards the work became the preserve of fewer firms, and while some seven firms were involved in occasional issues in the seventies the bulk of the business was undertaken by J. & E. Davy and Dudgeon. In the period 1971-81 J. & E. Davy handled nearly 100 issues and Dudgeon nearly 90.

The dormant state of share prices from 1945 to the early sixties (see chart 3 on p. 193) reflected not only the general behaviour of the economy but also certain characteristics of the market itself. Interest in the shares of Irish companies was limited due to the presence of only a few first class ones with consistent records of growth and good profits. There was not a great deal to entice local investors away from the great variety of equity investments available in London. Such Irish investments as were considered attractive tended, however, to be tightly held which resulted in relatively narrow markets, so that buyers and sellers might have to wait some time before their orders could be executed. In addition, companies did not set out to court the market with liberal dividend distribution policies, contenting themselves with traditional levels which seemed to have satisfied their long standing shareholders.[36]

However, since the mid-sixties the market has been much more active and has followed roughly the path displayed by its larger counterparts. Several factors may account for this. The Irish economy became much more open with companies getting a larger proportion of business by exporting and while this diversified their sources of income it also made their profits liable to the fluctuations of the international economy, which were particularly severe in the seventies. On the demand side, investors, both private and institutional, looked increasingly to ordinary shares as some sort of hedge for inflation, a factor which increased local interest in Irish shares, one which spread downwards from the market leaders to the better secondary shares. Even English investors were beginning to be attracted by good profits and, reportedly because in the mid-sixties "politics is less of a stock market issue".[37] Companies also made greater use of the market, not merely for obtaining capital by share and debt issues, but also for capitalising their past growth. All these factors helped to create interest in the market and generated greater dealing activity.

Significantly what also emerged in the late sixties, through growth and merger activity, were a handful of large companies, especially so when compared to earlier standards, whose capitalisations were sufficient to allow more institutional investment and dealing activity. Taking the six largest companies on the market in 1972 their combined equity capital represented some 53% of the total market capitalisation of the top 50 Irish companies. By 1982 the first six companies accounted for 66% of the capitalisation of the top 50.[38] But alongside this development it should be noted that the average capitalisation of quoted companies had not altered a great deal in the period 1972-82, the figure increasing from £6.0mn to £9.5mn. There is still a long tail of companies with small capitalisations; in 1982 there were 20 companies with capitals of less than £2.0mn. This compares with only 9 of under £1.0mn in 1972 when the share price index was half its 1982 level.[39] In 1985 the first five industrial companies were Smurfit, Cement-Roadstone, Waterford Glass, Irish Distillers Group and Carroll Industries. They accounted for 73% of the capital of the top 20 companies. There were some 35 companies with capitals of less than £6.0mn.

There is a large degree of concentration in the market, with reasonable dealing activity in the leading shares but only somewhat lethargic turnover in the smaller companies. The prospects for an increase in the number of large companies, or for frequent changes in their ranking, are however slight. This is due to the constraints imposed by the size of the home market, one of the largest sectors in the economy — agriculture — having a strong co-operative tradition, and of course, the state having a considerable interest in several trading activities, for example, sugar, turf and transport.

During recent years interest in shares and in the level of market activity has been periodically boosted by short lived speculative surges. The discovery of zinc and lead deposits by the Tara Exploration Co. (based in Canada) in 1973-74 brought a spurt of interest in Irish mining ventures. A more permanent benefit was that it also directed the attention of outsiders to other profitable investments on the Dublin market, which despite the oil crisis of the time, were benefiting from the growth of the economy.[40] But bigger speculative excitement was around the corner.

The arrival of oil exploration companies in 1979-80 gave the market floor a sudden "breath of fresh air". Companies such as Bula Resources and Atlantic Resources "seem to crystallize the Irish penchant for a flutter and without doubt attracted funds on to the Stock Exchange from quarters which never before would have dreamed of playing the market".[41] Indeed, such was the level of speculation in 1983 that the Irish government was reported to be concerned about the number of second mortgages raised in the Dublin area; the lure of large gains remains undiminished. The main company in the 1980 fever was Aran Energy which went from 200p. to 405p., to give it a capitalisation of £39.5mn. It later retreated from this peak and by the end of 1982 its stock market worth was £10.0mn, slightly smaller than Atlantic Resources worth £11.7mn, the next in line being Bula Resources with £7.5mn. But given the speculative nature of the shares and the wide swings which occur, the ranking of capitalisations is a shifting affair. During the 1983 boom in oil shares Atlantic Resources reached a heady 950p., having started its life at a mere 30p., but when the preliminary nature of the first oil strike had been appreciated, it relapsed to more sober levels. Most of these transactions are conducted under Rule 553 which permits dealings without companies having to comply with the requirements of the Unlisted Share Market, let alone the full panoply of the quotation requirements, which few of them could ever meet. Indeed the intention of these particular concessions is to encourage dealings in companies with a much greater, but recognised degree of risk.[42]

Detailed records on the level of market activity have only been available from 1974 onwards. Since that date the turnover of the market increased some fourfold, while the number of bargains recorded increased less rapidly. The size of the average bargain has also risen significantly over the period, from a level of £1,200 in 1974-76 to £4,000 in 1980-82. This increase is well in excess of the doubling of share values over these years, suggesting that there has been a greater degree of institutional participation in the market. The number of bargains per account is also greater than in earlier years, the average for three recent years being 1,700, compared with around 1,200 during 1974-76.

Outside interest in Irish shares has certainly grown over recent years, particularly so in companies which are also dealt in on the London floor, that is, Smurfit, Waterford and Cement-Roadstone. This is reflected in the proportion of capital now held outside the state. In the case of Smurfit the figure increased from 42% in 1972 to 47.8% in 1982, Cement-Roadstone went from 18.4% to 23.6%, while Waterford rose from 15% in 1975 to 22.5% in 1982. Part of this external interest no doubt comes from institutional investors and this is matched by growing institutional involvement within the country. Institutions hold a sizeable portion of the shares of the major companies, ranging from 27% in the case of Cement-Roadstone to 62% for Carroll Industries. However, the item nominee holdings may well contain a number of institutional owners of one sort or another, thereby putting the general level of institutional participation at about 60% or so. Within this figure the holdings of savings institutions (insurance and pension funds) probably account for about 20% to 30% of all shares, which is well below the figure for the United Kingdom. The bulk of the remaining shares are held by individuals who in the case of the major companies account for about 26-

33% of all shares outstanding; this is roughly the same proportion as for British companies. Numerically, of course, persons dominate the ranks of shareholders, representing about 90% of the total number. For the most part their holdings are under the £10,000 level; about 90% of the shareholdings in the large companies were below this figure. For small companies individuals dominate the share list, both by number and by virtue of the value of shares held. In their case about 90% of the capital is held within the country, a figure which suggests fairly low institutional participation. Indeed, the small capital outstanding would tend to preclude active institutional interest since they restrict themselves to a maximum of 5% of a company's capital. In the main, therefore, the shares of the numerous small companies on the market are in the ownership of the personal sector and they are reasonably firmly held at that.[43]

The present-day rules governing the quotation of a company are much more detailed than earlier requirements but the essential features remain the same. To ensure the maintenance of a reasonable market in the shares at least a quarter of any class of equity that is issued must be made available to the public, while the rules also stipulate a minimum market capitalisation. When the United Stock Exchange was formed in 1973 a company was expected to have a minimum market value of £250,000, and an individual security was to have an expected market value of £100,000. Since then these figures have been doubled but there is an important concession for regional markets, which is particularly vital for the Irish Unit, that "a lower initial capitalisation may be acceptable where the Council are satisfied as to marketability". The provisions set out in *Admission of Securities to Listing* are designed to ensure that not only will there be a reasonable market in the shares of a company but also that shareholders will be supplied with full information to enable them to make informed decisions when buying or selling. The general aim is to ensure marketability and safeguard the full disclosure of information. In addition companies are subject to the provisions of the Companies Act. Recently the Irish Unit was made the agency for implementing E.E.C. directives on listing and related matters.

Although such a comprehensive set of requirements is regarded as generally desirable it was seen as perhaps posing too formidable a hurdle for small companies in search of equity capital. To accommodate the needs of companies who did not want to place such a large fraction of their capital in public hands, and who had only a limited trading record, the Stock Exchange in 1980 introduced special regulations for the Unlisted Share Market. In this case there is no lower limit on the size of companies and they need only have been trading for three years compared with five for a full listing. Whereas a quarter of the equity capital needs to be made available for a full listing only ten per cent is required to be in public hands when dealings start on the U.S.M. Such shares can be made available to the public either by a placing (with an upper limit of £3.0mn), or by means of an offer for sale. To reduce the costs of issue only brief particulars are required to be advertised and there is a reduced level of reporting from accountants. However, all companies must sign the General Undertaking of the Stock Exchange which binds them to keep shareholders and the market informed as to its state of affairs. In 1985 six companies featured in the Dublin U.S.M. — Bula Resources, Memory Computer, Ennex International, Tuskar Resources, Flogas Plc. and F.I.I. Plc.

The use made of the U.S.M. has been a little disappointing and in order to attract non-oil companies to the market a new scheme was launched early in 1986 [Plate 6]. This is the Smaller Companies Market with simple and low cost facilities. The listing fee will be a modest IR£500 annually, waived for the first year. Eligible companies must be registered in the Republic, backed by a local stockbroker and be able to provide one year's audited accounts. Even companies which have just started can use its facilities if they have been assisted by the industrial development agency or obtained funds through the Éire Business Expansion Scheme. It is hoped to attract companies in the expanding field of electronics, chemicals and the financial services area. For investors it offers an opportunity to widen the range of shares in their portfolios, wider horizons having been denied to them by the presence of exchange controls since 1978.

# NOTES

1. *Banking Commission*, 1926, Second Interim Report, p. 32.
2. The Minister for Industry and Commerce, who gave the guarantee, was assisted by an Advisory Committee; *Commission of Enquiry into Banking, Currency and Credit*, 1938, Report, para. 445.
3. Both Banking Commissions advised against this kind of guarantee, the 1938 Commission suggesting that a government guarantee of the bonds of a lending institution would be preferable. Appendix 21 of its Report gives details of the loans guaranteed under the 1924 provisions.
4. ibid., para. 51. The £1 shares were quoted in the Dublin list. The prospectus appeared in *The Irish Times*, July 25 1925. At the time of setting up the I.T.C. the government already had guaranteed £150,000 of loans; the greater part of this business was transferred to the company.
5. L.M. Cullen, *An Economic History of Ireland since 1660*, (1972), pp. 178-79.
6. J. Meenan, *The Irish Economy since 1922*, (1970), p. 151. Examples are also given by the 1938 *Banking Commission* (Evidence, Vol. 2, p. 1,428) who were very critical of the policy of excluding foreign capital. In practice the prohibition was overcome by all sorts of agreements and undertakings.
7. *Company Taxation in Ireland*, (Prl. 2,628), 1972, p. 20.
8. The evidence of the Stock Exchange was presented by Mr. G.L. Kennedy, President, and Mr. J.F. Stokes, a member of the Committee; *Banking Commission*, 1938, Evidence, Vol. 1. Q. 2,926.

9. C.H. Murray, "Some Aspects of the Industrial Capital Market", *Journal of the Statistical and Social Inquiry Society of Ireland*, 1959-60, p. 113; *Company Taxation in Ireland*, op. cit., p. 20.

10. This was allowed under the Trade Loans (Guarantee) Amendment Act 1933. Particulars of the operation of the Acts are given in the *Banking Commission*, 1938, Evidence, Vol. 1, pp. 24-27.

11. Appendix 21 of the *Banking Commission*, 1938, Report, lists the guarantees given between 1932 and December 1936.

12. *Banking Commission*, 1938, Evidence, Vol. 1, Q. 19.

13. The 1938 *Banking Commission* claimed that facilities were present in Dublin for small or large issues by established companies, but conceded that little existed for newer firms.

14. *Statist*, March 10 1934, p. 362.

15. *Twenty-one Years of Industrial Financing*, (1955), p. 14.

16. *Statist*, December 1 1934, p. 859. In the issue of Ranks (Ireland) Butler & Briscoe offered £106,000 to the members of the Stock Exchange for underwriting; Dublin Stock Exchange, Minutes, February 27 1934.

17. The Stock Exchange practice was to divide the amount offered among the members, and if some was not taken up it would then be divided pro rata among the accepting members; Dublin Stock Exchange, Minutes, March 23, November 19 1934, July 18 1935.

18. *Banking Commission*, 1938, Report, p. 432.

19. *Banking Commission*, 1938, Evidence, Vol. 1, Q. 2,879.

20. ibid., Q. 3,000.

21. ibid., Q. 2,901.

22. Due to the paper shortage the Stock Exchange Committee relaxed the regulations governing advertising of the prospectus, regarding an abridged one or a statement in lieu of it as adequate; Minutes, November 18 1942.

23. This was done by the Encouragement of External Investment Act, 1958. However, the repeal of the Control of Manufactures Act was delayed so as not to break faith too sharply with companies who came in under its provisions. Foreign firms were also attracted, before 1973-74, by the relatively low level of Irish labour costs; Central Bank of Ireland, *Quarterly Bulletin*, March 1974, p. 30.

24. A sharp fall occurred in company savings from £29.2mn in 1965 to £22.5mn in 1966; *Company Taxation in Ireland*, op. cit., p. 129.

25. Quoted by Meenan, op. cit., p. 148. This probably arose from the habit of old businesses of looking to the banks when needing more capital, whether it was short term or long term; *Statist*, February 3 1951, "Financing Irish Industry", by J. C. Colbert, pp. 43-44.

26. *Company Taxation in Ireland*, op. cit., p. 51. While interest on bank borrowing was an allowable expense in arriving at taxable profit, this consideration was probably not decisive in accounting for the considerable importance of bank finance for Irish companies.

27. ibid., para. 48, p. 21. The relief is due to expire on April 5 1990. Mining profits were subject to similar relief.

28. *First Report of the Commission on Taxation: Direct Taxation*, (Prl. 617), 1982, p. 550.

29. *Statist*, February 3 1951, p. 43.

30. *Company Taxation in Ireland*, op. cit., p. 53.

31. Figures calculated from details given in *The Times Issuing House Year Book*.

32. These are set out in considerable detail in the Stock Exchange's *Admission of Securities to Listing*.

33.   For example Youghal Carpets was brought to the market in 1963 in this way.
34.   The directors of the Hibernian Industrial and General Investment Co. Ltd.
      were all members of the Stock Exchange. J.W. Freeman (Goodbody & Webb)
      was chairman, along with M. King-French (Boyle, Low, Murray & Co.), J.J.
      Davy (J. & E. Davy), J. McCann (James McCann & Son), E.C.G. Mulhern
      (Ryan & Dillon), and T.V. Murphy (L.A. Waldron & Co.). It handled two
      small public issues in 1948 and 1950. Tokenhouse Securities (Ireland) Ltd.
      was a subsidiary of the Dublin & General Trust Co. Ltd.
35.   They were P.W. Tunney & Co., Richard Pim & Son, Stewart & Kinsman,
      Moore, Gamble, Carnegie & Co., M. Dillon & Son, Ryan & Dillon, Boyle,
      Barton & Co., Bruce, Symes & Wilson, W. Wilson & Son, T.A. Brindley, and
      Lillis & Harrington.
36.   Murray, op. cit., p. 107. He referred to Irish companies having a more
      conservative attitude to dividend distributions than British ones, and he
      viewed this as an important explanation for the relative quiescence of the
      Dublin market. Like British companies Irish firms had been required to
      restrict their dividend distribution during the war, limiting them to the
      maximum payments made in 1938-40. Post-war relaxation, however, did not
      set Irish equities ablaze; companies simply built up reserves.
37.   *The Economist* later reported, "Many British investors took their money over
      to Dublin after Mr. Harold Wilson's election victory in 1964"; February 23
      1974, p. 105.
38.   Calculated from particulars contained in the useful *Irish Times* annual survey
      of Irish companies.
39.   Not only are some companies relatively small but only about $\frac{1}{4}$ to $\frac{1}{3}$ of the
      capital is in public hands.
40.   *The Economist*, February 23 1974, p. 105. Mineral exploration had been in
      progress since 1968.
41.   *The Irish Times*, December 31 1981.
42.   Under Rule 553(2) a broker who wishes to deal in the share concerned must
      get the approval of the presiding officer of the Exchange on each occasion. But
      if the company concerned meets certain requirements the shares can be dealt
      in under 553(3) whereby sanction does not have to be given for every deal.
43.   Information derived from *The Irish Times* annual surveys, and also kindly
      supplied by the main Irish companies quoted on the Stock Exchange Official
      List.

CHAPTER 11

# AMALGAMATION AND UNIFICATION

When the Irish Stock Exchange joined The Stock Exchange in March 1973 it represented the culmination of nearly one hundred years of varying degrees of formal co-operation between Irish markets and those in Britain. Even before the setting up of the Council of Associated Stock Exchanges in 1890, with Dublin as one of the founder members, the Dublin Stock Exchange had co-operated with other markets in such matters as special settlement dates, exchanging information on defaulters, settling disputes among brokers, and buying-in and selling-out between markets. These problems, while common to all markets, never proved of sufficient importance to merit the creation of a formal association. The impetus for this came from the Barton Fraud which was perpetrated in the stock of the North Western Railway Co. Its discovery in 1886 led the courts to order the company to reinstate the original owners' names on the company's register thus depriving many innocent parties of stock which they had bought in good faith. This legal decision produced widespread alarm, particularly since railway stocks were first class investments at the time. The episode prompted brokers to look into the question of their liability if they were involved in such unfortunate dealings, and from this concern sprang the initiative to form the Council of Associated Stock Exchanges which quickly proceeded to press for legislation to protect purchasers from losses due to forged transfers. The resulting legislation, the Forged Transfer Act of 1891, empowered companies to compensate shareholders for losses from forged transfers. However, companies were not compelled to adopt the provisions of the act, and in order to procure for shareholders the benefit of such protection the Stock Exchanges undertook an intensive campaign to persuade companies to do so, thereby making their certificates absolute evidence of title. In Ireland both Dublin and Cork campaigned effectively to get companies to adopt the provisions of the act, and companies who obliged were so marked in the Dublin list.[1]

With the Forged Transfer Act safely instituted the Council turned its attention to drawing up a general Code of Laws, not so much with the intention of securing absolute uniformity between markets but rather to seek "uniformity of principle in the conduct of exchange business", an aim supported by most member exchanges. During the inter-war years Dublin and Cork were involved in this process of adopting resolutions passed by the Council on such matters as rules on outside brokers (generally charging full commission if they operated in towns where there was a stock exchange), commission levels, quotation requirements (requesting companies to insert clauses in their articles of association for the protection of shareholders' interests), and those arising from the long drawn out and often difficult negotiations with London over access to London's dealing facilities. This involved markets outside London, including Dublin and Cork, agreeing to accept limits on telephone communications with non-members. Members of the Associated Exchanges were thus prevented from making net prices with any non-member jobber. All this was aimed at curtailing the widespread jobbing empire built up by Nicholson's of Sheffield, although this link was not used by Dublin and Cork brokers, in marked contrast to the useful service that Nicholson's rendered to the Belfast market (see Chapter 12).[2]

One matter, share pushing, which was discussed by the Council of Associated Stock Exchanges in the late thirties, was also causing concern to the Department of Finance and it took up the issue with the Stock Exchange. The Committee, of course, were already keenly aware of the effects of outside competition whether it came from established channels or the more recent outburst of share pushing. At the time the Stock Exchange did not divide commissions with anyone except outside brokers duly approved by the Committee; and neither did Dublin brokers divide commissions with the local banks.[3] In response to the approach by the Department of Finance the Stock Exchange suggested that one possible way of dealing with share pushing would be to require all brokers operating in the Irish Free State to be licensed by the government under a comprehensive system. By the terms of the 1799 legislation Stock Exchange members were required to take out a licence to deal in government securities, but the Committee pointed out that in practice "unlicensed brokers in other parts of the country have for years been dealing in such Government securities, so that the granting of a Licence does not afford protection to the Public or to the Stock Exchange". In addition, there was nothing to prevent a member of the public from "opening business in Dublin and transacting business in all securities other than Government securities and, in fact, such firms have from time to time operated in Dublin with unfortunate results to the public".[4] In the event the prospects of a major war and falling share prices deferred the need for change, and the general licensing of all brokers in the country had to wait for several decades.

It was not until the early sixties that a formal attempt was made to seek means of improving the collaboration between all the stock markets of Britain and Ireland. The war and post-war adjustment accounts for some of the lapse of time, while the full implications of trends in share ownership and changes in the structure of the market were only then becoming fully apparent. Although consideration was given to the formation of a united stock exchange as early as 1962 it was decided that a looser arrangement would best serve the diverse interests and contrasting practices of the many markets involved, and accordingly, in 1965, the Federation of Stock Exchanges in Great Britain and Ireland was set up. Its main aim was to achieve uniform minimum standards in certain areas of activity throughout all markets and within a short space of time this was achieved in such matters as membership qualifications, the administration of partnerships, branch offices of firms, compensation funds, and quotation requirements.

Dublin's first deliberations on whether to join the Federation took place in 1963 and the initial response was not to do so, the main stumbling block being the requirement that single member firms would have to be phased out. Sometime later the matter was again taken up, the Committee seeking the views of the Minister of Finance as to the desirability of their joining closely with an organisation outside the country. As it turned out the Minister had no objection to branch offices of outside firms appearing in Dublin, and no objection in principle to agreements between organisations in Ireland and those elsewhere provided that it was in the public interest. When the resolution to join was put before a special meeting of the members in 1965, the awareness of official approval and a recognition of the benefits of belonging to a large and powerful organisation produced an overwhelming majority in favour of such a step.[5]

At the same time the Cork Stock Exchange was also looking at the Federation prospectus. Not only was the matter discussed among Cork members but consultations were held with Dublin. Cork quickly formed the view that there was little alternative to joining. Had they opted to keep out of the Federation they would have been treated as outside brokers — "as a foreign Exchange" — and they could not have done business profitably on that basis. Their small clients would have suffered, while the larger ones would simply have transferred their business to Dublin. Certainly, they were keenly aware that their weakest point "was the lack of any compensation fund". The outcome was a decision by the members in June 1965 to join the Federation, and to get over the problem of no compensation fund a local one was hastily set up and a provision inserted in the rules to obtain additional contributions towards the central compensation fund.[6]

In addition to the formation of a collective organisation developments were also taking place in Britain aimed at the formation of strong regional units in contrast to the large number of separate markets, some sizeable, others very small indeed. Regionalisation was stimulated at the time by two considerations. First, the smaller markets had no effective dealing floors, they lacked compensation funds, and the standards of control and listing requirements were not always of the same quality as the larger markets could provide. Second, internal disquiet was intensified by the pronouncements of the Jenkins Committee on Company Law, of 1962, which recommended that the then Board of Trade should look at the list of stock exchanges with a view to reducing their number and increasing their size. This threat of external intervention in provincial affairs (from a body which had given them scant attention in the past) soon brought change from within. In 1964 the Scottish Stock Exchange was formed, followed by the Northern Stock Exchange in 1965, and the Midland & Western Stock Exchange a year later.

During the discussions which preceded the setting up of the Federation, the Joint Committee put forward the idea of a national stock exchange which would also embrace Dublin, Cork and Irish members of the Provincial Brokers Stock Exchange. Amalgamation within Ireland was also being considered and over the next few years several meetings were held between representatives of the Dublin and Cork markets with the aim of forming a single exchange. Complications arose at the beginning due to the constitution of the Dublin Stock Exchange and the need for Cork members to contribute to a Mutual Fund. By September 1967, however, a merger had been agreed in principle "in order to ensure co-operation in matters of common interest, to establish certain fundamental regulations governing stock broking in Ireland and to act on their behalf as a member of the Federation of Stock Exchanges of Great Britain and Ireland".[7] As part of the arrangements it was agreed to publish one Daily List, markings on the Cork floor being conveyed daily by telephone to the Dublin office for inclusion in the list. The Committee, with representatives from Cork, would deal with the usual matters relating to the organisation and running of the new body. The fusion took place in March 1971 when four Cork firms and those in Wexford, Limerick, Waterford and Galway were admitted to the newly titled Irish Stock Exchange, which was automatically admitted to the Federation. The Irish Stock Exchange thus embraced all stockbrokers operating within the Republic, and to conform to the provisions of the 1799 act the Department of Finance issued licences for the first time to brokers in Cork and those from the P.B.S.E.

More structural change was in the wind. Federation, of course, was seen as a stage towards a united stock exchange and its satisfactory working soon prompted proposals for full amalgamation. Between 1969 and 1971 a detailed scheme was drawn up to form a unified market called The Stock Exchange, consisting of the London Stock Exchange and the other members of the Federation. Within the new set-up there would be local administrative units each with its own rules to cover domestic matters. The general rules and regulations were to be based, with suitable amendments, on those of the London Stock Exchange, while its Deed of Settlement was to be altered to provide for the scheme of amalgamation and this was then to form the constitution of The Stock Exchange. Following discussions with the Department of Finance the Irish Stock Exchange voted unanimously to join the new organisation, which came into existence on March 25 1973.

Two general considerations lay behind this decision. First, to remain outside would have meant a significant loss of income for Irish brokers; dealing as outside brokers would have lost them concessions enjoyed under Federation, and no doubt many Irish investors would have switched to dealing directly with British brokers rather than go through a disadvantaged intermediary. Membership ensured direct access to other floors and particularly to London jobbers; of course, British brokers and jobbers were also entitled to access to the Dublin floor. For Irish investors it brought added protection in the form of the large central Compensation Fund of The Stock Exchange.[8] Second, the new organisation constituted the largest organised market in the E.E.C. and to remain outside would undoubtedly have reduced the prospect of obtaining funds from both British and European markets.

But, in view of the special position and workings of the Irish Stock Exchange, account was taken of certain important differences. The long standing requirement that brokers had to be licensed by the government continued to operate, while the Minister of Finance would also approve the rules and regulations relating to the Irish Unit. Special provisions applied to Irish government securities in that the procedure for issue was exempt from any control by The Stock Exchange, the government being able to create and sell additional tranches of existing loans without specifying an upper limit on the amount. Also, the Dublin floor could only be closed down with the consent not only of a majority of the local members but also of the Minister of Finance.

Since the Dublin floor employed a call over system involving broker to broker bargains, which conflicted with the single capacity basis of London with its jobbers, provisions were written into the rules permitting this mode of dealing. Thus broker to broker bargains were allowed in "Irish Government Securities, and Bonds, Government Guaranteed Securities and Corporation Stocks listed in The Stock Exchange Official List-Irish, and War Loan inscribed in the books of the Bank of Ireland". Also in "such securities as may be designated by the Council provided that ; (a) the securities are of a company whose Registered Office is situated in the Republic of Ireland, and (b) no Jobber is dealing in the security on a trading floor in the Republic of Ireland and (c) the bargain is done between members of the Irish Administrative Unit".[9] In July 1985 there were 97 designated securities on the Irish list. However, under the re-organisation scheme which comes into operation in the autumn of 1986 (the "Big Bang") the above designation of securities will end and Irish firms will become Registered Dealers in all Irish securities. This will ensure that the long established floor trading in Irish securities will continue.

While overall government of the Stock Exchange rests with an elected Council, certain powers and duties are delegated to the local administrative units. In the case of the Irish Unit these cover such matters as the control and supervision of the trading floor, publishing the list (the Irish Unit is the only one with its own list), granting quotations, providing facilities for settlement, although this is now done largely through TALISMAN (see below), adjudicating local disputes with an appeals channel to the Council, local membership, and "generally to do all such other things in connection with Stock Exchange business" as may be delegated to it by the Council, or seems conducive to the exercise of the powers accorded to it. The Committee of the Irish Unit consists of an elected President and Vice President (nowadays they usually serve for two years), eight other elected members and two ex-officio members, the Government Broker and the Unit's elected representative on the Council. To assist the Committee there are several sub-committees who deal with various technical aspects of stock exchange business. The office administration is presided over by a General Manager.

Members of the Unit pay an annual subscription and a local one to cover specific local expenditures. New entrants, of course, are faced with considerably larger outlays. Candidates are required to pay, in addition to the subscription, the sum of £1,000 to the Trustees of the Nomination Redemption Fund. They also need to complete three years training, with three months experience on the floor of the market, pass the relevant Stock Exchange examinations, and be separately proposed and seconded by members of at least four years standing and with at least two years acquaintance of the candidate. Clerks are also admitted to the market, but they cannot transact business as an accredited clerk until they have served with a firm for a year, with a minimum of six months experience on the floor. In 1985 the Irish Unit had five authorised clerks and nine unauthorised clerks. The membership of the Unit in March 1985 was 85 in 16 firms, with seven branch offices, one of them in London.[10]

Since the days of Federation the minimum number of partners in a firm has been two; single member firms were found more liable to financial problems. For the most part firms in the Irish Unit are partnerships, but a few firms are constituted as corporate members, registered under the provisions of the Companies Act. Recently those with limited corporate status have allowed outside institutions to take an interest in the firm (the ceiling at the present time is 29.9%, with the likelihood of 100% in the near future). In addition to the members and clerks, firms employ an office manager and the normal range of administrative and clerical assistance, the amount and nature depending on the volume of business handled. Larger firms have specialist staff engaged in research activity.

One feature of stockbroking during recent years has been the considerable reduction in the number of firms, a trend apparent in the Irish Unit particularly since 1973. In the regional markets of Britain a rapid programme of amalgamation took place in the late sixties, a consolidation inspired by the search for economies of scale, increased financial strength and in response to the changing investment market. Such firms, it was felt, could offer a larger range of specialist services, especially to institutional investors whose importance in the market place was increasing, and also to other investors who were widening their investment horizons beyond the local market. When the Irish Unit was formed over half the firms were two partner ones, a significantly higher proportion of small firms than existed in the other Units within the Stock Exchange. Their survival in Dublin probably arose due to lower costs of operation than elsewhere, but more so because until recently they benefited from the relative dominance of private client business in the market. Since 1973 the number of two partner firms has fallen markedly, to five in 1983, and the emergence of several larger units over these years has been in response to the influences noted above. There are now six firms with five or more partners.[11]

One of the benefits of Federation, and one which has been continued and refined under The Stock Exchange, is that of the prudential regulation of stockbroking. Not only has this brought added security to clients but it has also rendered individual firms more attentive to matters of cost and efficiency. Up to 1982 the appropriate margin of liquidity was set at £5,000 per partner but this did not have to be met on an individual basis merely at the firm level. However, the firm was obliged to maintain the required standard at all times. More recently an alternative basis of assessment was introduced, this time taking the form of a sum equivalent to two months of the annual audited expenditure of the firm, thereby taking account of the volume of business handled. Firms are then required to maintain that liquidity margin which is the greater.[12] Further financial monitoring, started in 1974, takes the form of quarterly returns of revenue and expenditure which permits a close surveillance of the trading performance of member firms. The financial position of each firm is also subject to periodic scrutiny by the Stock Exchange Inspector.

The distinctive feature of the Dublin floor is, of course, the continued use of the call over system for executing transactions. Once widely used on other local floors, where it has now been replaced by local dealers, Dublin remains its last refuge. However, broker to broker dealing is confined to Irish securities while transactions in U.K. securities are done by brokers contacting the appropriate dealers in London or the provinces, either directly or using the services of an agent on the London floor. With the introduction of exchange control in December 1978 the volume of business conducted in this way has been considerably reduced.

Dealings in Irish securities take place at two daily call over sessions. The morning call over takes place at 10.00, the afternoon one at 2.15. The only difference in procedure is that government funds are called first in the afternoon session. Generally the sessions last for about half an hour, slightly longer if certain sectors are the subject of greater investment interest than normal. The public can view the proceedings from the public gallery; during the oil share boom they flocked there.

Dealers from member firms sit at desks arranged in a circle on the floor of the market, with the President's chair, slightly raised, at the head [see Plate 5]. Most firms have a direct telephone link from the desk to their office, while there are also phone booths nearby to receive incoming calls. An official rings a bell to start the session. He then calls out in turn the name of each security listed on the large price boards situated to the left of the President's chair; the morning session begins with Land Bonds, then through to Corporation Stocks and Public Boards, to the banks, then general companies, and ending with the Unlisted Markets and dealings under special rules. As each stock is called the brokers proceed to deal in it until all their orders are completed. Buying brokers will indicate their intention to buy at a particular price, selling brokers, if any, will indicate their intention and price. Sometimes the buy and sell orders may coincide on price; if not then some slight movement may be necessary to bring the two together. It is assumed that deals are done in quotable amounts. Small bargains are so denoted on the boards and later in the Official List. Sometimes a broker will declare both price and quantity and it may be necessary in order to execute the deal to split the sum involved, for example, a single sale being divided between two buyers. When dealings in a stock are exhausted the next one is called, and so on through the list. For most of the stocks it is all a fairly orderly and sober procedure but the market can occasionally become very noisy if there is a great deal of interest in a particular stock or stocks. The recent surge of widespread interest in oil exploration stocks, both in 1981 and 1983, produced feverish activity with very agitated calling and bidding on the floor, the whole procedure watched by an equally concerned audience in the public gallery, occasionally overflowing down the stairs. When dealings in industrials are over the bell is rung again and in the morning session, the Government Broker posts his prices. These are ones at which he is prepared to deal, on behalf of the authorities, and in this capacity he is acting as a jobber. The brokers can, however, undertake deals in government stocks between themselves if they find that they can do so to the advantage of their client. When all business is done the bell is rung and any miscellaneous deals are then called, while the President requests market guide prices, as 'nominals' for the Boards, that is, bid and/or offer prices currently made in the market. The nominal prices are marked in green chalk, the actual prices at which bargains have been done in white. Once these have been checked a final bell marks the end of the dealing session. Bargains concluded at the checking stage can also be entered on the Boards. When a transaction is completed each broker enters it in his market book, and after the close of business brokers and their clerks confirm the details of the sessions business.

Broker to broker trading in an open call over only works under certain conditions, which happen to be fulfilled on the Dublin market. It can only work smoothly if all the dealers can meet at the same time and place and in moderate numbers. Also, it is crucial that bids and offers be fully audible to the participants and the number of securities dealt in has to be limited so as to keep the dealing session to a reasonable duration. The advantage of the system for the Dublin market is that since there is inadequate turnover to sustain a jobbing book, the call over concentrates orders into a short period of dealing which undoubtedly improves marketability. Rather than have spasmodic and thin dealing throughout the day, the market has greater depth for part of the time, but inevitably it means that market making is not going on continuously. However, transactions can be done, and are done, outside the call over but the prices agreed are closely related to those marked during the previous session, and should large deviations occur then the broker involved may be required to explain the circumstances surrounding the deal.

Prices arrived at during the afternoon call over constitute the closing prices of the day, and these together with any other prices marked on the Boards are inserted in the Official List-Irish. Prices of Irish securities dealt in on the London market are telexed there for the information of interested jobbers. The Official List gives details of business done and the closing quotations, and in the case of industrials the price and date of the previous bargains which is important for infrequently traded shares so that investors can see the exact timing of the price. Also, for industrials the Market Guide Prices are given. For many there are bid and offer prices, but invariably there are some with only bid prices, while if the market trend is downwards, only offer prices may appear. It also carries details of bargains done in the Unlisted Securities Market and those done under Rule 535. All prices are, of course, denominated in Irish currency.

Later in the day a contract note is prepared for the client in the broker's office giving details of the transaction — price and quantity, commission, and in the case of purchases, stamp duty (except for government stocks, bearer securities and certain corporation stocks and public boards) — and this is dispatched that evening. All transactions are duly entered on the client's records. For several years the commission on equities has stood at 1.65% on amounts up to £7,000, with a tapering scale for additional sums, while small bargains had a minimum charge.[13] After the autumn of 1986 commissions will be on a negotiated basis. As set out in the rules commission is divided with certain agents and with the banks; before 1973 Dublin did not share commission with the local banks on business they introduced. Stamp duty, generally regarded as an irritating survival of earlier fiscal practices, is levied at the rate of 1%.

Unless otherwise arranged, bargains in government stocks, corporation and other inscribed stocks are for settlement on the following business day. Bargains in other securities are usually made for the account, the dates of which are fixed by the Council for each year. Normally there are twenty four accounts, twenty of fourteen days duration, and four long accounts of three weeks. Dealing periods end on a Friday with settlement taking place on the Tuesday of the following week. The interval enables buyers to prepare their means of payment, while sellers have time to make available the relevant ownership documents. But the essence of the settlement procedure is that all bargains must be completed, and to ensure that this takes place the broker is bound by the rules, and indeed long established convention, to deliver either cash or securities even when his client proves a little dilatory. Should a client wish to continue an open position into the next account (that is postpone payment or the delivery of stock) then arrangements to do so can be made for a suitable charge.[14]

Until fairly recently the settlement procedure involved a considerable amount of paper work, the brokers to each bargain passing tickets to each other and by a process of endorsement only ultimate buyers and sellers were brought together, while the intermediate participants needed only to be concerned with the differences owing to them. This process was simplified by the fixing of "making up" prices by the General Manager based on the approximate average price of the last two days of the account. Delivery of stock in Irish registered companies was then assisted by the operation of a local Central Stock Payments Department. The introduction of TALISMAN to the Irish Unit in 1980-81 changed all that; but in the few securities not done through the TALISMAN channel, the time honoured method of passing tickets applies.

TALISMAN, or Transfer Accounting Lodgement for Investors, Stock Management for Jobbers, was introduced to the London market in 1979 in order to deal with the serious problem of cost and capacity which the old ticket system encountered in the face of mounting volumes and occasional peak loads. TALISMAN now also settles all bargains, for the account, in Irish registered securities. Briefly, the process is as follows. When the selling broker receives the share certificate and a signed transfer from his client, he deposits these in advance of Account Day with the TALISMAN centre of the Irish Unit. The documents are then checked, and the transfer information entered into the computer system. They then go to the company's registration office for transfer out of the clients name and into that of the Stock Exchange nominee company, SEPON Ltd. (Stock Exchange Pool Nominee). This is a single undesignated shareholding

1. The Commercial Buildings, Dame Street, Dublin

3. The Belfast Call Over after the War

5. Presiding at the Call Over; the late Brendan Briscoe (President 1979–81, Government Broker 1968-82), flanked by the General Manager and the Assistant General Manager

7.  The President and Deputy President (from the left) discuss the introduction of new technology against the background of the old

8. The Committee at work, 1986 (from the left: A.D. Nicholson, J.A. Garvey, R.J. Dennis, I.K. Martin, P.I. Gowran (General Manager), A.C.A. McDonnell (President) and K. Beaton

account in the register of every company participating in the scheme and is the foundation of the TALISMAN arrangement. The details of each sold bargain are held in the computer system, and while legal title passes to SEPON on registration, effective control of the stock remains with the client until delivery is made on Account Day. On this day ownership is transferred within the computer system to the buyer and the pool of stock held in the nominee account is available to meet the needs of individual buyers. The total of stock in the pool is the sum of all sales, which is equal to all purchases; the total is then apportioned out to satisfy each purchase. This, of course, does away with the old problem of perhaps splitting up a large sale to satisfy several smaller purchases, or making up a large purchase from several small sales. Once the apportionment is made to the various buyers the computer then provides bought transfers authorizing the removal of the stock from the SEPON account into the name of the buying client. Bought transfers then go to the company registrar and legal title passes from SEPON to the buyer who duly receives his share certificate.

Stamp duty is collected directly at the TALISMAN centre and paid over in total to the tax authorities. For member firms the computer system generates statements of their respective deliveries and apportionments of stock, and settlement between member firms is again made through a single account at the TALISMAN centre. The most recent technical aid to the working of the market was the introduction in 1983 of TOPIC, the Stock Exchange data viewing system [Plate 7]. This relays price and other up-to-date information between markets, and is also employed in brokers' offices as well as on the market itself.

All the technical advances which have taken place over recent years have helped to increase the efficiency of the market in performing its essential economic functions, both for the economy in general and for the borrower and investor. A stock exchange floor is, of course, like any other market, merely a place where buyers and sellers, in this case represented by brokers who specialize in executing transactions, come together to exchange money and assets at various prices. Both parties are interested in completing their transactions at the lowest possible cost, with the greatest expedition, and at an acceptable price. The operational efficiency of the market revolves around technical aspects and the cost of services. The qualitative question of the value placed on a security depends on the capacity of the market to reflect, in the price, all the relevant information which is publicly available to it. This requires the adoption by companies and public bodies of the stipulations set out in the Companies Act and the Stock Exchange rules on the vital matter of disclosure of information. In general then the market provides a location where assets of various kinds can be speedily obtained or disposed of at prices which reflect the evaluation of all available information by buyers and sellers, be they institutions with their expert analysts, or the individual investor.

But a stock market not only enables the total of wealth in the form of securities to be transferred easily between holders, it also provides an important mechanism for allocating the flow of new savings among the alternative uses open to it. The prices of existing securities indicate to those seeking new capital the terms on which new funds can be raised. If the market takes a favourable view of the prospects of a particular firm or industry then the price of those shares will rise and the yield will fall, which will facilitate the marketing of new shares in similar enterprises. And, of course, the knowledge that newly acquired shares can be easily and quickly sold through the market makes the investor more willing to commit his funds, often viewed as being short term, for the purpose of long term investment in industry.

However, to the extent that there are impediments to the acquisition and disposal of assets it is likely that the ability of the market to reflect the true value of a security will be impaired, and both turnover and marketability will suffer. As a result, investors may well find the returns from their investments reduced by the difficulty of adjusting their portfolio with complete flexibility, while borrowers may find the cost of funds higher than it otherwise would be, and the flow of capital into new investment will be correspondingly reduced.

Certain policy measures over recent years have probably prevented the market from providing the best service possible to Irish investors and borrowers. For example, the ability of Irish investors to deal in U.K. securities was substantially curtailed in December 1978 when the government, following on Ireland joining the European Monetary System, introduced regulations to impose exchange controls against the U.K. and several other countries. This greatly reduced the freedom of persons and institutions to invest in U.K. shares. But in response to pressure from several quarters, including the Stock Exchange, the authorities in 1979 allowed authorized insurers and pension funds to export a limited amount of funds for investment in foreign currency securities. Such purchases were allowed to the point where they brought an institution's holdings of foreign currency securities up to 10% of net actuarial liabilities. A further minor amendment followed in December 1979 when Irish residents were allowed to buy securities issued by official E.E.C. institutions. Attempts at this time by the Stock Exchange to persuade the Department of Finance to allow individuals to invest abroad up to £10,000 met with no success, although stockbrokers were allowed to obtain forward currency cover in respect of dealings in Irish shares in London. Overall, such a restraint has prevented investors from exercising the fullest degree of adjustment to their portfolios, and the longer the control persists then the greater the distortion in investment holdings will become. For the Stock Exchange it has, of course, already brought a reduction in business reflected in the reduced flow of orders channelled through Irish brokers to London.

The introduction of capital gains tax was another measure which undoubtedly had an inhibiting effect on the market. On grounds of equity there is a case for taxing realised gains since they constitute for the individual a stream of income, but in so doing the tax adversely affects the working of the capital market. In the case of risk investment much of the return takes the form of capital gain rather then dividend distributions, and the taxation of such gains discourages risk taking. Of course, it can be avoided by not realising any gains but that tends to immobilize risk taking capital. While its effects may be ameliorated by permitting losses to be placed against gains in arriving at the taxable charge, this is not always done. In general then, its imposition tends to discourage risk investment. But it also has effects on the flexibility and turnover of the market in industrial shares. The prospect of paying tax on realised gains will discourage the sale of shares and thus reduce the amount of switching between securities, which otherwise might occur. This reduction in turnover will affect the marketability of each share and the general liquidity of the market, all likely to contribute to a higher cost of capital for new and existing enterprises.

The Irish market first encountered capital gains tax in 1975 when the Capital Gains Act made gains realised from the disposal of assets on or after April 6 1974 subject to tax. Capital gains secured by institutional investors was already subject to tax since such gains arose from the nature of their trade; the new tax applied to casual gains made by individual investors. The taxable gain was arrived at after deducting the cost of the asset from the sale proceeds. This initial provision made no distinction between long or short term gains, and no allowance was made for inflation, that is, no attempt was made to establish "real" capital gains. An amendment in 1978, however, took account of the inflation question by deflating nominal gains by the change in the retail prices index, thus giving an indication of "real" gains. This Act also introduced a distinction between short (speculative!) and long term (investment!) gains by instituting reduced rates of tax on gains from disposals after the lapse of three years. From a basic level of 30% a tapering scale falling in three year steps applied, with total exemption after 21 years; holding a share that long would be more from neglect than design. The 1982 Act then brought in some swingeing changes. The tapering relief was abolished, the nominal rate of tax was raised to 40%, and short term gains were to be treated differently. Nominal gains obtained within 12 months of acquisition were made subject to a 60% rate, and real "gains" obtained within 2 or 3 years of acquisition were taxed at a 50% rate. But in order not to stifle activity altogether the annual exemption limits were raised for individuals from £500 to £1,000 in the case of single persons and from £2,000 to £4,000 for married couples.[15] These higher thresholds, secured after much lobbying, particularly by the Stock Exchange, undoubtedly helped small investors and marginally contributed to the volume of turnover, but the tax levels remain high by international standards and they are not likely to help procure more equity capital for Irish industry, a cry which has been heard not only from the Stock Exchange but also from some of the monetary authorities.

While the prospects for greater freedom in the selection of investments, and of obtaining more returns by a lowering of the tax burden seem distant, imminent changes will take place in the costs of transactions. From October 1986 the long standing practice of minimum commissions will end, to be replaced by negotiated rates. Based on the experience of similar changes in New York several years ago the London market expects that rates on small bargains will probably rise marginally, while those for large bargains will fall noticeably since these clients have considerable negotiating power to deploy against their brokers. The scope for similar changes in Ireland is, however, more limited. Small bargains may well cost a little more, but larger deals are unlikely to display the big reductions probable in London since the number of institutional participants are fewer and smaller, and the average size of institutional bargains is below that found in London. The prospects for rate changes are thus marginal rather than radical. If the Department of Finance could see its way to abolish ad valorem stamp duty (now 1%), then this would produce a significant reduction in the cost of dealing; at the moment that prospect seems distant.

More competitive conditions are also likely to bring some structural changes. The institutional arrangements differ from those in London with fewer opportunities for significant investment in broking concerns by outside financial institutions. To date four firms have been involved, with outside institutions taking a 29.9% interest in them. There may also be mergers involving some of the smaller firms which will strengthen their competitive position, but a big reduction in their number seems unlikely, at least in the short term, since most of the established firms have a reliable core of personal client business. The prospects are that the number of firms on the Dublin market may be reduced in number from the present fifteen to around ten.

# NOTES

1.  Dublin Stock Exchange, Minutes, February 2 1892, April 21 1895; Cork Stock Exchange, Minutes, January 2 1899. Cork joined the Council of Associated Stock Exchanges in 1899. For a full account of the Barton Fraud and the formation of C.A.S.E. see W.A. Thomas, *The Provincial Stock Exchanges*, (1973), pp. 193-95.
2.  For an account of these controversial negotiations see Thomas, op. cit., chapters 10 and 11.
3.  This matter was discussed at some length when the Stock Exchange

representatives gave evidence to the 1938 *Banking Commission*, Evidence, Vol. 2, pp. 414-16. Commissions have been divided with the banks since 1973. Before this the banks only put local business through the Dublin market, the rest going direct to London brokers. After the 1973 concession local brokers are extensively used by the banks.

4.   Dublin Stock Exchange, Minutes, December 17 1937.

5.   Dublin Stock Exchange, Minutes, October 31 1963, May 28 1965.

6.   Cork Stock Exchange, Minutes, June 16, July 19 1965.

7.   The Provincial Brokers' Stock Exchange was left out of the initial discussions so that its position could be clarified.

8.   In 1973 the Irish Compensation Fund was just under £25,000.

9.   *Rules and Regulations of the Stock Exchange*, p. 119.

10.  The total number employed in Stock Exchange business, including members, in the Irish Unit in 1985 was 268.

11.  The major firms, in terms of operations, are regarded as being Davy, Goodbody Dudgeon, Maguire, McCann, Morrison, Riada, and Solomons, Abrahamson; see *Business and Finance*, August 1983.

12.  The detailed requirements are set out in Rule 79a of the Rule Book. Slightly different requirements apply to limited corporate member firms.

13.  When the Irish Stock Exchange joined The Stock Exchange in 1973 it meant reducing the commission rate from $1\frac{1}{2}\%$ to $1\frac{1}{4}\%$, but this was absorbed on what was a bullish market at the time.

14.  For the details of carry-over procedures see J. Dundas Hamilton, *Stockbroking Today*, (1968), chapter 3.

15.  *First Report of the Commission on Taxation; Direct Taxation*, Prl. 617, pp.202-03.

CHAPTER 12

# THE BELFAST STOCK EXCHANGE

Belfast's first stockbroker, Josias Cunningham & Co., added share dealing to the trade of a general merchant in November 1843, while in the following year two more brokers appeared on the scene, namely, Jackson S. Stevenson and Theobald Bushell. These three served the dealing needs of investors during the spate of local railway promotion at the time, such lines as the Ulster, Belfast & Ballymena, Dublin & Belfast Junction and Belfast County Down, and no doubt they also assisted them in dealing in other Irish lines as well as British railways. While the market was nowhere near the scale of that in Dublin, it had its speculative fling especially in the 'light' stocks, and its price movements were regularly reported by the *Irish Railway Gazette* and the more distant *Economist* in London; Stevenson supplied the former's account, Cunningham the latter's. The brokers could execute clients' orders by matching them in their own offices, negotiating with each other, contacting correspondents in other markets, or by buying and selling on their own account; since a licence was not needed there was no legal restraint to prevent this.

By 1860 Josias Cunningham and Theobald Bushell had been joined by three more brokers, Orr & Co., Henry Reid, and William Robinson. In the next few years the limitation of the linen industry provided a new outlet for local investors and additional activity for the local share market. Its continued expansion into the mid 1870s and the beginnings of large scale shipbuilding with the formation of Harland and Wolff in 1862, together with the appearance of many ancillary firms, brought an unparalleled degree of expansion to the city with all that this entailed for the building, food and service activities needed to meet the needs of a rapidly growing population.

This was reflected in the quickening pace of limited company registrations. Between 1864 and 1882 nearly 130 limited companies were formed in Belfast itself. Many only survived for a short time and of the remainder comparatively few were large companies with over fifty shareholders. The addition of these new outlets for investment to the existing list of local railways, banks and a few miscellaneous shares, were probably sufficient to sustain the activities of half a dozen or so brokers, but in fact the number had increased to nineteen by 1880. It was undoubtedly the growth of savings in the rapidly expanding local economy (the population rose from 100,000 in 1851 to 250,000 in 1891) which provided sufficient investment turnover to sustain an enlarged body of brokers. They could channel local savings not only into Belfast companies but also into the shares of British companies and into foreign investments, particularly in North America.

With such a number of active brokers it is a little surprising that a stock exchange was not formed in the early 1880s. As *The Economist* observed in a survey of stock markets in 1884 — "in Belfast a number of important Ulster companies are represented, but there, as yet, no Stock Exchange is established".[1] Presumably the existing arrangements satisfied the brokers concerned in that they could conduct other commercial activities alongside broking (which Stock Exchange rules would no doubt have prohibited), and they were also free to advertise and supply their own prices to the local papers. However, the manner of transacting business in Belfast was not to the liking of some observers. An Irish financial periodical, *The Irish Insurance, Banking and Finance Journal*, commented critically that Belfast· brokers in 1882,

> ...are content as of old to carry the orders of their clients to the offices of their fellow brokers, and endeavour by a system of hawking to find a customer. Or, at times, they will neglect to do so, and by hanging up instructions depend on the appearance of a private client, so that they may cross the business within their own office, and thereby earn a double commission. Then, as regards the publishing of the daily transactions, that duty is left to individual and irresponsible firms. These firms can only name those bargains with which they themselves have been connected, or which have been reported. But others are constantly occurring outside their knowledge and so the record they supply is defective. Moreover the course of the market is seldom conveyed, or if conveyed at all it bears usually an indifferent relation to the actual facts — the 1st transaction in a security often appearing as the last, while the last may be set down as the first. Hence the public can form little idea whether prices are rising or falling, or whether the market be strong or weak.[2]

Added to which was the complaint, not a new one, that some people entered the trade merely to act as jobbers and were their "own most speculative client", earning further odium by encouraging investors to deal merely to extract commission from them. The result had been several defaulters.

Belfast brokers continued to conduct their business in an informal manner for another dozen years or so. Meanwhile, a further 270 limited companies made their appearance in the city (an average of around 20 a year in the 1890s), induced by the great developments in shipbuilding and its ancillary industries. Doubtless some of the new arrivals did not survive for long since many were small concerns, but several did later emerge as listed companies when the Stock Exchange put out its first list in 1897. In general, the widespread adoption of limited liability was seen as an important element in the remarkable development of Ulster, and Belfast in particular, at this time. A representative of the Belfast Chamber of Commerce, Thomas Sinclair, spoke glowingly of the record of Ulster companies to the 1877 House of Lords Select Committee on the Companies Bill,

> ...it has saved large industrial undertakings from being broken up on the retirement from business or on the death of successful owners; the success of such companies has induced men of ample means, protected by Limited Liability, to assist in establishing other industries in our neighbourhood, their capital thus being employed in Ulster instead of seeking investment elsewhere; in this way new industries have been successfully introduced and carried on in our great city and neighbourhood with great advantage to the general community, and especially to the labouring class, who on account of agricultural depression, are glad of an opportunity to earn a living in industrial pursuits. It is a remarkable fact that extremely few of our North of Ireland joint stock industrial companies have become insolvent, and almost every one of them which has gone into liquidation had paid its creditors 20s. in the £.[3]

But despite the private nature of the limited companies, exemplified by Harland & Wolff, sufficient business existed in the city in 1890 to sustain 22 broking concerns. Even so, the brokers were content to continue with their loose method of trading. Apparently, "values have been maintained but there is an absence of that briskness that denotes really good business and both buyers and sellers, at times, owing to the absence of a Stock Exchange, find great difficulty....in doing business". But the brokers maintained that no inconvenience was suffered by the public, a view not shared by one financial observer — "interested opinions from monopolists, such as many of these are, must be received with more than the proverbial grain of salt".[4]

When the move came to form a stock exchange in the mid-nineties, a period of active company promotion and considerable investment activity, the hesitancy of earlier years continued to be displayed. Following a meeting of nineteen brokers in January 1895, at the offices of Grubb & Coates, a committee was set up to consider the desirability of establishing a "stock exchange or similar institution".[5] When the brokers met a few days later at the offices of Messers Cunningham & Co., 41 Waring Street, the committee reported that it "could not at present recommend the formation of a Stock Exchange in Belfast", but it did think it would be desirable to rent a room, at a moderate rental,in which "the Brokers and their representative clerks can meet to transact business much as it is conducted on present lines".[6] Generously, Adam Duffin offered a rent free room in his Waring Street offices and Messers Grubb, Duffin and McKee were appointed to "have the room put in order". Significantly, it was decided that only those brokers, or their clerks, who had been invited to the preliminary meeting should be admitted to the room. The first dealing sessions were held on February 4th, with a morning meeting at 10.30 and an afternoon one at 2.30. The records are silent as to whether they had a call over or if they merely met informally to do business. Presumably it was the latter, but at least they did not have to trail to each other's offices in the cold weather.

Since the brokers found the daily assemblies in "The Room" in Waring Street eminently beneficial they decided to appoint another committee which was "to arrange for a suitable room for the transaction of business and to consider ways and means generally". After failing to obtain a room in the premises of the News Room, they settled for carrying on in "The Room" but now rented it from Adam Duffin for £60 a year. During the next few weeks the committee discussed the proposed rules for the association, which were modelled on those of Dublin. It was suggested that membership should be confined to those "doing business in Belfast", an annual subscription of £4 should be paid, and for new entrants a fee of £50 and the usual ballot ordeal. There would be a committee of five, plus an honorary secretary and treasurer to run the association. Commissions would be the same as those operating in Dublin, with no division to outsiders. The draft rules were approved in June and at a meeting held on July 25 1895, W. J. Coates was elected Honorary Secretary and B. J. Newett, Honorary Treasurer, while 32 members were admitted to the Association. A Committee was then elected to manage the affairs of the Stock Exchange and consisted of J. Cunningham, Adam Duffin, John Mckee, William Shaw and Francis Johnstone, with Adam Duffin in the Chair. Later meetings of the Committee discussed the local requirements for quotations and special settlements, while the settlement of accounts was instituted on well established stock exchange lines. They also proceeded to reject an application for membership on the grounds that the applicant firm was doing business of "too varied a nature to admit of their being accepted as members"; another was turned away since he had no "experience or training as a stockbroker". Of greater weight were the deliberations on the stocks to be "primarily admitted to quotation in the proposed Official List". At that juncture it was decided to close the Exchange for June, July and August, plainly obeying the old maxim of 'sell in May and go away'.[7]

As suggested earlier one of the reasons for the delay in setting up a formal Stock Exchange was that the brokers valued the freedom to indulge in a wide range of activities which the rules of an association might well prohibit. One such activity, carried on for many years by four leading brokers, was to supply reports on the state of the market to the local daily and weekly papers, and in return for "their troubles and expenditures" they got the "publicity of their names". This was a valuable privilege for those concerned, and at the time of setting up the Stock Exchange no challenge was made to its continuation. Had a rule prohibiting advertising been mooted at the outset then the formation of the association would probably have been further delayed. Early in 1897 such a rule was proposed but the four advertising brokers were only prepared to abandon their long standing and valued practice in return for certain other changes in the rules, and since they were well established and influential members of the Exchange their demands were met in full. They insisted that all advertising by brokers should stop, Dublin brokerage rates should apply to all business, and the entry requirements should be modified raising the entrance fee to £125, along with a £500 surety for three years, but with concessionary terms for the sons of members and for clerks of five or more years experience. Also, that a full time Secretary and Registrar should be appointed, and an Official List compiled and published. All the proposals were agreed to at a general meeting in May 1897 and the newspaper reports from individual brokers ceased to appear in October. Shortly afterwards Drummond Porter was appointed as Secretary and Registrar, and the Daily List made its appearance on October 22 1897.[8]

## Organisation

With the formation of the Stock Exchange the brokers changed from a system of itinerant trading to that of the well established call over. At agreed times they assembled in the market and the Registrar called through the list, with the Chairman of the day (a member of the Committee) presiding to ensure that orderly dealing took place. Bid and offer prices were made and the prices of completed bargains were duly recorded by the Registrar, who in consultation with the Chairman made up the list of closing prices. After the Official List had been finished the Registrar called the Supplementary

List, as arranged by the Committee, which consisted of stocks and shares not included in the main list. Finally, at the close of the morning session the Chairman went through the prices at which deals were done so that they were agreed to by all present; sometimes members had queried morning prices at the afternoon session. Prices marked were generally for marketable lots (£100 stock or £50 shares), but marks could be made in odd lots with the approval of the Chairman. If stock had not been publicly offered then no marking was allowed. Normally the business was conducted in an orderly fashion but occasionally the Chairman had reason to rebuke members for leaving their seats before the list was over.

The hours of business were fixed at 11.0 and 2.30. For a few years these times were satisfactory but in 1900 it was decided to alter the morning call over to 11.30 because it was felt that by such time "brokers would have their opening prices and more business would likely result".[9] With the large decline in business during the First World War the opening time was moved back, in 1917, to 11.0 o'clock so that business could be done locally rather than go elsewhere. Also, to facilitate local dealing wherever possible, the Secretary kept a register of the "intimations of members of Securities in which they may have dealings".[10] Given the circumstances it seemed reasonable to keep as much business as possible in Belfast. However, in 1923, with the return to more normal trading conditions, the morning call over reverted to 11.30. From 1931 until the Second World War the market also opened for a call over on Saturday morning.

To supplement local dealing facilities in the form of the call over, and to keep business in Belfast, a central switchboard with connections to brokers' offices was introduced on an experimental basis in the late twenties. Later, in 1932, a multiphone switchboard was installed so that all offices could be contacted collectively, or individually.[11] This facility enabled brokers to be in "constant touch with each other in the interval between the morning and afternoon meetings", thereby enabling them to test the local market. The hope was that it would "develop more active dealings in securities hitherto bought or sold in other markets."[12] While business in both local and national stocks was done through this channel, the Committee took the view that essentially it was an aid for dealings in national stocks whose main markets were elsewhere but local stocks should be done in the Room during the call over.[13] The widening of the market so produced did not always enable deals in national stocks to be speedily completed, but where a broker failed to get a local response and then sent the order to another market, the Committee suggested that he should "hold the business for about 10 minutes to enable [other] Brokers to get in touch with their principals". In general, it was felt that the switchboard had been of some value, especially to the smaller firms who lacked the telephone connections of their larger rivals, and it had succeeded in keeping a "great deal of business" from going out of the City.

It was during this period that Belfast became involved in one of the most thorny stock exchange issues of the whole inter-war period — Nicholson's "Belfast Venture". Belfast's acceptance of a price and dealing service from J. W. Nicholson & Son of Sheffield undoubtedly brought benefits to the market but it also put it at the centre of a bitter controversy. In 1928 the Stock Exchange was approached by Nicholson's with an offer to wire prices twice a day which would provide members "with additional facilities for dealing in active stocks". The Committee could see no objection and indeed several members were already doing business with Nicholson's, who had been dealing at net prices for some years with a large number of provincial brokers. The main link between the members and Nicholson's, and for supplying prices to the market, was through the firm of W.F. Coates & Co.[14] This avenue was later greatly supplemented by the installation of a teleprinter which gave up-to-date details of over 200 active stocks in which Nicholson's were prepared to make net prices. Thus, members had access to several price lists during the day, in addition to any direct calls they might make to Nicholson's. "Nicholson's prices" were also broadcast on the multiphone switchboard.[15] In effect the market had a rapid price service as well as a large jobbing facility put at its disposal. But not all members seemed entirely happy with this external incursion. One complained, not too convincingly, that members were dealing with Nicholson's at prices which could be obtained on the local floor. But there was little support for this mild condemnation and most were happy to use the additional market facility supplied by Nicholson's.

By 1939, however, there were signs that Belfast, along with other small provincial markets, might lose this valued dealing service. Growing unease among London dealers, and on some of the larger provincial markets as well, prompted the proposals incorporated in an agreement between the London Stock Exchange and the Council of Associated Stock Exchanges following a conference in 1939. London's frustration arose from the feeling that Nicholson's had diverted a great deal of business away from their floor, that they were dealing inside London margins, and that they sometimes used London as a market of "last resort". Accordingly, London adopted rules to enable it to declare a country dealer a non-member jobber and thus prohibit members from dealing with such a firm. The Belfast Committee viewed London's threat with considerable concern, the general feeling being that "Nicholson's was a godsend during the air raids in London when communications were so much delayed. If we lose our country jobber and send our business to London, we shall have to put up with bad prices. London prices are often wider than Nicholson's".[16]

Not only was Nicholson's declared a non-member jobber by London in 1941 but its difficulties were also increased when its teleprinters were commandeered by the military authorities and all private lines were taken over. It was left to do business through ordinary telephone exchange lines.

By this time the larger exchanges in the Council of Associated Stock Exchanges felt that they too would have to prohibit their members from having direct contact with Nicholson's and duly adopted rules to that end. The smaller exchanges, among them Belfast, were not so anxious to follow but felt that sooner or later they would have to fall in line otherwise business relations with London might be gravely injured. In the meantime Belfast continued to receive two telephone calls each day at fixed times from Nicholson's and the prices obtained were broadcast on the switchboard, while the secretary took orders from the members and transacted the business with Nicholson's. In the opinion of the Consultative Committee of the Council of Associated Stock Exchanges this practice contravened the rules adopted on the basis of the agreement made at the 1939 conference. Belfast, however, argued that they were in a different position to other Exchanges "owing to the great delay in telephone calls from this side".[17] Ultimately, in 1943, under pressure from London and the larger provincial exchanges, Belfast decided to adopt rules which would end direct market contact with Nicholson's, in particular that "a member is not permitted to use regularly booked time calls to or from a Non-member jobber for the purpose of providing a collective service to the Exchange." Although this put an end to the collective service, which in war conditions had been very useful to Belfast especially so in view of its isolated position, the members could however go direct to Nicholson's on normal exchange channels at their own expense.[18]

During the difficult war years of 1939-45 Belfast had to depend on its own call over mechanism, and the ancillary aid of the switchboard. It had to put up with considerable delays in communication with other exchanges, especially Glasgow with which it did a great deal of business. For example, for several months in 1944 it lost its telephone service to Britain which resulted in brokers not getting London and provincial prices till after mid-day, thus leaving them "in the dark" and unable to keep clients well informed about price movements. Peace, however, brought a gradual return of the established lines of communication, but it was now found that London prices were available earlier in the day and to accommodate this fact the Committee decided to change the call over from 11.30 to 11.15 in the hope of getting more business done on the Belfast floor. It was thought desirable that a local price should be established in leading stocks such as "Bats, Imp's or even Kaffirs, oil or rubber shares" in order to prevent this business from going to London.[19]

With the general revival of the economy after the war, and the accompanying desire on the part of investors to diversify their investments away from low interest trustee stocks, provincial brokers attempted to accommodate this trend by reviving a strong shunting network. They were prepared to deal in a wide range of stocks, much wider than they were intended to by the rules, and in effect they provided jobbing facilities to provincial markets by using fixed time calls, basing their operation on London prices. Fortunately for them London seemed to acquiesce since the scale of their activities was not sufficient to cause any irritation, and the market in general was expanding. In 1950 the Belfast firm of Carr, Workman decided to offer a shunting service in 23 blue chip stocks to the Belfast market. Since there was little hope of getting a private line and because timed calls were of little use for shunting purposes, the firm installed a teleprinter to link it with its Glasgow agent, McLean & Co. The expected London protest never came.

Carr, Workman began shunting-jobber operations in 1952, with Stanley Robinson in charge of this side of the business.[20] They made use of the "10/- jobber's stamp", a facility granted by the 1920 and 1931 Finance Bills to country dealers whereby they could hold stock for up to two months without paying ad valorem stamp duty.[21] The concession, in the case of Belfast, was obtained from the local Ministry of Finance, and London raised no objection on the understanding that Carr, Workman dealt only in local stocks. However, the initial list put out by the firm contained many national blue chip stocks and rather than provoke London a revised list of 23 stocks was drawn up consisting largely of local stocks, but it also included some national ones which had clear links with Belfast, such as Gallaher, Dunlop, Harland & Wolff, and Standard Motors.[22] The shares dealt in by Carr Workman, were called by the Secretary at the end of calling the Official List.

During the 1950s activity in local stocks gradually declined as some became nationally dealt in, while others languished reflecting the fortunes of their industries, all of which resulted in a dearth of business at the call over and on the switchboard. By the mid fifties the Committee was contemplating removing the switchboard entirely since it was seldom used for making bids or offers; it was largely used as a means to see if anything was "going". The step was finally taken in 1965. Also, by the late fifties it was found, during the call over, that the Secretary "laboriously" went through the list but there were only occasional deals in corporation and public authority stocks, a few in banks, while the spinning and textile section produced about ten deals a week, mostly in the shares of the York Street Flax Co. Thoughts of directing all dealing activity through Carr, Workman were rejected, however, and the call over remained but the Secretary was given greater discretion as to what was called. It was felt that since a company paid for a quotation then it was entitled to be called.

The prospects of keeping business in Belfast were made more difficult by the impetus given to regional jobbing by Regionalisation and Federation. Under these arrangements, especially the latter, certain firms were encouraged to emerge as jobbers, this side of the business being kept entirely separate from broking. In line with this Carr, Workman took out dual capacity registration thus enabling it to deal directly with any other country jobber but not with a London jobber — this could only be done through a registered London correspondent. However, after only a few years operation Carr, Workman ceased their jobbing activity in 1972, and a year later the long standing call over also came to an end. Dealing reverted to inter-broker contact for local stocks, and under The Stock Exchange arrangements, brokers could take national stocks direct to London jobbers, or use a London agent if they preferred — a system not unlike that of 1882.

By the time the Belfast Stock Exchange was set up, in 1895, procedures for settling bargains had been developed to a fine art. All that was needed was the adoption of established practices from the rule books of other exchanges. Essentially the practices adopted were the well tried ones with some concession to the small scale of the Belfast market. Bargains could be either for cash, for a specified date, or for the account. In the case of the first two, non fulfilment by one party to the transaction would lead to the customary buying-in or selling-out, which was done by the Secretary after due notice had been given to the market. Settlement for the account proceeded along familiar lines. Account days were taken as those fixed by the London Stock Exchange, although Belfast dispensed with the more organised aspects of settlement essential for the large turnover on other markets. The ticket system was used, with the buyer who was to take up securities at the end of the account issuing a ticket setting out the full particulars of the transferee, the consideration, and the member to whom the ticket was issued. It then passed through the hands of the various sellers during the account period until it came into the possession of the original seller, the intermediate parties merely being involved in the payment or receipt of differences. With the small number of brokers and turnover all this could be done without resorting to formal arrangements for meeting, but, of course, the usual deadlines applied.

Far more contentious than the mechanical matter of settlement was that of commissions. At the outset the Stock Exchange followed established practice and enacted that the commission charged to clients on transactions in Irish stocks and securities should be at a prescribed scale, the one used by the Dublin Stock Exchange. Also, that no division of commission was allowed except to recognised brokers; there was to be no sharing with bankers or solicitors. Most subsequent changes in the rules on commissions revolved around these two aspects, the level and the amount of rebating. Within a few years falling business led some of the members to undercut the published rate, prompting a stricture from the Committee that "full" rates only should be charged. Dealings with brokers in other markets were, of course, conducted on a free trade basis and when the London Stock Exchange proposed new commission scales in 1910, Belfast shared in the general provincial disapproval of its action. All agreed that a uniform scale for the public might be desirable but they objected to a fixed scale for provincial brokers dealing with London. Belfast accepted that London had cause for concern at the loss of certain business to the provinces but this had been because some London jobbers, using the telephone network and with the connivance of a few brokers, had pushed shares out to the provinces. This was not a complaint which could be levelled at Belfast.

London's response to better inter-market communication was not seen as in the best interests of security dealing generally; "the surest way of securing progress is to go one better rather than resort to the ancient methods of strangulation".[23] One small consequence of London's action was the decision of the Belfast Committee to soften its policy on rebates in that it decided not to censure members who divided with a bank on non-Irish securities in order to keep the business in the local market; better to bend the rules than lose business to London. The issue, however, continued to rear its head throughout the inter-war years, especially the early thirties when the fall in both turnover and share prices made brokers extremely conscious of any concessions. In the case of solicitors and banks brokers found that since they formally offered no rebate, business was being lost to other markets, but it sometimes came back if the shares were local. Belfast finally decided in 1941 to bring its practices on rebates into line with that of the mainland markets.[24]

Closely linked to commission levels was the delicate matter of relations with outside brokers. The general practice at the turn of the century was to regard those who operated within a certain radius (usually 5 miles) of an exchange as constituting undesirable competition (since they advertised widely) and therefore they should be afforded no concessions. Those outside the forbidden zone were usually granted concessions by way of rebates or dealings at net prices. Belfast adopted the same sort of stance towards outside brokers; there were four operating in Belfast in 1895. Those who applied to the Stock Exchange were granted provincial broker status, for the payment of a small annual fee, and they could even display on their contract notes that they were "Affiliated to the Belfast Stock Exchange".[25] But while the rules were quite clear about the class and location of outside brokers who could deal on concessionary terms with members, by the early 1900s the attention of the Committee was frequently drawn to lapses from the general code.[26] The usual admonitions to guilty members followed, but unlike Dublin, the Belfast Committee could not threaten the loss of a licence.

Some members favoured the prohibition of all dealings with outside brokers in Belfast, who at one time were rumoured to be thinking of setting up a rival exchange. Nothing came of either threat. During the inter-war years the irritation from outside brokers was reported as being greatly reduced, although by this time (1929) the exclusion zone for concessions had been extended from a five mile to a twenty mile radius. After the Second World War some outside brokers who indulged in widespread and highly questionable advertising did cause concern but the introduction of the

Prevention of Fraud Act, which involved a Stock Exchange veto to the Minister of Finance on outside broker registration, served to stifle the worst aspects of that kind of trade.[27] Also, in 1949, outside brokers in Northern Ireland were no longer permitted to use the phrase "Affiliated to the Belfast Stock Exchange" on their contract notes, and to get the long standing dealing concessions they had to qualify for inclusion on the General List of the London Stock Exchange, or join the Provincial Brokers Stock Exchange.

Most of the above practices, and the rules governing them, were suspended on the outbreak of war in 1914, and again in 1939. In August 1914 the Stock Exchange closed following London's action, and it remained so until London re-opened in January 1915, all markets being subject to the Temporary Regulations agreed with the Treasury.[28] Little business was done over these few months, just a few deals in local shares. When peacetime conditions returned, Belfast along with other markets favoured a fairly quick resumption of normal dealing facilities, especially the fourteen day account, but all markets had to be content to wait until May 1922. Somewhat similar procedures followed the outbreak of the Second World War, although the Stock Exchanges had a warning of things to come when the call over was suspended during the 1938 crisis. Again, following London's lead the Belfast market closed during early September and adopted the temporary regulations introduced by London.[29] By 1941, however, business had just about settled down to the new conditions, but Belfast also found its activities suffering from the wartime restraints imposed on Nicholson's and, for a time, by the heavy air raids inflicted on the City which caused considerable delays in communications with other markets.[30] In those raids several industrial and commercial companies suffered severe damage and the Stock Exchange found itself faced with enquiries as to what quotations were appropriate for such firms. By 1943, however, there was a welcome increase in business, which probably stood at treble the 1942 level judging by the number of certifications recorded.[31] The following year was marked by the complete cancellation for several months of the telephone service to Britain, and the resulting absence of price information prompted the Committee to think of going back to the telegraph service. Peace brought a revival of business, but it was not until 1947 that fortnightly settlements were restored, while speculative facilities had to wait another two years.[32]

## Domestic Matters

By the end of the nineteenth century the established stock exchanges had formulated admission rules which ensured that entrants possessed adequate professional knowledge, had sufficient financial reserves for immediate trading purposes along with an uncalled reserve for a limited period in the form of a surety requirement, and that they had no trading liabilities outside their main business. In addition, the terms of entry could be altered periodically to attract or discourage potential entrants, depending as to whether or not the membership wished to allow more competition. Belfast was no exception and quickly adopted rules designed to secure these general ends.

Prospective candidates were expected to have a place of business "within reasonable distance of the Stock Exchange, and not elsewhere", be over 21, and possess training experience as a stockbroker. Those who carried on "too varied a nature of business" with broking were excluded. Following a recommendation from two well established members, and having satisfied the Committee of their general suitability, candidates were then subjected to a ballot of the members. At the outset threequarters had to be in favour of entry, but this was later reduced to two-thirds. Then came the financial obligation. The original entrance fee was £50 but it was raised to £125 in 1897, with a concession for the sons of members (£50) and for clerks with five years experience (£75). Security had to be provided for three years to the sum of £500 deposited in either cash or securities (which predominated) with the Committee. Later the entrance fee was raised, occasionally after some debate on the virtues or otherwise of enlarging the membership, so that by 1929 the fee for an ordinary entrant was £1,000, clerks with five years experience paid £500, and the sons of members £200.[33] While the surety requirement had been raised to £1,000 for preferential entrants and to £2,500 for others, more taxing perhaps was the lengthening of the period to five years by 1929.[34] Up to 1914 the membership of the Exchange ranged from 32 at the formation to 39 in 1904. Jumping to 49 on the post 1918 boom, the total remained at this level until the onset of the thirties depression when it fell back to 41. War produced a fall to around thirty , where it remained for most of the post-war years. At the time of the formation of the Belfast Unit of the Stock Exchange the membership stood at 31.

As on other markets the members employed authorised or accredited clerks to attend in the market and deal on their behalf, on the payment of a small annual subscription. Their numbers ranged around 10 in the years up to 1914. Ordinary clerks could also enter the market but they could not deal on behalf of their employers.

The management of the Stock Exchange was entrusted to a Committee of nine members, elected annually, including the President and Vice-

President. It exercised the usual powers of formulating and interpreting the rules, acting as final arbiter in all disputes, regulating the general conduct of the market in all its aspects, ranging from fixing dealing times, granting quotation and special settlements, to the unpleasant business of declaring a member a defaulter. On such a small exchange there was no need to resort to a formal structure of sub-committees. While the Presidency was an annual office several holders were re-elected for successive terms. Adam Duffin, the first incumbent, held the office on five occasions between 1904 and 1920; A. H. R. Carr held it four times between 1900 and 1922, and Sir W. F. Coates was president four times between 1904 and 1926. The day to day administration of the Stock Exchange rested with the Secretary. Drummond Porter held the post from 1897 until his sudden death in 1911, when he was succeeded by James Carson. From 1920 to 1923 J. A. Fletcher held the office, to be replaced by Miss Gault. Robert Bell succeeded her in 1931 and was secretary to the Exchange for 40 years, retiring in 1971; he kept the most excellent of minutes.

"The Room" in Adam Duffin's offices at 7, Waring Street, where the brokers met informally for a short while, became on the formation of the Stock Exchange, the market place. Within a year or so it was found unsuitable despite the fact that the distraction of outside noise had been muted by paving the street with wood, the Stock Exchange contributing £5 towards the cost. Thoughts of purpose built accommodation in the High Street on land owned by the Earl of Shaftesbury proved short lived — it would have imposed a very heavy financial burden on a small association. To meet their needs suitable premises were found in Lombard Street and leased from the Anglo American Oil Co., the additional expense involved necessitating an increase in the annual subscription.[35] For over sixty years these premises served as the Stock Exchange, until, in 1963, the association leased space in the Northern Bank Buildings which contained suitable office accommodation, and a market room was fitted up with boards, members' chairs and a chairman's desk.

Shortly after the formation of the Stock Exchange, Adam Duffin and the Secretary called on the Post Master in Belfast to discuss means of speeding up the transmission of telegraph messages between Belfast and London. Such delays were familiar to brokers everywhere, and indeed were a perennial problem for several more years. In Belfast's case messages were sent on a direct wire between the General Post Office and the London Stock Exchange, and while the service was interrupted during the First World War, it was resumed in the early twenties. Normally, the service was regarded as satisfactory but subject to greater delays in winter due to storms. By the twenties, of course, the telephone had taken over much of the inter-market links, but even this new medium was not without its difficulties. Apart from casual connections, an important use of the telephone was for putting through fixed time calls, especially to Glasgow, so as to obtain price information and transmit orders. For a time in the mid-twenties such calls were suspended, to the considerable inconvenience of members, because of the congestion caused on the limited number of circuits available between Belfast and Glasgow. The only other major complaint against the telephone service of the time related to charges. When the first instrument was installed in the Stock Exchange in 1898 it was free of rent, but by 1921 Belfast, along with other Exchanges, was protesting against proposed increases, asserting that they were "wholly unjustified and entirely due to the extravagance in management, which gives at the same time a far from efficient service and that this bears especially heavily on Stockbrokers whose business involved a constant use of the telephone".[36] Apart from the interruption of services due to the heavy air raids suffered by Belfast in the early years of the Second World War, the telephone service seems thereafter to have been generally satisfactory for the conduct of inter-market business.

Within the activities of the Belfast Stock Exchange the multiphone switchboard occupied an important role, but perhaps not that which was hoped for when it was installed in the late twenties. While it proved useful in the dissemination of price information outside market dealing times, not many deals were done over it. This was probably due to the considerable price and dealing service which the Nicholson teleprinter rendered to the market in the thirties. The system was retained for some time after the last war and may have covered its costs in terms of saved commissions in other markets, but by the early sixties the level of use did not warrant its retention. It was finally removed in 1965.

Undoubtedly the oldest firm on the Belfast market is J. Cunningham & Co. with an unbroken record of trading in securities since 1843, and always with a member of the family involved in the business. Darbishire, Malcomson & Coates had links with the early days through Herbert Darbishire & Co. who started trading in May 1884. In 1985 these two firms merged to form J. Cunningham & Co.(Inc. Darbishire, Malcomson & Coates). The firm of Carr, Workman, Patterson, Topping & Co. also had links to the 1890s through A.H.R. Carr & Co. and R. Workman & Co. In 1985 it merged with the London brokers, Laing & Cruickshank. The other surviving firm from the founding days is Wm. F. Coates & Co., whose founder was later knighted. The only other founding firm to continue in existence through to the early seventies was A.J. McIlwaine & Co.; John McKee & Co. ceased trading some years earlier.

The Stock Exchange's most famous member only kept his connection for a comparatively short time. James Craig, later Viscount Craigavon, learnt the broking business as an apprentice with Foster & Braithwaite of the London Stock Exchange during 1890-92. Returning to Belfast he set up his own business in April 1892 under the title of Craigs & Co., mysteriously adding an "s". While he was one of the founding members of the Stock Exchange and a successful broker, apparently "he felt little urgency about broking" and left the business in 1900 to join the Royal Irish Rifles. He was Prime Minister of Northern Ireland from 1921 until his death in 1940.[37]

## Gilt Edged and other fixed interest stocks

In June 1922 the Treasury informed the newly created Department of Finance of the Irish Free State that it intended to close the Dublin register of British government stocks kept at the Bank of Ireland, and for the benefit of Northern Ireland stockholders it was going to open a register at the main branch of the Bank of Ireland in Belfast. The successful opposition to the proposed closure of the Dublin register has been related in Chapter 7. Corresponding to the fight to keep the Dublin facility open, lobbying and canvassing on an equal scale was taking place in Belfast to ensure the introduction of similar facilities there.

The Belfast Stock Exchange and its Committee played a leading part in the campaign to get the register to Belfast — they "left no stone unturned". The Committee wrote to the newly formed government of the province urging that the necessary arrangements should be made for establishing a register in Belfast since it would be in the interests of all resident stockholders. This was followed by a deputation (consisting of Adam Duffin, J. Richardson and J. Taylor) to meet the Minister of Finance to discuss the proposed facility at the Donegall Place branch of the Bank of Ireland. The Committee also enlisted the support of the local banks. Given the intention of the London Treasury to make such an introduction, the sustained pressure from Belfast quickly produced results and in March 1923 the Chief Clerk of the Bank of Ireland appeared at the Stock Exchange to explain the working of the new register as from March 19 1923.

The advantages to local investors of the new register was the local payment of dividends, together with speedy and accessible transfer facilities, especially bearing in mind that much of the stock at that time was in inscribed form. Thus, a broker who received, for example,

> ....on a Monday morning, a selling order in Inscribed stock, is able to sell the stock and forward to the seller the relative P/A for signature on the same day. So that if the Power [of Attorney] is returned to the broker by first post, it can be acted upon the following day and the client paid on Thursday; which means that only four days need elapse between receipt of the order and payment to the client. Sales of Registered Stock can also be

completed within the same time, provided the client furnishes the broker with the relative stock certificate and returns the transfer without delay.[38]

To get the full benefit of the new register, therefore, it was important that as many stocks as possible should be placed on it, and dealing facilities in Belfast should be such that transactions could take place locally.

At the time the new Register was opened the market in gilt edged was dominated by 5% War Loan, some £1,900mn out of the total nominal debt of £5,500mn. While this stock, and other leading stocks such as the famous 2½% Consols, 3½% Conversion Loan, 4% Funding Loan, and 4% Victory Bonds, were obvious candidates for inclusion, the Stock Exchange Committee was anxious that action should be taken to "preserve and extend the register through the addition of all future new issues, registered or inscribed". In response to a request from the Stock Exchange, the Chancellor of the Exchequer gave an assurance that all future issues of government stocks would be registered at the Bank of Ireland, Belfast. In line with this promise, 4½% Conversion Stock 1940-44 issued in 1924, was transferable at the Donegall Place branch of the Bank of Ireland as from February 1925. However, when the prospectus of 5% Treasury Bonds 1933-35 appeared in 1928 no provision was inserted for Belfast transfers. After protests from the Stock Exchange, and representations from the Bank of Ireland, the Treasury gave an assurance "that appropriate arrangements would be made at the Bank of Ireland in respect of all future long dated securities of importance".[39] Over the ensuing years, with the rapid expansion of the debt during wartime, post-war nationalisation and its gradual increase later, the number of stocks on the Register in 1985 had reached well over a 100, with a total nominal value of £180mn. Since January 1943 all transfers have been in registered form.

The success of the Register depended very much on local market facilities. To ensure a reasonably free market in the leading stocks the firm of W. J. Richardson & Co. offered to act as jobbers, initially in 5% War Loan, and later they were authorised to make prices in other stocks. But on such a limited market it would not be possible to run a jobbing account without an assurance of support from all members of the Exchange. Therefore, the members entered into an "honourable agreement", that they would not cross orders in their offices in stocks in which the jobber was authorised to make prices, and that in cases where the consideration was over £2,000 they would give the jobber plenty of advance warning so that he could see the extent of the market on that day. Also, brokers were urged to forgo a margin if they had an order with an impractical limit from the client so that the business could be done on the local market and then put through the Belfast Register. In general the members adhered to the "honourable agreement" and when occasional lapses were brought to the attention of the Committee the view was forcibly put to a transgressor that the jobber should always be fully supported because of the importance of the local Register to the Belfast market. After all they had, along with Dublin, a fairly privileged facility, one which "large cities across the water would give a great deal to have".[40] "Enjoying...the distinction of its own register for British government securities at its own doors, this Exchange", the President explained in 1933, "naturally gives pride of place to dealings in British government securities in which there is an active daily market, and, as we have our own jobber, we are practically independent of other markets in such stocks".[41]

During peacetime, and with reasonable turnover, Richardson's seems to have been willing to deal on the basis of $\frac{1}{8}$% jobbing turn, increasing to $\frac{3}{16}$% when markets became less active. With the coming of war, which brought a considerable reduction in turnover and greater risks, the spread was widened to $\frac{1}{4}$%. This action did not meet with the approval of all the members, but Richardson's argued that in the difficult conditions of 1940-41 they had little alternative, promising to make a $\frac{3}{16}$% price when more normal circumstances returned. Certainly Richardson's had problems with trading in such conditions and these were reflected in the low profit obtained on the jobbing book — for three months operations in the middle of 1943 they made a profit of £143 on turnover of £234,000, a return of $\frac{1}{16}$%.

After the war Richardson's increased the number of stocks in which they were prepared to deal, usually on the basis of a $\frac{3}{16}$% margin, on the understanding that the "honourable agreement" adopted in 1923 for War Loan would apply to all stocks. By doing so it was generally agreed that the presence of a local jobber was of considerable assistance to the members. By the sixties, however, activity in gilt edged had fallen off, a decline linked to the attraction of alternative investments with some degree of inflation hedging, and to the higher and more variable interest rates, all of which was reflected in the fall in the amount of stock on the local register. In 1972 Richardson's decided to cease operating as a jobber in gilt edged (the firm had taken out dual capacity under the Federation arrangements).[42] By this time the total of nominal stock on the register had fallen to just £100mn. After the formation of The Stock Exchange in 1973 gilt edged transactions were channelled directly to London jobbers, or to a provincial jobber, most of the business going to the former. In this period gilt edged increased in popularity with the higher yields, so that the total on the local register in 1985 stood at £180mn. As can be seen from the figures in Appendix 8 the value of turnover in gilt edged over recent years has averaged about £100mn, the average bargain size varying from around £14,500 to £30,000, suggesting that this is predominantly a personal sector market, with little or no regular institutional involvement. The number of transfers on the local register was 13,000 in 1982, with about 10,000 a year for 1983-85. Such transfers can also be made between the Belfast Register and the Bank of England and the National Savings Stock Registers. For the few gilt edged stocks still on the Dublin Register, these can be transferred to Belfast but they must be routed through the Bank of England.

Following the establishment of the government of Northern Ireland in 1921 various issues were made on the market, the early ones for cash and the later ones for cash and conversion purposes. During the twenties four issues of Ulster Loan $4\frac{1}{2}\%$ Stock were made, for a total of £4.0mn, most of it offered to the market at a price of about 10% below par, with the balance of £44,000 taken up by the Minister of Finance for various departmental funds. As with later issues the stock was transferable both in London (Midland Bank) and in Belfast (Belfast Banking Co.), with free transfers between the two registers. Over the years, however, the amount of stock on the Belfast register declined, largely because London registered stock was more acceptable on the market.

Taking-in part of an issue for departmental funds, a well established practice, was a feature of most issues but there was an interesting departure from it with the issue of £2.5mn of Northern Ireland $3\frac{3}{4}\%$ stock in 1939. In this instance the £2.5mn was subscribed by the banking houses of Glyn, Mills & Co. and Barings, who then offered the stock to the market at £98 10s.[43] This offer for sale basis (a temporary reversion to the contractor system) may have been prompted by the uncertainty of the time, or perhaps that the money was needed fairly quickly to discharge bank advances which had been made to the Northern Ireland Road Transport Board. Due to the method of issue used the brokers on the Stock Exchange were not directly involved, but they were offered and accepted part of the underwriting of most other government loans, the underwriting arrangements being in the hands of the London firm, Messrs R. Nivison & Co.[44] But they did not always get what they would have liked. In May 1940, for example, they were induced to protest after having been offered only £100,000; the protest brought them a promise of more generous treatment in future. In later issues the underwriting they were offered ranged between £200,000 and £300,000, rising to £1.0mn in the case of the largest offer made in Northern Ireland, the issue of £20.0mn of 7% Exchequer Stock in 1967.[45]

In 1936 three Northern Ireland government stocks featured in the Belfast Share List, with a total nominal value of £7.8mn, and with low interest rates at the time the $4\frac{1}{2}\%$ and 5% Ulster Loans displayed attractive premiums of 10% and 16% respectively. After the war the total of quoted stock had risen a little to £9.8mn and the premium was still there. By 1974 the nominal value of the three quoted stocks amounted to £32mn, but in marked contrast to earlier times of low interest rates and premium prices, the stocks stood at considerable discounts. From the early seventies no separate issues were made for Northern Ireland and the last stock quoted, £20.0mn of 7% Exchequer Stock was redeemed in May 1984.[46]

Belfast Corporation had been making issues on the market for many years before the government came on the scene. Prior to 1889 the City had

obtained funds on mortgage (at rates varying from $3\frac{1}{2}$% to 4%) but an act of
that year allowed the Corporation to consolidate its outstanding mortgages
into loan stock. The first issue under the 1889 Act was for £200,000 of $3\frac{1}{2}$%
Redeemable Stock, offered, as was the general practice for local authority
stocks at the time, by tender with allocations of stock to the "highest
bidders". Various tranches followed over the next few years, along with
three other issues of stock of around £200,000 each, all by tender. The offers
were handled by the Belfast Banking Co. who received the tenders and also
acted as registrar for the stocks. The issues were made to repay earlier loans
and to finance various municipal capital projects. Within a short space of
time the Corporation had borrowed some £2.0mn from the market, in the
process issuing six separate stocks. This feature of City borrowing
prompted the Stock Exchange to urge that these small loans should be
consolidated into one denomination of stock,

> The multiplicity of the existing issues, at various rates of interest
> and maturing at different periods is a source of confusion and
> inconvenience to the investing public and renders the smaller
> issues especially difficult to deal in and, at times, practically
> unmarketable. This tends to make the Belfast Corporation Stocks
> unpopular in comparison with other similar securities and renders
> them less attractive for trustee investment for which indeed many
> of the short dated are altogether unsuitable.[47]

The City fathers did not oblige instantly with a consolidation of the
outstanding miscellaneous issues, but at least in the next major round of
borrowing between 1905 and 1910 they did take note of the strictures. In
1905 they issued £1.0mn of $3\frac{1}{2}$% Redeemable Stock 1935, followed by three
tranches to give a total outstanding of £1.7mn. By 1913 the City had a
quoted debt of £3.7mn, nearly half in $3\frac{1}{2}$% stock. In contrast to earlier loans
those after 1905 were made on a fixed price basis and underwritten, a
practice which had become widespread in the capital market by then. The
change in the case of local authority issues was probably induced by the
larger loans and the diminished receptiveness of the market. Whatever the
reasons it brought additional income for the brokers who participated in the
underwriting by way of a commission of 1%.[48] However, with these larger
loans the centre of gravity of borrowing shifted to London and the Union of
London & Smith Bank acted as agents, along with the Belfast Banking Co.
The transfer registers shifted to London thereby making the stock more
attractive to British investors, but dividends paid to local holders could still
be cashed in Belfast by special arrangements.

## Industrial and Commercial Share Markets

When the first joint stock companies act made its appearance in 1844 Belfast could only display a few companies established on corporate lines, apart from railways and the three Belfast Banks (see Chapter 8). They were involved in either shipping, public utilities or provisions. Shipping was represented by the Belfast Steam Packet Co. and the Belfast New Steam Tug Co., public utilities by the Belfast Gas Light Co., the Belfast Commercial Buildings, and the famous White Linen Hall Co. (opened in 1785 and financed by a public subscription of £10,000), and the staple of life by the Belfast Flour & Bread Co.[49] The next twenty years saw only three successful registrations of Belfast companies under the new acts, the largest company built the Ulster Hall (in 1859, with paid up capital of £13,300), the other grew flax in India (1860; £6,000), while in 1858 the Belfast Flour & Bread Co. was incorporated with a paid up capital of £1,208 in £2 shares and 276 shareholders. All this, of course, was small fry in relation to what followed in the early 1860s in the linen industry.

Linen had a long association with Belfast and the surrounding area. In the second half of the eighteenth century the bleachers of the Lagan Valley had sent their linen through Belfast for export, much of it handled in the White Linen Hall. But the beginning of factory production followed on the burning down of Thomas Mulholland's cotton spinning mill in 1828. In the rebuilding he decided to apply steam power to flax spinning, using the "wet process", and his York Street Mill opened in 1830 with 8,000 flax spinning spindles. His success brought a rush of new capital into this side of the industry; by 1850 there were 29 mills spinning flax, with only four in cotton. By 1861 the number of spindles had increased to 590,000, compared with only 250,000 in 1841. The application of power to weaving started a little later, but the diffusion was slow with fewer than 3,000 power looms in Belfast in 1862.

The American Civil War changed the picture greatly. With raw cotton supplies cut off, demand surged for linen goods and the industry responded. The number of flax spindles rose from 500,000 in 1862 to 724,000 by 1868, the number of power looms increased from 3,000 to 9,000, and the labour force jumped from 33,500 to 57,000 over the same period.[50] The boom produced, for many companies, handsome returns on the capital employed, doubling them in several cases.[51] This, of course, induced the construction of new mills, but from a capital market viewpoint it prompted several of the well established concerns to be incorporated under the limited liability acts. As in all such booms some private owners were easily persuaded to sell off their business to the public, while more often than not keeping a considerable interest themselves; it enabled others to raise capital for expansion.

In and around Belfast there were 13 registrations of spinning companies during 1864-66, the nominal capital of the companies ranging from £60,000 to £500,000. The largest, by called up capital, the Ulster Spinning Co., was registered in June 1866 and of its nominal capital of £500,000, £213,000 was called up, mostly in £10 shares from 104 shareholders. York Street Flax Spinning Co., registered in 1864, also had a nominal capital of £500,000 but only £100,000 was called up, again in £10 shares from 112 shareholders. Next in line came the Brookfield Linen Co., nominal capital £400,000, with £80,000 called up from 115 shareholders, followed by Falls Flax Spinning Co., registered in 1865, which had a nominal capital of £100,000 with £19,850 called up from its 45 shareholders. Finally, Edenderry Spinning Co., registered in 1864, had a mere £14,000 called up from the nominal capital of £70,000, but it had only 13 shareholders. Whiteabbey Flax Spinning Co., registered in 1866, had a nominal capital of £200,000, while Island Spinning Co., also registered in 1866, had a nominal capital of £60,000. Some of these were, in fact, integrated concerns engaged in spinning and weaving, which not only produced greater profits than solely spinning but they also survived the later depression, unlike some of their more specialised smaller rivals.[52] But incorporation was not universal. The earlier partnership form continued to dominate the industry since many owners were reluctant to adopt limited liability. They felt there was little risk and they did not lack capital. By 1887 only 23 out of 500 concerns in the linen industry had taken out incorporation.[53]

While six out of the above companies were to occupy an important place in the spinning share section of the Belfast list in 1895, they were not, however, frequently dealt in from the mid-sixties to the eighties despite the reasonable number of shareholders in some of them. According to the evidence given to the 1886 Royal Commission on Depression of Trade and Industry by a linen trade representative, the capital was largely held by the owners of the mills at the time of conversion to limited status, while the remainder "is also pretty largely held by the persons engaged in working the mills who in many cases were junior partners when they changed hands", while the "general public hold a proportion of the shares".[54] By the end of the century the ownership had become more diverse and the shares were one of the specialities of the Belfast market.

The expansive financial climate of the early 1860s also suited the ambitions of the promoters of financial companies. Belfast witnessed a few of these, one of which survived to appear in the Stock Exchange list of 1896. The first arrival was the Belfast and Provincial Building & Investment Co., which in addition to building houses also lent money. It displayed the usual features of such companies — a nominal capital greatly in excess of paid up capital, in this case £100,000 compared with £4,850, it had £25 shares but only £2 10s. called up, and it could muster 197 shareholders. A more lasting rival, the Belfast Discount Co., was registered in 1865 and its stated objects clearly indicate the capacious financial intent of such concerns. Its objects were "Lending and borrowing money, dealing in lands, tenements, and securities, receiving money on deposit, granting letters of credit and transacting the business of bankers". To this end it had a modest nominal capital of £20,000, with £2,500 paid from 500 £10 shares, £5 called up, and acquired by 20 shareholders. By the mid-nineties the paid up capital had risen to £10,180, with an additional small preference issue. One more finance company arrived on the scene just before 'Black Friday', May 11 1866, namely, the Royal Land, Building & Investment Co., again to borrow money, lend on property and deal in securities. The returns of the Registrar of Companies indicates that it had a nominal capital of £100,000 in £10 shares, but there are no other details. It probably succumbed in the aftermath of the Overend, Gurney crash.

But the 1866 crisis did not altogether dampen Belfast's inclinations in this direction. A few finance companies appeared over the next decades but on the whole they emerged only in boom periods and invariably had very small capitals. The only large arrival was the Discount Corporation of Ireland, in September 1878, essentially a bill broker. It had the familiar financial structure — a large nominal capital, £500,000, but only £33,212 was called up with 10s. paid on the £2 shares held by 253 shareholders. It was still operating at the turn of the century with a modest increase in paid up capital.[55]

During the seventies and eighties the number of registrations fluctuated with the level of activity, both the local and national economy. From a handful in depressed years, such as 1868, 1876, 1886, the number rose to a dozen or so in prosperous ones, such as 1873 and 1883. But, in addition, as the extent of Belfast's industrialization and that of the surrounding areas increased with the growth of the shipbuilding industry, centred on Harland & Wolff, Workman, Clark & Co., and MacIlwaine & McColl, the annual figures of registration rose every year as more companies were formed and took limited liability. Even so, the adoption of limited liability over the period was somewhat gradual, due not so much to a reluctance to turn away from the unlimited partnership form but rather because the markets in which companies operated were restricted and required no great injections of capital. A few relatively large companies were formed but the market could not sustain many, and the industries which did produce a large number of quoted companies were generally those which were able to export a significant portion of their output.

Company registrations in this period reflected the growth of the leading industries of the City, namely shipbuilding and linen, and of course those meeting the needs of a large and growing population by way of services, housing and provisions. Among the registrations of the seventies and eighties there were companies involved in manufacturing, some of them related to the main industries, such as machine makers, iron foundries and ropeworks. In the building trade there were builders, cement, timber and felt merchants; in services there were tugs, ferries, tramways, hotels, marine insurance, printing, newspapers, carriers, cafes and temperance restaurants, rinks and halls; in provisions, curers, grocers, warehousemen (of several kinds), hardware merchants, mineral waters, drapers, shirt makers, wines and spirits, and distilleries. Of the companies later listed on the Belfast Stock Exchange, several date from this period. Among the service companies were Belfast Street Tramways (registered in 1872), Belfast Steamship Co. (1872), Ulster Steamship Co. (1877), Cave Hill Tramways (1881), and Irish Shipowners (1883). Breweries and distilleries had Dunville (1879), J. & J. McConnell (1883), and Robertson, Ledlie, Ferguson & Co. (1879). The Belfast Ropework Co. was formed in 1876 to provide a reliable supply of ropes to Harland & Wolff.[56] Most of these were included by Josias Cunningham in his share list, printed in Belfast newspapers during the mid-eighties, as companies whose shares were periodically dealt in by local brokers.

By the 1890s shipbuilding dominated the local economy with the premier company, Harland & Wolff, building the world's greatest and most elegant liners for the White Star Line. Lesser vessels came from the yards of Workman, Clark and MacIlwaine & McColl, two companies which merged in 1893. While shipbuilding sustained a large workforce it also needed support and supplies from a number of ancillary firms in engineering and other products. Similarly, the continued growth of the city required the services of a wide range of industries. In the expansionary climate of the decade company registrations in the Belfast area ran at over twenty a year, dipping slightly in 1894, and in the peak year of activity, 1897, reaching 40 registrations. The benefit to the Stock Exchange list was that during 1891-98 a further fifteen companies emerged which were of sufficient size and nature to warrant a quotation. With a few exceptions these were companies in the provision and service industries. In the early nineties came the Antrim Iron Ore Co. (registered 1891, paid up capital in 1897 of £26,000), The Irish News (1891; £15,000), Leahy, Kelly & Leahy (1891; £25,000 — makers of cigars and tobacco), Olley & Co. (1891; £5,500 — newspapers), J. Wilson & Son (1890; £25,000 — wines and spirits), Wilson & Strain (1892; £35,000 — bakers), Wm. Cowan Ltd. (1893; £100,000 — wines and spirits), and Bernard Hughes Ltd. (1893, £70,000 — millers). With only two recruits in the next few years — Warden Ltd. (1895; £70,000 — theatre) and McConnells Distillery Ltd. (1895; £300,000) — the boom of 1897-98 brought five more companies to the fore, namely, D. Allen & Sons (1897; £85,000 — printers), Lagan Valley Estates (1897; £55,000 — brick manufacturers), Brewsters Ltd. (1897; £40,000 — millers and bakers in Londonderry), John Fulton & Co. (1898; £75,000 — bleachers, dyers and finishers), and Martin Estates (1898; £100,000).

Thus, by 1898, the industrial and commercial section of the Belfast list carried six milling and bakery companies (total paid up capital £280,000;

# BELFAST STOCK EXCHANGE DAILY LIST.

PUBLISHED BY AUTHORITY OF THE COMMITTEE.

Printed at the "Northern Whig" Office, Belfast.

No. 300. THURSDAY, DECEMBER 29, 1898.

**MEMBERS:**

ADELEY, W. J., 32, Rosemary Street.
BARR, J. B. (Osborne & Barr), 13, Waring Street.
BROWNE, G. B. (Herbert Darbishire & Co.), 9, Royal Avenue.
CALVERT, W. H. (Taylor, Calvert & Co.), 6, Royal Avenue.
CARR, A. H. R. (A. H. R. Carr & Co.), Ulster Buildings, Waring Street.
CARR, THOMAS J. (A. H. R. Carr & Co.), Ulster Buildings, Waring Street.
COATES, WM. F. (Wm. F. Coates & Co.), 3, Lombard Street.
CRAIG, JAMES (Craigs & Co.), 36, Rosemary Street.
CUNNINGHAM, JAMES (Josias Cunningham & Co.), 41, Waring Street.
CUNNINGHAM, SAMUEL (Josias Cunningham & Co.), 41, Waring Street.
DARBISHIRE, HERBERT (Herbert Darbishire & Co.), 9, Royal Avenue.
DUFFIN, ADAM (Adam Duffin & Co.), 9, Waring Street.
GUNNING, S., 3, Donegall Street.
HAMPTON, WILLIAM, 1, Skipper Street.
JOHNSON, ABRAHAM (Johnson, Mahony & Co.), 82, Royal Avenue.
JOHNSTONE, C. J., 29 & 31, Donegall Street.
JOHNSTONE, FRANCIS, 21, Waring Street.
JOHNSTON, PHILIP (Morell & Johnston), 9, Rosemary Street.
JOY, ROBERT (Shaw & Joy), 29, Rosemary Street.
MILLIKEN, WILLIAM (Steen & Milliken), 64, Royal Avenue.
MORELL, JAMES (Morell & Johnston), 9, Rosemary Street.
M'GIFFIN, RICHARD, Ulster Buildings, Waring Street.
M'KEE, JOHN (John M'Kee & Co.), 100, High Street.
M'KEE, ROBERT (John M'Kee & Co.), 100, High Street.
NEWETT, B. J. (Robinson & Newett), 63, Royal Avenue
OSBORNE, ALFRED (Osborne & Barr), 13, Waring Street.
RICHARDSON, WALTER J., 47, Rosemary Street.
ROBINSON, E. A. (Robinson & Newett), 63, Royal Avenue.
SHAW, WILLIAM (Shaw & Joy), 29, Rosemary Street.
STEEN, COCHRANE (Steen & Milliken), 64, Royal Avenue.
TAYLOR, JAMES (Taylor, Calvert & Co.), 6, Royal Avenue.
WORKMAN, WILLIAM (R. Workman & Co.), 8, Corporation Street.
WORKMAN, JAMES (R. Workman & Co.), 8, Corporation Street.

**Members of the Belfast Stock Exchange are not allowed to advertise for business purposes, or to issue Circulars to others than their own principals. Persons doing so are not members of the Exchange, nor are they under the control of the Committee.** DRUMMOND PORTER, *Registrar.*

## BANKS.

| Amount of Stock or No. of Shares. | Amt. | Paid. | Dividends Payable. | Last Two. | | When Ex. Div. | Name. | Last Price. | Business Done. |
|---|---|---|---|---|---|---|---|---|---|
| 5,000 | 125 | 25 | Feb. Aug. | a50/- | a50/- | 12 Aug. | Belfast Banking Company Limited—Old ... | 127 | 127¼ |
| 11,000 | 125 | 25 | Feb. Aug. | a20/- | a20/- | 12 Aug. | Do. —New ... | 51 | |
| 25,000 | 50 | 10 | Mar. Sept. | a11/- | a11/- | 15 Sep. | Northern Banking Company Limited—A ... | 27 | |
| 15,000 | 50 | 10 | Mar. Sept. | a5/6 | a5/6 | 15 Sep. | Do. —B ... | 13⅛ | |
| 5,000 | 50 | 11 | Mar. Sept. | a... | a... | 15 Sep. | Do. —New ... | 15 | |
| 180,000 | 15 | 2½ | Mar. Sept. | a5/- | a5/- | 15 Sep. | Ulster Bank Limited ... | 12$\frac{3}{16}$ | 12$\frac{3}{16}$,¼ |
| 40,000 | 100 | 12½ | Feb. Aug. | a12/6 | a12/6 | 14 July | Provincial Bank Limited ... | 30¼ | |
| 150,000 | 50 | 10 | Jan. July | a9/- | a9/- | 28 July | National Bank Limited ... | 21⅛ | |
| 100,000 | 80 | 20 | Feb. Aug. | a44/- | a44/- | 12 Aug. | London and County Limited ... | 105¼ | |
| 120,000 | 100 | 15 | Jan. July | a15/- | a15/- | 28 July | London Joint Stock Limited ... | 34¼ | |
| 140,000 | 100 | 20 | Jan. July | a26/- | a30/- | 28 July | London and Westminster Limited ... | 61 | |
| 40,000 | 100 | 25 | Apl. Oct. | a40/- | a40/- | 13 Oct. | Standard of South Africa Limited ... | 68 | |
| 110,000 | 100 | 15½ | Jan. July | a15/6 | a18/6 | 28 July | Union of London Limited ... | 37⅛ | |

## RAILWAYS.

| Amount of Stock or No. of Shares. | Amt. | Paid. | Dividends Payable. | Last Two. | | When Ex. Div. | Name. | Last Price. | Business Done. |
|---|---|---|---|---|---|---|---|---|---|
| £3,567,165 | Stock | 100 | Mar. Sept. | 67/6 | 62/6 | 31 Aug. | Great Northern Railway—Ordy ... | 177⅛ | |
| £2,023,285 | Stock | 100 | Jan. July | 40/- | 40/- | 14 July | Do. —4 per cent. Deb ... | 141 | |
| £1,204,575 | Stock | 100 | Mar. Sept. | 40/- | 40/- | 31 Aug. | Do. —4 per cent. Pref ... B | 140 | |
| £872,763 | Stock | 100 | Mar. Sept. | 65/- | 55/- | 31 Aug. | Belfast and Northern Counties Railway—Ordy | 157 | 156 |
| £739,502 | Stock | 100 | Jan. July | 40/- | 40/- | 29 June | Do. —4 per c. Deb | 138 | |
| £937,450 | Stock | 100 | Mar. Sep. | 40/- | 40/- | 31 Aug. | Do. —4 per c. Pref B | 136 | |
| £109,000 | Stock | 100 | Mar. Sep. | 30/- | 30/- | 31 Aug. | Do. —3 per c. Pref B | 103⅛ | |
| £381,650 | Stock | 100 | Mar. Sep. | 65/- | 65/- | 12 Aug. | Belfast and County Down Railway—Ordy | 163 | |
| £181,686 | Stock | 100 | Jan. July | 40/- | 40/- | 29 June | Do. —4 per cent. Deb | 140 | |
| £138,000 | Stock | 100 | Jan. July | 30/- | 30/- | 29 June | Do. —3 per cent. Deb | 105 | |
| £50,000 | Stock | 100 | Jan. July | 45/- | 45/- | 29 June | Do. —4½ per cent. Pref B | 148 | |
| £248,141 | Stock | 100 | Mar. Sep. | 50/- | 50/- | 12 Aug. | Do. —5 per cent. Guar | 168 | |
| £200,000 | Stock | 100 | Mar. Sep. | 40/- | 40/- | 12 Aug. | Do. —4 per cent. Pref B | 134⅛ | |
| £4,971,155 | Stock | 100 | Mar. Sep. | 55/- | 50/- | 31 Aug. | Great Southern & Western Railway—Ordy .. | 134¼ | |
| £2,321,487 | Stock | 100 | Jan. July | 40/- | 40/- | 14 July | Do. —4 per cent. Deb | 141⅛ | |
| £1,329,100 | Stock | 100 | Mar. Sep. | 40/- | 40/- | 31 Aug. | Do. —4 per cent. Guar | 140 | |
| £2,370,000 | Stock | 100 | Mar. Sep. | 45/- | 40/- | 12 Aug. | Midland Great Western Railway—Ordy ... | 108⅛ | |
| £1,326,014 | Stock | 100 | Jan. July | 40/- | 40/- | 29 June | Do. —4 per cent. Deb | 138¼ | |
| £885,750 | Stock | 100 | Mar. Sep. | 40/- | 40/- | 12 Aug. | Do. —4 per cent. Pref B | 136 | |
| £700,150 | Stock | 100 | Mar. Sep. | nil | nil | Aug. '96 | Dublin, Wicklow, and Wexford Railway—Ordy | 26 | |
| 11,951 | 50 | 50 | Mar. Sep. | nil | 5/- | 11 Mar. | Waterford and Limerick Railway—Ordy | 30⅞ | |

## CORPORATION STOCKS.

| Amount of Stock or No. of Shares. | Amt. | Paid. | Dividends Payable. | Last Two. | | When Ex. Div. | Name. | | | Last Price. | Business Done. |
|---|---|---|---|---|---|---|---|---|---|---|---|
| £150,000 | Stock | 100 | | ... | ... | 29 Sep. | Belfast Corporation | 3½ per cent. | 1921 | 109¼ | |
| £200,000 | Stock | 100 | Quarterly | ... | ... | 29 Sep. | Do. | do. | 1928 | 112 | |
| £100,000 | Stock | 100 | Jan. | ... | ... | 29 Sep. | Do. | 3½ per cent. | 1912 | 105 | |
| £150,000 | Stock | 100 | April | ... | ... | 29 Sep. | Do. | do. | 1915 | 105 | |
| £200,000 | Stock | 100 | July | ... | ... | 29 Sep. | Do. | 3½ per cent. | 1924 | 106 | |
| £200,000 | Stock | 100 | Oct. | ... | ... | 29 Sep. | Do. | 3 per cent. | 1955 | 104¼ | |
| £1,120,344 | Stock | 100 | Jan. July | ... | ... | 1 Dec. | Dublin Corporation | 3½ per cent. | 1944 | 110⅛ | |
| £547,970 | Stock | 100 | Apl. Oct. | ... | ... | 29 Sep. | Belfast Water Comm. | 3½ per cent. | 1938 | 114⅛ | |
| £425,000 | Stock | 100 | Jan. July | ... | ... | 29 June | Do. | 3 per cent. | 1953-56 | 105¼ | |
| £1,081,814 | Stock | 100 | Apl. Oct. | ... | ... | 29 Sep. | Belfast Harbour Comm.— | 3½ per cent. | 1953 | 110¼ | |

## STEAM AND SHIPPING.

| Amount of Stock or No. of Shares. | Amt. | Paid. | Dividends Payable. | Last Two. | | When Ex. Div. | Name. | Nos. | Last Price. | Business Done. |
|---|---|---|---|---|---|---|---|---|---|---|
| 1,000 | 50 | 50 | Mar. Sep. | nil | 10/- | 30 Mar. | Belfast Steamship Co., Limited... | 1-1,000 | 37⅛ | |
| 15,000 | 10 | 5 | Mar. Sep. | nil | 1/- | 30 Mar. | Do. —"A" ... | 1-15,000 | †3¼ | |
| £585,950 | Stock | 100 | May Nov. | a20/- | a20/- | 30 Nov. | City of Dublin S. Packet Co., Ld. | ... | 68⅛ | |
| 14,100 | 10 | 10 | Apl. Oct. | a2/6 | a2/6 | 29 Sep. | Dundalk&NewryS.PacketCo.Ld. | ... | 4⅛ | |
| 500 | 100 | 100 | May Nov. | a50/- | a40/- | 30 Nov. | Irish Shipowners Company, Ltd. | 1,501-2,000 | 73 | |
| 1,500 | 100 | 50 | May Nov. | a25/- | a20/- | 30 Nov. | Do. do. ... | 1-15,000 | 36 | |
| 24,000 | 10 | 5 | Feb. Aug. | a3/- | a3/- | 31 Aug. | Ulster Steamship Co., Limited... | 1-24,000 | 6⅛ | |

## BAKERY SHARES.

| Amount of Stock or No. of Shares. | Amt. | Paid. | Dividends Payable. | Last Two. | | When Ex. Div. | Name. | Nos. | Last Price. | Business Done. |
|---|---|---|---|---|---|---|---|---|---|---|
| 2,947 | 1 | 15/- | February | 1/6 | Yearly | 10 Feb. | Belfast Bread Consumers Co. Ltd. | 1-2,947 | 24/- | |
| 4,000 | 5 | 5 | Feb. Aug. | 3/- | 3/- | 31 Aug. | Brewsters, Limited—Ordinary ... | 5,335-8,000 | 5⅛ | |
| 4,000 | 5 | 5 | Feb. Aug. | 2/6 | 2/6 | 31 Aug. | Do. —5 per cent.—Pref | 1,335-4,000 | 5⅛ | |
| 4,668 | 5 | 5 | June Dec. | 4/- | 4/- | 30 Nov. | Bernard Hughes, Limited—Ordy | 9,333-14,000 | 8⅛ | |
| 4,668 | 5 | 5 | June Dec. | 3/- | 3/- | 30 Nov. | Do. —6 per cent.—Pref | 2,333-7,000 | 7$\frac{7}{16}$ | |
| 2,332 | 10 | 10 | May Nov. | 5/- | 5/- | 27 Oct. | Do. —5 per cent.—Deb | 1,169-3,500 | 13⅛ | |
| 8,000 | 5 | 5 | June Dec. | 6/- | 4/- | 30 Nov. | Inglis & Co., Limited —Ordy | 9,001-17,000 | 9¼ | |
| 9,000 | 5 | 5 | June Dec. | 3/- | 3/- | 30 Nov. | Do. —6 per cent.—Pref | 1-9,000 | 7⅛ | |
| 9,000 | 5 | 5 | May Nov. | 2/6 | 2/6 | 27 Oct. | Do. —5 per cent.—Deb | 1-9,000 | 6⅛ | |
| 1,485 | 2 | 2 | November | a2/- | Yearly | 15 Dec. | Old Public Bakery, Limited ... | 1-1,485 | *28/- | |
| 3,000 | 5 | 5 | Jan. July | 3/- | 3/- | 28 July | Wilson & Strain, Limited —Ord | 1-3,000 | 6$\frac{7}{16}$ | |
| 4,000 | 5 | 5 | Jan. July | 3/- | 3/- | 28 July | Do. —6 per cent.—Pref | 1-4,000 | 6⅞ | |

## BREWERIES AND DISTILLERIES.

| Amount of Stock or No. of Shares. | Amt. | Paid. | Dividends Payable. | Last Two. | | When Ex. Div. | Name | Nos. | Last Price. | Business Done. |
|---|---|---|---|---|---|---|---|---|---|---|
| 170,000 | 10 | 10 | Mar. Sep. | a14/- | a24/- | 31 Aug. | Arthur Guinness, Son, & Co. Ltd. .. | | 57⅛ | |
| 200,000 | 10 | 10 | Mar. Sep. | 6/- | 6/- | 31 Aug. | Do. —6 per cent.—Pref ... | | 19 | |
| 50,000 | 10 | 10 | Apl. Oct. | a13/- | a17/- | 27 Oct. | Dunville & Co., Ltd. ... ... | 1-50,000 | 25¼ | |
| 5,000 | 10 | 10 | Feb. Aug. | 6/- | 6/- | 28 July | Irish Distillery, Ltd—6 p.c.—Pref ... | | 13 | |
| 500 | 100 | 100 | Jan. July | 50/- | 50/- | 14 July | Do. —5 per cent.—Deb ... | | 110 | |
| 7,500 | 10 | 10 | Jan. July | 6/- | 6/- | 29 June | J. & J. M'Connell, Limited—Pref | 1-7,500 | 14⅞ | |
| 3,000 | 10 | 10 | ... | ... | ... | ... | M'Connell's Distillery, Ltd.-5 p.c. Pref.- | 1-3000 | 11 | |
| 10,000 | 10 | 9 | May Nov. | a9/- | a13/6 | 11 Nov. | Mitchell&Co.of Belfast, Ld.-Ordy | 1-10,000 | 18¼ | |
| 5,000 | 10 | 10 | Jan. July | 5/- | 5/- | 29 June | Do. —5 per cent.—Deb | 1-5,000 | 11 | |
| 6,700 | 10 | 10 | May Nov. | a8/- | a6/- | 11 Nov. | Wm. Cowan, Limited—Ordy ... | 1-6,700 | 12 | |
| 3,300 | 10 | 10 | May Nov. | 6/- | 6/- | 11 Nov. | Do. —6 per cent.—Pref | 1-3,300 | 13¼ | |
| 10,000 | 10 | 8 | Feb. Aug. | 8/- | 8/- | 31 Aug. | Young, King, & Co., Limited ... | 1-10,000 | 14¼ | |

## SPINNING SHARES.

| Amount of Stock or No. of Shares. | Amt. | Paid. | Dividends Payable. | Last Two. | | When Ex. Div. | Name | Nos. | Last Price. | Business Done. |
|---|---|---|---|---|---|---|---|---|---|---|
| 8,000 | 50 | 25 | May. Nov. | 10/- | 10/- | 11 Nov. | Brookfield Linen Co., Limited ... | 1-8,000 | 15¼ | |
| 2,000 | 10 | 10 | Nov. | a5/- | Yearly | 11 Nov. | Edenderry Spinning Co., Ltd. ... | ... | ... | |
| 10,000 | 10 | 9 | Nov. | a4/6 | ,, | 11 Nov. | Do. do. ... | ... | ... | |
| 2,000 | 50 | 25 | January | 25/- | Yearly | 27 Jan. | Falls Flax Spinning Co., Ltd. ... | 1-2,000 | 15 | |
| 5,350 | 10 | 7½ | November | 9/- | Yearly | 11 Nov. | Island Spinning Co., Ltd. ... | 1-5,350 | ... | |
| 13,000 | 7½ | 6 | Apl. Oct. | 3/7½ | 3/7½ | 11 Nov. | Philip Johnston & Son, Ltd. ... | 1-13,000 | 6⅛ | |
| 12,650 | 3 | 3 | Apl. Oct. | nil | nil | ... | Whiteabbey Flax Sp. Co., Ltd... | 1-12,650 | 2 | |
| 12,000 | 25 | 25 | Jan. July | a15/- | a15/- | 28 July | York St. Flax Sp. Co., Ltd.-Ord | 25,001-37,000 | 33 | |
| 25,000 | 10 | 10 | Jan. July | 6/- | 6/- | 28 July | Do. —6 per cent.—Pref | 1-25,000 | 15¼ | |
| £250,000 | Stock | 100 | Jan. July | 45/- | 45/- | 29 June | Do. —4½ per cent.—Deb | ... | 116⅛ | |
| 300,000 | 10 | 10 | Apl. Oct. | 20/- | 40/- | 11 Nov. | J. & P. Coats Limited ... ... | 1-300,000 | 72⅛ | |
| 565,230 | 1 | 1 | Jun. Dec. | ... | 9d | 15 Dec. | English Sewing Cotton—Ordy—1-80 & 184,931-750,080 | | *34/6 | 35/-,35/3 |
| 565,150 | 1 | 1 | ... Sep. | ... | -/7⅛ | 29 Sep. | Do. —5 p.c. Cum. Pref.—184,851-750,000 | | 22/3 | |
| 888,900 | 1 | 1 | Jun. Dec. | ... | 6.96d | 30 Nov. | Fine Cotton Spinners and Dblrs. —Ordy ... | 1-888,900 | 31/3 | 31/9,32/- |
| 888,900 | 1 | 1 | Jun. Dec. | ... | 3.12d | 30 Nov. | Do. —5 per cent. Cum. Pref.... ... | 1-888,900 | 22/3 | |

## MISCELLANEOUS.

| Amount of Stock or No. of Shares. | Amt. | Paid. | Dividends Payable. | Last Two. | | When Ex. Div. | Name | Nos. | Last Price. | Business Done. |
|---|---|---|---|---|---|---|---|---|---|---|
| 6,000 | 2 | 2 | Mar. Sep. | a6d | a1/- | 31 Aug. | Antrim Iron Ore Co., Ltd—"A" | 1-6,000 | 30/- | |
| 8,955 | 3 | 2 | Mar. Sep. | a6d | a1/- | 31 Aug. | Do —"B" ... ... | 6,001-14,955 | 28/6 | |
| 2,000 | 10 | 10 | January | a8/- | Yearly | 27 Jan. | Belfast Commercial Buildings, Ld | 1-2,000 | 11 | |
| 2,000 | 5 | 5 | November | 12/6 | Yearly | 30 Nov. | Belfast Mineral Water Co., Ltd. | 1-2,000 | 10⅛ | |
| 24,600 | 10 | 10 | Feb. Aug. | a7/6 | a7/6 | 31 Aug. | Belfast Street Tramways Co. .. | 1-24,600 | 16⅞ | |
| 2,500 | 100 | 75 | Feb. Aug. | a37/6 | a52/6 | 12 Aug. | Belfast Ropework Co., Ltd. ... | 21-2,500 | 90¼ | c90⅛ |
| 1,500 | 100 | 25 | ... | ... | ... | ... | Do. —New | 2,501-4,000 | 36⅛ | 37 |
| 10,000 | 10 | 10 | Mar. Sep. | 5/- | 5/- | 31 Aug. | Do. —5 per cent.—Pref | 1-10,000 | 12$\frac{13}{16}$ | |
| 2,030 | 10 | 5 | June Dec. | a2/- | a2/- | 14 July | Belfast Discount Company, Ltd. | ... | 41/- | |
| 302 | 5 | 5 | June Dec. | 2/6 | 2/6 | 14 July | Do. 5 per cent.—Pref | ... | 4⅛ | |
| 2,000 | 50 | 25 | December | nil | nil | ... | Coey & Company, Limited .. | ... | ... | |
| 1,500 | 50 | 50 | Apl. Oct. | 25/- | 25/- | 27 Oct. | Do. —5 per cent.—Deb | ... | 46 | |
| 6,000 | 1 | 1 | Feb. Aug. | 6d | 6d | 12 Aug. | Cave Hill Tramways Company... | 1-6,000 | 27/6 | |
| £85,000 | 100 | 100 | Jan. July | 45/- | 45/- | 29 June | D. Allen & Sons, Ltd-4½pc.-Deb | ... | 107⅛ | 107¼ |
| 8,000 | 10 | 10 | April | a17/- | Yearly | 15 Apl. | Forster Green & Co., Limited ... | 1-8,000 | 20⅛ | |
| 20,000 | 1 | 15/- | July | 1/10½ | Yearly | 29 June | The "Irish News," Limited ... | 1-20,000 | 25/- | |
| 15,000 | 5 | 4 | Mar. Sep. | nil | 1/7½ | 15 Sep. | John Arnott & Co. of Belfast, Ltd. | 1-15,000 | 4⅛ | |
| 466 | 50 | 50 | Feb. Aug. | 22/6 | 22/6 | 28 July | Do. —4½ per c.—Deb | 1,466 | 56 | |
| 8,000 | 5 | 5 | ... | ... | ... | ... | John Fulton & Co, Ltd.—5½ p.c.—Pref | 1-8,000 | 5$\frac{11}{16}$ | |
| 1,000 | 10 | 10 | January | 12/- | Yearly | 10 Feb. | Kirker & Company, Limited ... | 1-1,000 | 10 | |
| 54,658 | 1 | 1 | May Nov. | a6d | a6d | 29 June | Lagan Vale Estate, &c., Co. Ltd. | 1-54,658 | 22/6 | |
| 4,000 | 5 | 5 | Jan. July | 5/- | 3/- | 12 Aug. | Leahy, Kelly & Leahy, Ord 1,001-95 & 2,996-6,000 | | 8⅛ | |
| 1,000 | 5 | 5 | Jan. July | 3/- | 3/- | 12 Aug. | Do. —6 per cent.—Pref | 1-1,000 | 6¼ | |
| 6,000 | 10 | 8 | Mar. Sep. | 4/9½ | 8/- | 15 Sep. | James Lindsay & Company, Ltd. | 1-6,000 | 16⅛ | |
| 7,500 | 10 | 8 | Feb. Aug. | 3/2½ | 3/2½ | 31 Aug. | Lindsay Brothers, Limited ... | 1-7,500 | 7⅛ | |
| 400 | 50 | 50 | Jan. July | 22/6 | 22/6 | 14 July | Do. —4½ per cent.—Deb | 1-400 | 57 | |
| 666,667 | 1 | 1 | ... | ... | 1/- | 13 Oct. | Lipton, Limited—Ordy | 1,333,334-2,000,000 | 50/- | 50/-,51/- |
| 666,667 | 1 | 1 | ... | ... | 5.69d | 29 Sep. | Do. —5 p.c.—Cum. Pref | 333,334-1,000,000 | 24/- | 55/- |
| 15,490 | 6 | 6 | August | nil | nil | ... | Marcus Ward & Co. Ltd. ... | 1-15,490 | 3⅛ | 3⅛ |
| 10,000 | 10 | 10 | Jan. July | ... | ... | ... | Martin Estates Co. Ltd.—4 p.c. Deb | 1-10,000 | 10⅛ | |
| 353 | 50 | 50 | August | 6 p.c. | ... | 15 Aug. | "Northern Whig," Limited ... | 1-353 | 53 | |
| 1,100 | 5 | 5 | October | 10/- | Yearly | 13 Oct. | Olley & Co., Limited. ... ... | 1-1,000 | 7 | |
| 15,000 | 10 | 8 | Mar. Sep. | a10/- | a10/- | 15 Sep. | Robertson, Ledlie, Ferguson&Co. Ld. | 1-15,000 | 22⅛ | |
| 50,000 | 2 | 6/- | January | 10 p.c. | Yearly | 13 Jan. | Ulster Marine Insurance Co. Ltd. | 1-50,000 | 7/6 | |
| 8,318 | 2 | 2 | ... | nil | nil | ... | Ulster Hall Company, Limited ... | 1-8,318 | 10/- | |
| 7,000 | 5 | 5 | Jan. July | 4/- | 4/- | 14 July | Warden, Limited—Ordy ... | 7,001-14,000 | 3⅞ | |
| 7,000 | 5 | 5 | Jan. July | 2/6 | 2/6 | 14 July | Do. —5 per cent.—Pref | 1-7,000 | 4¼ | |
| 25,000 | 1 | 1 | May Nov. | 6d | 6d | 11 Nov. | J. Wilson & Son, Belfast, Ld-5 p.c.-Pref | 1-25,000 | 19/6 | 19/6 |
| 60,000 | 10 | 10 | Feb. Aug. | 6/- | 5/- | 28 July | A. & S. Henry & Co. Limited ... | 1-60,000 | 11¼ | |

* Ex. Div. *a* Free of Income Tax. † Exceptional amount at special price. ‡ Ex. Rights. B Dividend contingent on the profits of each separate year. C For Cash.

Dividends recommended or declared.

Business Hours—11 o'clock a.m. and 2-30 p.m. No meeting on Saturdays.
Account Days—December 30th and January, 13th, 1899.
Bank Rate 4 per cent.

Stock Exchange will be CLOSED on Monday, 2nd January, 1899.

*Fig. 9: Belfast Stock Exchange Daily List, 1898*

average per company £46,690), seven breweries and distilleries (£1,025,000; £146,428), seven spinning companies (£1,316,075; £188,000), four shipping companies (£511,000; £127,750) and 28 miscellaneous companies (£2,312,332; £82,582), involving in all a total paid up capital of £5,444,000 (average capital per company £104,692). As expected capital intensive activities, such as brewing and shipping, displayed larger capitalisations, with lower levels for bakers and millers, and also in the range of miscellaneous companies. The lowest capitalisations in the list, however, were well below the average levels indicated above. There were ten companies with paid up capitals of less than £20,000. In a few cases only the preference and debenture capital was quoted, the vendors of the company keeping all or most of the equity. The only national companies in the list in 1898 were such household names as Guinness, English Sewing Cotton, J. & P. Coats, Lipton, and Fine Cotton Spinners & Doublers.

After this surge of company formation the first years of the new century witnessed a marked slowing down in the rate of registrations, partly due to greater legal regulation imposed by the Companies Act of 1900. However, the promotion boom of the last years of the decade soon re-established the high levels of the mid-nineties and, indeed, by 1912 surpassed them. But all this had little effect on the Belfast Stock Exchange list. Few additions appear to it by the eve of the First World War. In the spinning section five additional companies are quoted, one an established firm from the 1870s, Richardson, Sons & Owden, while the others were fairly recent registrations. There was at this time a tendency to incorporate as the fortunes of the industry waned. The bakery section lost four companies and gained one. Shipping remained the same, while breweries gained three including Old Bushmills Distillery, registered in 1896.[57] The biggest changes took place in the miscellaneous section with the departure of eleven local companies and the inclusion of twelve new ones, several of them in industries characteristic of Belfast. Thus, by 1913, the number of local companies in the list stood at 62, with a total nominal capital of £9.1mn. Several of these firms, however, had quite small capitalisations of around £20,000 and dealing in their shares was very infrequent. Furthermore, 20 of them had taken advantage of a provision in the 1908 Companies Act enabling them to register as a private company, and thus while they continued to be listed (suitably identified) they did not supply an annual balance sheet and statement of accounts to the Stock Exchange. To qualify for this change in status the number of shareholders had to be less than 50.[58]

Four years of war brought a boom in shipbuilding and an added demand for linen, some of it for the production of aeroplane canvas. It was, however, but a short prelude to a prolonged period of depression for the main industries of Northern Ireland. By the mid-twenties severe recession had set in reaching a low point in 1933 when Harland & Wolff did not launch a ship, while in the following year Workman, Clark went out of business.

Neither was it a particularly opportune time for Harland & Wolff to grace the Belfast list. While the business had started in 1858 it was not registered as a limited company until December 1885, under the name of Queens Island Shipbuilding & Engineering Co. Ltd. It then had a nominal capital of £350,000 in £1,000 shares held by seven shareholders. The name was changed to Harland & Wolff Ltd. in 1888. It was then converted into a private company in October 1908, and later, registration was transferred from Dublin to Belfast under the Government of Ireland Act, 1920. It finally became a public company in July 1924 with an offer to the public of £4.0mn 6% First Cumulative Preference Shares of £1 each at par (the total issued capital of the company at the time stood at £10.3mm).[59] It was to prove an unhappy existence. From the start the shares traded at a discount, falling gradually to a low of 15s. in 1928. In 1929 the company paid no preference dividend, and by 1931 the share price had collapsed to 9d. Although the price recovered to 12s. by 1936, no dividend was paid. The introduction of the ordinary stock to the market before the Second World War proved a more profitable involvement for investors, the price rising from 15s. to 25s. after the war. But again it was short lived. By the mid-sixties no dividend was paid and the early seventies saw the shares languishing at 15s.

A happier arrival on the Belfast market, and on London, was made by Gallaher Ltd. A long established business founded about 1859 by Thomas Gallaher, it was acquired in 1896 by Gallaher Ltd. It had a nominal capital of £1.0mn in £100 shares, £10 paid, with £83,000 called up from twelve shareholders. Converted into a private company in 1908 it became a public company again in 1928. In January 1929 one million 6½% Cumulative Preference Shares of £1 each were offered to the market, at an issue price of 20s. 6d., by the merchant bankers Edward de Stein & Co.; the Belfast broker to the issue was W. F. Coates & Co.[60] Apart from a low of 18s. 9d. in 1931 the shares commanded a respectable premium in later years. When the ordinary shares of the company came to the market in 1930 they proved a handsome investment. The £1 ordinary shares moved from 23s. in 1930 to over £7 in 1936.

The fate of the other sectors of the Belfast list was fairly mixed in the inter-war years. Linen faced strong competition from cotton and foreign supplies, the fortunes of the quoted firms reflecting these difficulties. Within a few years of the end of the First World War, linen share prices fell and soon dividends were cut, and for some years, especially the early thirties, none was paid. Quoted prices were for the most part purely nominal, recovery coming only with the prospect of extra orders as the Second World War approached. The worst experience probably fell to the York Street mills. From £32 its £25 shares fell to just over £3 in 1929 (the dividend had stopped in 1926), and then to £1 in 1931 where they froze for several years. The capital was restructured in 1937 with £20 written off the

£25 shares and the remaining £5 subdivided into £1 units; these fluctuated between 3s. 6d. and 18s. 3d. over the next few years. By 1946 its fortunes had recovered somewhat and a more buoyant share price resulted.[61]

On balance other Belfast shares had a more stable record over these difficult years. The best were those associated with consumer durables, particularly bakeries and cigarettes. For example, Bernard Hughes, Inglis and Leahy, Kelly & Leahy displayed stable prices for most of the depression years, advancing strongly in the thirties with a very good dividend record. The representatives of the warehousing trade — Arnott's, Ledlie & Ferguson, and Robinson & Cleaver, the printing industry — McCaw, Stevenson & Orr, and building — Lagan Valley Estates, all reflected the gradual improvement in the economy to 1929, then they fell off sharply with the onset of the depression but recovered quite quickly afterwards. Some reduced their dividends but only one or two passed them for very short periods.

The post-war years saw a gradual contraction of the Belfast list due to the difficulties faced by the local economy and the trend towards amalgamation. In the case of textiles the half dozen or so linen quotations of the immediate post-war period had been reduced by the mid-seventies to just two, Henry Campbell & Co. (who acquired Island Spinning Co. Ltd in 1959) and Frazer & Haughton Co. Ltd. The bakery section still boasted the presence of Hughes (Bernard) Ltd. and Inglis & Co., but all the local distilleries had given way to national names. The shipbuilding giant, Harland & Wolff, survived in the list until it ran into difficulties in the early seventies, while the other leading local share of earlier years, Gallaher, was taken over in 1980 by the American Tobacco International Corporation. Leahy, Kelly & Leahy still continued to represent a local interest in the manufacture of cigars and cigarettes, with Arnott (John) & Co. Ltd (of Belfast), and Young & Anderson keeping the local stores section alive. But the miscellaneous representation had by the mid-seventies dwindled to a mere seven companies. Thus, when the last Belfast list appeared in June 1974 the local industrial and commercial section amounted to fifteen companies, with a total nominal value of £2.9mn and a market value of £3.6mn. Few of these companies transferred to The Stock Exchange Daily Official List.

All the companies granted a quotation in the Belfast list had to comply with the requirements laid down by the Committee. For the first two years after its formation, in 1895, the Exchange judged requests for a quotation against the requirements used by Dublin, setting out its own rules in 1897. This, of course, merely involved adapting well tried and standard set of rules to its own special needs. Basically such rules were designed to ensure that a company was duly constituted and an adequate proportion of the capital was made available to the public to make a market (that two thirds or more of the nominal amount of each security was fairly and unconditionally allotted to the public). Also, that details were available of other shares allotted, and the relevant documents to verify that the money from the issue had been duly received by the company were to be made available for inspection. A company normally used the services of a broker in its dealings with the Committee. By 1889, in most respects, the Belfast rules followed the practices of Dublin, Liverpool and London.[62] As on other exchanges the Committee was not slow to exercise its powers. For example, it refused to quote companies whose prospectus had not been put to the public in a satisfactory manner, or where the allotment of shares had been improperly executed, or where the acquisition of assets by the company had not been completed. The most frequent complaint against companies usually arose, however, after they were quoted in that they did not always keep their promise to supply copies of accounts and reports before the annual general meeting, and the Committee's remedy was a threat to suspend the quotation. If the Committee felt that the market would benefit from quoting a particular company it would do so provided it was satisfied as to the bona fide character of the concern and that it was of "sufficient magnitude and public importance and that $\frac{2}{3}$ of the issue in question has been acquired by the public".[63] By the 1920s the procedures were virtually identical to those of London, and in 1947 the market formally adopted London rules on quotations and permission to deal.

## The Stock Exchange — Northern Ireland

By the early sixties the membership of the Exchange stood at 32. Business revolved around a diminishing list of local companies, several trustee stocks, and dealings channelled by brokers to other markets. Relative to other provincial markets Belfast was thus a small entity and there was little prospect of an increase in membership or turnover. At that time the Jenkins Committee on Company Law reported and among its recommendations was one which greatly concerned the stock exchanges. It recommended that the Board of Trade should look at the list of stock exchanges with a view to reducing their number and increasing their size. In addition, it drew attention to the need to ensure that all markets had adequate compensation funds for the protection of the public. To meet the criticism on size several markets in England, Wales and Scotland were successfully regionalised into stronger units, but the opportunities available to Belfast were limited, as it was impractical to go in with the Scottish market, and politically difficult to join with the Irish Stock Exchange. Thus to ensure some strength through collective participation it readily joined in the arrangements for setting up the Federation of Stock Exchanges in Great Britain and Ireland in 1965.[64]

To meet the other demand of the Jenkins Report the Belfast Committee set up a Compensation Fund in 1962, indeed it had been actively looking into this matter well before the Jenkins threat appeared. In 1965 the Fund stood at around £5,500, reaching £11,800 in 1968. To increase the viability of the market members were urged to use local jobbing facilities set up under the dual capacity arrangements embodied in Federation.

Gradually, however, opinion within the Federated exchanges was moving towards forming one Stock Exchange, and following detailed discussions over several years The Stock Exchange came into being in 1973. Under this new structure Belfast became a separate Unit with its own local organisation, while local investors had the benefit of the protection of the central Compensation Fund. The dealing channel for stocks now leads directly to the London or regional jobbers, except in a few designated stocks, while the settlements procedures are incorporated into the TALISMAN network. Three firms now operate in Belfast, namely, Coates (Wm. F.) & Co., Laing & Cruickshank, and Josias Cunningham & Co. (Inc. Darbishire, Malcomson & Coates).

# NOTES

1. *The Economist*, April 19, 1884, p. 480.
2. *The Irish Insurance, Banking and Finance Journal*, December 1882, p. 4.
3. Select Committee of the House of Lords on the Companies Bill, B.P.P., 1897(X), Q. 285.
4. *Finance Union*, November 11 1893.
5. The members were B.S. Newett, James Cunningham, Adam Duffin, R.C. Grubb, John McKee, C.I. Johnstone and William Shaw.
6. Belfast Stock Exchange, Minutes, January 23, 30 1895.
7. Belfast Stock Exchange, Minutes, February 25 to October 19 1896.
8. Belfast Stock Exchange, Minutes, February 22 to May 27 1897.
9. Belfast Stock Exchange, Minutes, May 24 1900.
10. Belfast Stock Exchange, Minutes, June 14 1917.
11. Belfast Stock Exchange, Minutes, December 7 1932.
12. *Financial News*, August 28 1933.
13. Belfast Stock Exchange, Minutes, July 5 1933. In September the Belfast postal authorities informed the Stock Exchange that inter-connection between brokers on the switchboard was illegal. But they were later advised from London that the agreement contained no clause to prohibit such use of the switchboard.
14. The phone in this office was also used for links with Dublin, but the brokers did not make much use of the facility.
15. Belfast Stock Exchange, Minutes, May 1936. At the height of the operation Nicholson's could handle some 3,000 bargains a day, and they used for that time an advanced system of punch card accounting. For details of Nicholson's

operations see W.A. Thomas, *The Provincial Stock Exchanges*, (1973), pp. 237-39; see also *Nicola: A Story of the Nicholson Family and their Stockbroking Business*, by H.C. Nicholson (privately printed), pp. 30-35.

16. Belfast Stock Exchange, Minutes, February 26 1941.

17. Belfast Stock Exchange, Minutes, October 28 1942.

18. In 1941 Nicholson's divided into two firms, the jobbing side being carried on by Cyril Nicholson & Sons. Due to restricted activity it was forced to close down in 1953.

19. Belfast Stock Exchange, Minutes, May, June 7 1950.

20. Carr, Workman set up a nominee company to deal with transfers for the jobbing side of the business. This meant they could use the company's seal rather than more laborious personal signatures.

21. For details of the campaign to obtain this valuable concession see Thomas, op. cit., p. 221.

22. Belfast Stock Exchange, Minutes, May 21 1952.

23. Belfast Stock Exchange, Minutes, January 22 1912.

24. Belfast Stock Exchange, Minutes, May 28 1941. Dublin did not rebate to the banks until the early seventies.

25. During 1900-11 the number of outside brokers recognised by the Committee rose from 5 to 12. Several firms in Londonderry were accorded such status. In 1933 there were eight brokers in the City, one of whom, T.S. Magee & Son, dated from 1863; the others were far more recent formations.

26. Under the 1910 Finance Act a stamp duty concession was given to contracts between brokers, and outside brokers registered with the Minister of Finance were then granted half commission terms. To obtain such registration outside brokers needed the support of members of the Stock Exchange.

27. The Act was passed in 1939 but was not really operative until after the war. The provision made it an offence to "carry on or purport to carry on the business of dealing in securities" without a licence from the Board of Trade or from the Minister of Finance in Northern Ireland.

28. For detailed coverage of the episode see E.V. Morgan and W.A. Thomas, *The Stock Exchange: Its History and Functions*, (1962), pp. 218-21.

29. See Thomas, op. cit., pp. 239-41.

30. Belfast Stock Exchange, Minutes, May 28 1941.

31. The number of certifications in 1943 was 6,466 compared with 2,272 in 1942: Belfast Stock Exchange, Minutes, May 26 1943.

32. Thomas, op. cit., p. 241.

33. The fees for preferential entry were raised by £100 all round in 1938.

34. Belfast Stock Exchange, 1929 Rule Book, Rules 46-79.

35. Belfast Stock Exchange, Minutes, May, November 30 1901.

36. Belfast Stock Exchange, Minutes, January 1921. The Post Office charged rent from 1907 onwards.

37. St. John Irvine, *Craigavon, Ulsterman*, (1949), pp. 52-55. Three members who served for over 50 years were W.H. Workman, joined 1905; Josias Cunningham, joined 1924; and J.A. Barr, joined 1928.

38. Belfast Stock Exchange, Minutes, November 13 1922, January 19, 30, March 8 1923. The quotation is from *Financial News*, August 28 1933.

39. Belfast Stock Exchange, Minutes, November 5, 11 1924, January 20 1928.

40. Belfast Stock Exchange, Minutes, May 24 1923, May 22 1936.

41. *Financial News*, August 28 1933.

42. The original founder of the firm, W.J. Richardson, retired from the Stock Exchange in 1942. He had conducted the firm's jobbing activity since 1923, and he was a founder member of the Exchange as well.

43.  *The Times' Book of Prospectuses of New Issues*, May 31 1939.
44.  Nivison's also offered Belfast brokers an underwriting interest in the issues of public utility stocks they handled e.g., in 1955 they got £175,000 of underwriting in the issue of £2.0mn, Northern Ireland Electricity Stock and a further £250,000 in 1957 in a further issue of the same stock.
45.  Belfast Stock Exchange, Minutes, January 6 1967. There was an underwriting commission of 1% and ¼% overriding commission.
46.  Only £1.7 mn of this stock was on the Belfast Register and half of this was in four names.
47.  Belfast Stock Exchange, March 13 1898.
48.  Belfast Stock Exchange, Minutes, May 13 1910. In the case of the 1910 tranche of 3½% stock, 1935, the Stock Exchange underwrote some £60,000 out of £120,000.
49.  *Return of all joint stock companies under 7 and 8 Vict. c. 110*, B.P.P., 1845, (577), XLVII.
50.  E. Boyle, "'Linenopolis': the rise of the textile industry", in *Belfast, The Making of a City*, ed. by J.C. Beckett (1983), pp. 46-47.
51.  E. Boyle, "The Economic Development of the Irish Linen Industry, 1825-1913", unpublished Ph.D. Thesis, Q.U.B., 1979, p. 95. In the case of H. Campbell the rate of return, as measured by profit over fixed and variable assets, increased from 14% to 32.6% between 1861 and 1864; similarly Beesbrook rose from 6.4% to 27.1% over 1862 to 1864.
52.  Ibid., p. 94. Among the integrated 'giants' were York Street, Blackstaff and Smithfield.
53.  Ibid., p. 178.
54.  *Royal Commission on Depression of Trade and Industry*, B.P.P., 1886(XXI), Q. 7027.
55.  Two other small finance companies formed in 1869 and 1871 were still operating in 1900 — The Ulster Loan & Discount Co., and City Loan and Discount Co.
56.  At the time of registration Belfast Ropework had a paid up capital of £17,000 from 10 shareholders. The Stock Exchange granted its shares a special settlement and quotation in October 1895. In 1972 the name was changed to McCleery, L'Amie Group Ltd.
57.  The Stock Exchange had granted old Bushmills Distillery shares a special settlement in October 1896 but not a quotation, being concerned as to which market they were "chiefly dealt in". In the event, the special settlement did not take place until January 1898, the same date as in Manchester, since the latter Exchange had requested changes in the company's articles of association; Belfast Stock Exchange, Minutes, October 19 1896, January 24 1898.
58.  Other stipulations were that they did not raise capital from the public and that the articles of association restricted the right to transfer shares. Their continued presence in the list was more for publicity purposes than any guide to the value of their shares arrived at by active trading. For details of this legal change see P.L. Cottrell, *Industrial Finance 1830-1914*, (1980), p. 74.
59.  It was quoted in Belfast, Glasgow and London. The issue was underwritten by the London Maritime Investment Co. at a commission of 1½% and overriding commission of ½% on the nominal amount of the shares offered for subscription.
60.  Edward de Stein & Co. had a subsidiary which handled the issuing activity, namely, Constructive Finance & Investment Co. Ltd.
61.  Share price details for this period are conveniently available, in summarized form in the *Stock Exchange (London and Provincial) Ten Year Record*.

62. Belfast Stock Exchange, Minutes, October 1899. It revised the code for quotations using London and Liverpool rules as a guide.
63. Belfast Stock Exchange, Minutes, August 21 1900.
64. For details of these developments see Thomas, op. cit., pp. 266-68.

# APPENDIXES

## Appendix 1

### Public Loans raised in Ireland 1760 to 1793

| Year | Description of Loans | Amount of Loans £ Irish | Amount of Loans £ British | Debentures created: £ British 3½% | Debentures created: £ British 4% | Debentures created: £ British 5% | Annuities created: £ British |
|------|----------------------|------------------------|---------------------------|----------|----------|----------|-----------|
| 1760 | 4% Debentures at par | 150,000 | 138,462 | – | 138,462 | – | – |
| 1760 | 5% Debentures at par | 150,000 | 138,462 | – | – | 138,462 | – |
| 1761 | 5% Debentures at par | 50,000 | 46,154 | – | – | 46,154 | – |
| 1762 | 5% Debentures at par | 200,000 | 184,615 | – | – | 184,615 | – |
| 1763 | 5% Debentures at par | 100,000 | 92,308 | – | – | 92,308 | – |
| 1766 | 4% Debentures at par | 100,000 | 92,308 | – | 92,308 | – | – |
| 1769 | 3½% Debentures at par | 30,000 | 27,692 | 27,692 | – | – | – |
| 1770 | 4% Debentures at par | 50,000 | 46,154 | – | 46,154 | – | – |
| 1770 | 4% Debentures at par | 50,000 | 46,154 | – | 46,154 | – | – |
| 1771 | 4% Debentures at par | 100,000 | 92,308 | – | 92,308 | – | – |
| 1772 | 4% Debentures at par | 100,000 | 92,308 | – | 92,308 | – | – |
| 1773 | Tontine Life Annuities | 265,000 | 244,615 | – | – | – | 14,677 |
| 1775 | Tontine Life Annuities | 175,000 | 161,538 | – | – | – | 9,692 |
| 1777 | Tontine Life Annuities | 300,000 | 276,923 | – | – | – | 20,769 |
| 1778 | 4% Debentures at par | 166,000 | 153,231 | – | 153,231 | – | – |
| 1780 | Lottery Loan, 4% Debentures at 105 | 200,000 | 184,615 | – | 193,846 | – | – |
| 1781 | Lottery Loan, 4% Debentures at 105 | 100,000 | 92,308 | – | 96,923 | – | – |
| 1782 | 4% Debentures at par | 260,000 | 240,000 | – | 240,000 | – | – |
| 1784 | 4% Debentures at par with 10% premium money | 15,250 | 14,077 | – | 14,077 | – | – |
| 1785 | 4% Debentures at par, with Short Annuity of £1.10s for 12 years | 150,000 | 138,462 | – | 138,462 | – | 2,077 |
| 1787 | 4% Debentures at par | 183,700 | 169,569 | – | 169,569 | – | – |
| 1787 | 3½% Debentures at par | 200,000 | 184,615 | 184,615 | – | – | – |
| 1789 | 3½% Debentures at par | 918,240* | 847,606 | 847,606 | – | – | – |
| | £ | 4,013,190 | 3,703,484 | 1,059,913 | 1,513,802 | 461,539 | 47,215 |

\* Including £518,240 borrowed from Bank of Ireland.

*Source*: "Accounts Relating to the Public Income and Expenditure of Great Britain and Ireland", B.P.P., 1868-69, Vol. 35, Accounts and Papers (2) Appendix 13, p.542.

Appendix 2

## Irish Tontine Annuities (1773, 1775, 1777): Distribution of Subscriptions

|  | 1773 | | | 1775 | | | 1777 | | |
|---|---|---|---|---|---|---|---|---|---|
|  | Number | Amount IR£ | % | Number | Amount IR£ | % | Number | Amount IR£ | % |
| Ireland: |  |  |  |  |  |  |  |  |  |
| Dublin | 65 | 21,900 | 8.3 | 64 | 16,600 | 9.5 | 126 | 29,000 | 9.6 |
| Rest of Ireland | 39 | 13,400 | 5.1 | 40 | 7,700 | 4.4 | 102 | 21,900 | 7.3 |
| Britain: |  |  |  |  |  |  |  |  |  |
| City of London | 83 | 45,600 | 17.2 | 74 | 20,400 | 11.7 | 55 | 12,800 | 4.3 |
| Middlesex | 184 | 90,900 | 34.3 | 178 | 47,700 | 27.2 | 145 | 45,400 | 15.2 |
| Surrey | 27 | 18,000 | 6.8 | 12 | 3,700 | 2.1 | 30 | 5,900 | 2.0 |
| Rest of Britain | 176 | 54,700 | 20.6 | 155 | 56,800 | 32.4 | 272 | 62,000 | 20.6 |
| Europe: |  |  |  |  |  |  |  |  |  |
| Geneva | 20 | 4,300 | 1.6 | 61 | 9,400 | 5.4 | 187 | 100,000 | 33.3 |
| Rest of Europe | 33 | 16,200 | 6.1 | 44 | 12,700 | 7.3 | 93 | 23,000 | 7.7 |
|  | 627 | £265,700 | 100 | 628 | £175,000 | 100 | 1010 | £300,000 | 100 |

*Source*: Journals of the Irish House of Commons, Vol. 10, 1779, Appendix cccxxvi–ccccxii

*Note*: The lists give names of nominees and the sums involved for each. Where names from the same family have been nominated for small amounts this has been taken as representing one subscription. The 1777 figure for Geneva overstates the actual number of subscribers due to the operation of investment clubs.

## Appendix 3

## Public Loans raised in Ireland 1793 to 1814

£ British

| Year | Description of Loan: Rate per £100 Cash at which Stock created | Amount of Loan | Debentures or Stock Created | | | Terminable Annuities created | Rate % at which Loan raised |
|---|---|---|---|---|---|---|---|
| | | | 3½% | 4% | 5% | | |
| 1793 | 5% Debentures at par | 184,615 | – | – | 184,615 | – | 5.0 |
| 1793 | 5% Debentures at par | 138,462 | – | – | 138,462 | – | 5.0 |
| 1794 | 5% Debentures, with Short Annuity of £1 for 15 years | 950,446 | – | – | 950,446[1] | 9,504 | 5.55 |
| 1795 | 5% Debentures, with Short Annuity of £1.5s for 15 years | 1,469,231 | – | – | 1,469,231[2] | 16,670 | 5.63 |
| 1796 | 5% Debentures, with Short Annuity of £1.5s for 15 years | 590,769 | – | – | 590,769 | 7,385 | 5.71 |
| 1797 | 5% Debentures, with Short Annuity of £4.15s for 13½ years | 300,000 | – | – | 300,000[3] | 14,250 | 8.04 |
| 1797 | 5% Debentures, at £158.15s | 369,277 | – | – | 586,154 | – | 7.93 |
| 1797 | 5% Debentures, at par from Bank of Ireland, with Short Annuity of £3.12s.6d for 19 years | 461,538 | – | – | 461,538 | 16,731 | 7.75 |
| 1798 | 5% Debentures, at £163.7s | 184,690 | – | – | 302,769 | – | 8.20 |
| 1798 | 5% Debentures at £163.18s.8d. | 966,212 | – | – | 1,583,954 | – | 8.20 |
| 1799 | 5% Debentures, at par and £24.15s Treasury Bills | 1,846,154 | – | – | 1,846,154 | – | 6.24 |
| 1800 | 5% Debentures, at par and £15 Treasury Bills | 2,307,692 | – | – | 2,307,692 | – | 5.77 |
| 1802 | 3½ per Cents, at £108.18s.9d | 1,500,000 | 1,634,061 | – | – | – | 3.81 |
| 1804 | 5 per Cents, at £112.7s.3d | 1,153,846 | – | – | 1,296,490 | – | 5.62 |
| 1806 | 3½ per Cents, at £139 | 1,846,154 | 2,566,154 | – | – | – | 4.86 |
| 1808 | 3½ per Cents, at £135 | 692,308 | 934,615 | – | – | – | 4.73 |
| 1808 | 5% Loan from Bank of Ireland, at par | 1,153,846 | – | – | 1,153,846 | – | 5.0 |

## Appendix 3 (continued)

| Year | Description of Loan: Rate per £100 Cash at which Stock created | Amount of Loan | Debentures or Stock Created | | | Terminable Annuities created | Rate % at which Loan raised |
|------|------|------|------|------|------|------|------|
| | | | 3½% | 4% | 5% | | |
| 1809 | 3½ per Cents, at £120, and £9.2s.6d Treasury Bills | 1,153,846 | - | - | 1,384,615 | - | 4.65 |
| 1811 | 3½ per Cents, at £120, and £11.15s Treasury Bills | 2,307,692 | - | - | 2,769,231 | - | 4.79 |
| 1812 | 3½ per Cents at £100, 5 per Cents at £20, and £10 Treasury Bills | 1,384,615 | 1,384,615 | - | 276,923 | - | 5.0 |
| 1813 | 3½ per Cents at £100, 5 per Cents at £20, and £11.15s Treasury Bills | 1,846,154 | 1,846,154 | - | 369,231 | - | 5.09 |
| 1814 | 3½ per Cents at £90, and 4 per Cents at £30.15s | 2,769,231 | 2,492,308 | 851,538 | - | - | 4.38 |
| | £ | 25,576,778 | 15,011,753 | 851,538 | 13,818,274 | 64,540 | - |

[1] including £500,000 payable in London at the Bank of England

[2] including £1,100,000 payable in London at the Bank of England

[3] payable in London at the Bank of England

Source: "Accounts relating to the Public Income and Expenditure of Great Britain and Ireland", B.P.P., 1868-69, Vol. 35, Accounts and Papers (2) Appendix 13, p. 551.

## Appendix 4

# Loans raised in Great Britain for Ireland 1798 to 1816

| Year ending | Amount of Loan | Amount of Stock created | Rate % at which loan raised* |
|---|---|---|---|
| *Before the Union* | | | |
| March 25 1798 | 1,500,000 | 2,925,000 | 6.34 |
| March 25 1799 | 2,000,000 | 4,000,000 | 6.24 |
| To January 5 1800 | 3,000,000 | 5,250,000 | 5.25 |
| January 5 1801 | 2,000,000 | 3,140,000 | 4.71 |
| *After the Union to 1816* | | | |
| January 5 1802 | 2,500,000 | 4,393,750 | 5.27 |
| January 5 1803 | 2,000,000 | 2,639,000 | 3.96 |
| January 5 1804 | 2,000,000 | 3,200,000 | 5.10 |
| January 5 1805 | 4,500,000 | 8,190,000 | 5.46 |
| January 5 1806 | 2,500,000 | 4,300,000 | 5.16 |
| | 1,500,000 | 360,000 | 5.82† |
| January 5 1807 | 2,000,000 | 3,320,000 | 4.98 |
| January 5 1808 | 2,000,000 | 3,012,000 | 4.83 |
| | 1,000,000 | 2,409,625 | 4.82 |
| January 5 1809 | 2,500,000 | 2,954,375 | 4.73 |
| January 5 1810 | 3,000,000 | 3,600,000 | 4.64 |
| January 5 1811 | 4,000,000 | 5,615,000 | 4.21 |
| | 1,400,000 | 2,005,250 | 4.21 |
| January 5 1812 | 4,500,000 | 6,300,000 | 5.77 |
| January 5 1813 | 4,350,000 | 7,636,000 | 5.28 |
| January 5 1814 | 6,000,000 | 10,200,000 | 5.53 |
| January 5 1815 | 5,500,000 | 7,342,000 | 4.60 |
| January 5 1816 | 9,000,000 | 16,560,000 | 5.62 |

* Interest payable and annuity created over amount received.

†Contributors received £360,000 of Navy Five per cents and an annuity of £5 for 54¾ years.

*Source*: "Notes from 1786 to 1890, relating to the National Debt, and the duties imposed by various enactments upon the National Debt Commissioners", Report by the Secretary and Comptroller General of the Proceedings of the Commissioners for the Reduction of the National Debt from 1796 to 1890, B.P.P., 1898(6539), Vol. XLVIII, pp. 298-307.

## Appendix 5

## Transfers of Stock between Ireland and England 1818 to 1863

| Year to Jan. 5th | From England to Ireland £ | From Ireland to England £ |
|---|---|---|
| 1818 | 62,800 | – |
| 1819 | 2,855,500 | – |
| 1820 | 2,570,075 | – |
| 1821 | 287,016 | – |
| 1822 | 142,992 | 9,694 |
| 1823 | 1,517,735 | 17,232 |
| 1824 | 809,030 | NIL |
| 1825 | 2,172,961 | 27,652 |
| 1826 | 3,536,888 | 254,323 |
| 1827 | 1,672,643 | 839,276 |
| 1828 | 524,186 | 1,199,234 |
| 1829 | 1,364,030 | 756,452 |
| 1830 | 1,151,808 | 758,122 |
| 1831 | 2,065,219 | 1,373,032 |
| 1832 | 1,311,650 | 515,646 |
| 1833 | 811,595 | 511,176 |
| 1834 | 607,391 | 1,060,942 |
| 1835 | 561,691 | 1,400,951 |
| 1836 | 1,333,600 | 618,277 |
| 1837 | 1,457,825 | 644,840 |
| 1838 | 742,346 | 788,403 |
| 1839 | 357,628 | 514,348 |
| 1840 | 934,964 | 297,540 |
| 1841 | 603,459 | 592,182 |
| 1842 | 652,036 | 462,083 |
| 1843 | 1,825,304 | 869,137 |
| 1844 | 1,540,373 | 516,578 |
| 1845 | 1,459,597 | 326,439 |
| 1846 | 1,834,630 | 196,801 |
| 1847 | 1,350,547 | 245,881 |
| 1848 | 2,644,854 | 1,384,482 |
| Year ending Dec. | | |
| 1848 | 2,006,499 | 1,680,586 |
| 1849 | 1,160,560 | 1,959,268 |
| 1850 | 1,104,616 | 1,201,831 |
| 1851 | 1,040,571 | 754,794 |
| 1852 | 732,722 | 2,646,157 |
| 1853 | 2,310,376 | 704,383 |
| 1854 | 1,403,344 | 1,625,429 |
| 1855 | 2,190,839 | 458,799 |

## (Appendix 5, continued)

| Year to Jan. 5th | From England to Ireland £ | From Ireland to England £ |
|---|---|---|
| 1856 | 1,991,084 | 579,106 |
| 1857 | 1,950,909 | 807,506 |
| 1858 | 440,510 | 2,452,301 |
| 1859 | 1,135,812 | 1,016,301 |
| 1860 | 1,006,434 | 1,031,358 |
| 1861 | 1,134,931 | 2,274,867 |
| 1862 | 743,079 | 1,720,367 |
| 1863 | 710,638 | 2,067,773 |

*Sources*: "Notes from 1786 to 1890, relating to the National Debt, and the duties imposed by various enactments upon the National Debt Commissioners", Report by the Secretary and Comptroller General of the Proceedings of the Commissioners for the Reduction of the National Debt from 1796 to 1890, B.P.P., 1898(6539), Vol. XLVIII, pp. 308, 310; "Account of the amount of stock transferred between England and Ireland 1826-30", B.P.P., 1830-31, v.353; for 1831-40, B.P.P., 1841(361), xiii,219; for 1837-47, B.P.P., 1847-48(196), xxxix,571; and for 1848-63, B.P.P., 1864(341), xxiv,395.

Appendix 6

## Large Limited Company Registrations in Ireland, 1887 to 1897, Dublin and Cork

| Year of Registration | Company | Business | Nominal Capital £ | Share Denomination £ | Amount Paid-up £ | Value of Vendors' Shares £ | Number of Shareholders* |
|---|---|---|---|---|---|---|---|
| DUBLIN | | | | | | | |
| 1888 | J.G. Mooney & Co. | Wines & Spirits | 60,000 | 5 | 41,724 | 15,000 | 479 |
| 1888 | Bolands, Ltd. | Millers | 205,000 | 5 | 161,670 | 43,330 | 1,493 |
| 1889 | Merchants' Warehousing Co. | Warehousemen | 50,000 | 1 | – | 49,150 | 157 |
| 1890 | A. & R. Thwaites & Co. | Mineral waters | 60,000 | 5 | 40,005 | 19,995 | 460 |
| 1890 | Dublin Brick & Tile Co. | Brickmakers | 30,000 | 1, 5 | 21,500 | 5,000 | 171 |
| 1890 | Castlebellingham & Drogheda Breweries, Ltd. | Brewers | 175,000 | 10 | 116,062 | 58,000 | 647 |
| 1890 | Kinahan & Co. | Wines and Spirits | 200,000 | 10 | 106,620 | 53,320 | 457 |
| 1890 | Switzer & Co. | Drapers | 65,000 | 5 | 30,010 | 14,990 | 292 |
| 1890 | Alexander Thom & Co. | Printers | 150,000 | 5 | 30,140 | 107,860 | 740 |
| 1890 | Dublin & Wicklow Manure Co. | Chemicals & Manure | 61,000 | 1 | 61,000 | – | 126 |
| 1890 | Thomas Dockrell, Sons, & Co. | Contractors | 30,000 | 5 | 20,000 | 10,000 | 112 |
| 1891 | Ferrier, Pollock & Co. | Drapers | 75,000 | 5 | 35,000 | 35,000 | 76 |
| 1891 | Kehoe, Donnelly & Pakenham, Ltd. | Meat curers | 80,000 | 5 | 49,920 | 30,000 | 197 |
| 1891 | John Jameson & Son, Ltd. | Distillers | 450,000 | 10 | – | 450,000 | 11 |
| 1892 | Crowe, Wilson & Co. | Drapers | 100,000 | 5 | 48,000 | 22,000 | 256 |
| 1892 | S. Davis, Sons, & Goodbody, Ltd. | General Trading | 70,000 | 10 | 30,500 | 19,500 | 268 |
| 1893 | Wallace Bros., Ltd. | Coal merchants | 50,000 | 5 | 26,000 | 14,000 | 111 |
| 1893 | Edward & John Burke, Ltd. | Bottlers and exporters | 600,000 | 5 | 420,000 | 180,000 | 496 |
| 1893 | Grappler Pneumatic Tyre & Cycle Co. | Tyre and cycle makers | 75,000 | 1 | 40,515 | 25,000 | 1,180 |
| 1894 | Bagots, Hutton & Co. | Tea, wine and spirit merchants | 60,000 | 5 | 40,000 | 20,000 | 350 |
| 1894 | H. Williams & Co. | Grocers | 50,000 | 1 | 35,000 | 15,000 | 527 |
| 1894 | Dolphin Hotel & Restaurant Co., and Michael Nugent, Ltd. | Hotel keepers | 60,000 | 5 | 40,000 | 20,000 | 407 |
| 1894 | Inglis & Co. | Millers & Bakers | 85,000 | 5 | 56,670 | 28,330 | 411 |

| Year | Company | Business | | | | | |
|---|---|---|---|---|---|---|---|
| 1894 | J. Shanks & Co. | Mineral waters | 45,000 | 1 | 18,210 | - | 191 |
| 1895 | Arnott & Co. Dublin, Ltd. | Drapers | 150,000 | 5 | 120,000 | - | 1,476 |
| 1895 | J. McCormick & Co. | Coal merchants | 200,000 | 5 | 74,956 | 35,000 | 277 |
| 1895 | Todd, Burns & Co. | Drapers | 100,100 | 5 | 66,992 | - | 478 |
| 1895 | W. Drummond & Sons. Ltd. | Seed merchants | 120,000 | 5 | 50,000 | 50,000 | 289 |
| 1896 | Pile, Ltd. | Fishmongers | 24,000 | 1 | - | 24,000 | 961 |
| 1896 | Drogheda Chemical Manure Co. | Chemical manures | 60,000 | 5 | 24,950 | 25,000 | 179 |
| 1896 | Thos. Heiton & Co. | Coal and iron merchants | 140,000 | 5 | 69,970 | 60,000 | 396 |
| 1896 | Dublin United Tramways (1896), Ltd. | Tramways | 1,200,000 | 10 | 755,390 | - | 2,940 |
| 1896 | Hely's, Ltd. | Stationers | 100,000 | 1 | 53,326 | 26,666 | 449 |
| 1896 | Maguire & Gatchell, Ltc. | Builders | 75,000 | 5 | 35,000 | 25,000 | 290 |
| 1896 | Edmond Johnson, Ltd. | Jewellers | 80,000 | 5 | 39,982 | 25,000 | 225 |
| 1897 | A. Armstrong & Co. | Paper merchants | 60,000 | 1 | 40,000 | 20,000 | 261 |
| 1897 | Clarence Hotels, Ltd. | Hotel keepers | 30,000 | 1 | 14,900 | 15,000 | 105 |
| 1897 | Tedcastle, McCormick & Co. | Coal merchants | 300,000 | 5 | 133,340 | 66,660 | 864 |

### CORK

| Year | Company | Business | | | | | |
|---|---|---|---|---|---|---|---|
| 1887 | Guy & Co. | Stationers | 30,000 | 1 | 8,000 | 17,000 | 121 |
| 1889 | Imperial Hotel, Cork, Ltd | Hotel keepers | 30,000 | 5 | 25,000 | - | 324 |
| 1891 | Dwyer & Co. | Warehousemen | 100,000 | 5 | 25,000 | 30,000 | 203 |
| 1894 | W. & H.M. Goulding, Ltd. | Chemical manures | 250,000 | 5 | 171,000 | - | 764 |
| 1894 | F.H. Thompson & Son, Ltd. | Bakers | 75,000 | 5 | 16,670 | 38,330 | 262 |
| 1894 | Dobbin Ogilvie & Co. | Grocers | 90,000 | 5 | 20,000 | 30,000 | 224 |
| 1895 | John Daly & Co. | Alcohol merchants | 95,000 | 5 | 41,025 | 53,975 | 597 |
| 1895 | Keane & Turnbull, Ltd. | Clothiers | 40,000 | 5 | 15,000 | 12,500 | 243 |
| 1896 | Cork Chemical & Drug Co. | Chemists | 60,000 | 5 | 17,000 | 25,000 | 431 |
| 1897 | Cork Brick Manufacturing Co. | Brickmakers | 20,000 | 1 | 11,975 | 5,000 | 140 |
| 1897 | J. Macarthy & Sons, Ltd. | Alcohol merchants | 60,000 | 5 | 25,000 | 20,000 | 318 |
| 1897 | Cork Timber & Iron Co. | Timber and iron merchants | 100,000 | 5 | 34,775 | 45,000 | 378 |

* At the time of registration

Source: Return Relating to Joint Stock Companies, &c., "Companies formed and registered in Ireland, under the Companies Act, 1862 (25 & 26 Vict. c.89), as Limited Companies".

## Appendix 7

### Turnover on The Stock Exchange – Irish*

£ 000

| Year | Irish Government Securities | | Irish Company Securities | | Gilt Edged | | Other Securities |
|------|---------|------------|----------|------------------|---------|------------|------------|
|      | 0-5 yrs | Over 5 yrs | Ordinary | Fixed Interest   | 0-5 yrs | Over 5 yrs |            |
| 1974† | 1,116,524 | 450,524 | 38,876 | 2,916 | 2,167 | 8,613 | 59,519 |
| 1975 | 2,464,480 | 1,171,924 | 44,541 | 14,010 | 9,453 | 69,895 | 53,625 |
| 1976 | 2,645,498 | 1,287,181 | 39,276 | 7,604 | 12,226 | 29,506 | 43,675 |
| 1977 | 5,436,319 | 3,129,411 | 65,380 | 16,305 | 17,222 | 22,057 | 71,447 |
| 1978 | 5,316,487 | 3,558,052 | 95,594 | 14,495 | 69,641 | 13,953 | 64,624 |
| 1979 | 4,226,620 | 3,648,117 | 98,537 | 6,467 | 7,207 | 15,704 | 39,536 |
| 1980 | 4,247,310 | 3,188,423 | 144,162 | 14,698 | 9,421 | 6,396 | 102,954 |
| 1981 | 4,733,942 | 2,769,917 | 176,908 | 44,676 | 16,416 | 34,283 | 141,332 |
| 1982 | 8,975,417 | 5,640,322 | 140,343 | 7,206 | 22,005 | 61,070 | 185,737 |
| 1983 | 8,329,724 | 5,570,177 | 701,541 | 49,898 | 39,079 | 45,555 | 291,697 |
| 1984 | 8,760,513 | 6,761,513 | 922,432 | 60,456 | 30,623 | 11,421 | 282,007 |
| 1985 | 6,750,445 | 10,087,757 | 702,113 | 11,721 | 28,115 | 47,239 | 212,797 |

* Figures represent the sum of purchases and sales by stockbrokers with their personal and corporate clients.

† Figures for 22 account periods.

*Sources*: The Stock Exchange; Central Bank of Ireland *Quarterly Bulletin*.

## Appendix 8

### Turnover on The Stock Exchange – Northern Ireland*

£ millions

| Year | Gilt Edged | Local Authority Securities | Other Fixed Interest | Ordinary Shares |
|------|-----------|---------------------------|----------------------|-----------------|
| 1969 | 24.43 | 2.79 | 4.06 | 29.52 |
| 1970 | 47.10 | 2.30 | 4.25 | 26.01 |
| 1971 | 101.27 | 2.77 | 4.07 | 43.95 |
| 1972 | 70.87 | 4.16 | 4.33 | 50.63 |
| 1973 | 117.31 | 2.59 | 2.72 | 34.60 |
| 1974 | 83.87 | 3.69 | 1.81 | 21.00 |
| 1975 | 83.06 | 4.67 | 2.46 | 26.22 |
| 1976 | 94.07 | 3.37 | 2.12 | 24.05 |
| 1977 | 96.29 | 5.33 | 2.66 | 40.17 |
| 1978 | 108.33 | 7.45 | 2.97 | 35.74 |
| 1979 | 104.70 | 6.11 | 2.00 | 43.45 |
| 1980 | 82.25 | 5.07 | 2.41 | 63.01 |
| 1981 | 57.53 | 5.39 | 2.03 | 54.57 |
| 1982 | 133.31 | 7.23 | 6.53 | 60.10 |
| 1983 | 140.99 | 7.03 | 7.00 | 99.67 |
| 1984 | 60.78 | 7.64 | 6.14 | 118.82 |
| 1985 | 48.58 | 3.08 | 4.58 | 117.68 |

* See note to Appendix 7.

*Source*: The Stock Exchange – Northern Ireland.

# INDEX

Allan, C.F., 95
Allied Irish Investment Bank, 196
Aran Energy, 198
Arnott & Co., 150
Ashenhurst, John T., 51, 86
Atlantic Resources, 197, 198

Bainbridge, Thomas, 120
Baldwin, Henry, 80
Bank finance, 192
Banking Commission (1926), 183, 186
Banking Commission (1938), 171, 185,
    188, 189
Bank of England:
  interest payable at, 7
  Irish stocks transferable at, 7
  stock transfers, 121-22
  suspension of convertibility (1797), 10
Bank of Ireland:
  Bank stock, 6, 61, 65
  Belfast gilt edged register, 130, 234-37
  capital, 6, 9, 19, 135-36
  discounting lottery prizes, 32
  gilt edged holdings, 128, 129
  gilt edged register, 129-31
  government accounts, 3, 4
  loans on debentures, 17
  loans on Treasury bills, 9-10
  loans to contractors, 42-43, 44
  loans to government, 9, 117-18
  London agent, 7
  National Loans, 165
  public notary, 48
  stock transfers, 121-22, 124-25, 128
  subscriptions to, 136
  surrender of debentures, 18
  Transfer Office, 18
Bantry Bay, 7
Baring Bros., 237
Barton Fraud, 203
Beaton, Kenneth, 96
Belfast Banking Co., 148, 237, 238
Belfast companies, 239
Belfast Corporation stocks, 237-38
Belfast Ropework Co., 242
Belfast Stock Exchange:
  call over, 223-24, 227
  clerks, 231
  commissions, 228-29
  Compensation Fund, 248
  emerging jobbers, 227-28
  formation, 221-23
  gilt edged dealings, 234-37
  hours of business, 224, 226
  informal markets, 219-21
  links with Nicholson's, 225-26

listed companies, 242-44, 246
management, 231-32
membership, 231
outside brokers, 229-30
premises, 232
quotation requirements, 246-47
settlement, 228
shunting, 226-27
switchboard dealings, 224, 227, 233
telegraph, 232-33
wartime dealing, 226, 230
Belfast Street Tramways Co., 112, 150-51
Belfast Unit, 247-48
Bell, Robert, 232
Beresford, J.C., & Co., 42, 49
Biddulph, Cocks & Co., 46
"Big Bang", 208
Bills of exchange, 11
Bish & Co., 28
Bland, Barnett & Hoare, 46
Bloxham, Henry C., 95
Bloxham, Toole & Co., 95
Bloxham, Toole, O'Donnell, 94-95
Board of First Fruits, 46
Bogle French, Borrowes, Canning, 40, 43
Boldero, Kendall, Adey & Co., 22, 24,
    42, 46
Borrowes, Walter, 42
Boyce, Joseph, 102
Boyle, Alexander, 57, 81, 100, 126
Boyle, Low, Pim & Co., 57, 79, 100
Boyle, R.H., 86, 90
Brennan, Joseph, 165
Brockhouse Nominees, 188
Brookfield Linen Co., 240
Brown, Collinson & Co., 22
Briscoe, Brendan, 96
Briscoe, Herbert, 96
Bruce, Halliday, 94, 141
Bruce, Samuel, 12, 51, 75, 94
Bruce & Symes, 56, 81, 94, 102, 126
Bruce, Symes & Williams, 94
Bruce, Symes & Wilson, 94
Bubble Act (1720), 135
Bula Resources, 197, 200
Bushell, Theobald, 108, 219
Bushell, Tobias, 108
Butler & Briscoe, 96, 170, 188, 196
Butler, Desmond, 96
Butler, J. P., 96

Campbell, Henry, & Co., 246
Canals, 136-37
Capital gains tax, 215
Carr, A.H.R., 232, 233
Carr, George, 102, 111

Carr, Workman & Co., 227-28
Carr, Workman, Patterson, Topping &
Co., 233
Carroll Industries, 197, 198
Carroll, J.H., 151
Carson, James, 232
Castlereagh, Lord, 116, 117
Cazenove & Co., 102
Cement Ltd., 188, 189
Cement-Roadstone, 197, 198
Central Bank of Ireland, 174, 175, 176-
77, 191
Chamber of Commerce, 82
City of Dublin Merchants' Stock &
Sharebrokers' Association, 106-7
City of Dublin Steam Packet Co., 142-43,
144, 145
City of Glasgow Bank, 148
Clements, H.T., 23, 46, 135
Coates, W.F. & Co., 225, 245
Coates, Sir W.F., 232, 233
Coates, W.J., 222
Code of Laws, 204
Colbert, J. P., 187
Colles, Isaac, 30
Collins, Michael, 130, 165
Commercial Buildings, 51, 89, 106, 107
Commercial Buildings, Cork, 108
Commercial Insurance Co., 94, 141
Commissioners for the Reduction of the
National Debt, 46-48, 119
Commissioners for Wide Streets, 46
Committee on Insurance Associations
(1856), 144
Companies Act (1844), 143-44
Companies Act (1862), 144
Company formation (before 1914):
banking and finance, 146-47, 149,
240-41
boom of 1825, 140-41
boom of 1835-36, 141-42
breweries and distilleries, 149
cycle companies, 153-57
dairy companies, 151
flax companies, 147-48
hotels and restaurants, 147, 149
mining, 146
public utilities, 146
rubber plantations, 158
share denominations, 153
shipbuilding, 241, 242, 244
shipping, 146, 149, 150
volume of, 144-45, 241-44
warehousing companies, 149-50
Committee of Inquiry into Taxation on
Industry (1956), 192
*Company Taxation in Ireland* (1972), 192-
93

Connell, William, 108
Consolidated Fund, 4
Control of Manufactures Acts (1932-34),
185
Co-Partnership Act (1782), 138-40
Cope & Co., 28
Cork Stock Exchange:
brokers' clerks, 56
brokers' licences, 206
commissions, 65
crisis of 1914, 70
Daily List, 60, 149
early railway shares, 105, 108
Federation, 205
fines, 58
formation, 151-53
market hours, 57
membership, 55, 83
outside brokers, 67-68
premises, 90
quotation requirements, 159
Registrar, 60
settlement, 62
telephone, 92
Corporation debentures, 131-32
Cory, Isaac, 40, 43, 49
Cotter, Rogerson, 22, 24
Council of Associated Stock Exchanges,
68, 70, 203-4, 225, 226
Cox Merle & Co., 42
Craig, James, 233-34
Croft, Blackwell, Roberts & Croft, 46
Crofton, James, 12
Croker, Darling & Co., 75
Croker, John, 106
Crosthwait, Leland, 12, 89, 125, 136
Crosthwait, Thomas, 80
Cumming, Hugh, 51
Cunningham, Josias, 108, 109, 219, 222,
242
Cunningham, Josias, & Co., 219, 222,
233, 248
Curtis, Patrick, 94, 126
Curtis, Robert, 7
Curtis & Woodlock, 94
Cycle share speculation, 153-57

Daniel, Thomas, 89
Darbishire, H., & Co., 233
Darbishire, Malcomson & Coates, 233,
248
Davy, J. & E., 188, 196
Deey, Christopher, 28, 30, 31, 46, 136,
137
Deey, Robert, 12, 28, 30, 31, 46, 47, 51,
74, 137
Deey, William, 12
Depreciation allowances, 192

Designated Securities, 207-8
De Stein, Edward, & Co., 245
Dick, Quintin, 126
Dick, Samuel, 89, 135
Dillon, M., & Son, 95, 188
Dillon & Waldron, 95
Dividend tax abatement, 185-86
D'Olier, Jeremiah, 46
Drummond Commission (1838), 101
Du Bedat, William G., 79, 106
Dublin Corporation stocks, 131-32, 166, 167
Dublin Distillers Co., 149
Dublin Royal Exchange Stock & Share-brokers' Association, 79-81, 106
Dublin Stock Exchange:
  account periods, 61-63
  agency business, 66
  brokers' clerks, 56, 83, 86
  brokers' licences, 74-75, 81-82, 204-5, 206
  call over, 57-58
  Clearing Room, 63
  commissions, 63-65, 123, 129, 204
  Commission of Enquiry (1849), 48, 80-82, 106
  committees, 86, 88
  companies quoted, 145-46
  Compensation Fund, 94
  crisis of 1914, 68-70
  crisis of 1931, 68
  Daily List, 59-60
  dealings in government stocks, 128-29
  dealing practices, 56-58
  defaulters, 92-93
  early transfer procedures, 60, 81
  entrance fees, 83
  Federation, 205
  fines, 58
  first Rule Book, 75
  formation in 1799, 49-51
  founding members, 48-49, 51
  government stock transfers, 123, 125-26
  indentured clerks, 78
  market hours, 57
  marketable lots, 58
  membership, 55, 75-83, 208
  Mutual Guarantee Fund, 93
  outside brokers, 65, 67-68
  parliamentary act (1799), 49-51
  premises, 51, 89-90
  President, 86
  public admission, 55-56
  quotation requirements, 158-59
  Registrar, 58-59, 88
  Second World War, 70-71
  settlement, 60-63
  shunting, 66-67, 91
  telegraph, 90-92
  telephone, 92
  Voluntary Association (1793), 48-49
  women members, 86
Dublin United Tramways Co., 95, 112, 113, 150
Dudgeon, Henry, 95
Dudgeon, Herbert, 95
Dudgeon, Hume, 95
Dudgeon, H.J., 95
Dudgeon, James, 95
Dudgeon & Sons, 95, 188, 196
Duffin, Adam, 222, 232
Dunville & Co., 149

Economic Development (1958), 172, 190
Edenderry Spinning Co., 240
Egan, J.C., 107
Egmont, Earl of, 126
Electric Telegraph Co., 90
English, Henry, 140
English lotteries, 24
Exchange controls, 214
Exham, Thomas, 108
Exshaw, John, 31

Falls Flax Spinning Co., 240
Federation of Stock Exchanges in Great Britain and Ireland, 205, 247-48
Finance Act (1932), 185
Finance, Department of, 70-71, 82, 86, 130, 165-66, 168, 174, 176-77, 204, 206, 207, 214, 216, 234
Finlay, James, 48, 51
Fitzgerald, Vasey, 119
Fitzgerald, William, 95
Fitzwilliam Securities Ltd., 196
Fletcher, J.A., 232
Forbes, John, 4
Foreign securities, 131
Forged Transfers Act, 203-4
Foster, John, 2, 3, 23, 28, 39, 46, 117, 138
Foster & Braithwaite, 233
Fox, Edward, 107
Frank & Co., 28

Gallaher Ltd., 227, 245, 246
Gault, Miss, 232
General Estates Trust Co., 188
Gibbons, James, 12, 31, 42, 51, 74
Gibbons & Williams, 42, 125
Gladstone, W. E., 143
Glyn, Mills & Co., 237
Goodbody & Co., New York, 95
Goodbody, Denis, 95
Goodbody, Donald Carter, 95
Goodbody Dudgeon, 95, 196

Goodbody, Jonathan, 95
Goodbody, Robert, 95
Goodbody & Webb, 95, 188, 196
Goodbody, W.W., 95
Government bonds:
   holdings, 173-74, 175, 177
   market, 174, 176-77
   turnover, 178
   yields, 178-79
Government Broker, 96, 170, 171, 174-
   75, 176, 179, 208, 210
Government debentures:
   compared with inscribed stock, 17-18,
   41
   demand for, 44
   method of issue, 39-41
   nature of, 17
   Robert Shaw's loan (1796), 43-44
Government stocks, transfers in:
   amounts transferred, 126-28
   arbitrage, 123
   benefit from, 122-23
   holdings in Ireland, 128
   legislation, 120
   methods, 121-22
   price differences, 123-24
   users, 124-26
Grand Canal, 113, 136-37, 145
"Grappler" Pneumatic Tyre & Cycle Co.,
   154, 156
Grattan, Henry, 2, 117
Grattan's Parliament, 2, 4-5
Gray, Robert, 125
Grubb & Coates, 222
Griffin & Macdougall, 157
Guinness, Arthur, & Co., 145
Guinness, Mahon & Co., 125, 188, 195

Harland & Wolff, 219, 221, 227, 241,
   242, 244-45, 246
Hamilton, W. G., 2-3
Hayes, Edward, 151
Herries, Roberts & Co., 46
Hibernian Bank, 107, 140-41, 148
Hibernian Fire & Life Assurance Co., 94
Hibernian Industrial & General Invest-
   ment Co., 195
Higginbottom, Thomas, 124
Hill, Charles, 81
Hogan, Patrick, 86
Hone, Nathaniel, 89, 125
House of Industry, 46
Hughes (Bernard) Ltd., 242, 246
Hull, Fawcett & Hill, 81

Imperial Tobacco Co., 189
Indian stocks, 131
Industrial Credit Co., 187-88, 195

Industrial finance (inter-war):
   dividend tax abatement, 185-86
   guaranteed loans, 183-84, 186
   protection measures, 184-85
   sources of funds, 191-93
Industrial Trust Co., 183-84, 186
Investment Bank of Ireland, 196
Irish Distillers Group Plc., 197
Irish Dunlop Co., 188
Irish Exchequer, 3, 9, 11-12, 18
Irish Free State:
   Conversion Loan 1935, 168
   early finances, 164
   finance during 1939-45, 171-72
   Financial Agreement Loan, 168
   Government Broker, 170
   Land Bonds, 170
   National Loans, 165-69
Irish Stock Exchange, 203, 206
Irish Sugar Co., 187, 188
Irish Temperance League, 90
Irish Unit:
   administration, 208
   broking firms, 209, 216
   call over, 209-11
   clerks, 208
   commissions, 211-12, 216
   Compensation Fund, 207
   formation, 207-8
   membership, 208
   Official List, 211
   prudential aspects, 209
   settlement, 211-13
   special provisions, 207-8
Irish Volunteers, 2

Jameson, William, & Co., 149
Jenkin, Caleb, 30, 136
Jenkins Committee on Company Law
   (1962), 206, 247
Johnstone, Francis, 222
Joint Stock Companies Act (1856), 144
Jones, Griffith, 46
Joplin, Thomas, 141

Kennedy & Gordon, 188
Keogh, Dona Mary Irene, 86
Keogh, James, 188
Keshan, John, 106
Kirwan, James, 107

Labertouche & Co., 102
Laing & Cruickshank, 248
Lanauze, Henry, 75, 102
Land Bonds, 128, 170
La Touche, Messers, 42
La Touche, Robert, 125
Law, Bonar, 130

Law, Robert, 125
Lawrence, Pierce & Co., 102
Lawrence & Waldron, 188
Leahy, Kelly & Leahy Ltd., 242, 246
Leydon, John, 186
Lillis & Harrington, 188
Limited Liability Act (1855), 144
Linen companies, 239-40, 245-46
*Listing, Admission of Securities to*, 199
Little Theatre, 31
Liverpool & Manchester Railway, 99
Loan contractors, 39-40, 41-42
London Stock Exchange:
  commission rules (1912), 67
  crisis of 1914, 68-70
  Irish Land Bonds, 170
  non-member jobbers, 225
  Second World War, 70-71
  single capacity, 67
Lotteries:
  contractors, 26-28
  conversion of 1787-88, 6-7, 25
  discounting of prizes, 32
  division of tickets, 30-31
  drawing of prizes, 31
  in aid of loans, 25
  insurance, 32-34
  issuing of tickets, 28-29
  Lottery Commissioners, 28, 46
  lottery loans, 6
  Lottery Offices, 29
  methods of issue, 26
  office keepers, 30
  prizes, 25
  revenue raised, 25-26
Low, Francis, 100
Low, Nathaniel, 124, 137
Lullin, Masbore, Aubert & Co., 45

McCann, James, 95, 188
McCann & Naish, 95
McDonnell, John, 80
McElligott, J.J., 165, 166, 169, 171
MacIlwaine & McColl, 241, 242
McIlwaine, A.J., & Co., 233
McKee, John, 222
McKee, John, & Co., 233
McLean & Co., 227
Magee, John, 30
Magee, William, 30
Magnetic Telegraph Co., 90-91
Maguire, McCann, Morrison & Co., 95
Mahoney, Pierce, 105
Manifold & Hines, 157
Maquay, John Leland, 125
Martin & Co., 46
Mazarin, Cardinal, 20
Mercantile Law Commission (1854), 139

Merrill Lynch, 95
Midland & Western Stock Exchange, 206
Midland Great Western Railway, 137
Miller & Symes, 89
Mineral exploration companies, 197
Mocatta, Abraham De Mattos, 46
Molony & Murray, 157
*Money Market Report* (1968), 164, 173-74,
  177, 178
Moore, Ponsonby Arthur, 144
Moore, Gamble, Carnegie & Co., 95
Morrogh, A.D., 96
Morrogh, Dominic C., 96
Morrogh, Walter, 96
Morrogh & O'Callaghan, 96
Morrogh, W.& R., 196
Mulholland, Thomas, 239
Munster Bank, 147
Munster & Leinster Bank, 132
Murphy, T.V., 95
Murray, Robert, 123
Music Hall, 31

Naish, Richard, 95
National Bank, 141
National City Bank, 183, 186
National Debt Commissioners (British),
  22, 121
National Debt of Ireland:
  Commissioners for the Reduction of,
    47-48, 119
  conversion of 1787-88, 6-7, 25
  early loans, 16
  growth of, 6-10
  in 1797, 8
  inscribed stock, 17-18
  interest on, 5
  'Irish Fives', 18
  issues at a discount, 8-9
  life annuities, 19-20
  loans raised after 1801, 117-18
  London issues, 7-8, 9
  'old Four per cents', 18
  payment of interest in London, 7, 19
  remittance of London loans, 10-12
  short annuities, 19
National Loans:
  First National Loan, 165
  Five per cent National Loan, 166
  Fourth National Loan, 167
  holders of, 170
  market in, 170-71
  National Security Loan, 167
  New York offer, 167
  Second National Loan, 166-67
  Sinking Funds, 166, 169, 171
  Third National Loan, 167
  underwriting, 169

Newcomen, Sir William Gleadowe, 12, 46, 49, 137
Newett, B.J., 222
New Royal Canal Co., 137
New Stock Exchange, 107-8
Nesbitt & Steward, 28
Nicholson, J.W., & Sons, 67, 204, 225-26
Nivison, R., & Co., 237
Non-Conformist Ministers, Board of, 46
North Kerry Proprietary Co., 188
North Western Railway Co., 203
Northern Banking Co., 42, 148
Northern Bank Finance, 196
Northern Ireland government stocks, 237
Northern Stock Exchange, 206

O'Brien & Toole, 196
O'Connell, Daniel, 141
O'Connor, Valentine O'B, 81
O'Donnell & Fitzgerald, 95, 188
O'Donnell, James, 94
O'Gorman, Richard, 107
Oil exploration shares, 197-98
Old Bushmills Distillery, 244
Old Exchange Coffee House, 89
Orr & Co., 219
Ouzel Galley Society, 89
Overend, Gurney & Co., 146, 148

Parker, Alexander, 81
Parnell, Sir Henry, 142
Parnell, Sir John, 3, 8, 17, 32, 47
Pasavant & Co., 45
Pearson, P. B., 96
Pim, George, 81
Pim, James, 100, 109, 122, 123, 126
Pim, Joseph, 125
Pim, Joshua, 89
Pim, R., 124
Pim, Richard, 130
Pitt, William, 39, 47, 117
Pittar, Samuel John, 51
Porter, Drummond, 223, 232
Power, John, 94
Price, Dr. Richard, 20
Price, Rowland, 124, 126
Provincial Bank, 141
Provincial Brokers' Stock Exchange, 206, 230
Public Capital Programme, 172
Public notaries, 48, 51
Puget & Bainbridge, 11, 22, 24, 46
Puget, John, 7, 10, 40

Quotation requirements, 158-59, 246-47

Railways:
  boom promotions, 101-2

Córas Iompair Éireann, 113, 137
  dealings in English markets, 104
  debentures, 112
  early Belfast share dealings, 108-9, 219
  early promotions, 100
  English interest, 110-11
  light railways, 112, 150-51
  location of subscribers, 109-10
  preference shares, 111-12
  Railways Act (1924), 113
  rival share markets, 105-7
  share issues, 102-3
  share price movements, 101-2, 103-5
  speculative dealings, 103, 104-5
Ranks (Ireland) Ltd., 187, 188
Regionalisation, 206
Reid, Henry, 219
Republic of Ireland:
  annual National Loans, 172, 175
  government finances, 172-73, 175
  overseas borrowing, 175
Revenue Commissioners, 3, 46
Richardson, W.J., & Co., 235-36
Roberts, Curtis & Were, 28, 42
Robinson, John, 51
Robinson, William, 219
Roe, George, 80
Roose, D. Charles, 126
Rourke, John, & Son, 108
Royal Bank of Ireland, 141, 148
Royal Canal, 137
Royal Exchange, 11, 12, 28, 89, 106, 107

Salts (Ireland) Ltd., 188, 189
Scottish Stock Exchange, 206
SEPON, 212-13
Shannon, Edward, 51
Share issues (since 1945):
  costs, 195
  facilities, 188-89, 195-96
  methods, 194-95
  volume, 184, 191-92, 193-94
Share market turnover, 198
Share ownership, 198-99
Share price movements, 182, 189-90, 191, 196
Share pushing, 204
Shaw's Bank, 141
Shaw, Robert, 7, 40, 43, 46, 135
Shaw, Robert, Junior, 43-44
Shaw, William, 222
Sinclair, Thomas, 221
Sinking funds, 18, 46-47, 166, 169, 171
Smaller Companies Market, 200
Smith, Adam, 20
Smurfit (Jefferson) Group Plc., 197, 198
Sneyd, Edward, 46
Standard Motors, 227

Stephens, Joseph J., 106
Stevenson, Jackson S., 108, 219
Stokes & Kelly, 94
Stokes & Kelly, Bruce, Symes & Wilson, 94
Symes, George, 56, 81, 94, 126

TALISMAN, 208, 212-13, 248
Taylor, J., 234
Teller of the Exchequer, 3
Thellusson & Co., 23, 45
Thompson, J. Norris, 31
Thomson, Poulett, 142
Tisdall, Charles, 75
Tokenhouse Securities (Ireland) Ltd., 195
Tone, Wolfe, 8
Tonti, Lorenzo, 20
Tontine Committee (1812), 23
Tontine of 1773, 20-21
Tontine of 1775, 21
Tontine of 1777, 21
Tontines:
    attractions of, 19-20
    English, 20
    holders, 44-46
    London agent, 22
    payment of interest, 21-22
    problems, 22-24
    use in Ireland, 6
TOPIC, 213
Townsend, W. H., 108
Trade Loans (Guarantee) Act 1924, 183
Trading Companies Act (1834), 143
Tramways, 112-13, 150-51
Treasury bills, 6, 9-10, 40, 42, 46
Treasury Commissioners, 4, 51, 57, 74
Trevor, Hugh, 125
Turner, Timothy, 51
Tunney, P. W., & Co., 188

Ulster Banking Co., 148

Ulster Spinning Co., 148, 240
Underwriting, 194, 195
Union, Act of:
    amalgamation of Exchequers, 119
    burden imposed, 117
    financial terms, 116-17
United Irishmen, 8
United Stock Exchange, 206-7
Unlisted Securities Market, 199-200, 210, 211

Vickers, Jeremiah, 47

Waldron, L.A., & Co., 95
Walker, Henry, 30
Walker, T., 30
Ward, John and George, 28
Waterford Glass, 197, 198
Watson, Solomon, 125
Webb, Albert, 95
Webb, Theodore R., 95
White Linen Hall Co., 239
White, Luke, 28, 30, 39, 42-43, 136
Whitestone, W.H., 30
Wilkinson & Faulkner, 95
Williams, Henry J., 100
Williams, James, 30
Williams, Richard, 12, 75, 86, 100, 102, 125
Williams, Thomas, 74
Wilson, Hill, 28, 74
Wilson & Son, Moffat, 183
Wilson, Thomas, 80, 122, 125
Wilson, Thomas H., 106
Woodlock, Thomas, 95
Woolworth, F.W., & Co., 189
Workman, Clark & Co., 241, 242, 244
Workman, R., & Co., 233

York Street Flax Spinning Co., 148, 227, 239, 245-46